# PandoraHearts

Jun Mochizuki

CONTENTS



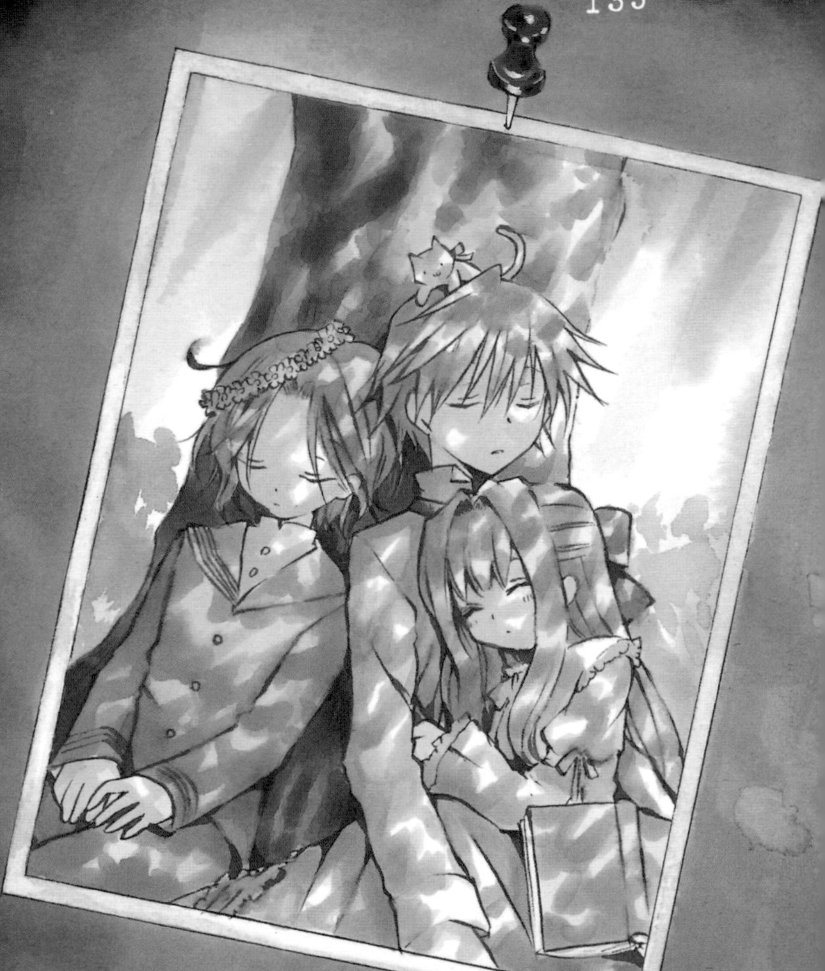

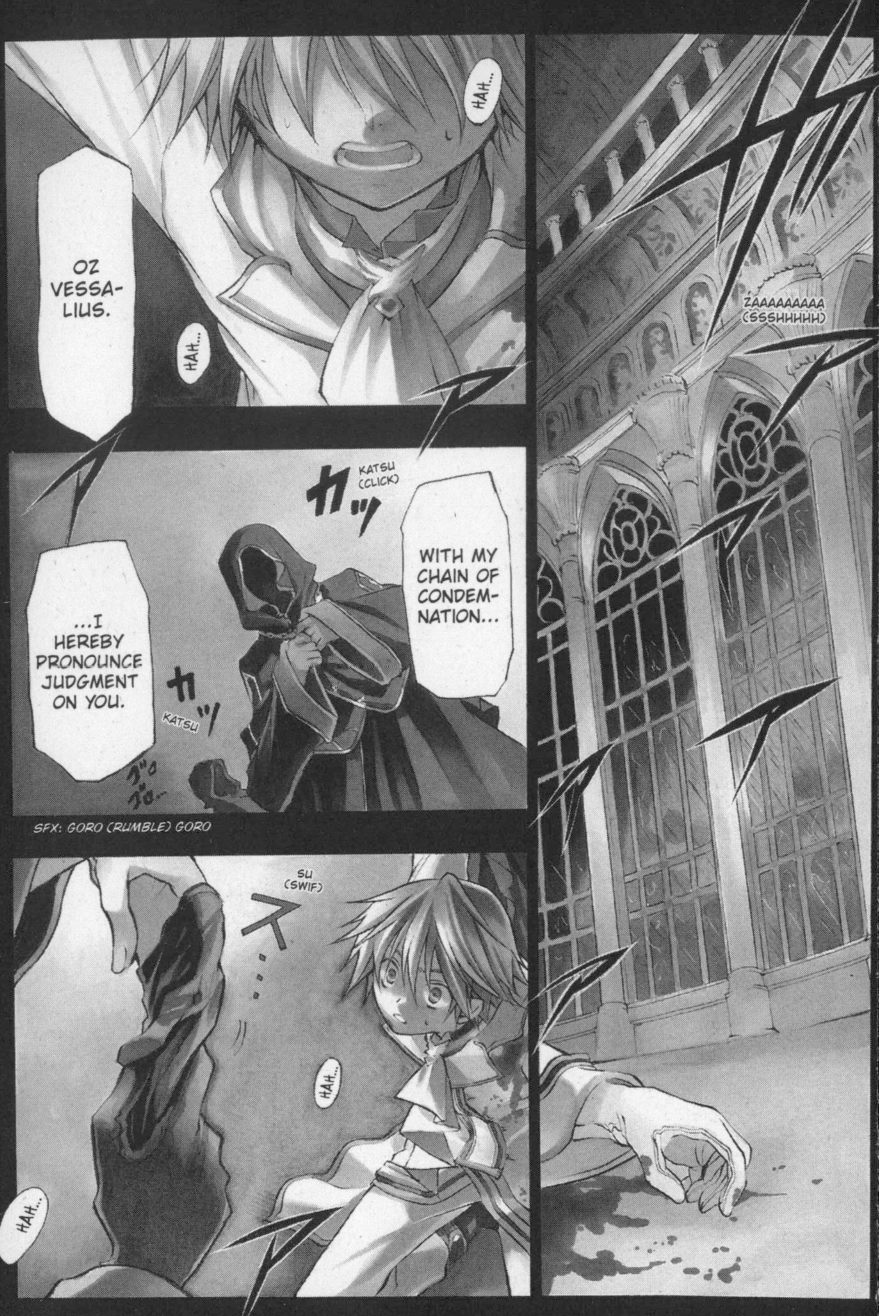
ZAAAAAAAAA
(SSSHHHHH)
HAH...
OZ VESSA-LIUS.
HAH...
KATSU
(CLICK)
カッ
WITH MY CHAIN OF CONDEM-NATION...
...I HEREBY PRONOUNCE JUDGMENT ON YOU.
カッ
KATSU
SFX: GORO (RUMBLE) GORO
SU
(SWIF)
ス
HAH...
HAH...

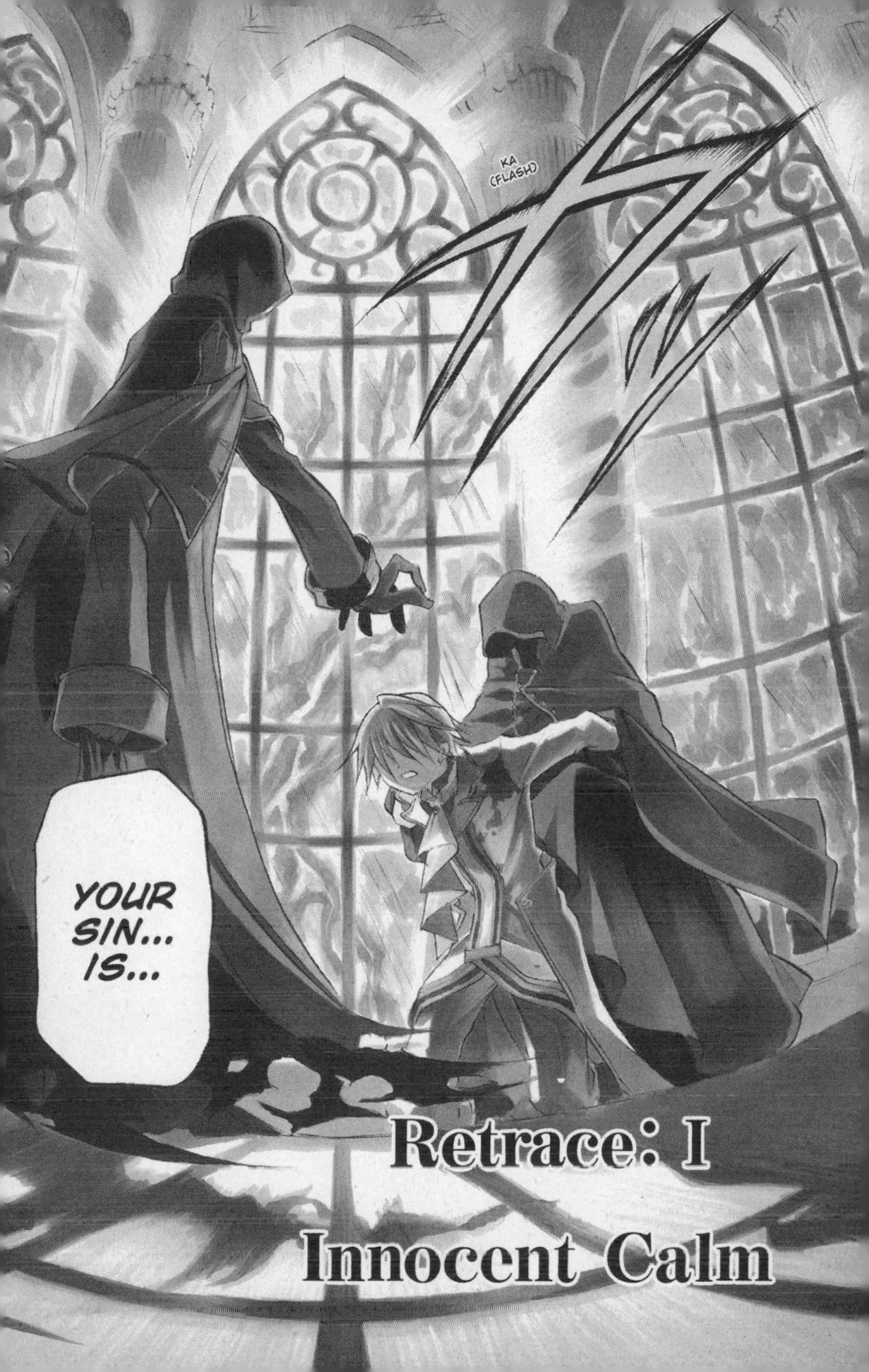
KA
(FLASH)
YOUR SIN... IS...
Retrace: I
Innocent Calm

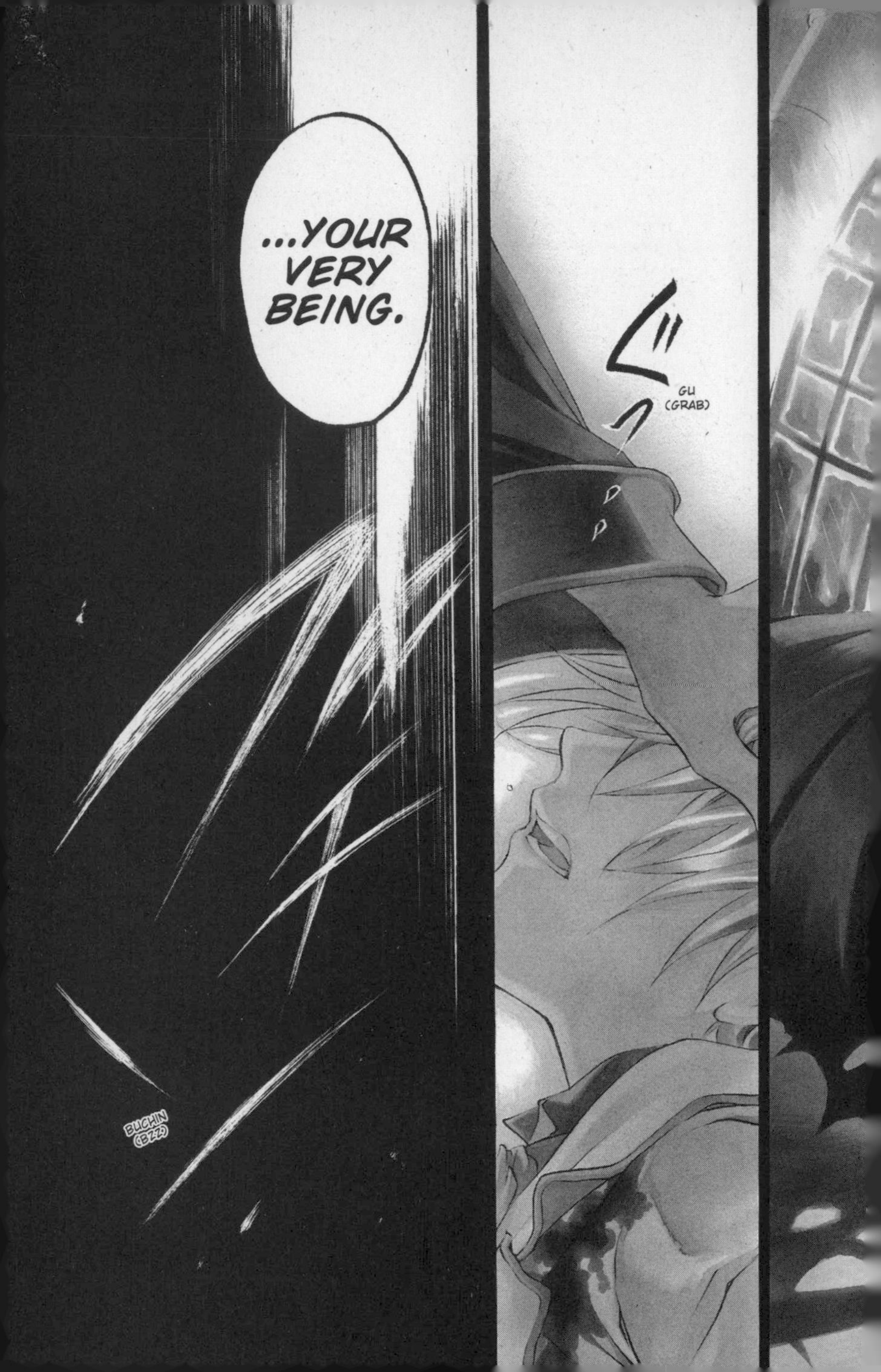
GU (GRAB)
...YOUR VERY BEING.
BUCHIN (BZZ)

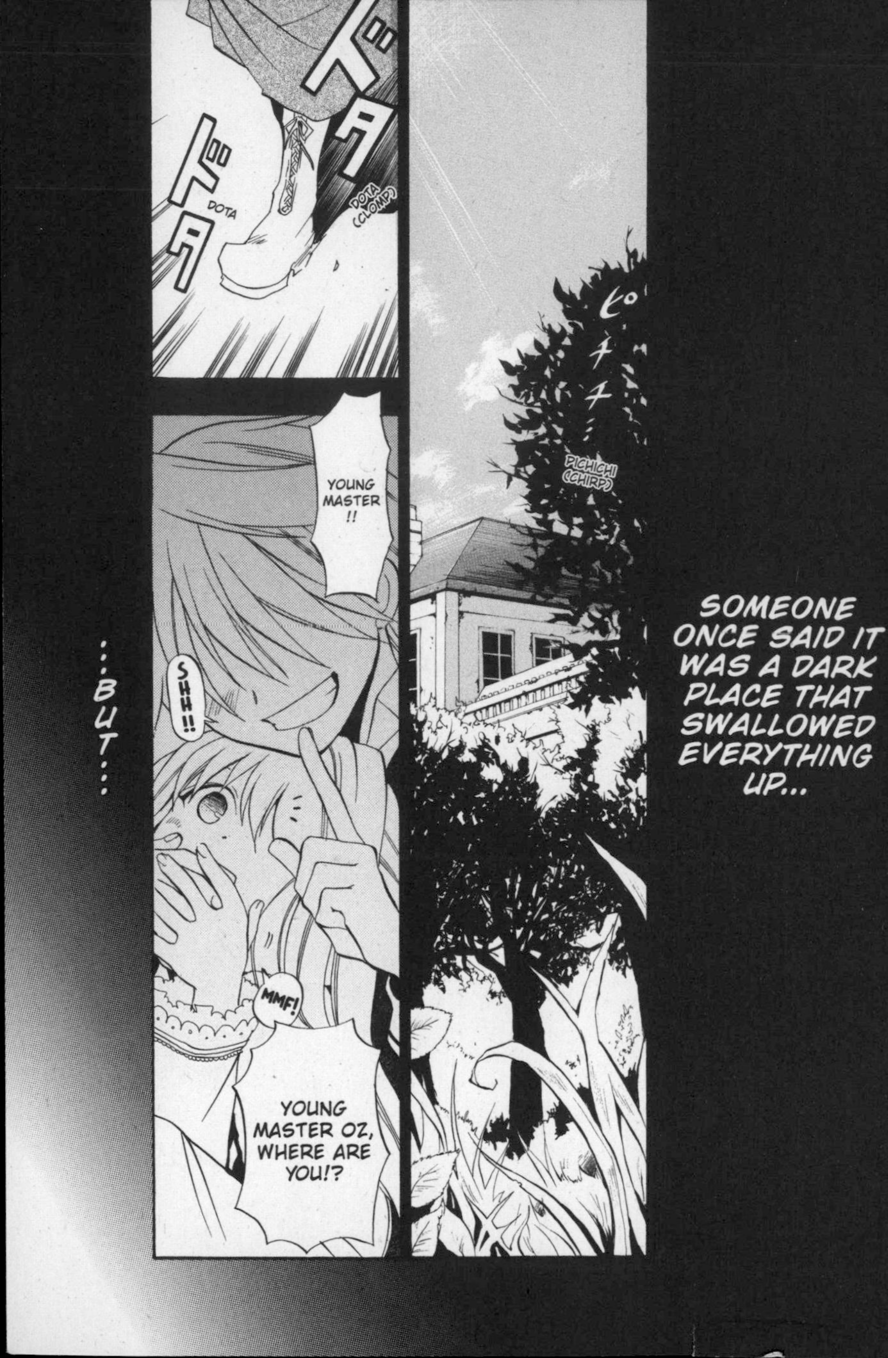
SOMEONE ONCE SAID IT WAS A DARK PLACE THAT SWALLOWED EVERYTHING UP...
PICHICHI (CHIRP)
DOTA (CLOMP)
DOTA
YOUNG MASTER !!
SHH!!
MMF!
YOUNG MASTER OZ, WHERE ARE YOU!?
...BUT...

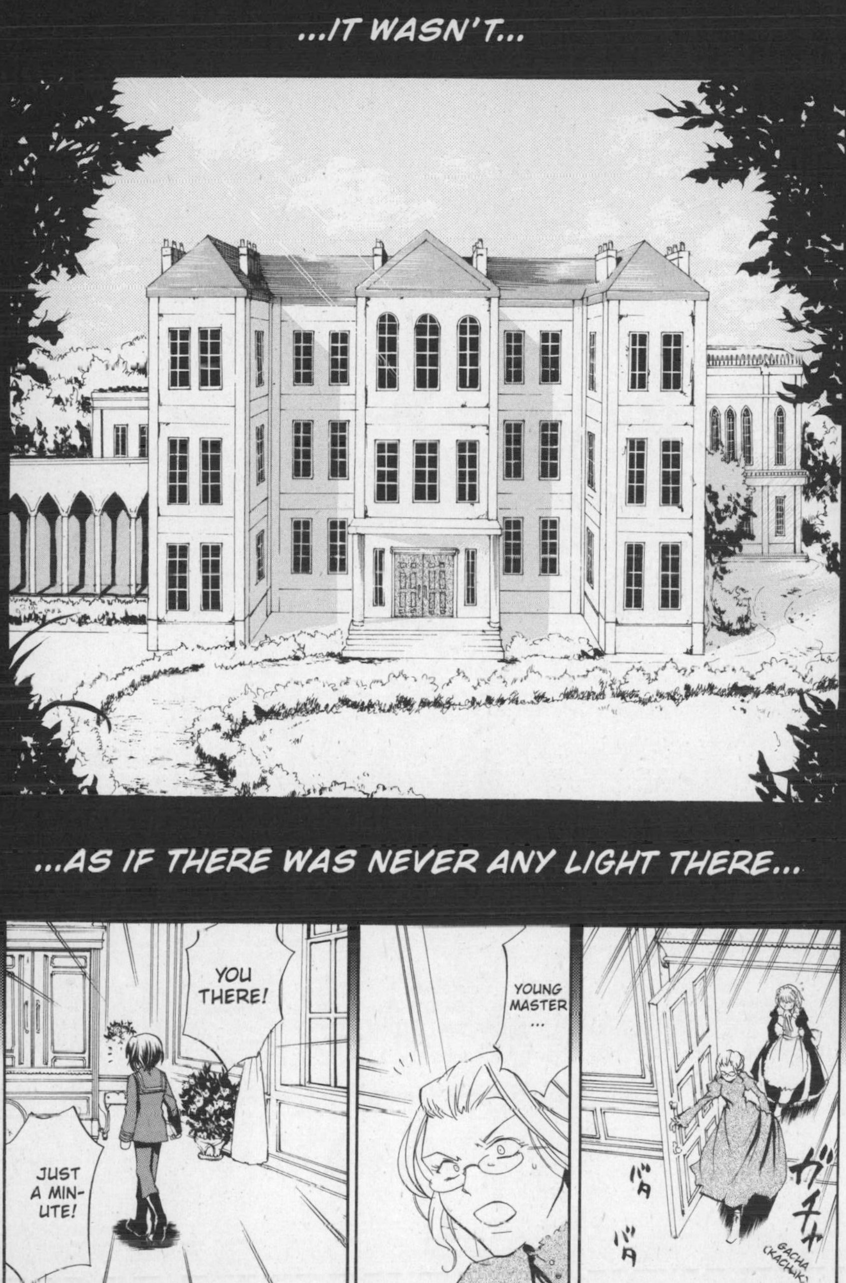
...IT WASN'T...
...AS IF THERE WAS NEVER ANY LIGHT THERE...
GACHA (KACHAK)
YOUNG MASTER ...
YOU THERE!
JUST A MIN-UTE!

SFX: BATA (STOMP) BATA

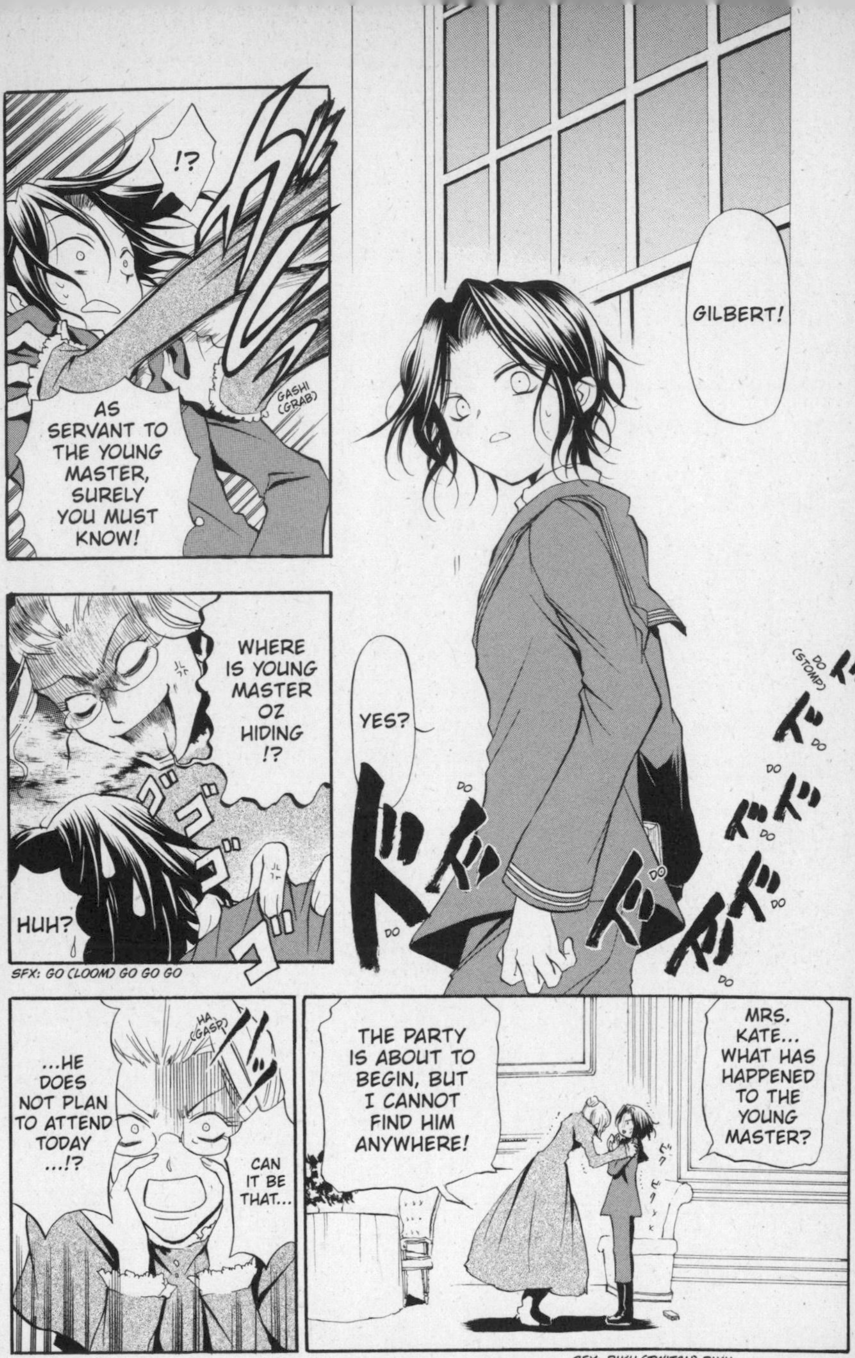
GILBERT!
YES?
DO (STOMP) DO DO DO DO DO DO DO DO DO
!?
GASHI (GRAB)
AS SERVANT TO THE YOUNG MASTER, SURELY YOU MUST KNOW!
WHERE IS YOUNG MASTER OZ HIDING !?
HUH?
MRS. KATE... WHAT HAS HAPPENED TO THE YOUNG MASTER?
THE PARTY IS ABOUT TO BEGIN, BUT I CANNOT FIND HIM ANYWHERE!
HA (GASP)
CAN IT BE THAT...
...HE DOES NOT PLAN TO ATTEND TODAY ...!?

SFX: GO (LOOM) GO GO GO

SFX: BIKU (TWITCH) BIKU

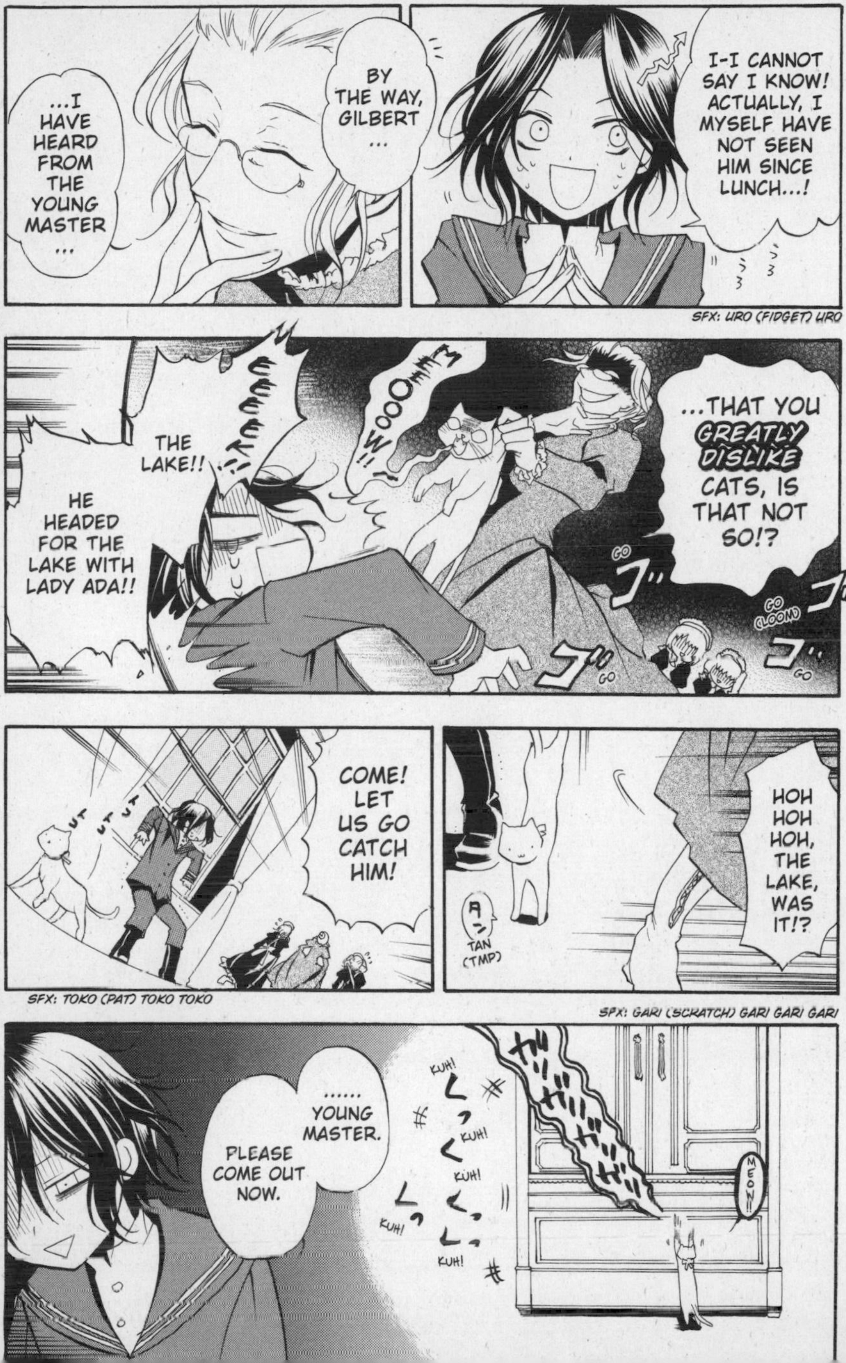

I-I CANNOT SAY I KNOW! ACTUALLY, I MYSELF HAVE NOT SEEN HIM SINCE LUNCH...!
BY THE WAY, GILBERT...
...I HAVE HEARD FROM THE YOUNG MASTER...
...THAT YOU GREATLY DISLIKE CATS, IS THAT NOT SO!?
GO GO (LOOM) GO GO
MEEEOOOW!!
EEEEEK!!
THE LAKE!!
HE HEADED FOR THE LAKE WITH LADY ADA!!
HOH HOH HOH, THE LAKE, WAS IT!?
TAN (TMP)
COME! LET US GO CATCH HIM!
MEOW!!
KUH! KUH! KUH! KUH! KUH!
......YOUNG MASTER.
PLEASE COME OUT NOW.

SFX: URO (FIDGET) URO

SFX: GARI (SCRATCH) GARI GARI GARI

SFX: TOKO (PAT) TOKO TOKO

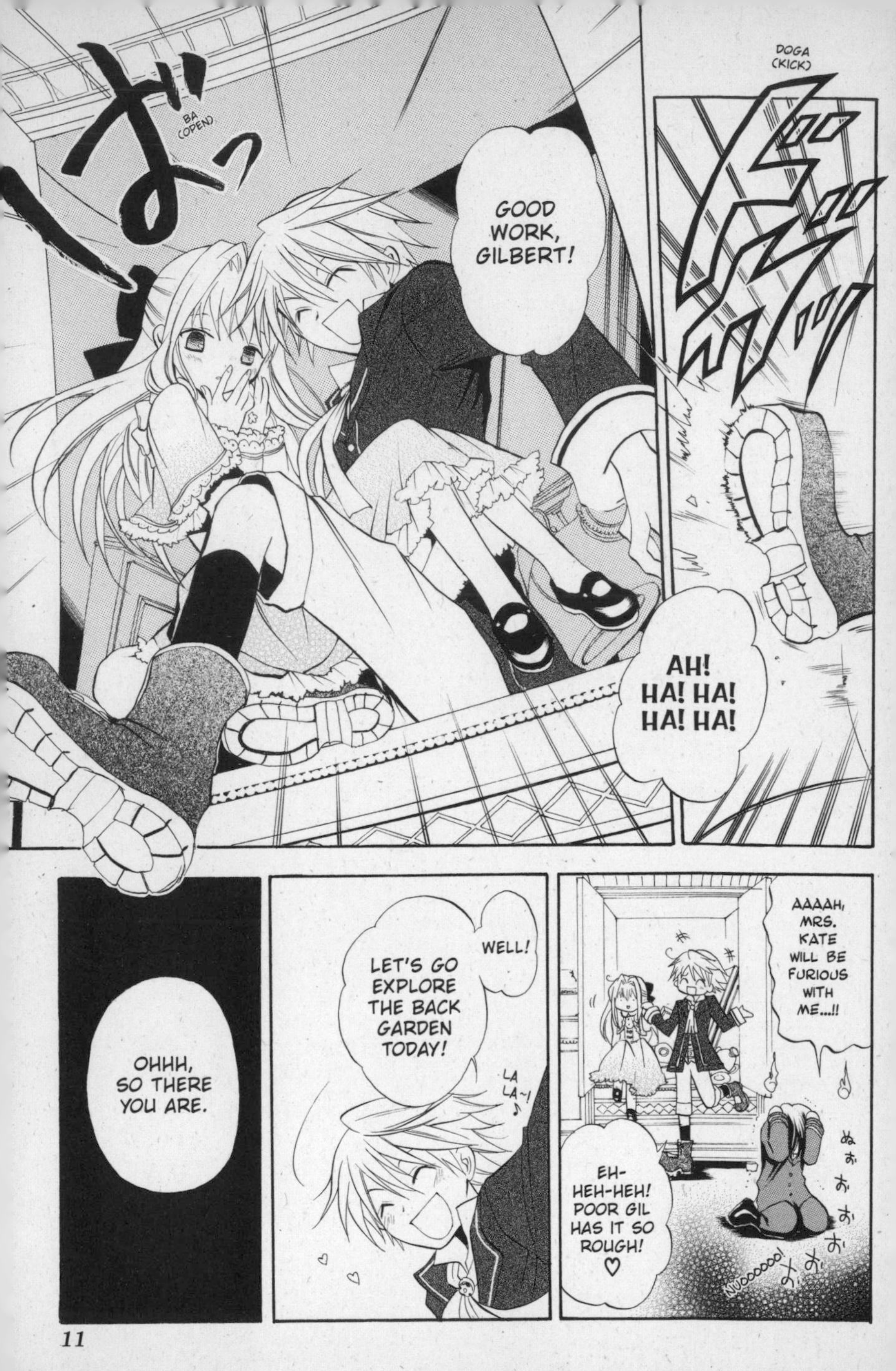
DOGA (KICK)
AH! HA! HA! HA! HA!
BA (OPEN)
GOOD WORK, GILBERT!
AAAAH, MRS. KATE WILL BE FURIOUS WITH ME...!!
NUOOOOOO!
EH-HEH-HEH! POOR GIL HAS IT SO ROUGH! ♡
WELL!
LET'S GO EXPLORE THE BACK GARDEN TODAY!
LA LA~! ♪
OHHH, SO THERE YOU ARE.

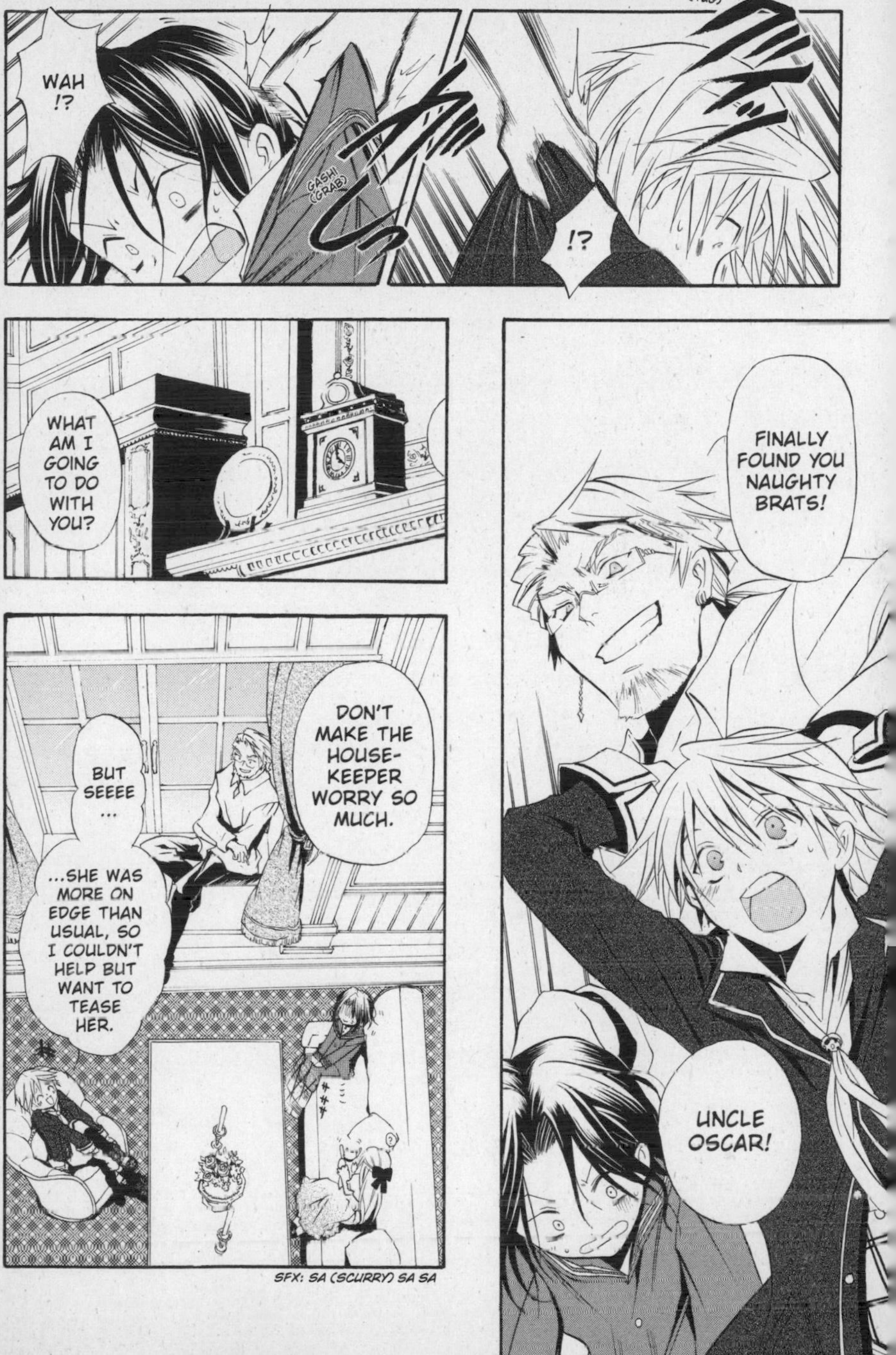
GUI (TUG)
!?
WAH !?
GASHI (GRAB)
FINALLY FOUND YOU NAUGHTY BRATS!
UNCLE OSCAR!
WHAT AM I GOING TO DO WITH YOU?
DON'T MAKE THE HOUSE-KEEPER WORRY SO MUCH.
BUT SEEEE ...
...SHE WAS MORE ON EDGE THAN USUAL, SO I COULDN'T HELP BUT WANT TO TEASE HER.
SFX: SA (SCURRY) SA SA

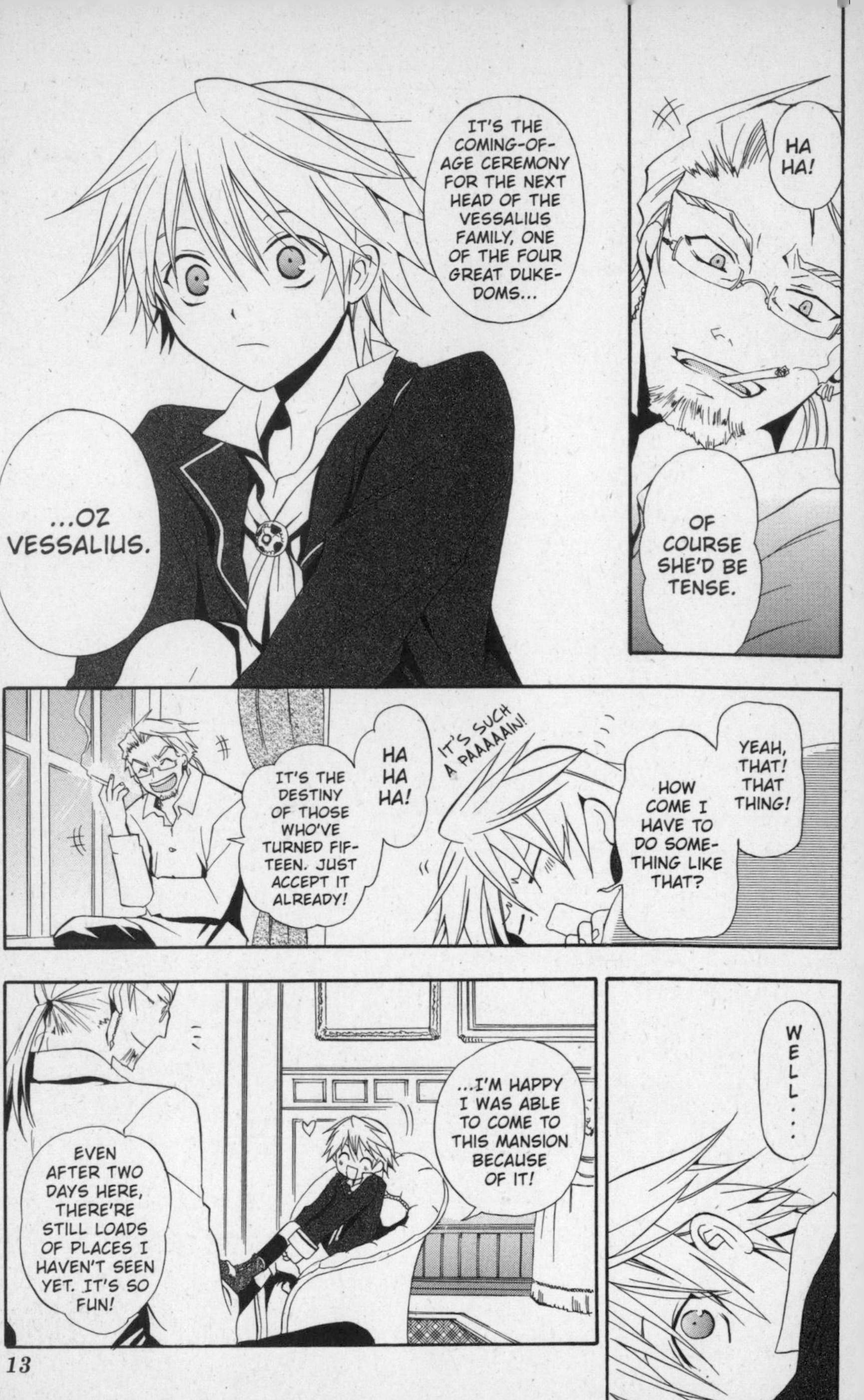
HA HA!
OF COURSE SHE'D BE TENSE.
IT'S THE COMING-OF-AGE CEREMONY FOR THE NEXT HEAD OF THE VESSALIUS FAMILY, ONE OF THE FOUR GREAT DUKE-DOMS...
...OZ VESSALIUS.
YEAH, THAT! THAT THING!
HOW COME I HAVE TO DO SOME-THING LIKE THAT?
IT'S SUCH A PAAAAAIN!
HA HA HA!
IT'S THE DESTINY OF THOSE WHO'VE TURNED FIF-TEEN. JUST ACCEPT IT ALREADY!
WELL...
...I'M HAPPY I WAS ABLE TO COME TO THIS MANSION BECAUSE OF IT!
EVEN AFTER TWO DAYS HERE, THERE'RE STILL LOADS OF PLACES I HAVEN'T SEEN YET. IT'S SO FUN!

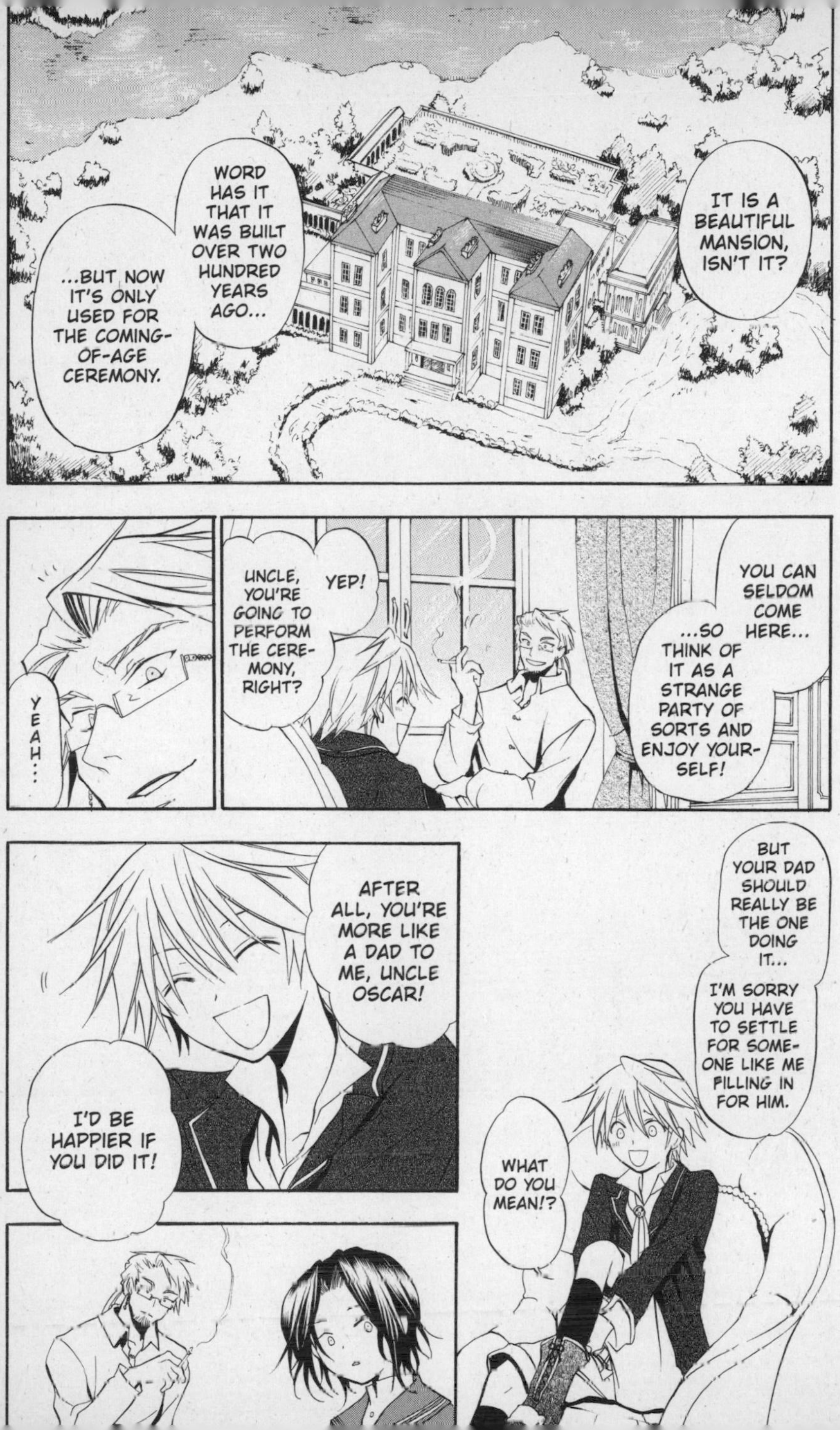
IT IS A BEAUTIFUL MANSION, ISN'T IT?
WORD HAS IT THAT IT WAS BUILT OVER TWO HUNDRED YEARS AGO...
...BUT NOW IT'S ONLY USED FOR THE COMING-OF-AGE CEREMONY.
YOU CAN SELDOM COME HERE...
...SO THINK OF IT AS A STRANGE PARTY OF SORTS AND ENJOY YOUR-SELF!
YEP!
UNCLE, YOU'RE GOING TO PERFORM THE CERE-MONY, RIGHT?
YEAH...
BUT YOUR DAD SHOULD REALLY BE THE ONE DOING IT...
I'M SORRY YOU HAVE TO SETTLE FOR SOME-ONE LIKE ME FILLING IN FOR HIM.
WHAT DO YOU MEAN!?
AFTER ALL, YOU'RE MORE LIKE A DAD TO ME, UNCLE OSCAR!
I'D BE HAPPIER IF YOU DID IT!

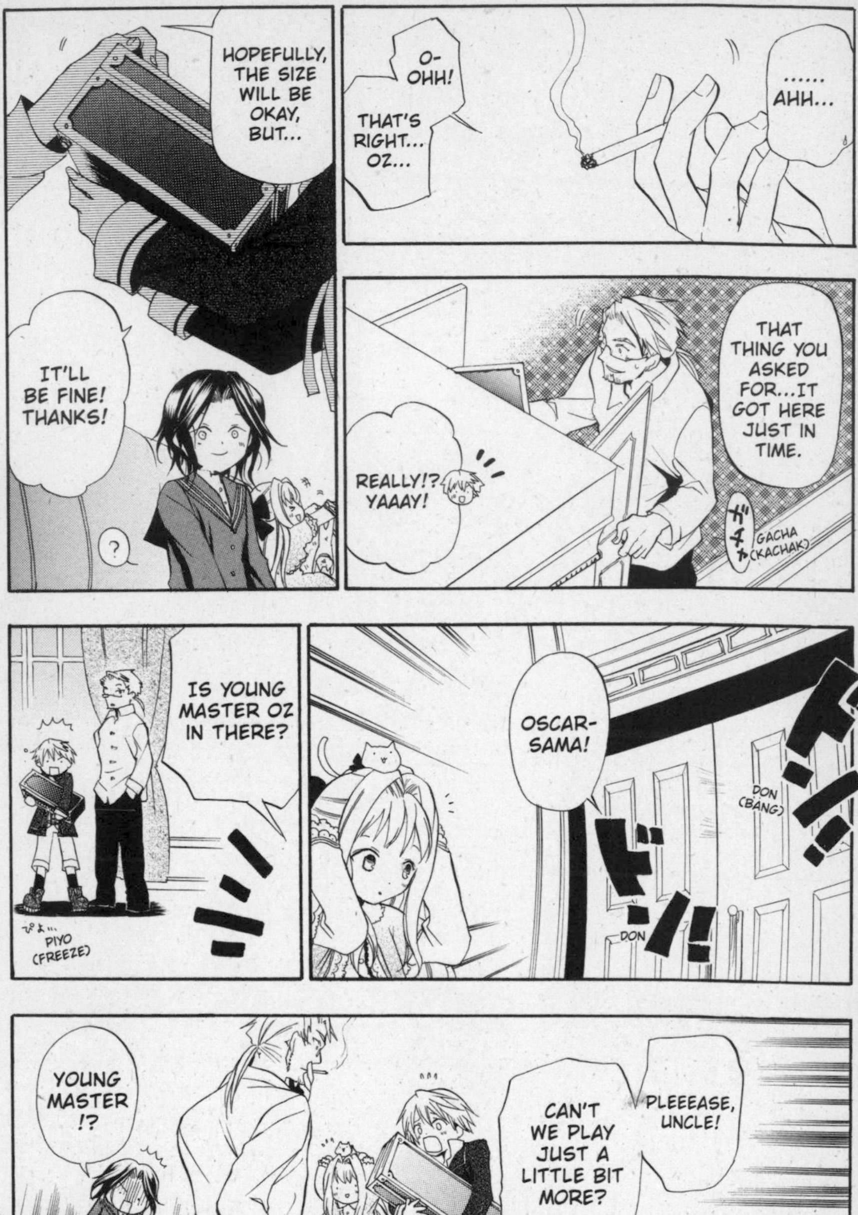

......
AHH...
O-OHH!
THAT'S RIGHT... OZ...
THAT THING YOU ASKED FOR...IT GOT HERE JUST IN TIME.
ガチャ
GACHA (KACHAK)
REALLY!? YAAAY!
HOPEFULLY, THE SIZE WILL BE OKAY, BUT...
IT'LL BE FINE! THANKS!
?
DON (BANG)
OSCAR-SAMA!
DON
IS YOUNG MASTER OZ IN THERE?
ぴよ...
PIYO (FREEZE)
PLEEEASE, UNCLE!
CAN'T WE PLAY JUST A LITTLE BIT MORE?
YOUNG MASTER !?

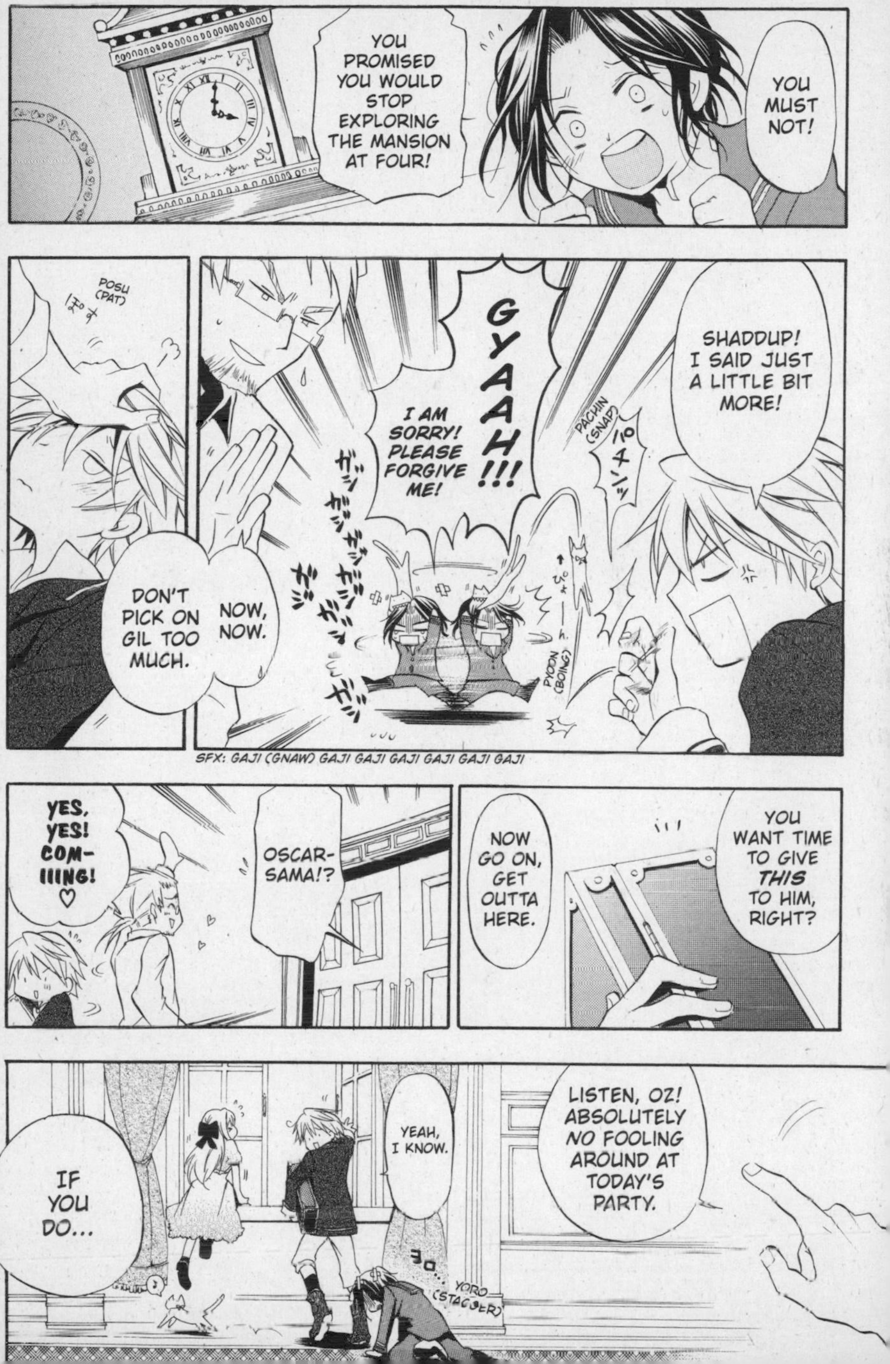
YOU MUST NOT!
YOU PROMISED YOU WOULD STOP EXPLORING THE MANSION AT FOUR!
SHADDUP! I SAID JUST A LITTLE BIT MORE!
PACHIN (SNAP)
GYAAAH!!!
I AM SORRY! PLEASE FORGIVE ME!
PYOON (BOING)
POSU (PAT)
NOW, NOW.
DON'T PICK ON GIL TOO MUCH.
SFX: GAJI (GNAW) GAJI GAJI GAJI GAJI GAJI GAJI
YOU WANT TIME TO GIVE *THIS* TO HIM, RIGHT?
NOW GO ON, GET OUTTA HERE.
OSCAR-SAMA!?
YES, YES! COM-IIING! ♡
LISTEN, OZ! ABSOLUTELY NO FOOLING AROUND AT TODAY'S PARTY.
YEAH, I KNOW.
YORO (STAGGER)
IF YOU DO...

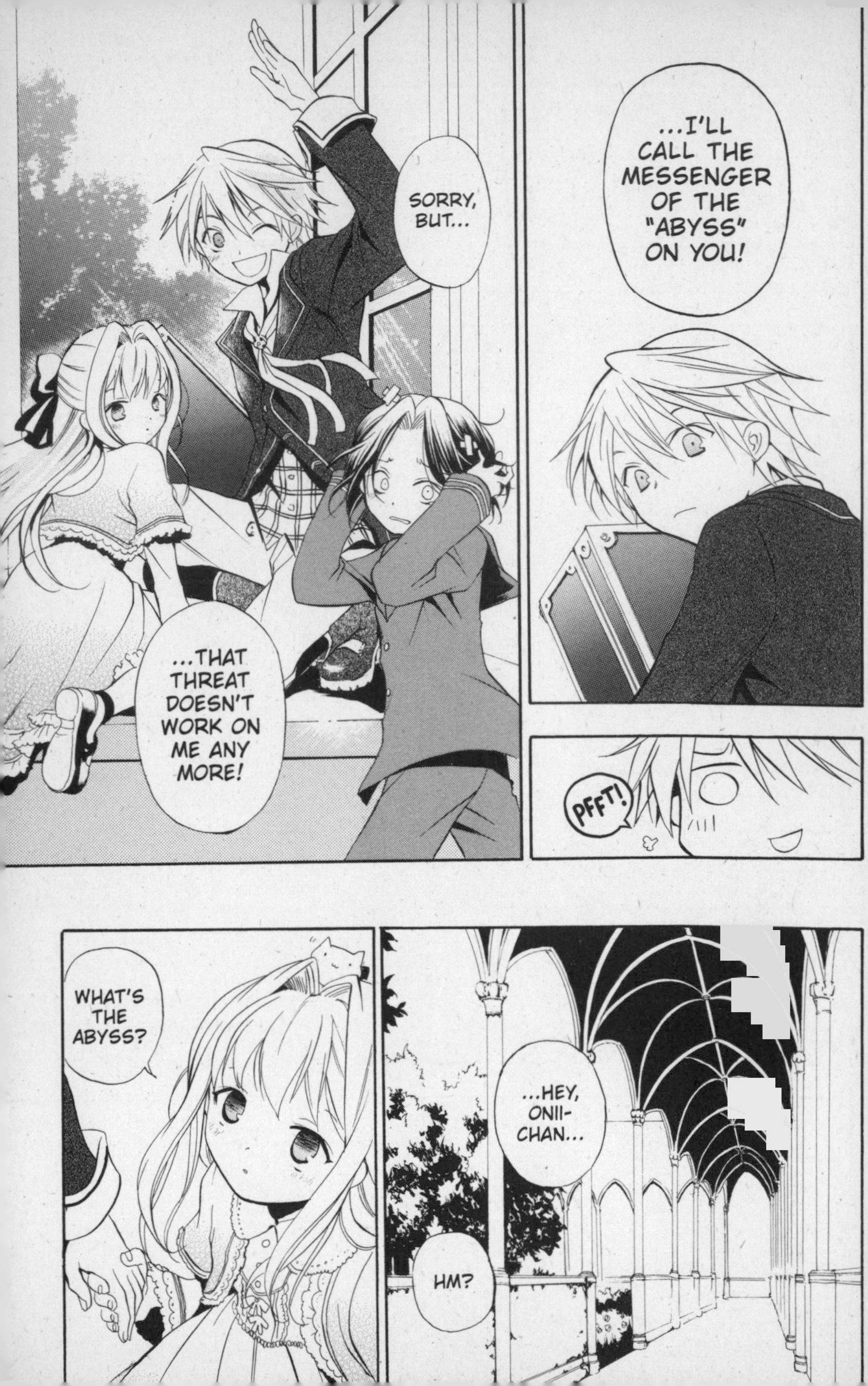
...I'LL CALL THE MESSENGER OF THE "ABYSS" ON YOU!
PFFT!
SORRY, BUT...
...THAT THREAT DOESN'T WORK ON ME ANY MORE!
...HEY, ONII-CHAN...
HM?
WHAT'S THE ABYSS?

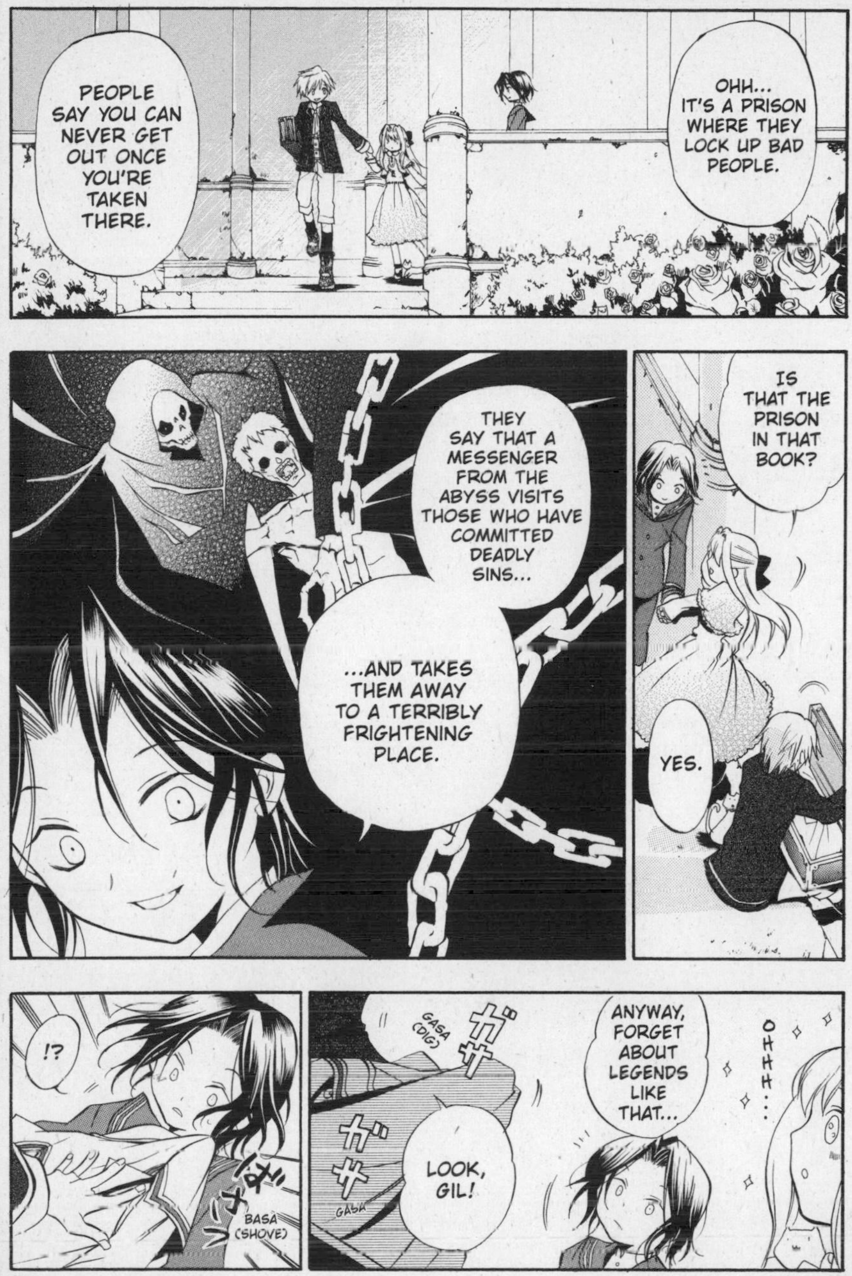

OHH... IT'S A PRISON WHERE THEY LOCK UP BAD PEOPLE.
PEOPLE SAY YOU CAN NEVER GET OUT ONCE YOU'RE TAKEN THERE.
IS THAT THE PRISON IN THAT BOOK?
YES.
THEY SAY THAT A MESSENGER FROM THE ABYSS VISITS THOSE WHO HAVE COMMITTED DEADLY SINS...
...AND TAKES THEM AWAY TO A TERRIBLY FRIGHTENING PLACE.
OHHH...
ANYWAY, FORGET ABOUT LEGENDS LIKE THAT...
GASA (DIG)
LOOK, GIL!
GASA
!?
BASA (SHOVE)

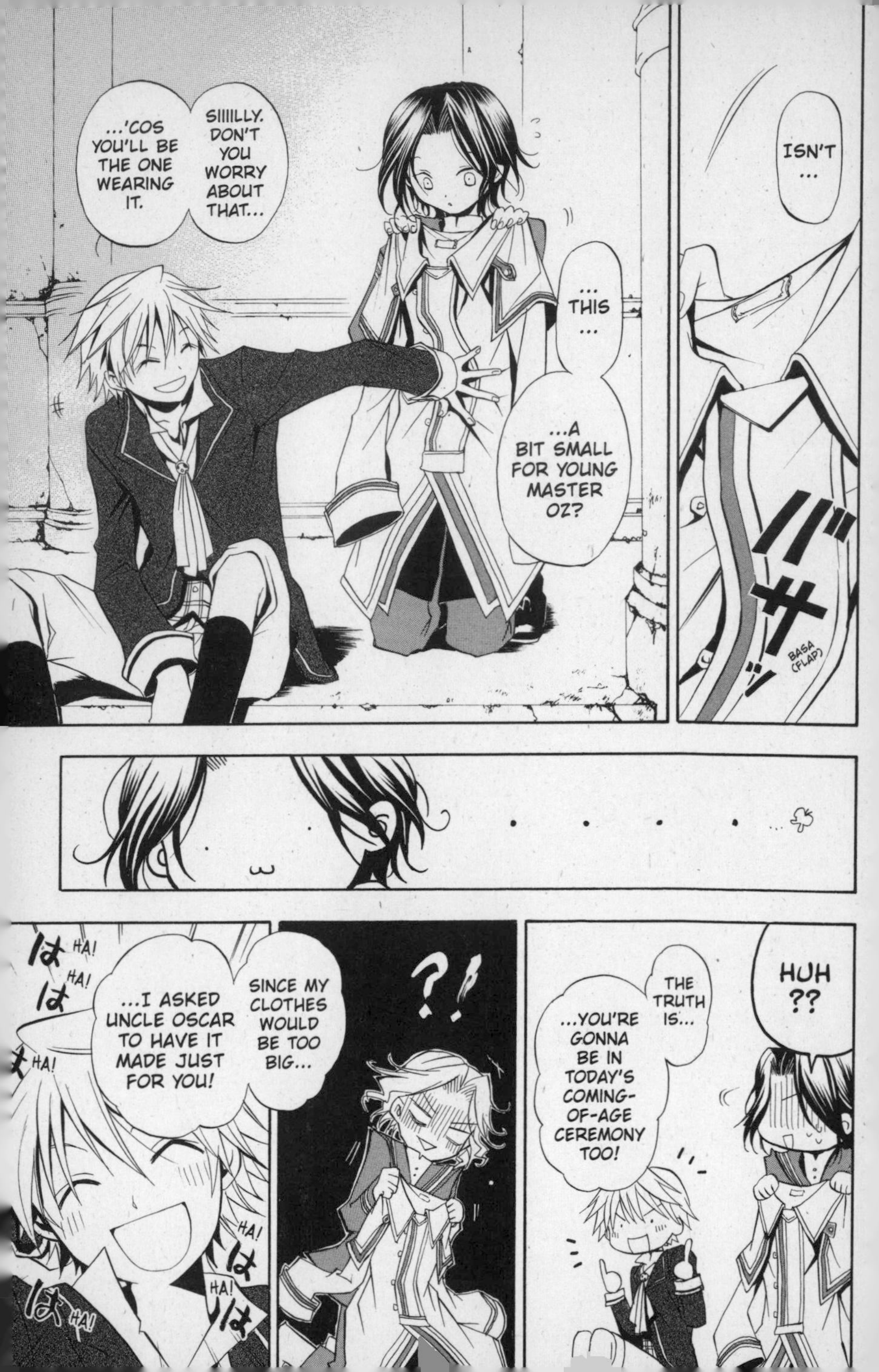
ISN'T ...
バサ
BASA (FLAP)
... THIS ...
...A BIT SMALL FOR YOUNG MASTER OZ?
SIIIILLY. DON'T YOU WORRY ABOUT THAT...
...'COS YOU'LL BE THE ONE WEARING IT.
HUH ??
THE TRUTH IS...
...YOU'RE GONNA BE IN TODAY'S COMING-OF-AGE CEREMONY TOO!
?!
SINCE MY CLOTHES WOULD BE TOO BIG...
...I ASKED UNCLE OSCAR TO HAVE IT MADE JUST FOR YOU!
は HA! は HA! は HA!
は HA! は HA! は HA!

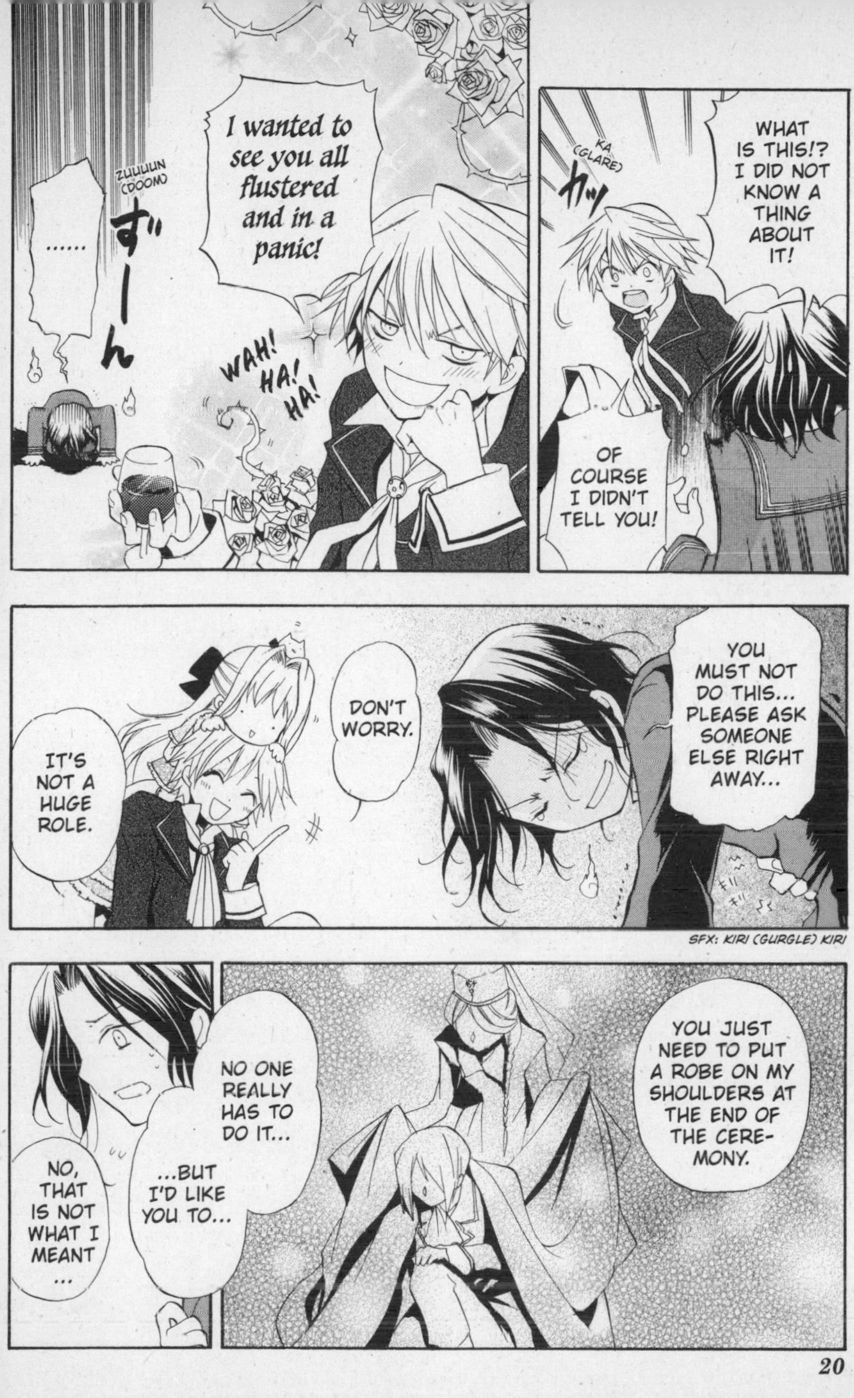

WHAT IS THIS!? I DID NOT KNOW A THING ABOUT IT!
KA (GLARE)
カッ
OF COURSE I DIDN'T TELL YOU!
I wanted to see you all flustered and in a panic!
WAH! HA! HA!
ZUUUUN (DOOM)
ずーん
......
YOU MUST NOT DO THIS... PLEASE ASK SOMEONE ELSE RIGHT AWAY...
DON'T WORRY.
IT'S NOT A HUGE ROLE.
SFX: KIRI (GURGLE) KIRI
YOU JUST NEED TO PUT A ROBE ON MY SHOULDERS AT THE END OF THE CERE-MONY.
NO ONE REALLY HAS TO DO IT...
...BUT I'D LIKE YOU TO...
NO, THAT IS NOT WHAT I MEANT ...

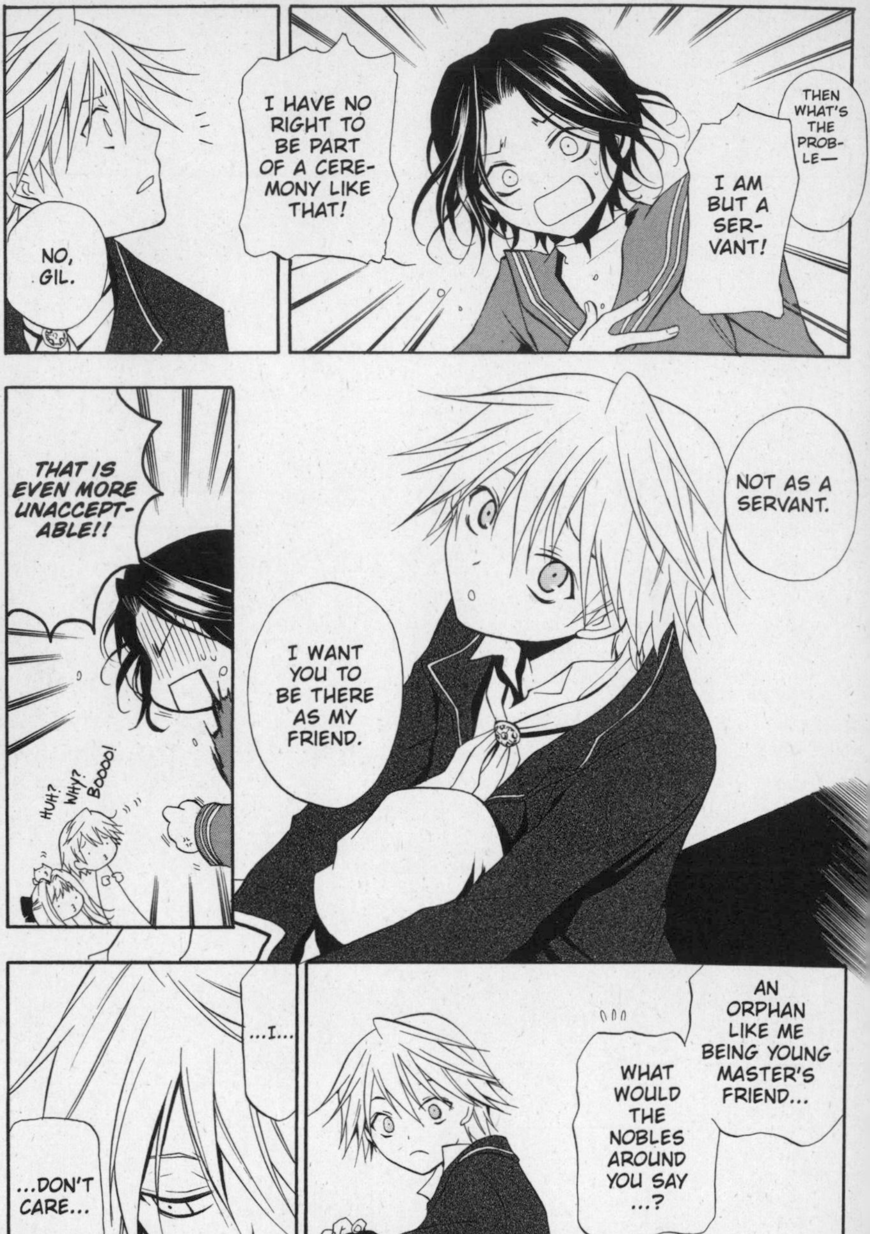
THEN WHAT'S THE PROBLE—
I AM BUT A SERVANT!
I HAVE NO RIGHT TO BE PART OF A CEREMONY LIKE THAT!
NO, GIL.
NOT AS A SERVANT.
I WANT YOU TO BE THERE AS MY FRIEND.
THAT IS EVEN MORE UNACCEPTABLE!!
HUH? WHY? BOOOO!
AN ORPHAN LIKE ME BEING YOUNG MASTER'S FRIEND...
WHAT WOULD THE NOBLES AROUND YOU SAY ...?
...I...
...DON'T CARE...

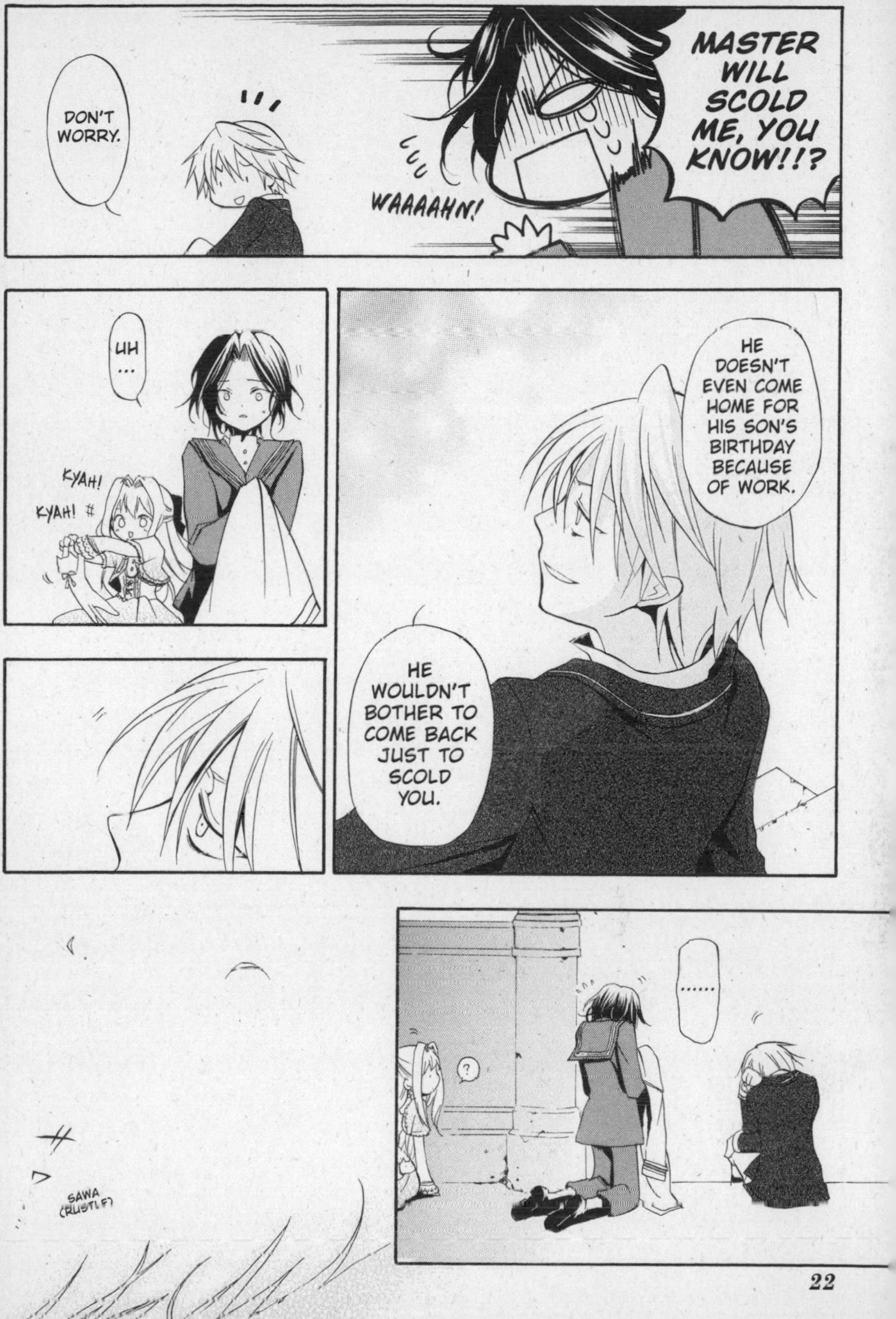
MASTER WILL SCOLD ME, YOU KNOW!!?
WAAAAHN!
DON'T WORRY.
HE DOESN'T EVEN COME HOME FOR HIS SON'S BIRTHDAY BECAUSE OF WORK.
HE WOULDN'T BOTHER TO COME BACK JUST TO SCOLD YOU.
UH ...
KYAH!
KYAH!
......
?
SAWA (RUSTLE)

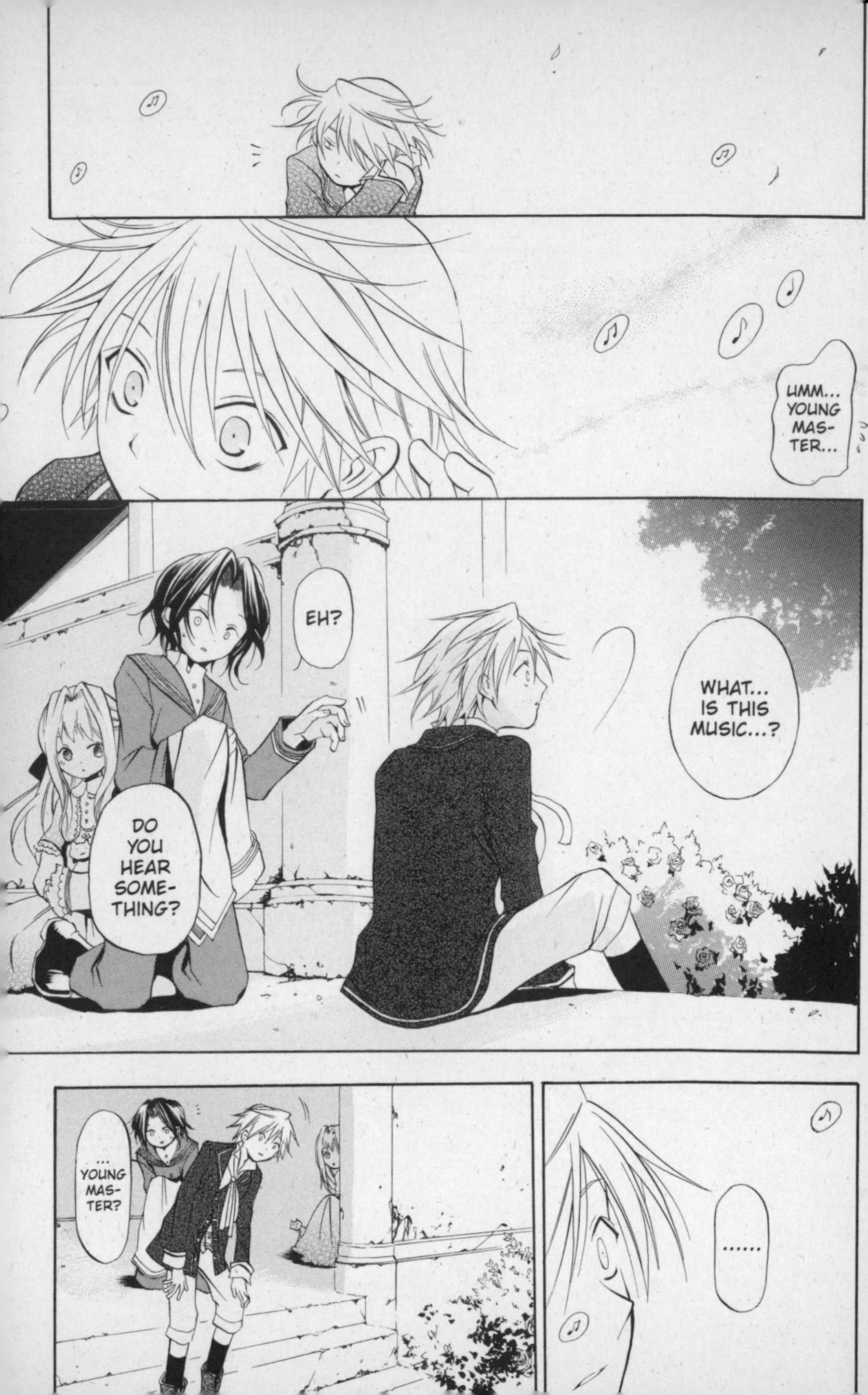
UMM... YOUNG MASTER...
WHAT... IS THIS MUSIC...?
EH?
DO YOU HEAR SOMETHING?
......
... YOUNG MASTER?

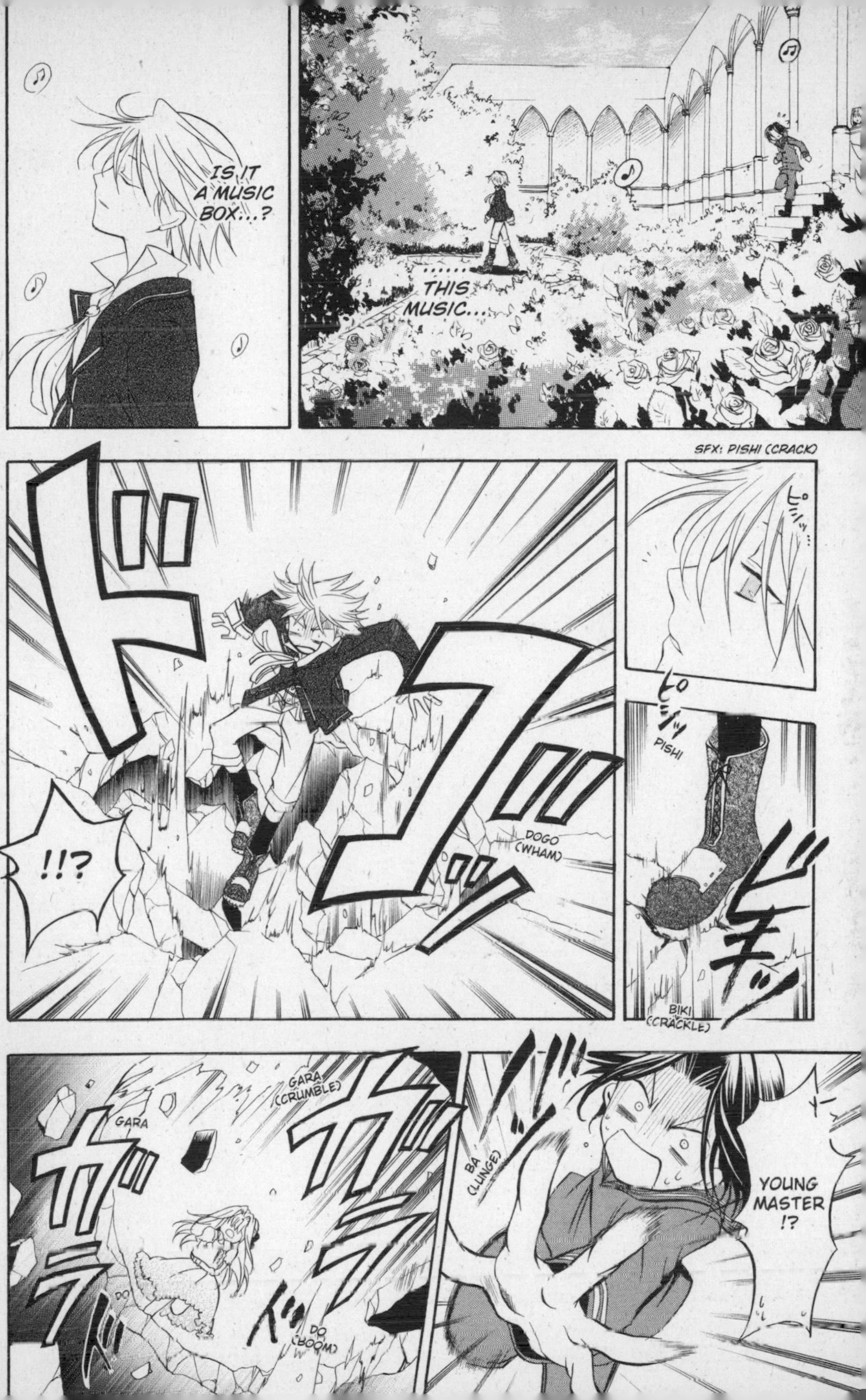
……THIS MUSIC…
IS IT A MUSIC BOX…?
SFX: PISHI (CRACK)
PISHI
BIKI (CRACKLE)
DOGO (WHAM)
!!?
YOUNG MASTER !?
BA (LUNGE)
GARA (CRUMBLE)
GARA
DO
DO (BOOM)

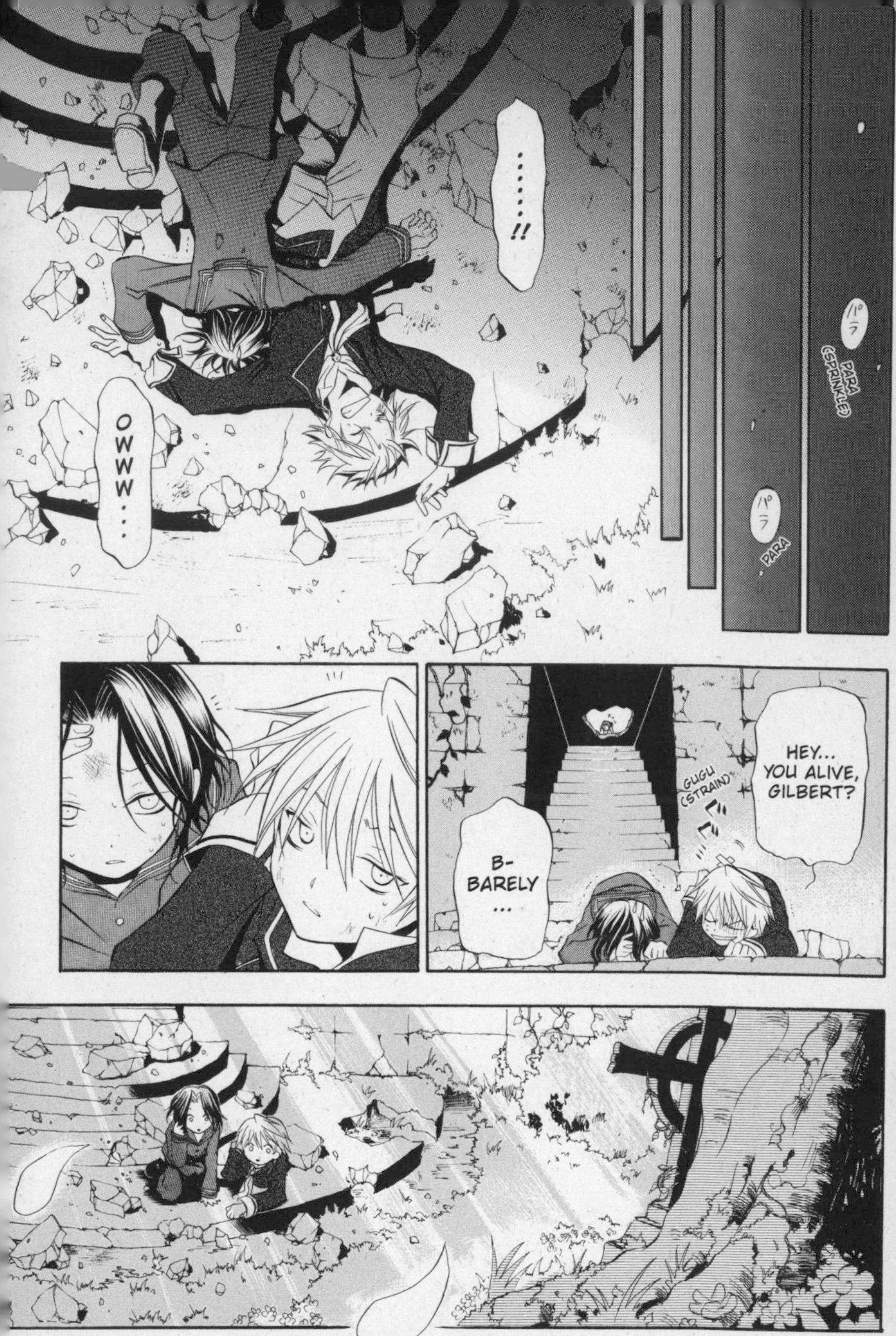
パラ
PARA (SPRINKLE)
パラ
PARA
......!!
OWWW...
HEY... YOU ALIVE, GILBERT?
GUGU (STRAIN)
B-BARELY ...

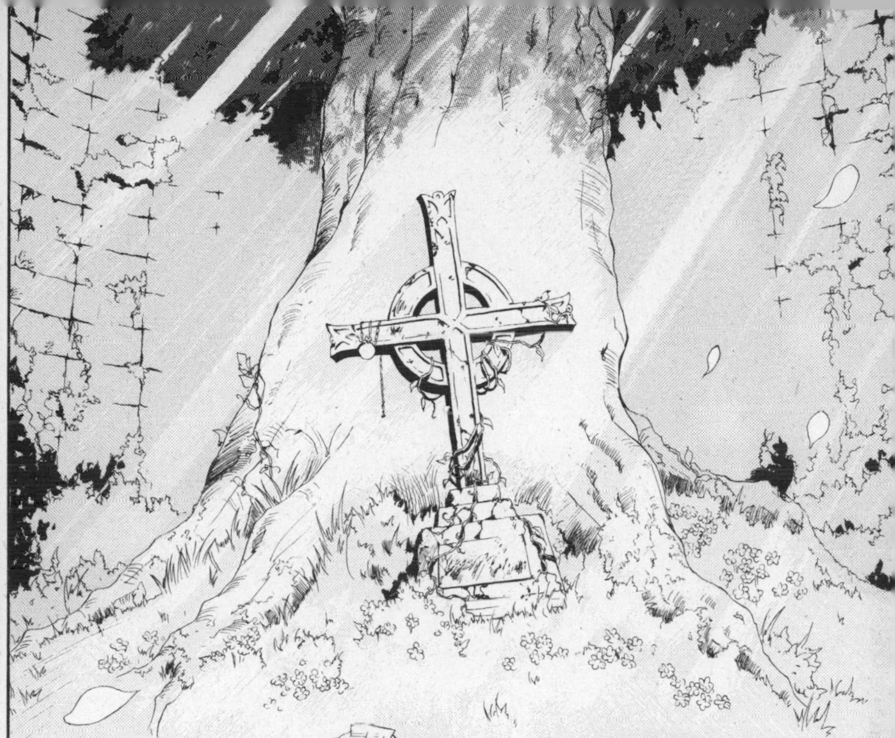

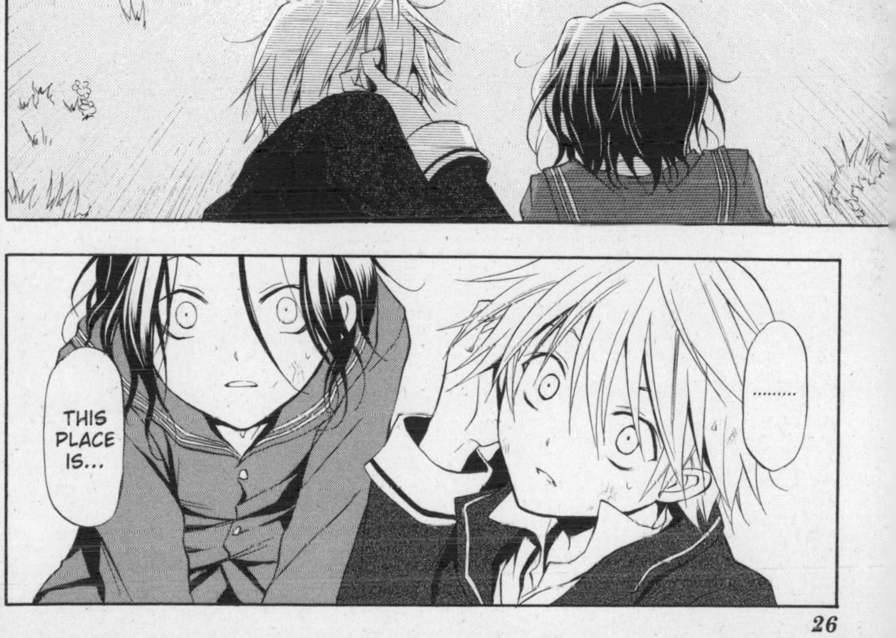
.........
THIS PLACE IS...

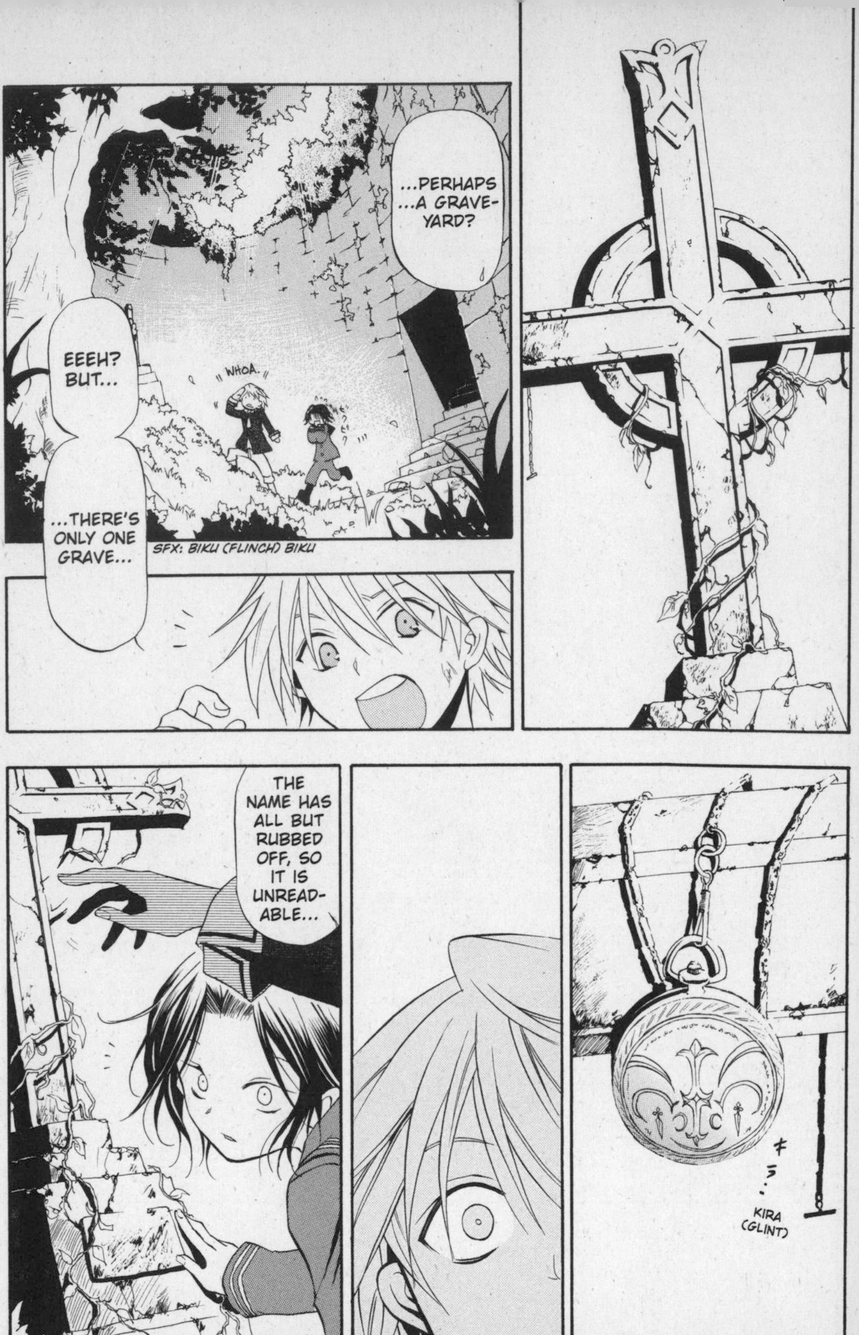
...PERHAPS ...A GRAVE-YARD?
EEEH? BUT...
WHOA.
...THERE'S ONLY ONE GRAVE...
SFX: BIKU (FLINCH) BIKU
KIRA (GLINT)
THE NAME HAS ALL BUT RUBBED OFF, SO IT IS UNREAD-ABLE...

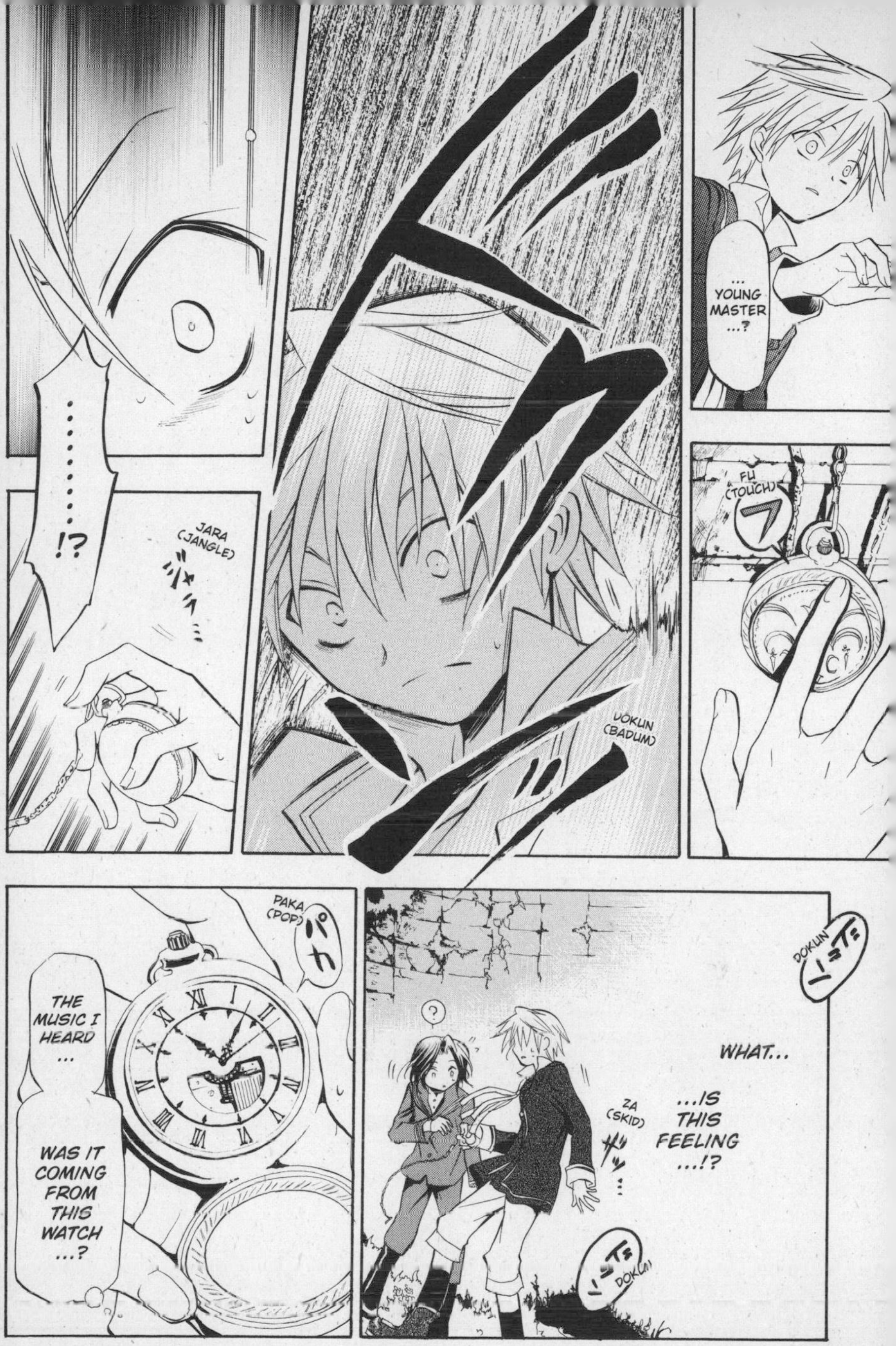
...YOUNG MASTER...?
FU (TOUCH)
DOKUN (BADUM)
......!?
JARA (JANGLE)
DOKUN
WHAT...
...IS THIS FEELING...!?
ZA (SKID)
DOKUN
PAKA (POP)
THE MUSIC I HEARD...
WAS IT COMING FROM THIS WATCH...?

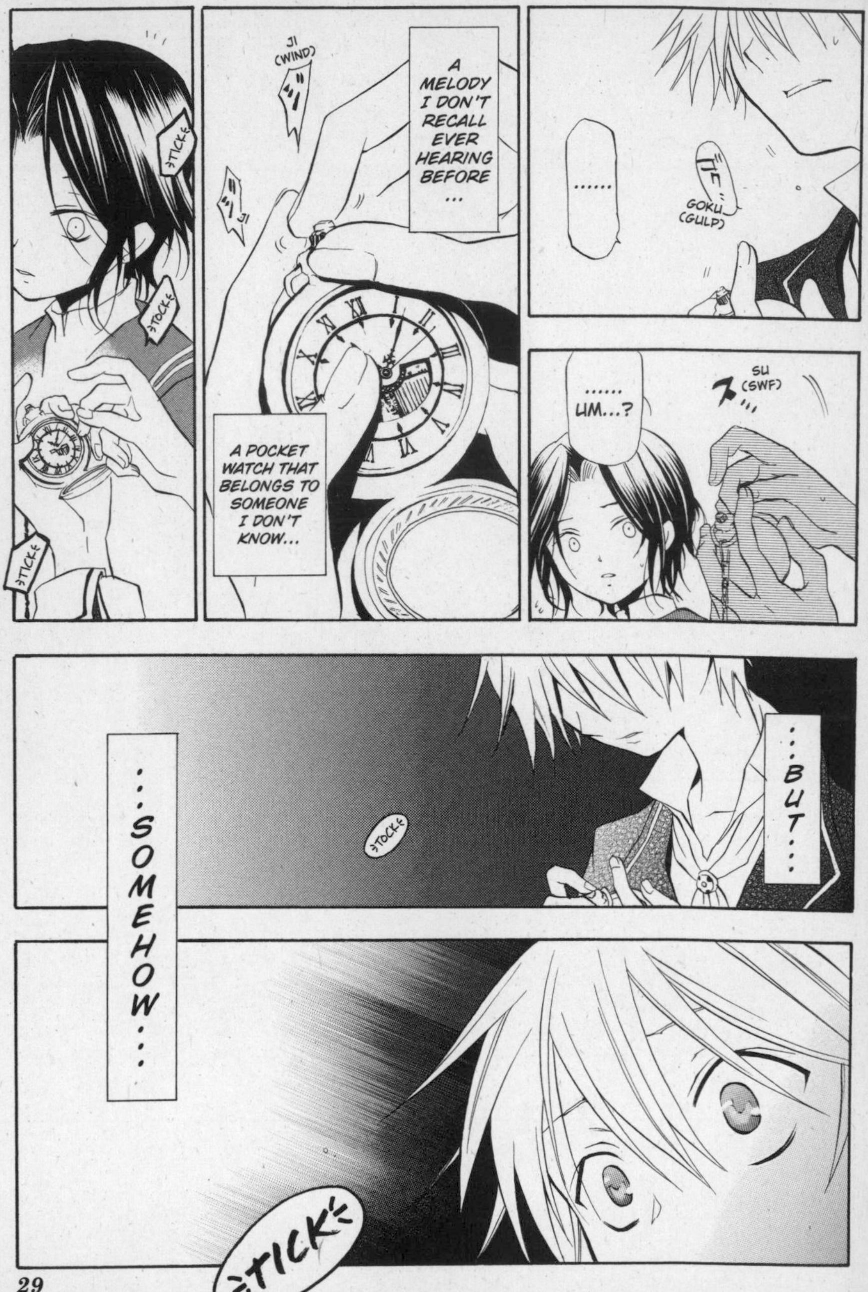
......
GOKU (GULP)
......
UM...?
SU (SWF)
A MELODY I DON'T RECALL EVER HEARING BEFORE...
JI (WIND)
JI
A POCKET WATCH THAT BELONGS TO SOMEONE I DON'T KNOW...
TICK
TOCK
TICK
...BUT...
TOCK
...SOMEHOW...
TICK

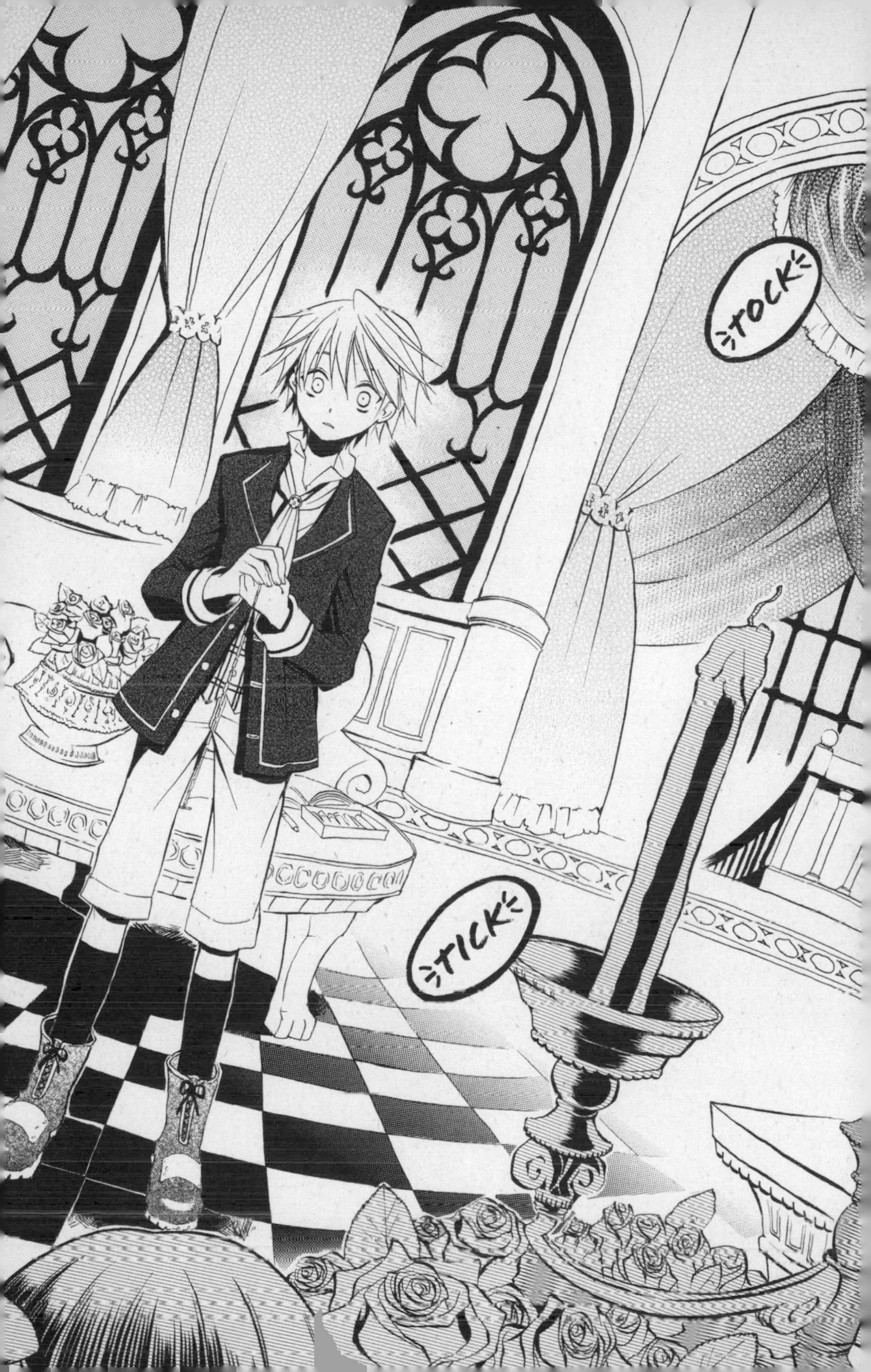
TOCK
TICK

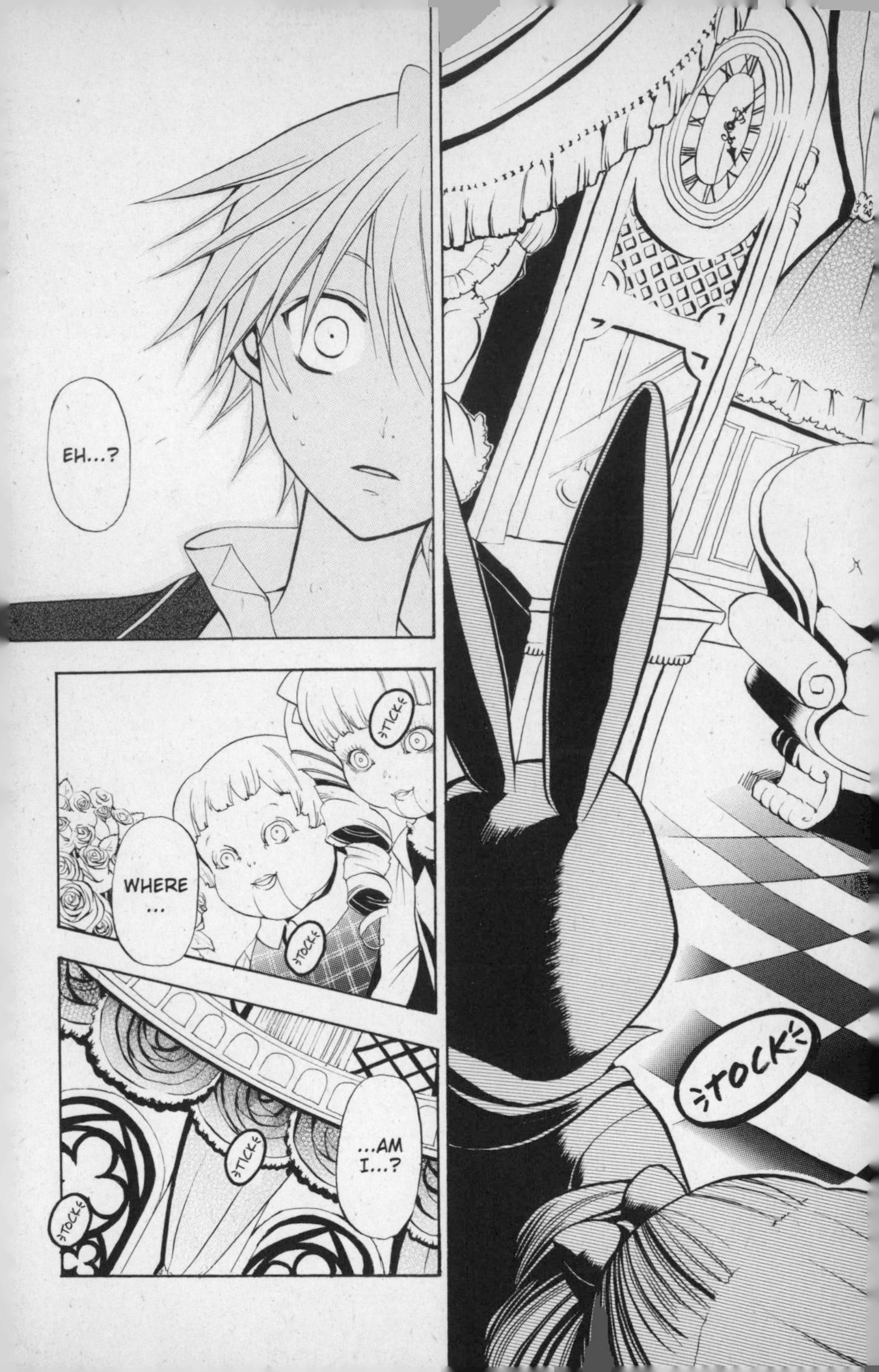
TOCK
EH...?
TICK
WHERE ...
TOCK
...AM I...?
TICK
TOCK

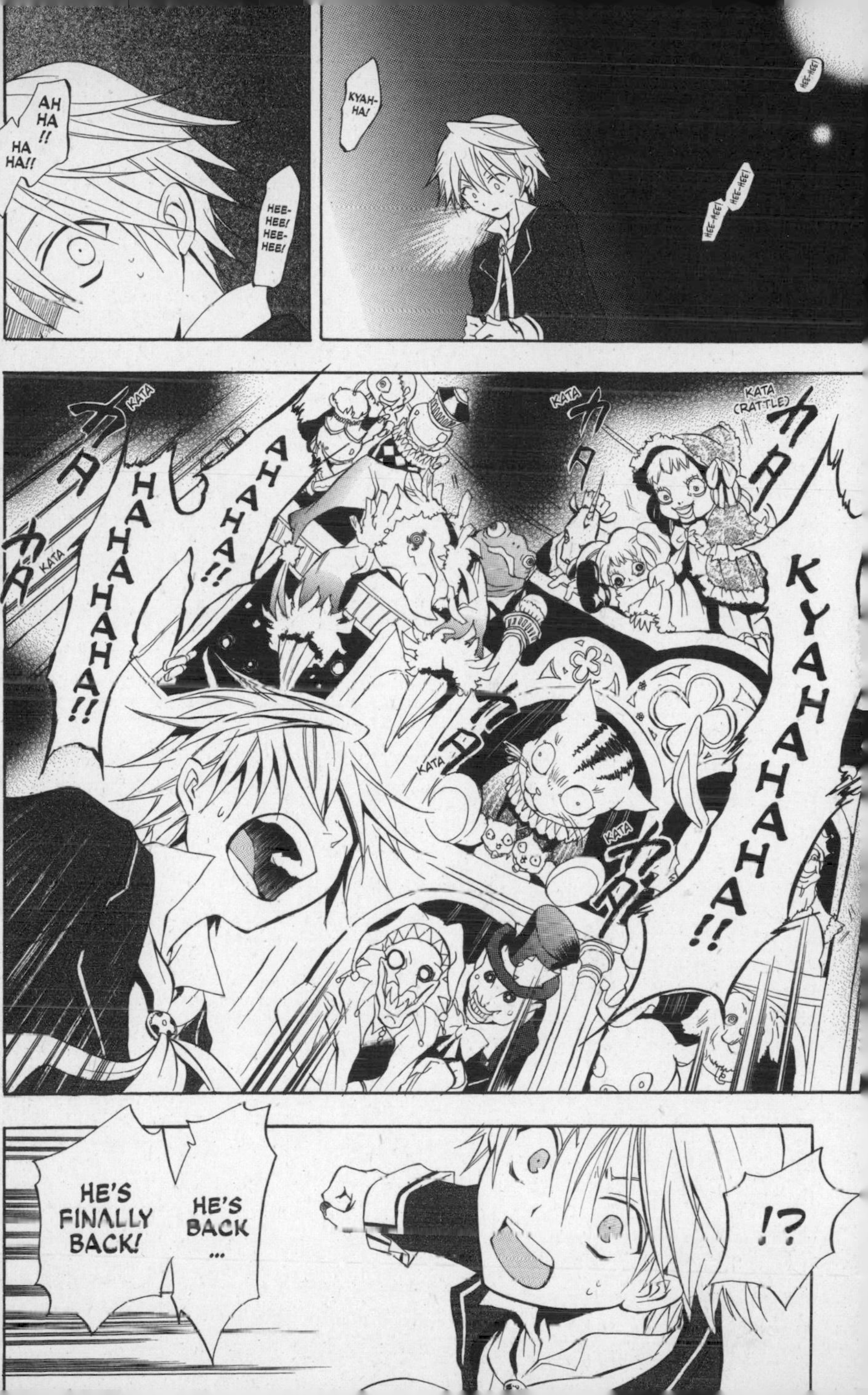
HEE-HEE!
HEE-HEE! HEE-HEE!
KYAH-HA!
HEE-HEE! HEE-HEE!
AH HA!! HA HA!!
KATA (RATTLE)
KYAHAHAHAHA!!
KATA
KATA
KATA
AHAHAHA!!
HAHAHAHAHA!!
KATA
KATA
!?
HE'S BACK...
HE'S FINALLY BACK!

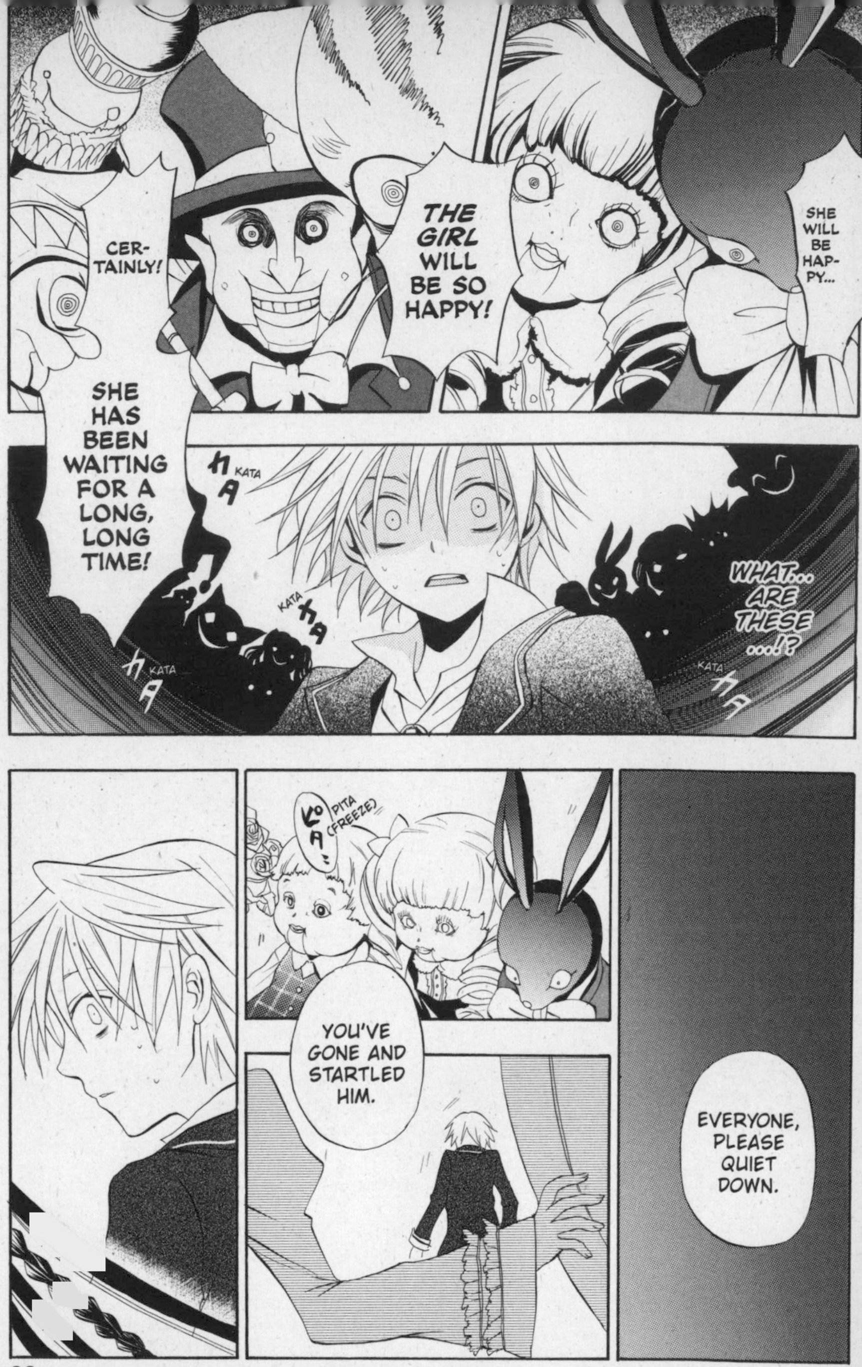
SHE WILL BE HAPPY...
THE GIRL WILL BE SO HAPPY!
CER-TAINLY!
SHE HAS BEEN WAITING FOR A LONG, LONG TIME!
KATA
KATA
KATA
KATA
WHAT... ARE THESE ...!?
EVERYONE, PLEASE QUIET DOWN.
PITA (FREEZE)
YOU'VE GONE AND STARTLED HIM.

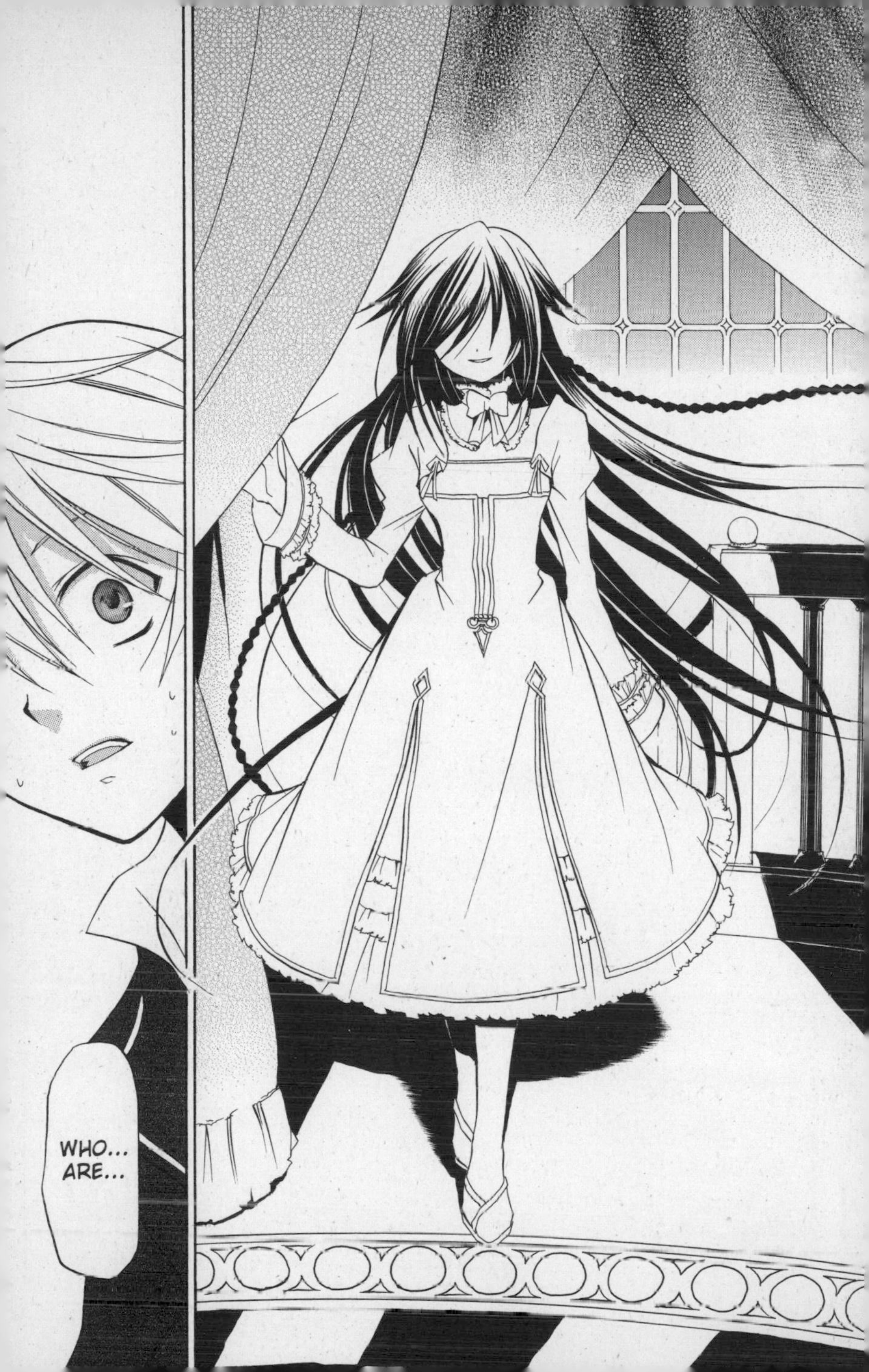
WHO... ARE...

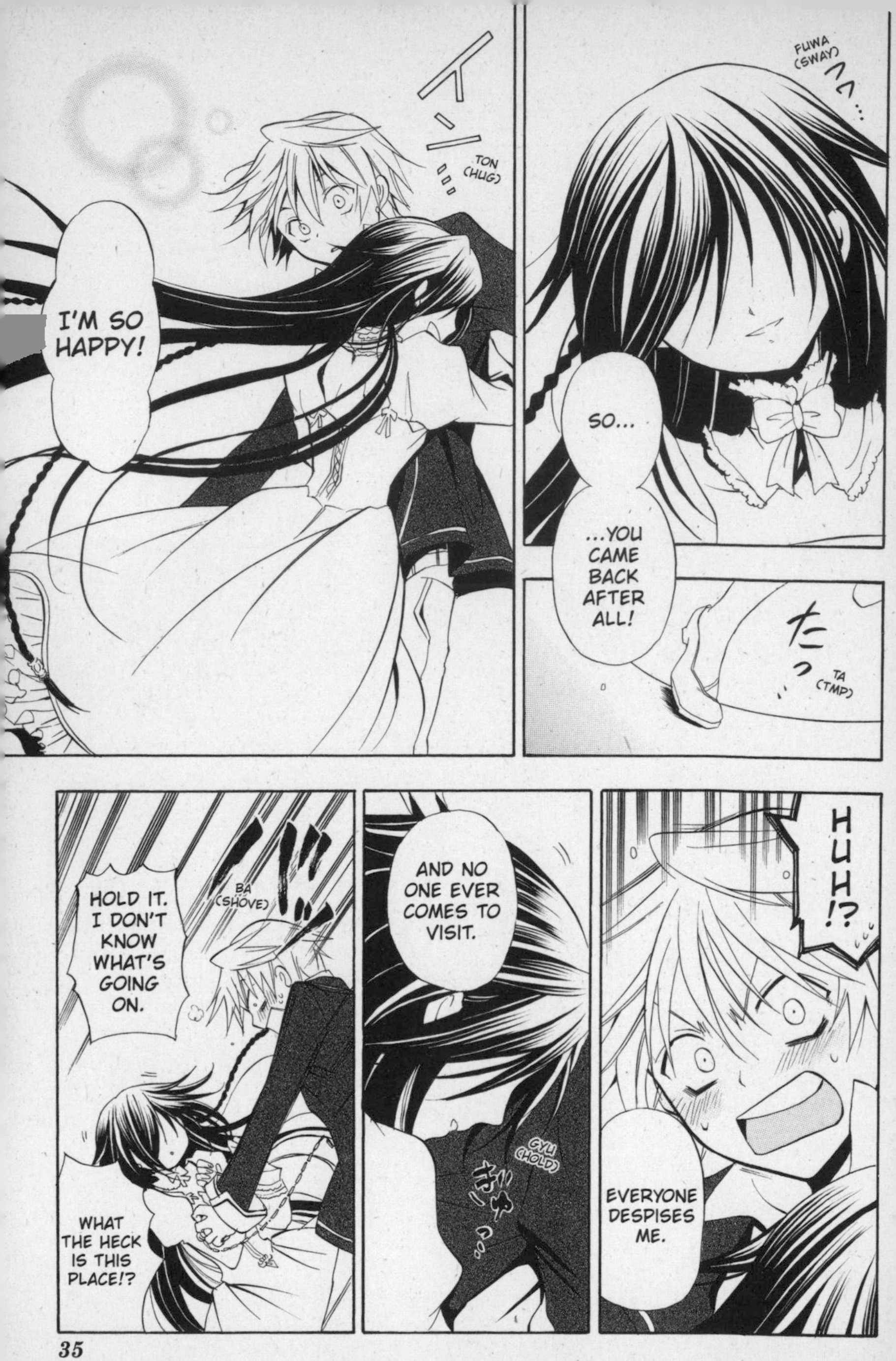
FUWA (SWAY)
SO...
...YOU CAME BACK AFTER ALL!
TA (TMP)
TON (HUG)
I'M SO HAPPY!
HUH!?
EVERYONE DESPISES ME.
AND NO ONE EVER COMES TO VISIT.
GYU (HOLD)
BA (SHOVE)
HOLD IT. I DON'T KNOW WHAT'S GOING ON.
WHAT THE HECK IS THIS PLACE!?

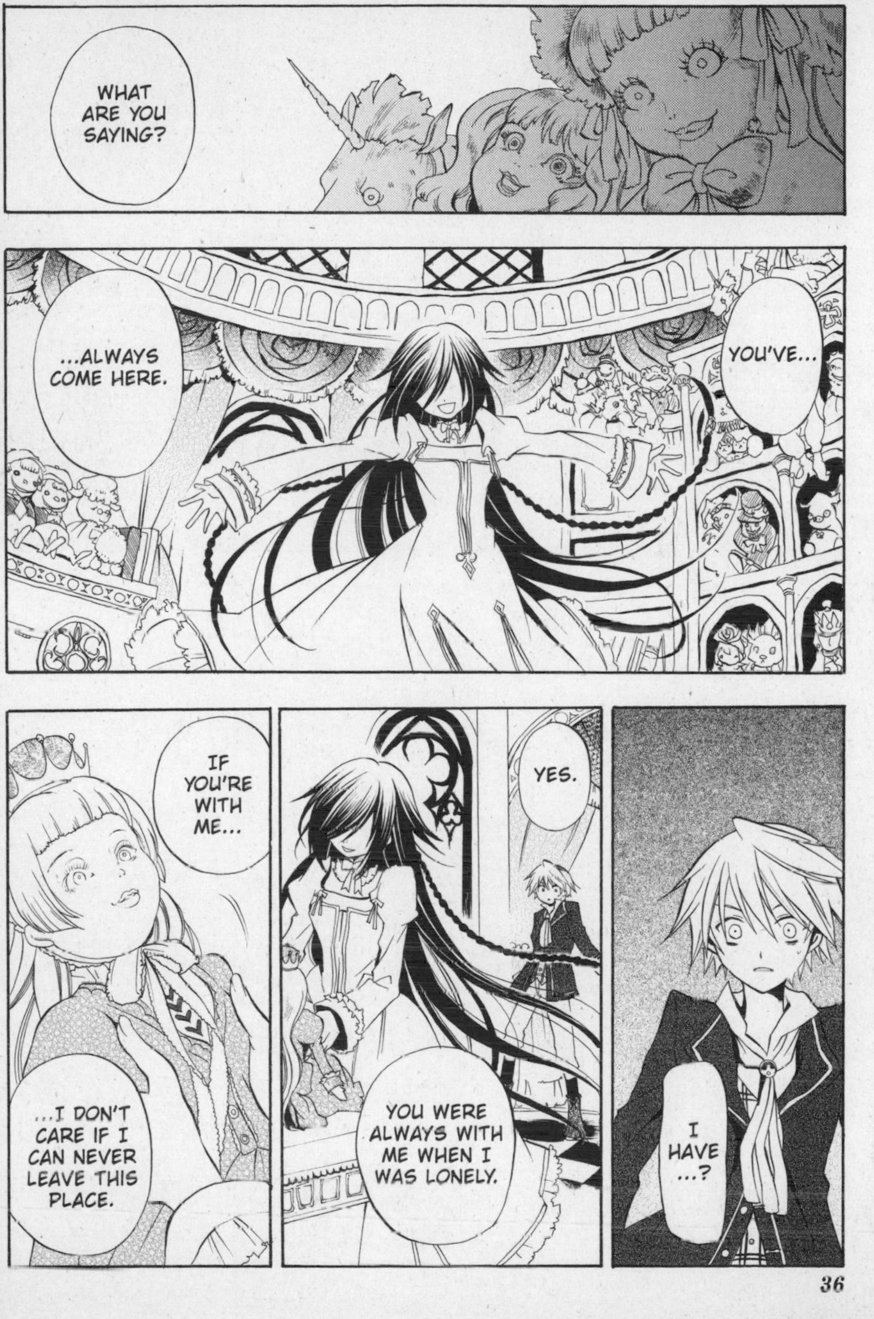
WHAT ARE YOU SAYING?
YOU'VE...
...ALWAYS COME HERE.
I HAVE ...?
YES.
YOU WERE ALWAYS WITH ME WHEN I WAS LONELY.
IF YOU'RE WITH ME...
...I DON'T CARE IF I CAN NEVER LEAVE THIS PLACE.

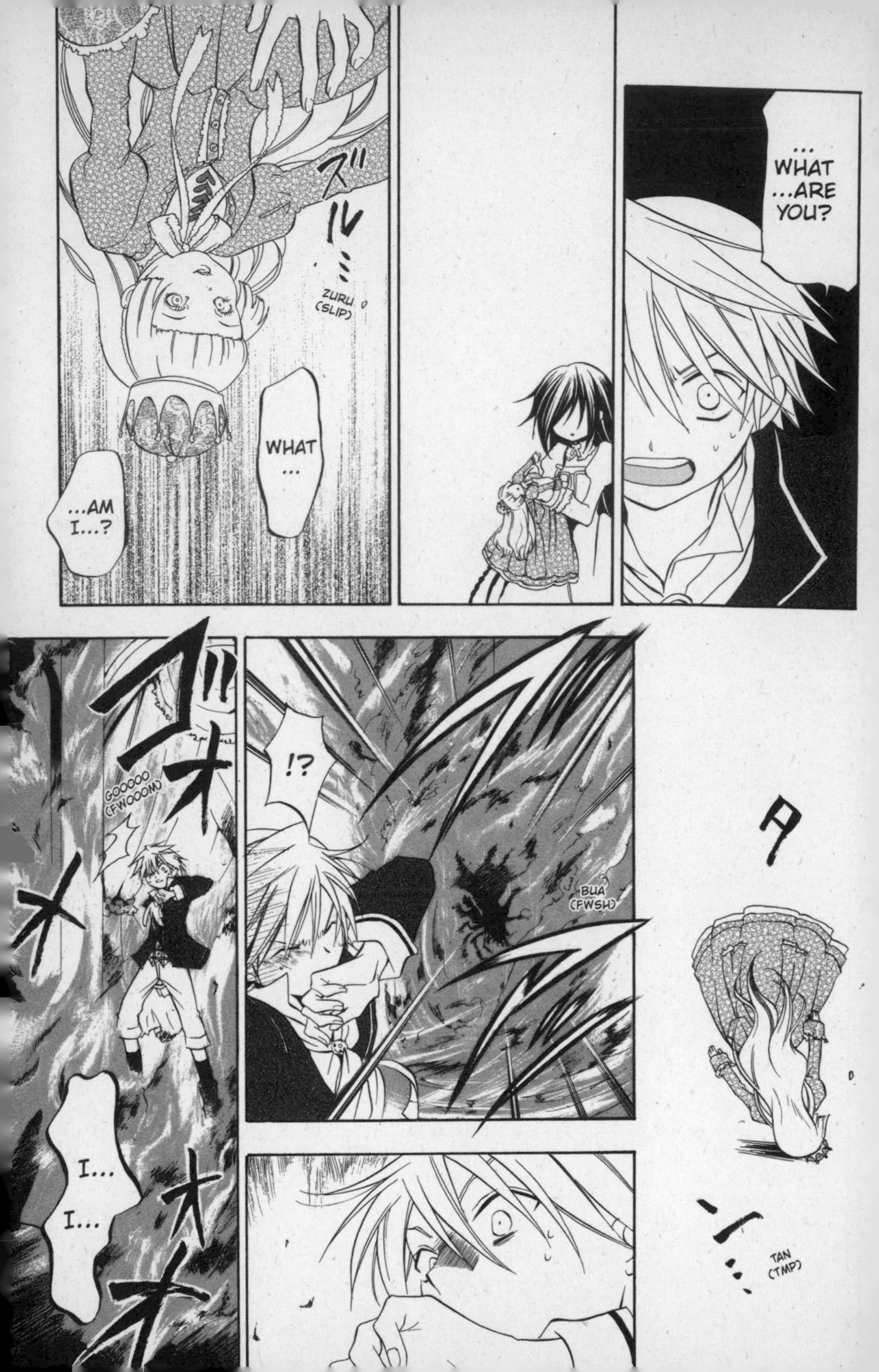

...
WHAT
...ARE
YOU?
ズル
ZURU
(SLIP)
WHAT
...
...AM
I...?
タン
TAN
(TMP)
!?
BUA
(FWSH)
ゴオオオ
GOOOOO
(FWOOOM)
I...
I...

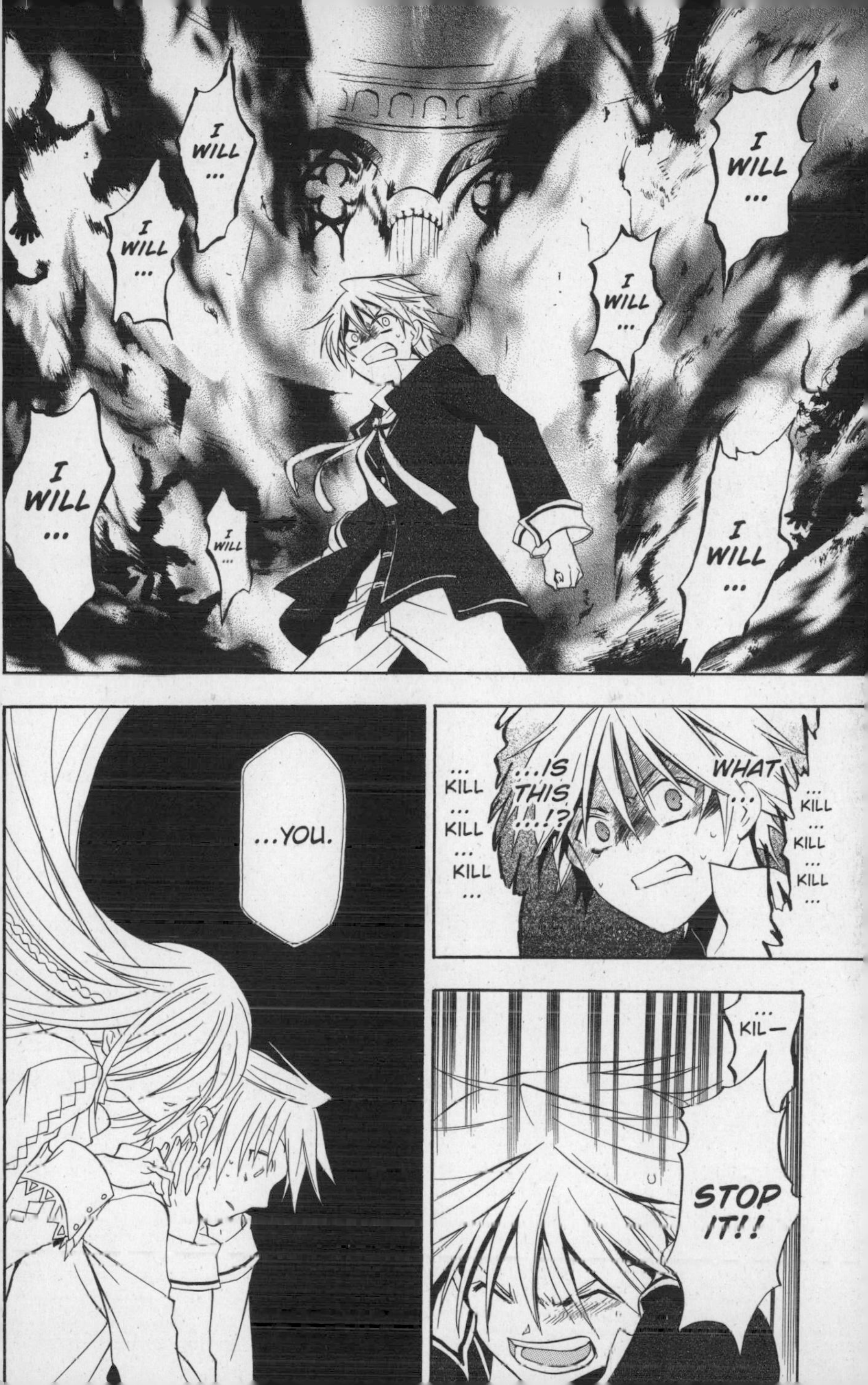
I WILL ...
I WILL ...
I WILL ...
I WILL ...
I WILL ...
I WILL ...
I WILL ...
... KILL ... KILL ... KILL ...
WHAT...
...IS THIS...!?
... KILL ... KILL ... KILL ...
... KIL—
STOP IT!!
...YOU.

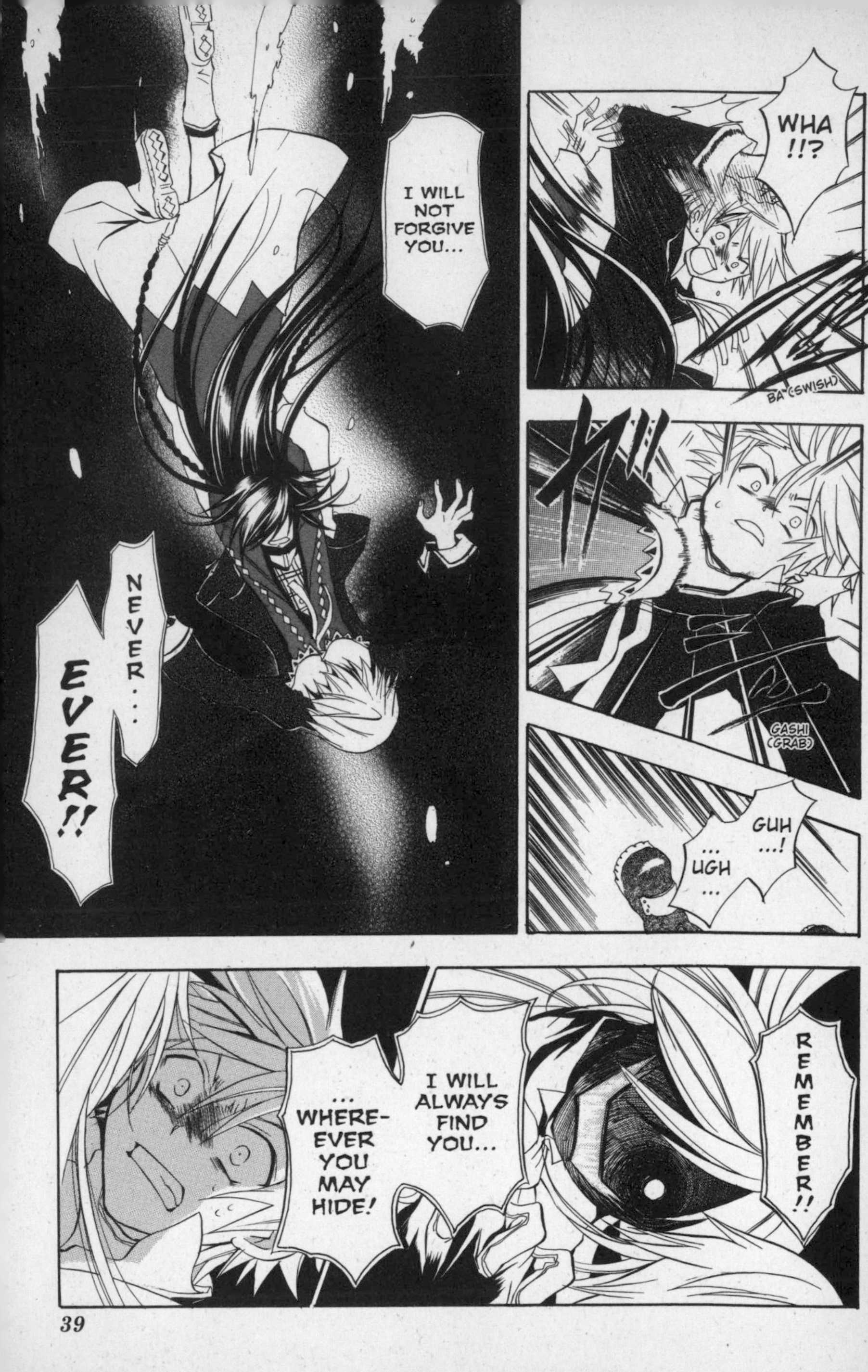
WHA !!?
BA (SWISH)
GASHI (GRAB)
GUH ...!
... UGH ...
I WILL NOT FORGIVE YOU...
NEVER...
EVER!!
REMEMBER!!
I WILL ALWAYS FIND YOU...
... WHEREVER YOU MAY HIDE!

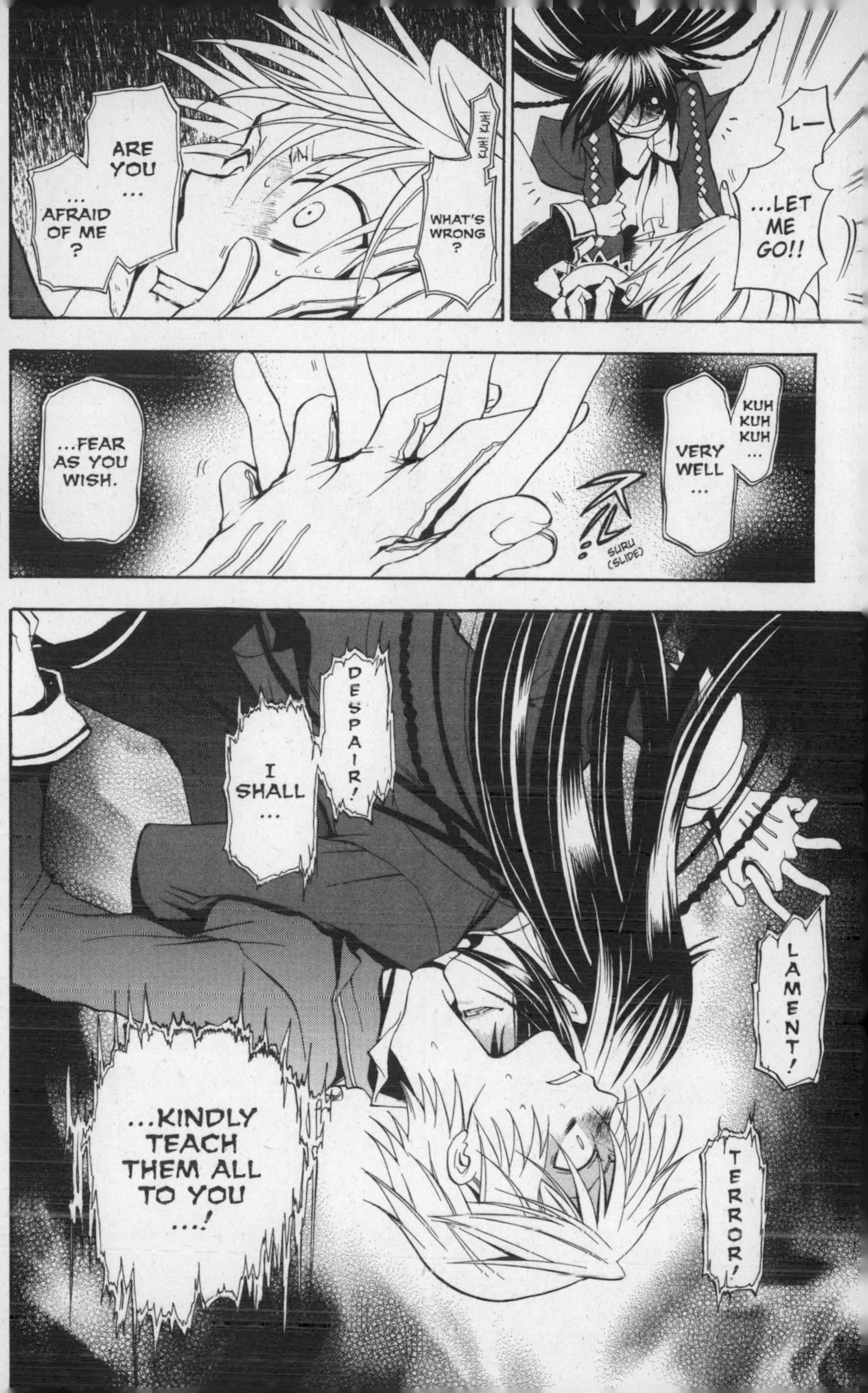
L—
...LET ME GO!!
KUH! KUH!
WHAT'S WRONG?
ARE YOU ... AFRAID OF ME?
KUH KUH KUH ...
VERY WELL ...
SURU (SLIDE)
...FEAR AS YOU WISH.
DESPAIR!
I SHALL ...
LAMENT!
TERROR!
...KINDLY TEACH THEM ALL TO YOU ....!

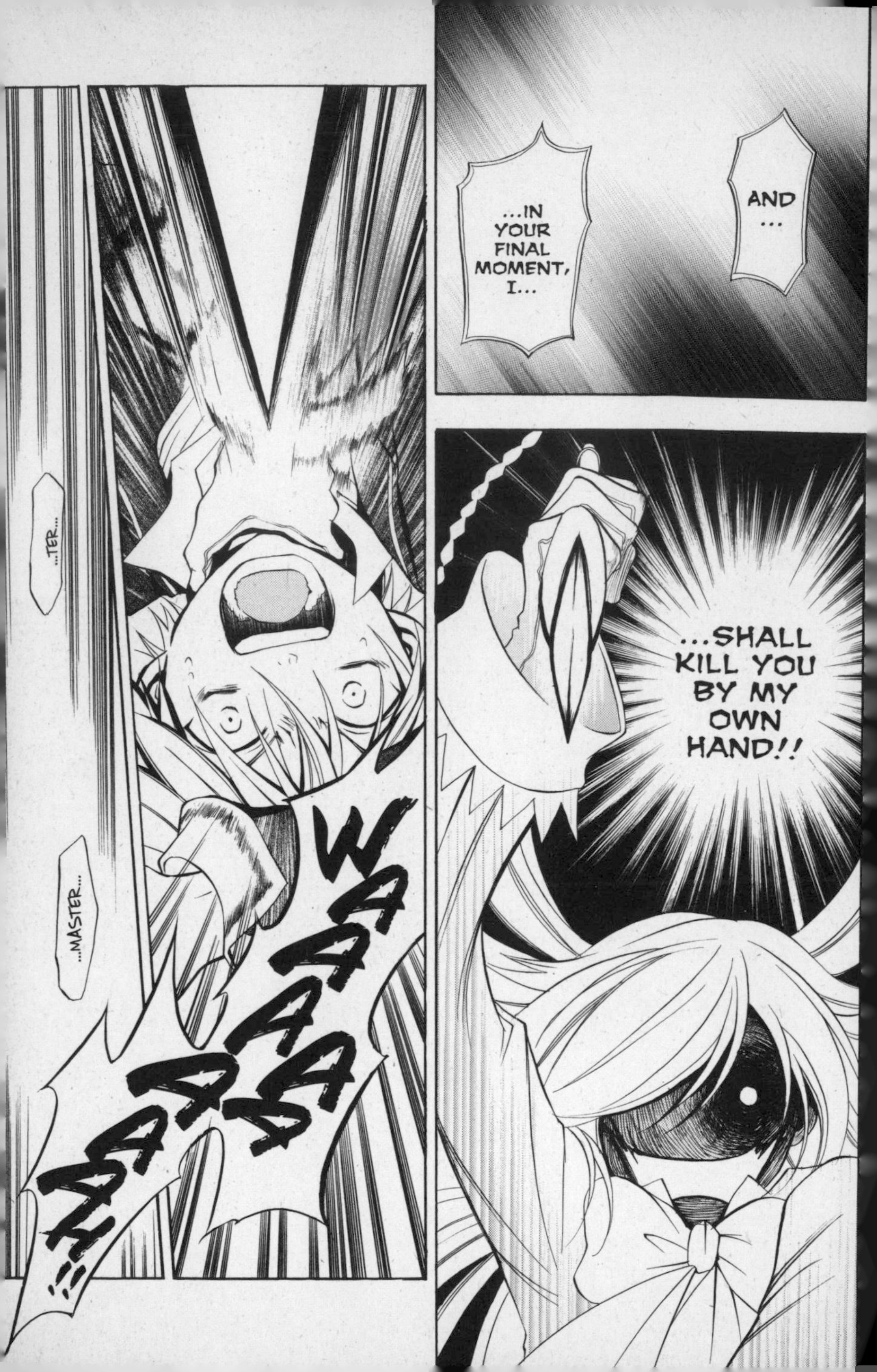
AND...
...IN YOUR FINAL MOMENT, I...
...SHALL KILL YOU BY MY OWN HAND!!
...TER...
...MASTER...
WAAAAAAAH!!

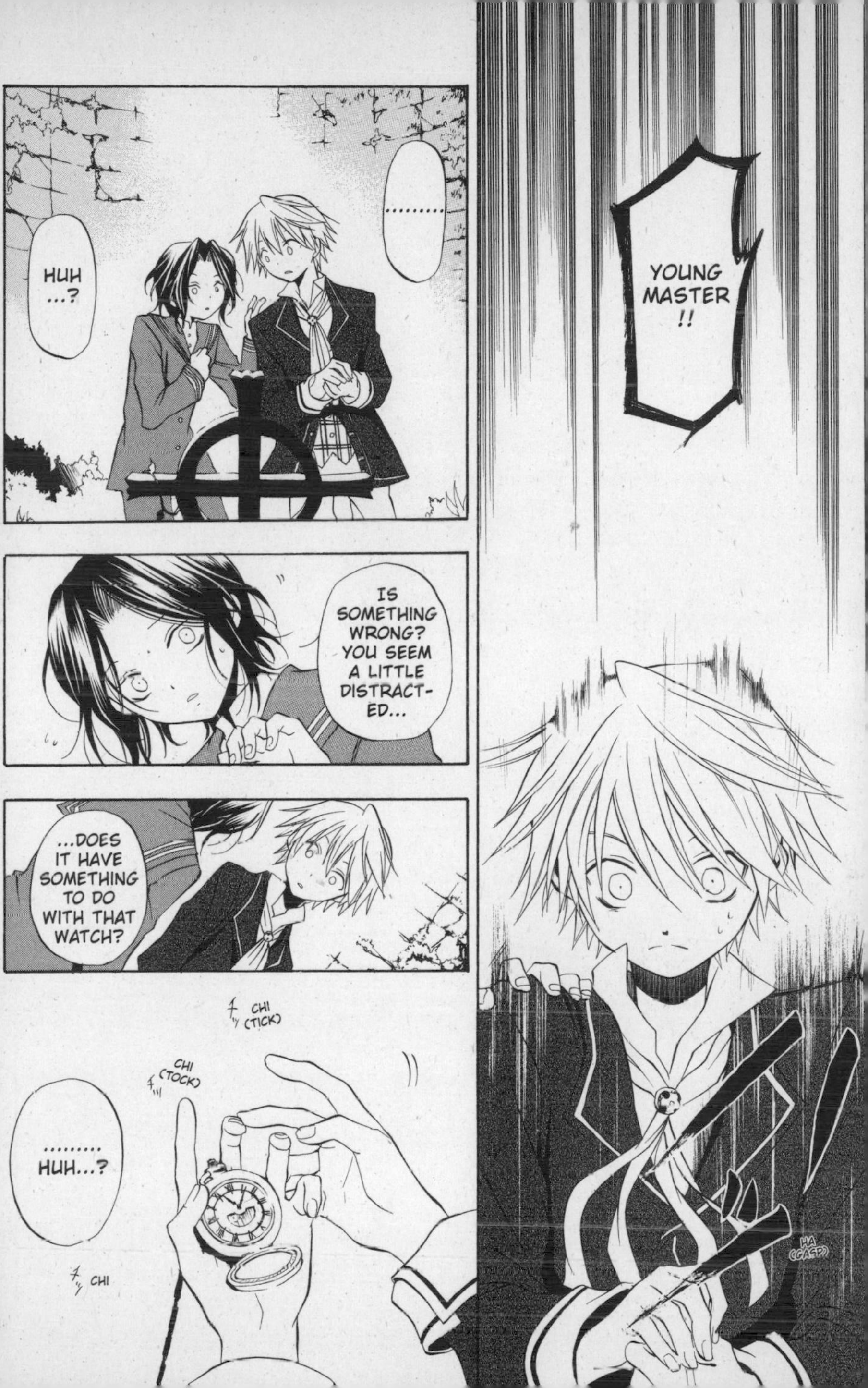
YOUNG MASTER !!
HA (GASP)
.........
HUH ...?
IS SOMETHING WRONG? YOU SEEM A LITTLE DISTRACT-ED...
...DOES IT HAVE SOMETHING TO DO WITH THAT WATCH?
チッ CHI (TICK)
チッ CHI (TOCK)
......... HUH...?
チッ CHI

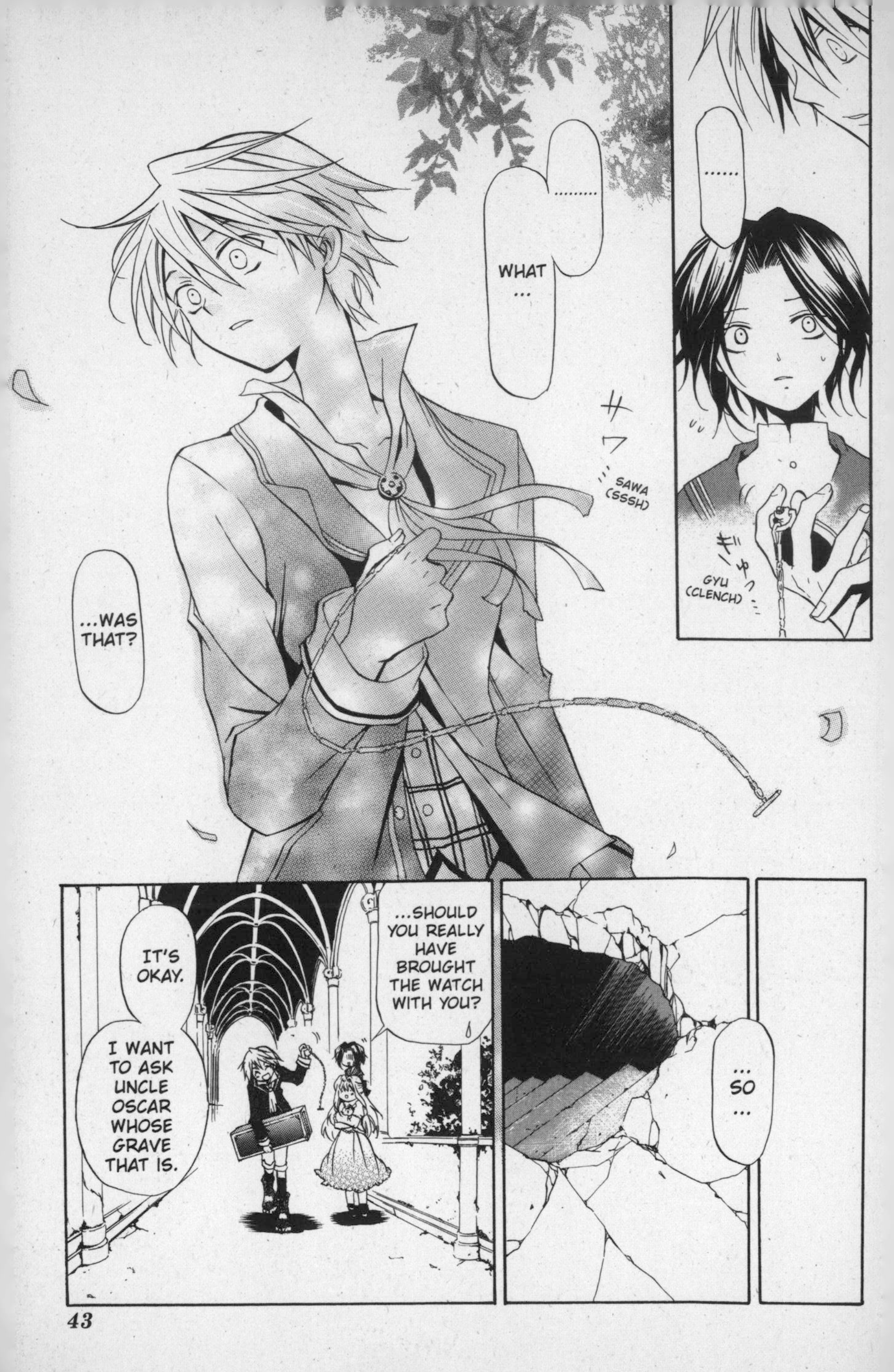
……
ぎゅっ
GYU (CLENCH)
………
WHAT …
ザワ
SAWA (SSSH)
…WAS THAT?
… SO …
…SHOULD YOU REALLY HAVE BROUGHT THE WATCH WITH YOU?
IT'S OKAY.
I WANT TO ASK UNCLE OSCAR WHOSE GRAVE THAT IS.

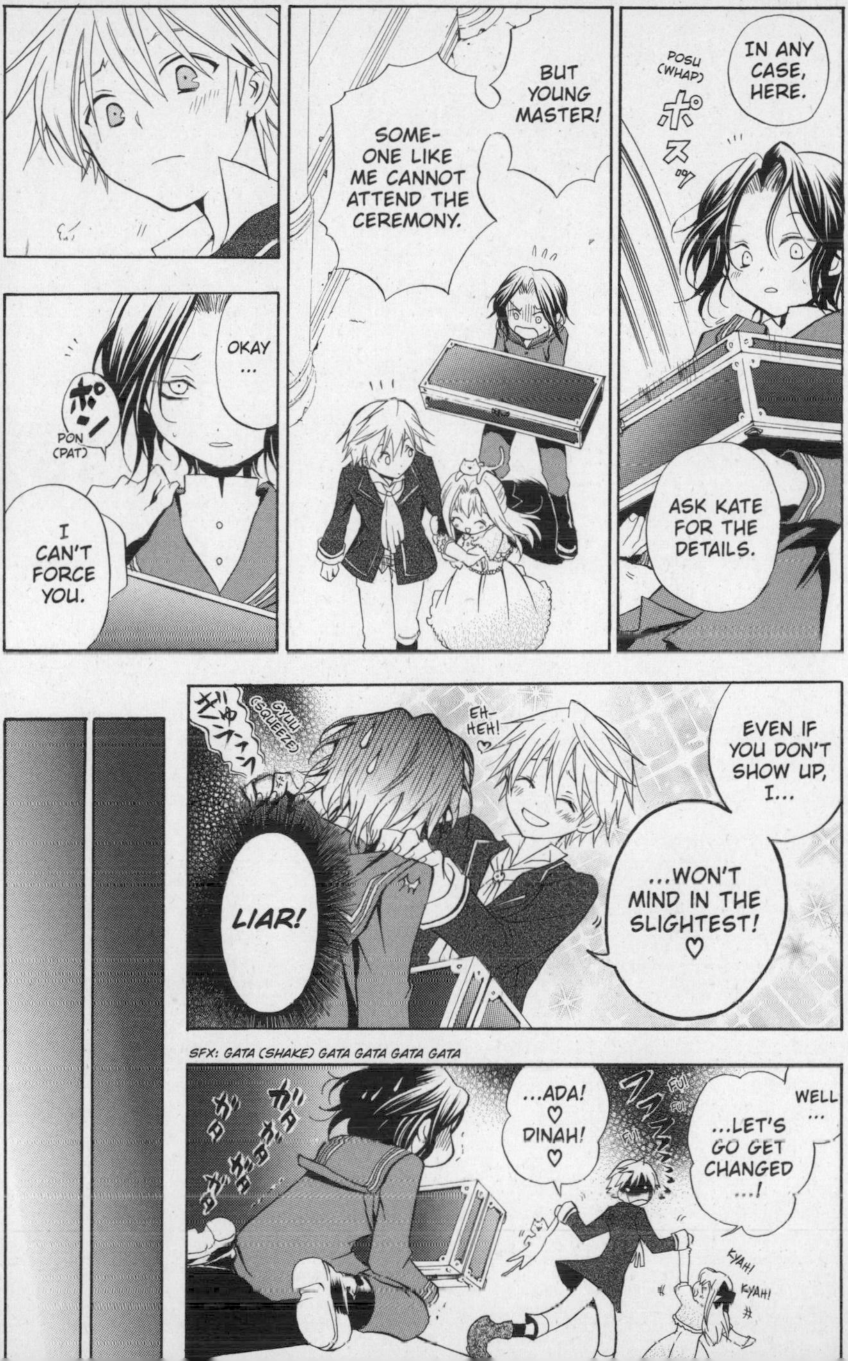
IN ANY CASE, HERE.
POSU (WHAP)
ASK KATE FOR THE DETAILS.
BUT YOUNG MASTER!
SOME-ONE LIKE ME CANNOT ATTEND THE CEREMONY.
OKAY ...
PON (PAT)
I CAN'T FORCE YOU.
EVEN IF YOU DON'T SHOW UP, I...
...WON'T MIND IN THE SLIGHTEST! ♡
EH-HEH! ♡
GYUU (SQUEEZE)
LIAR!
SFX: GATA (SHAKE) GATA GATA GATA GATA
WELL ...
...LET'S GO GET CHANGED ...!
...ADA! ♡ DINAH! ♡
FU! FU! FU!
KYAH! KYAH!

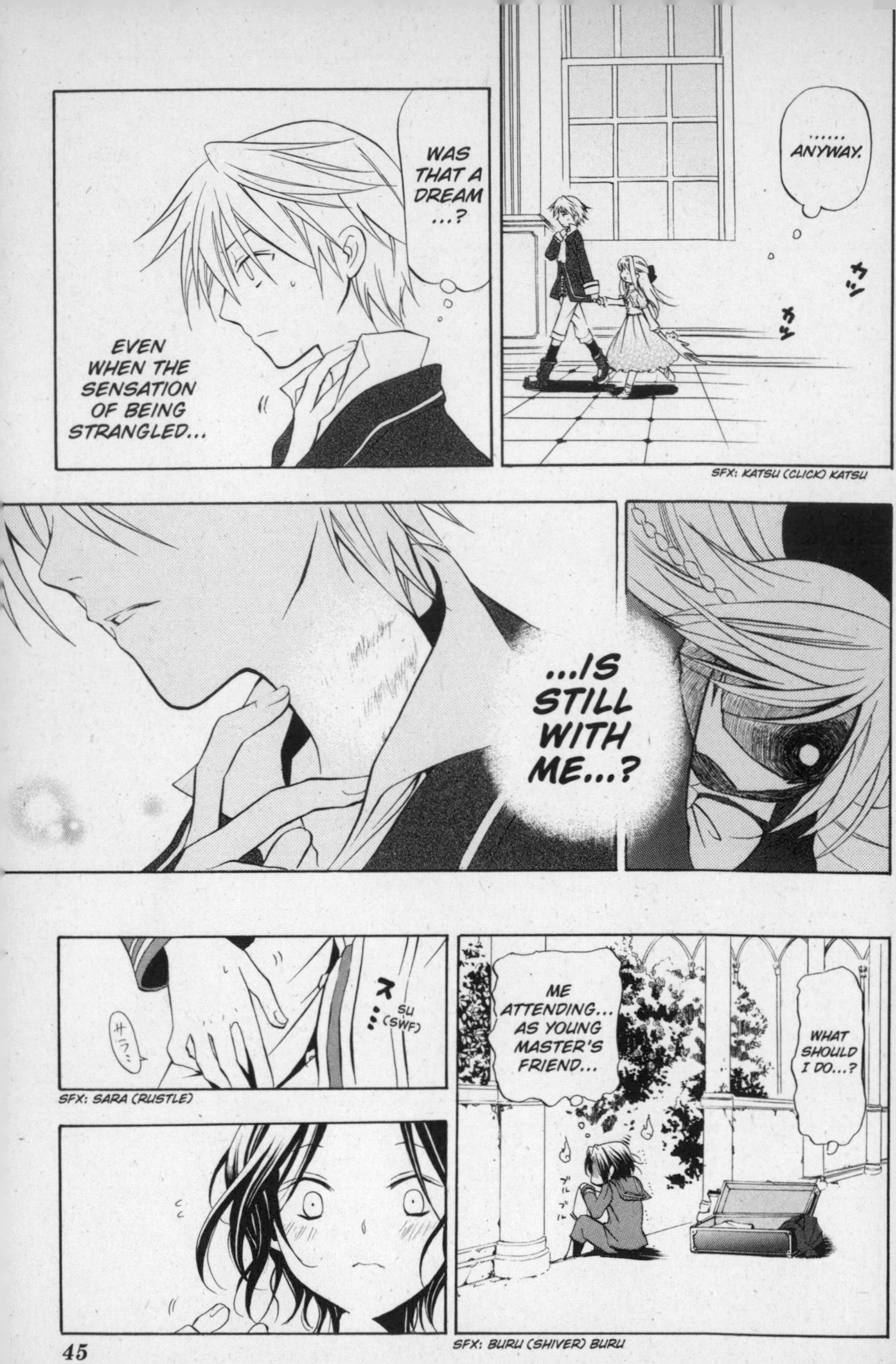
...... ANYWAY.
カッ
カッ
SFX: KATSU (CLICK) KATSU
WAS THAT A DREAM ...?
EVEN WHEN THE SENSATION OF BEING STRANGLED...
...IS STILL WITH ME...?
ME ATTENDING... AS YOUNG MASTER'S FRIEND...
WHAT SHOULD I DO...?
SFX: BURU (SHIVER) BURU
ス...
SU (SWF)
サラ...
SFX: SARA (RUSTLE)

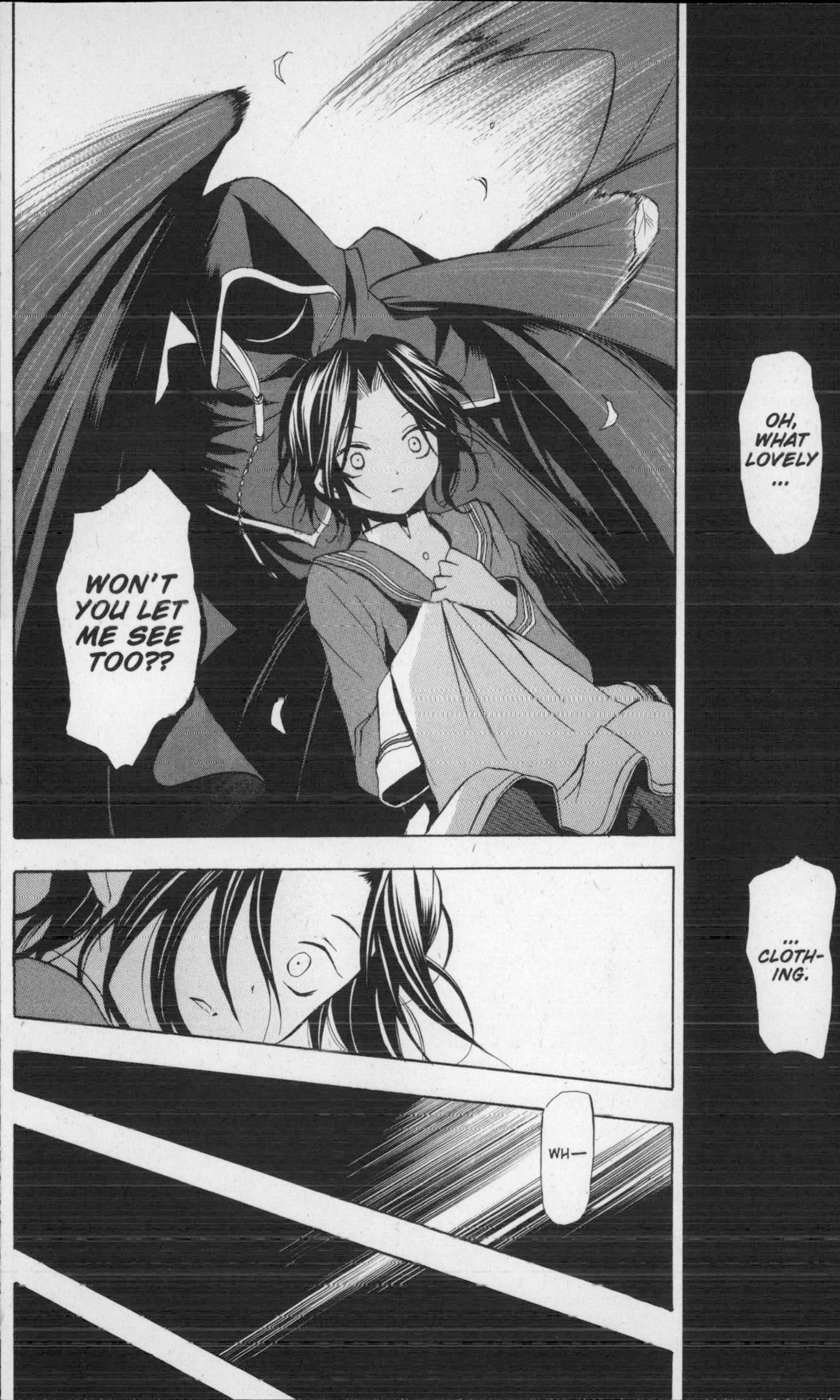
OH, WHAT LOVELY ...
... CLOTHING.
WON'T YOU LET ME SEE TOO??
WH—

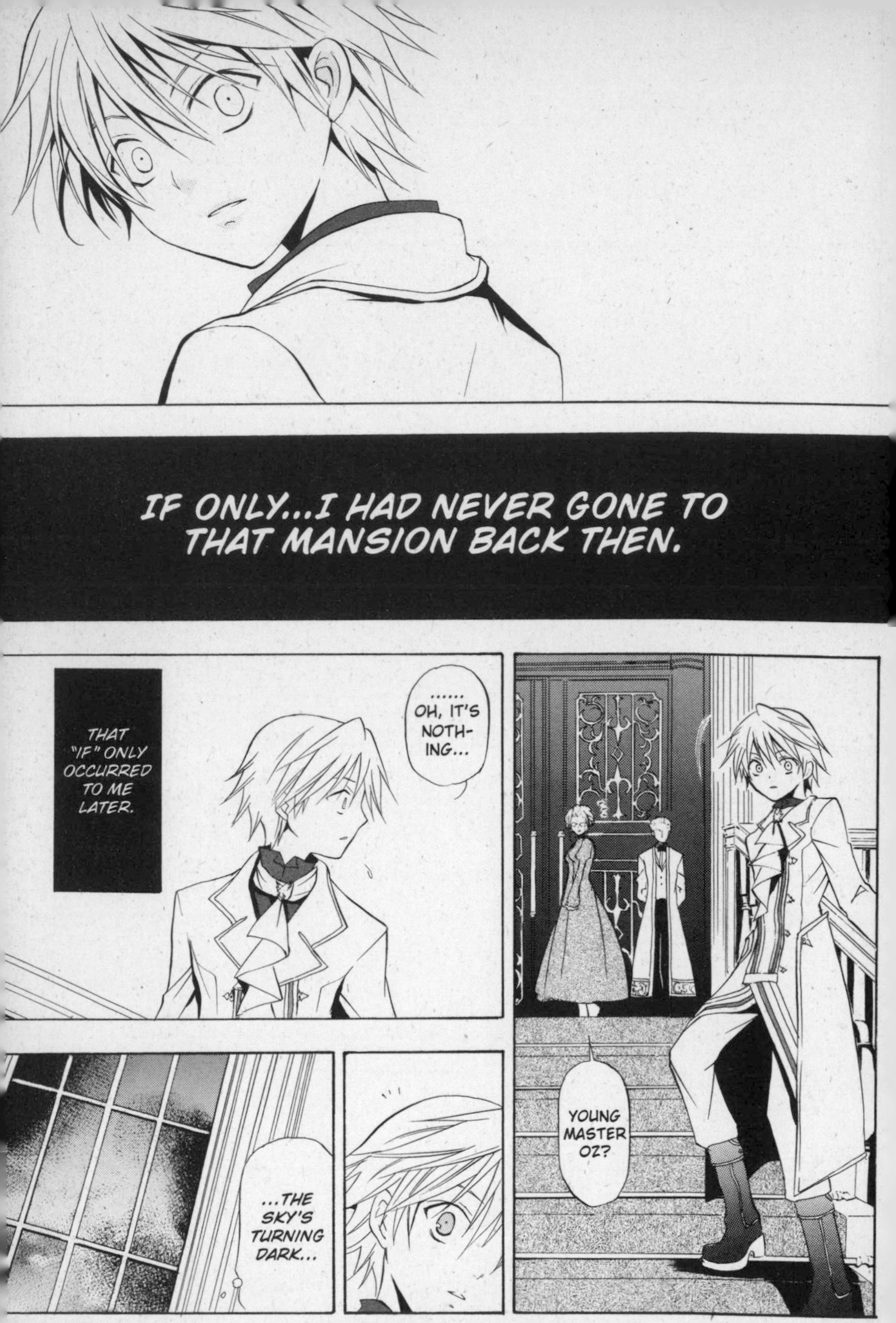
IF ONLY...I HAD NEVER GONE TO THAT MANSION BACK THEN.
YOUNG MASTER OZ?
...... OH, IT'S NOTHING...
THAT "IF" ONLY OCCURRED TO ME LATER.
...THE SKY'S TURNING DARK...

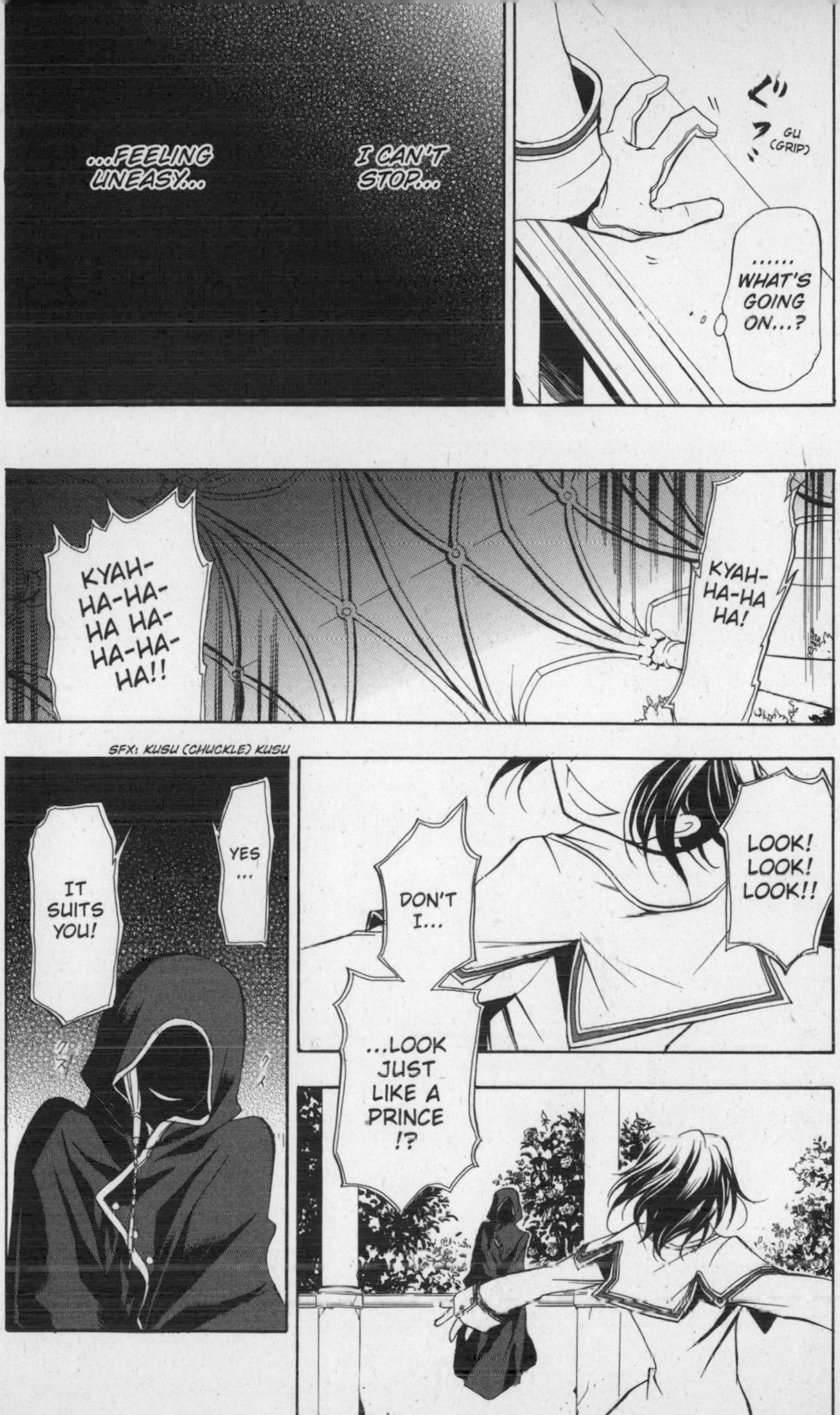
GU (GRIP)
...... WHAT'S GOING ON...?
I CAN'T STOP...
...FEELING UNEASY...
KYAH-HA-HA HA!
KYAH-HA-HA HA HA-HA-HA-HA!!
SFX: KUSU (CHUCKLE) KUSU
LOOK! LOOK! LOOK!!
DON'T I...
...LOOK JUST LIKE A PRINCE!?
YES ...
IT SUITS YOU!

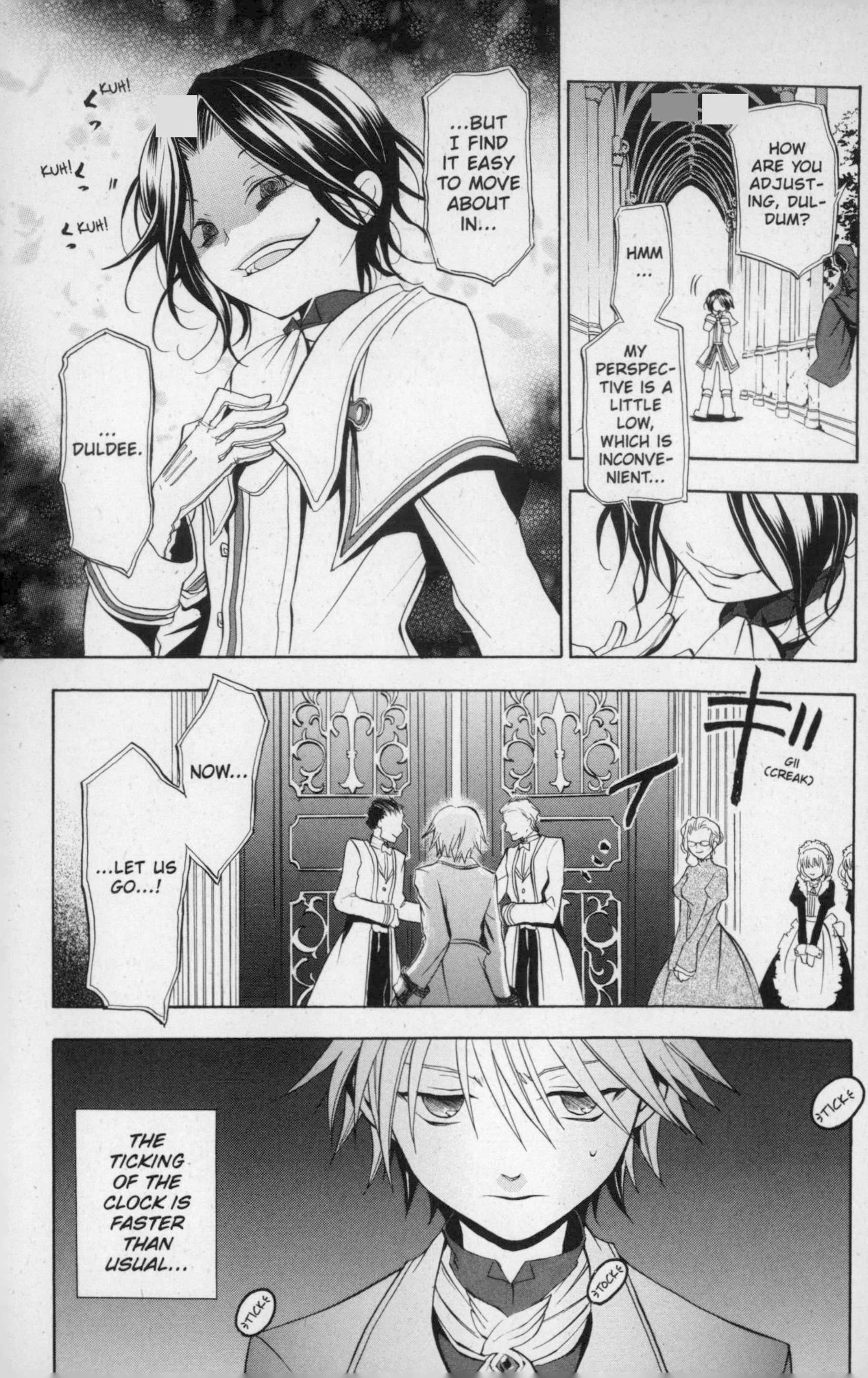
HOW ARE YOU ADJUSTING, DULDUM?
HMM...
MY PERSPECTIVE IS A LITTLE LOW, WHICH IS INCONVENIENT...
...BUT I FIND IT EASY TO MOVE ABOUT IN...
KUH!
KUH!
KUH!
...DULDEE.
GII (CREAK)
NOW...
...LET US GO...!
TICK
TICK
TICK
THE TICKING OF THE CLOCK IS FASTER THAN USUAL...

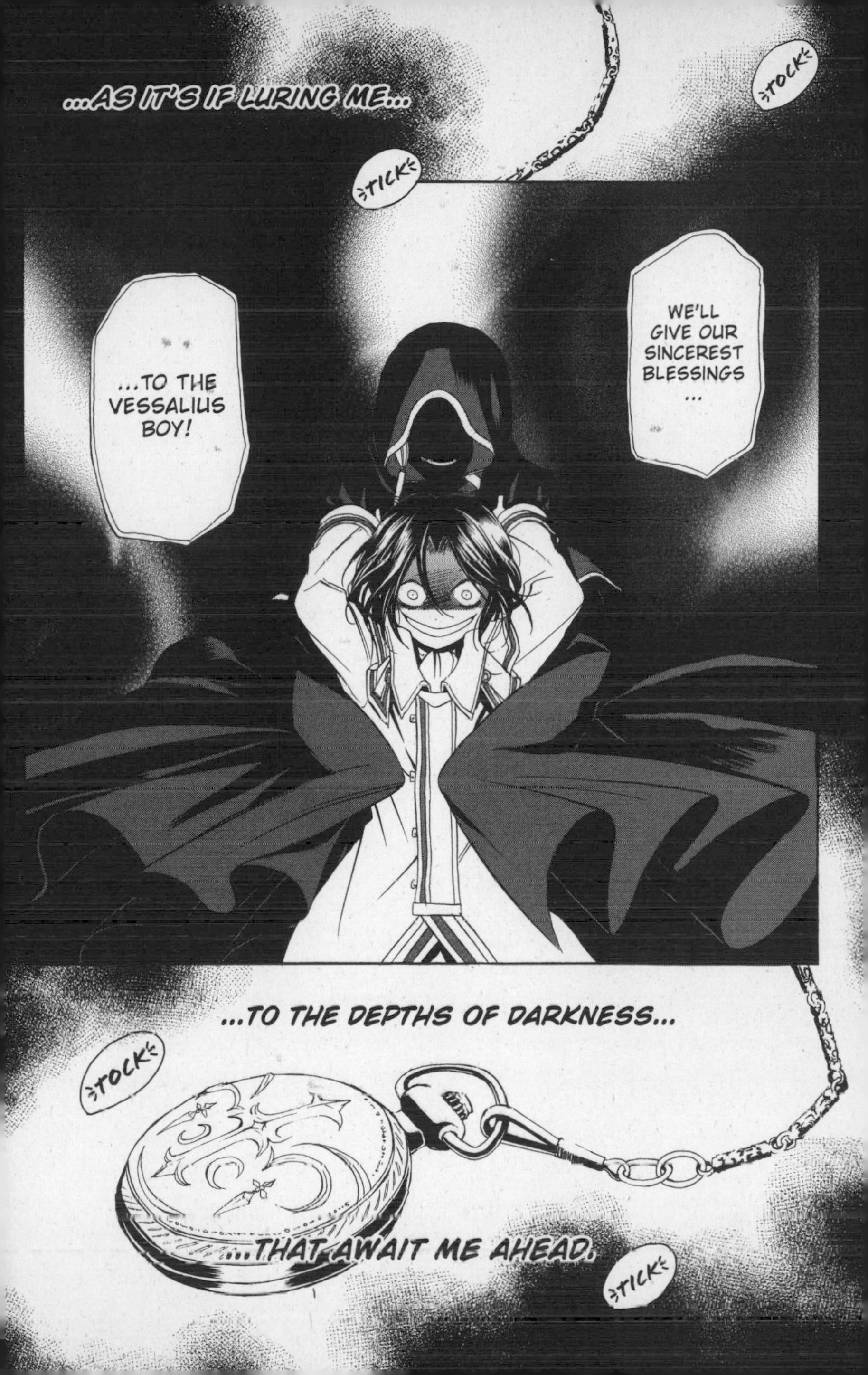
TOCK
...AS IT'S IF LURING ME...
TICK
WE'LL GIVE OUR SINCEREST BLESSINGS ...
...TO THE VESSALIUS BOY!
...TO THE DEPTHS OF DARKNESS...
TOCK
...THAT AWAIT ME AHEAD.
TICK

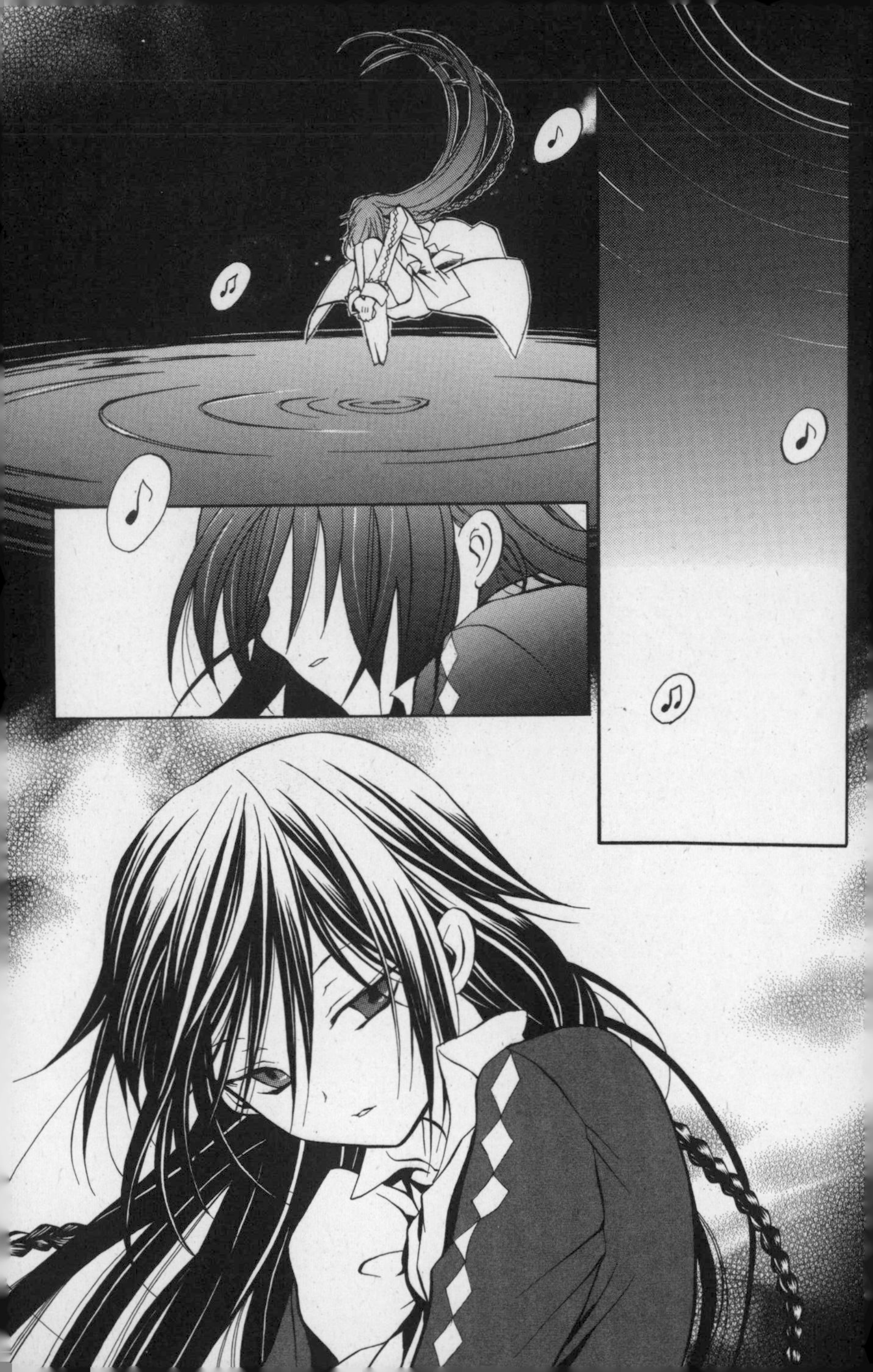

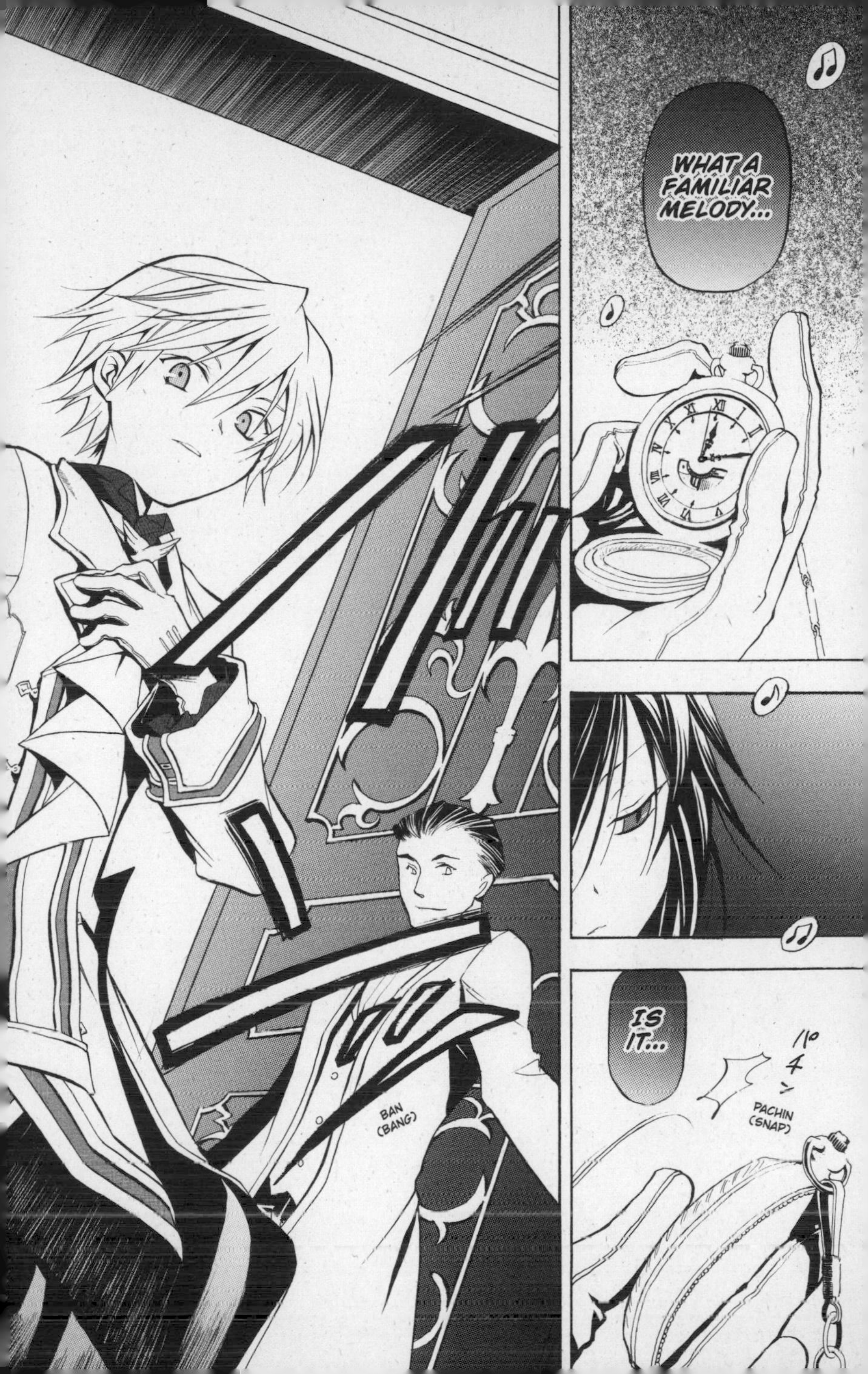
WHAT A FAMILIAR MELODY...
IS IT...
パチン
PACHIN (SNAP)
BAN (BANG)

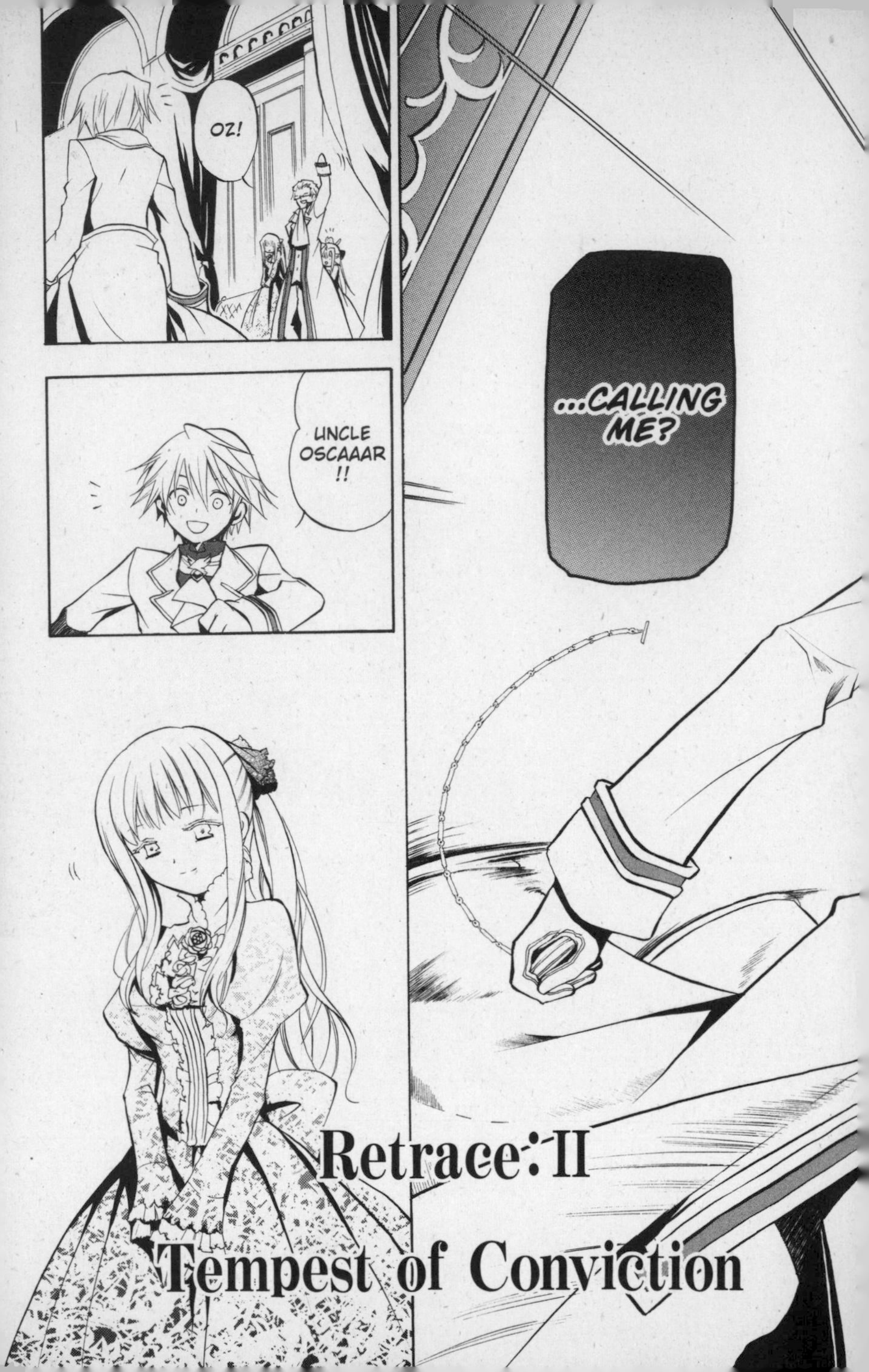
...CALLING ME?
OZ!
UNCLE OSCAAAR !!
Retrace: II
Tempest of Conviction

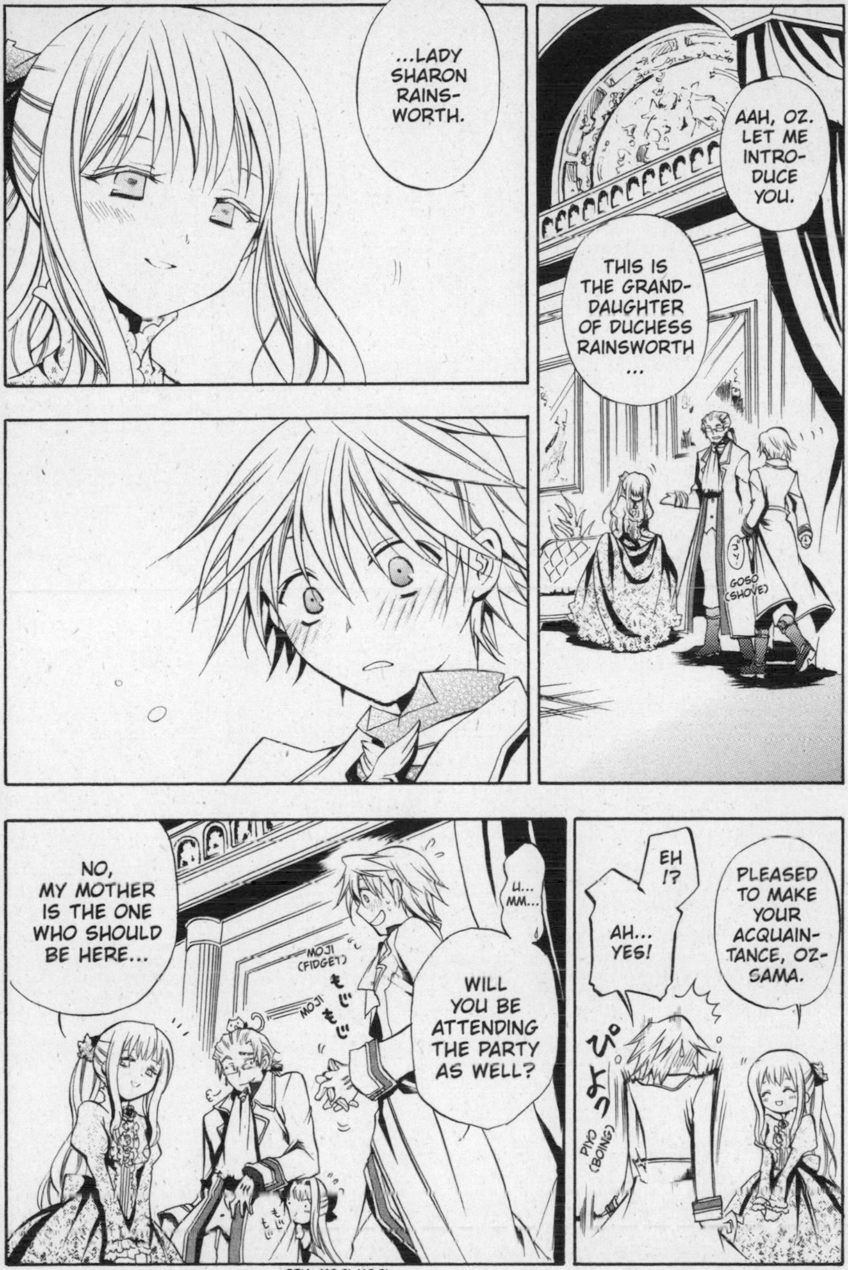
AAH, OZ. LET ME INTRO-DUCE YOU.
THIS IS THE GRAND-DAUGHTER OF DUCHESS RAINSWORTH ...
GOSO (SHOVE)
...LADY SHARON RAINS-WORTH.
PLEASED TO MAKE YOUR ACQUAIN-TANCE, OZ-SAMA.
EH !?
AH... YES!
PIYO (BOING)
U... MM...
WILL YOU BE ATTENDING THE PARTY AS WELL?
MOJI (FIDGET)
MOJI
NO, MY MOTHER IS THE ONE WHO SHOULD BE HERE...

SFX: MOJI MOJI

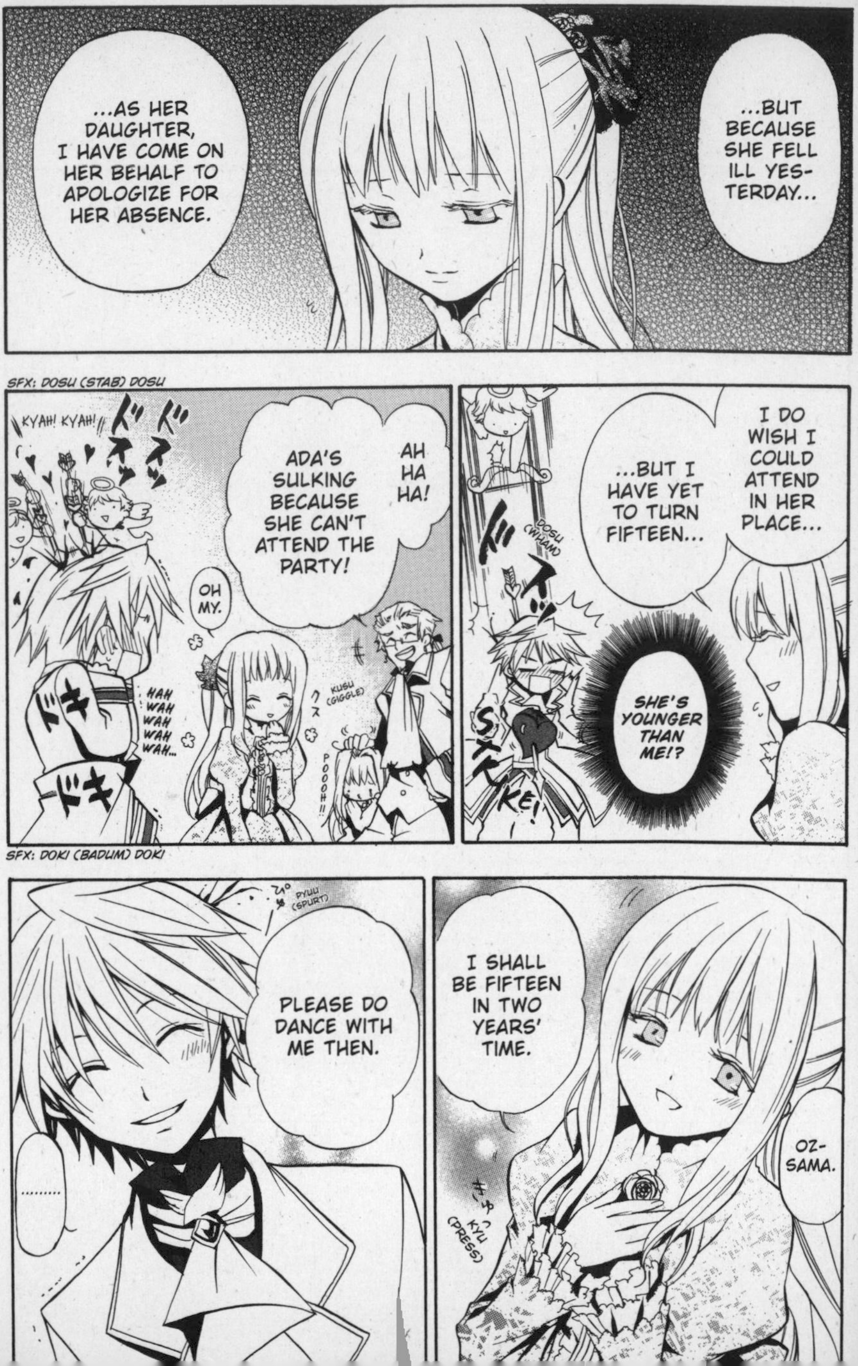
...BUT BECAUSE SHE FELL ILL YESTERDAY...
...AS HER DAUGHTER, I HAVE COME ON HER BEHALF TO APOLOGIZE FOR HER ABSENCE.
SFX: DOSU (STAB) DOSU
I DO WISH I COULD ATTEND IN HER PLACE...
...BUT I HAVE YET TO TURN FIFTEEN...
DOSU (WHAM)
SHE'S YOUNGER THAN ME!?
AH HA HA!
ADA'S SULKING BECAUSE SHE CAN'T ATTEND THE PARTY!
KYAH! KYAH!
OH MY.
KUSU (GIGGLE)
POOOOH!!
HAH WAH WAH WAH WAH...
SFX: DOKI (BADUM) DOKI
OZ-SAMA.
I SHALL BE FIFTEEN IN TWO YEARS' TIME.
KYU (PRESS)
PYUU (SPURT)
PLEASE DO DANCE WITH ME THEN.
........

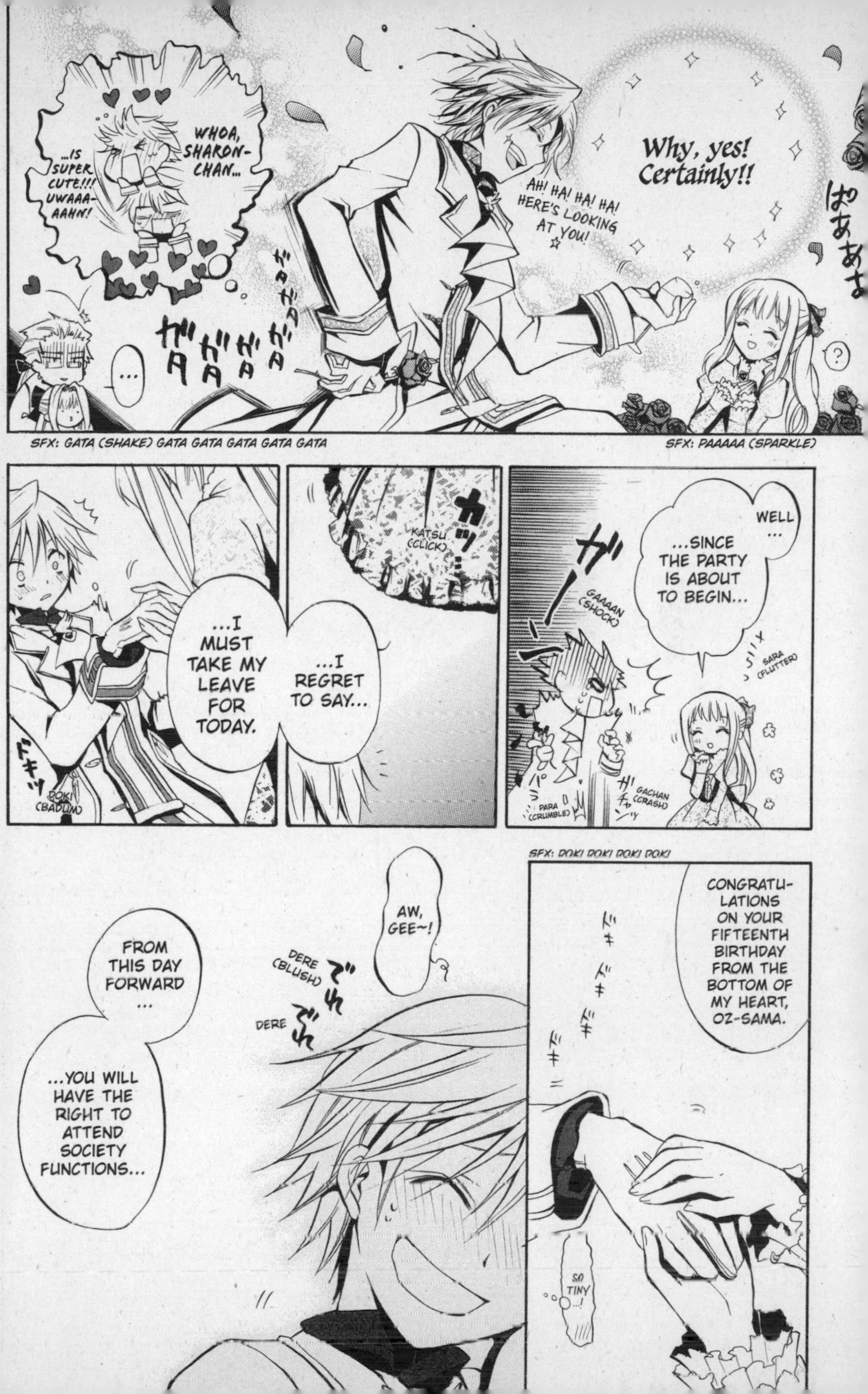
Why, yes! Certainly!!
AH! HA! HA! HA! HERE'S LOOKING AT YOU! ☆
?
WHOA, SHARON-CHAN...
...IS SUPER CUTE!!! UWAAA-AAHN!
...
SFX: PAAAAA (SPARKLE)
SFX: GATA (SHAKE) GATA GATA GATA GATA GATA
WELL...
...SINCE THE PARTY IS ABOUT TO BEGIN...
GAAAAN (SHOCK)
SARA (FLUTTER)
GACHAN (CRASH)
PARA (CRUMBLE)
KATSU (CLICK)
...I REGRET TO SAY...
...I MUST TAKE MY LEAVE FOR TODAY.
DOKI (BADUM)
SFX: DOKI DOKI DOKI DOKI
CONGRATULATIONS ON YOUR FIFTEENTH BIRTHDAY FROM THE BOTTOM OF MY HEART, OZ-SAMA.
SO TINY...!
AW, GEE~!
DERE (BLUSH)
DERE
FROM THIS DAY FORWARD...
...YOU WILL HAVE THE RIGHT TO ATTEND SOCIETY FUNCTIONS...

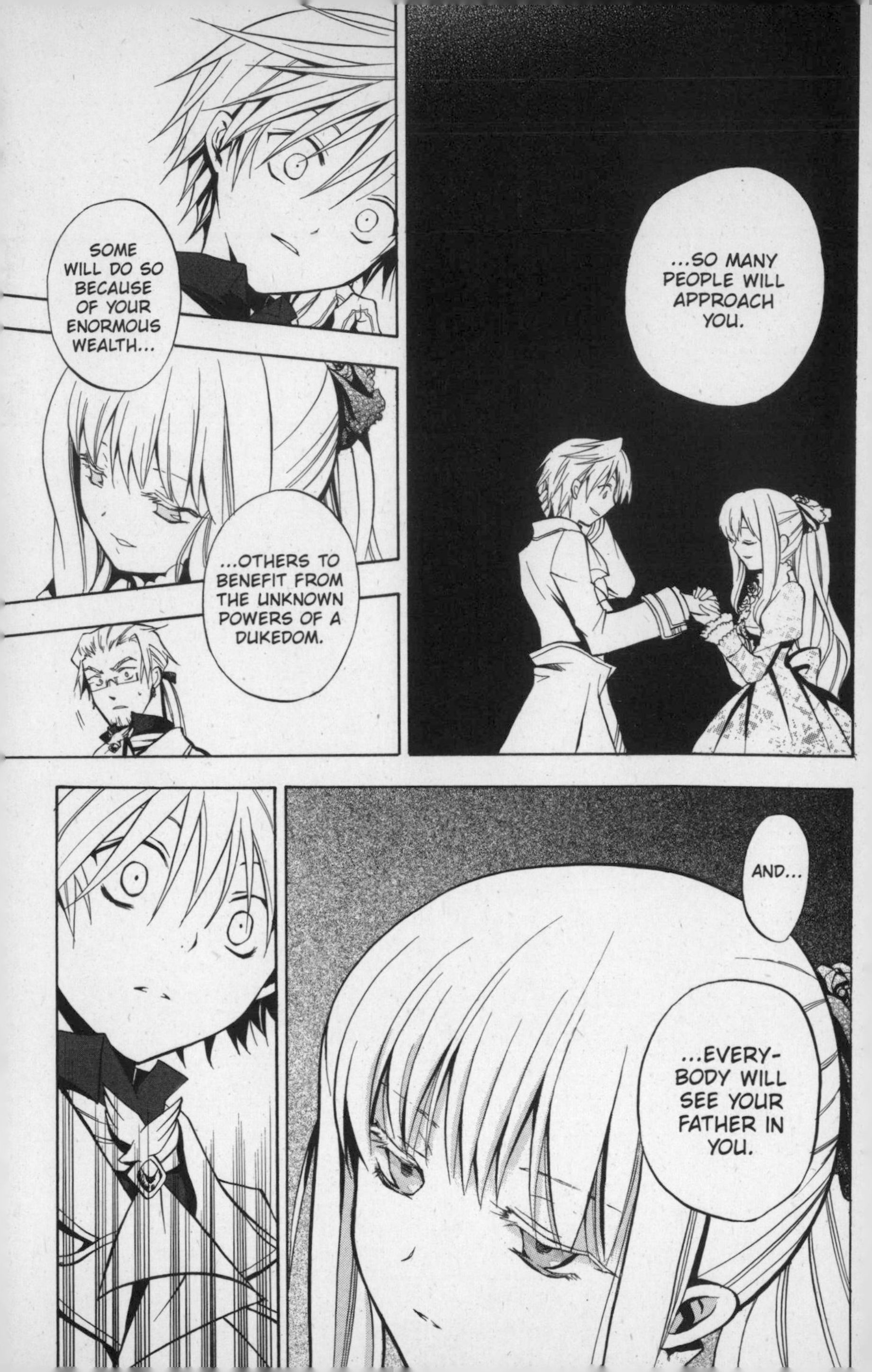
...SO MANY PEOPLE WILL APPROACH YOU.
SOME WILL DO SO BECAUSE OF YOUR ENORMOUS WEALTH...
...OTHERS TO BENEFIT FROM THE UNKNOWN POWERS OF A DUKEDOM.
AND...
...EVERY-BODY WILL SEE YOUR FATHER IN YOU.

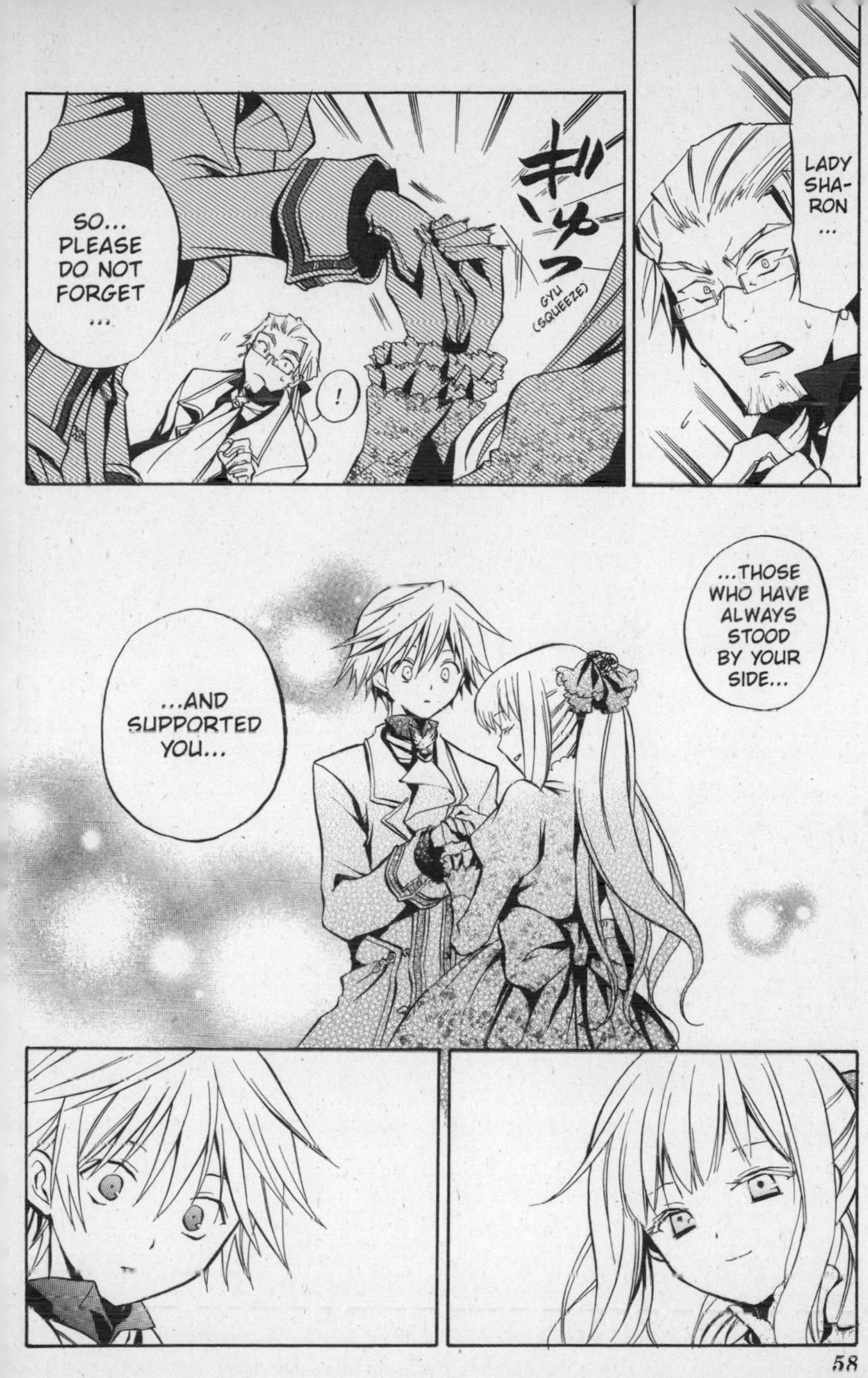
LADY SHARON ...
ギュッ
GYU (SQUEEZE)
SO... PLEASE DO NOT FORGET ...
!
...THOSE WHO HAVE ALWAYS STOOD BY YOUR SIDE...
...AND SUPPORTED YOU...

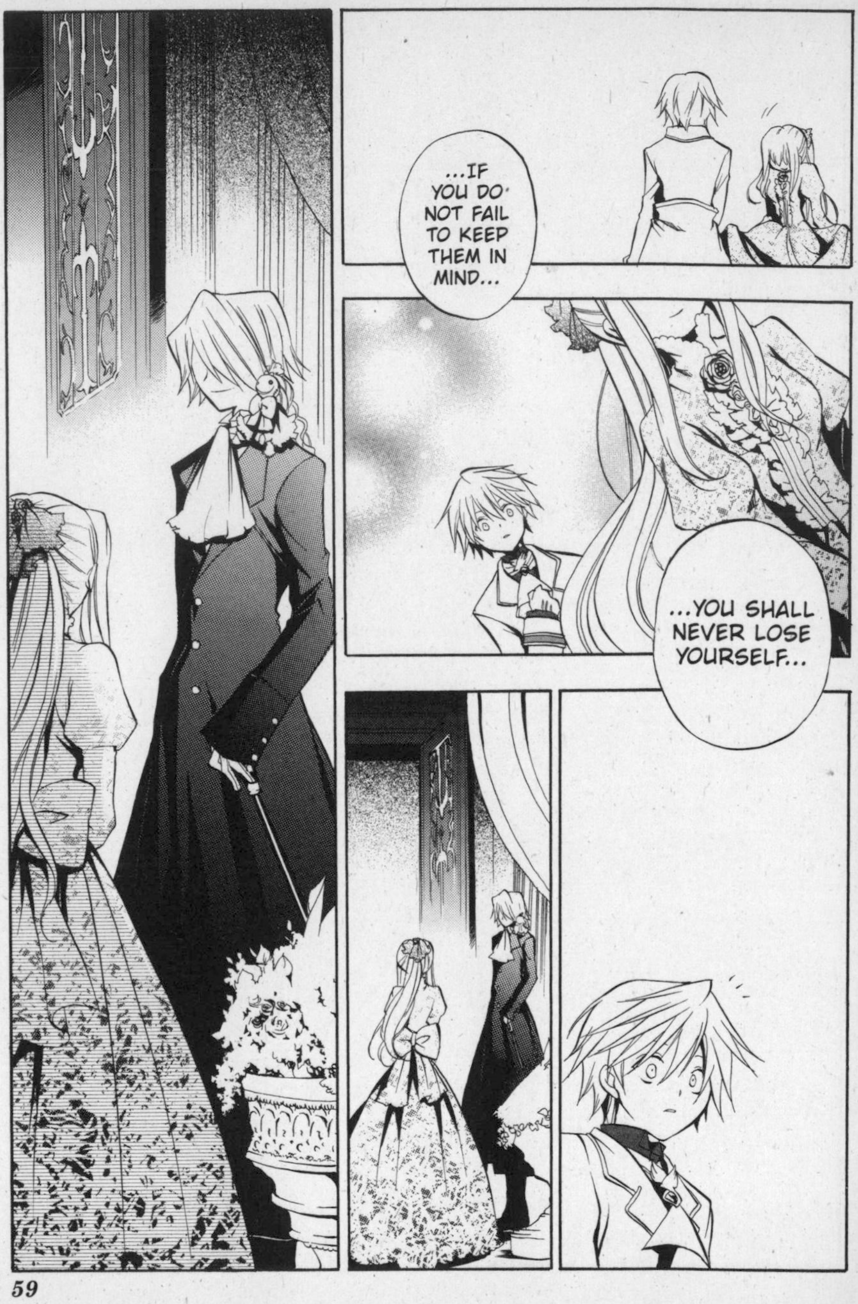
...IF YOU DO NOT FAIL TO KEEP THEM IN MIND...
...YOU SHALL NEVER LOSE YOURSELF...

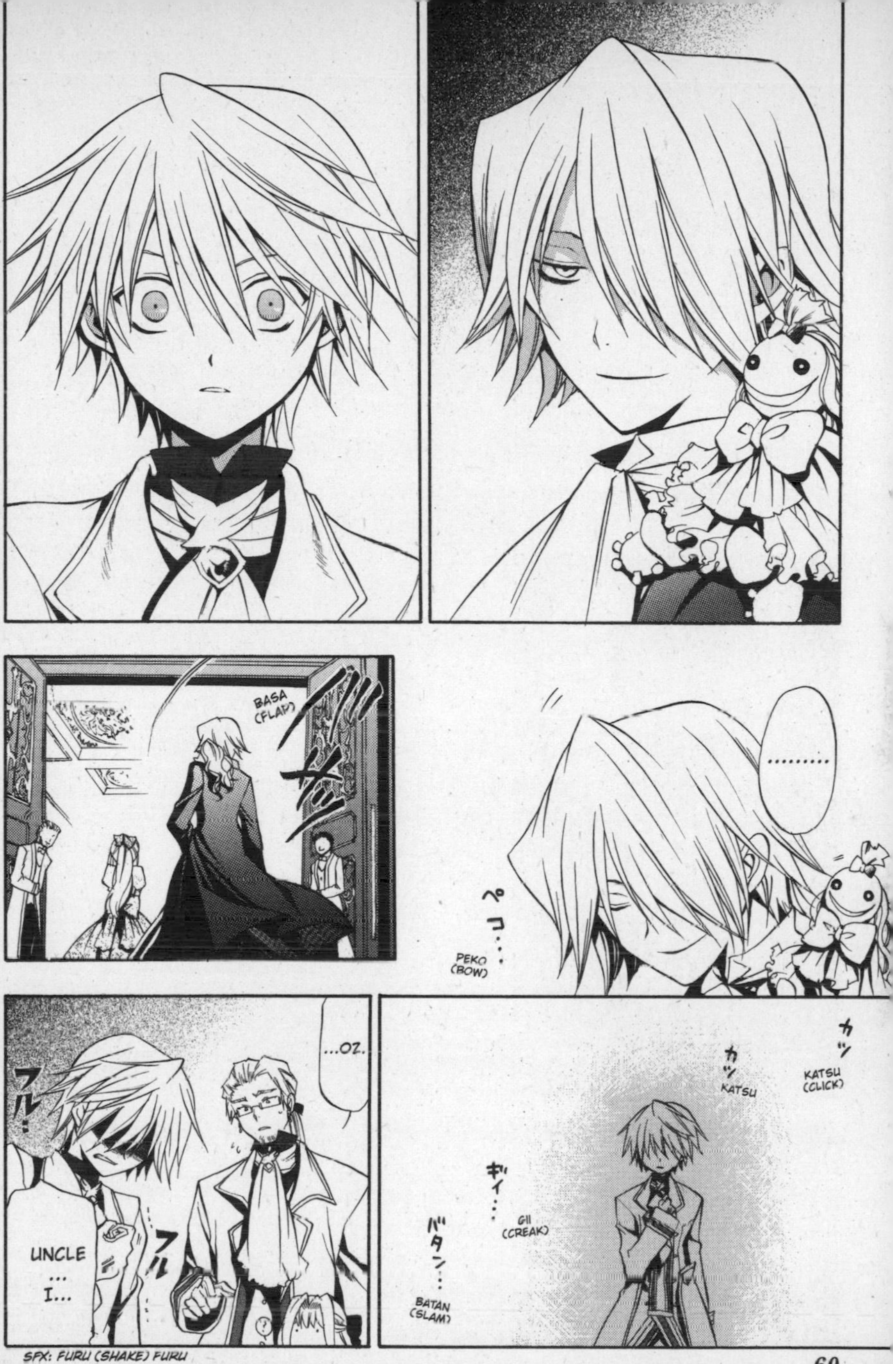
........
ペコ…
PEKO (BOW)
BASA (FLAP)
カツ
KATSU (CLICK)
カツ
KATSU
ギィ…
GII (CREAK)
バタン…
BATAN (SLAM)
...OZ.
フル
UNCLE ... I...
フル

SFX: FURU (SHAKE) FURU

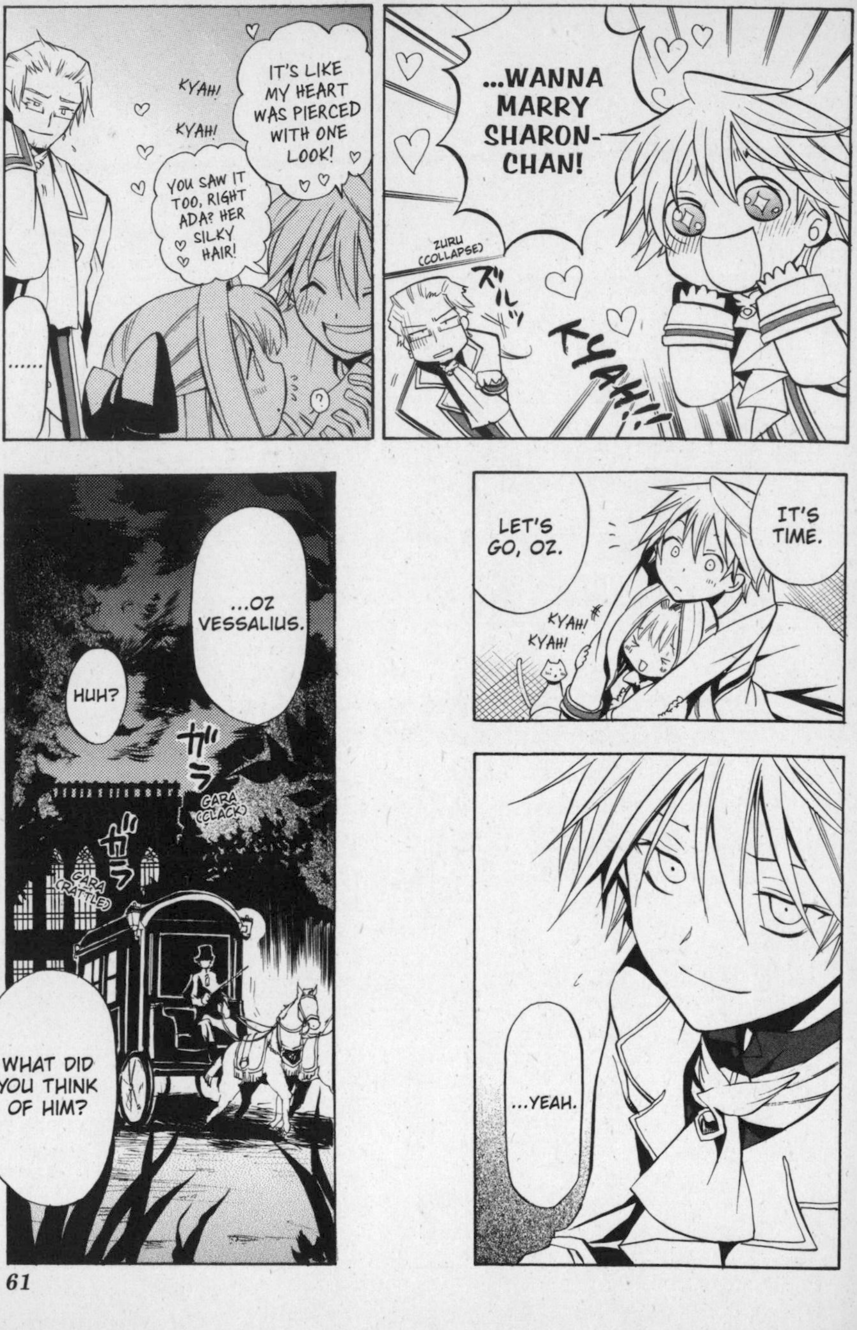
...WANNA MARRY SHARON-CHAN!
ズルッ
ZURU (COLLAPSE)
KYAH!!!
IT'S LIKE MY HEART WAS PIERCED WITH ONE LOOK!
KYAH!
KYAH!
YOU SAW IT TOO, RIGHT ADA? HER SILKY HAIR!
......
?
IT'S TIME.
LET'S GO, OZ.
KYAH!
KYAH!
...YEAH.
...OZ VESSALIUS.
HUH?
ガラ
GARA (CLACK)
ガラ
GARA (RATTLE)
WHAT DID YOU THINK OF HIM?

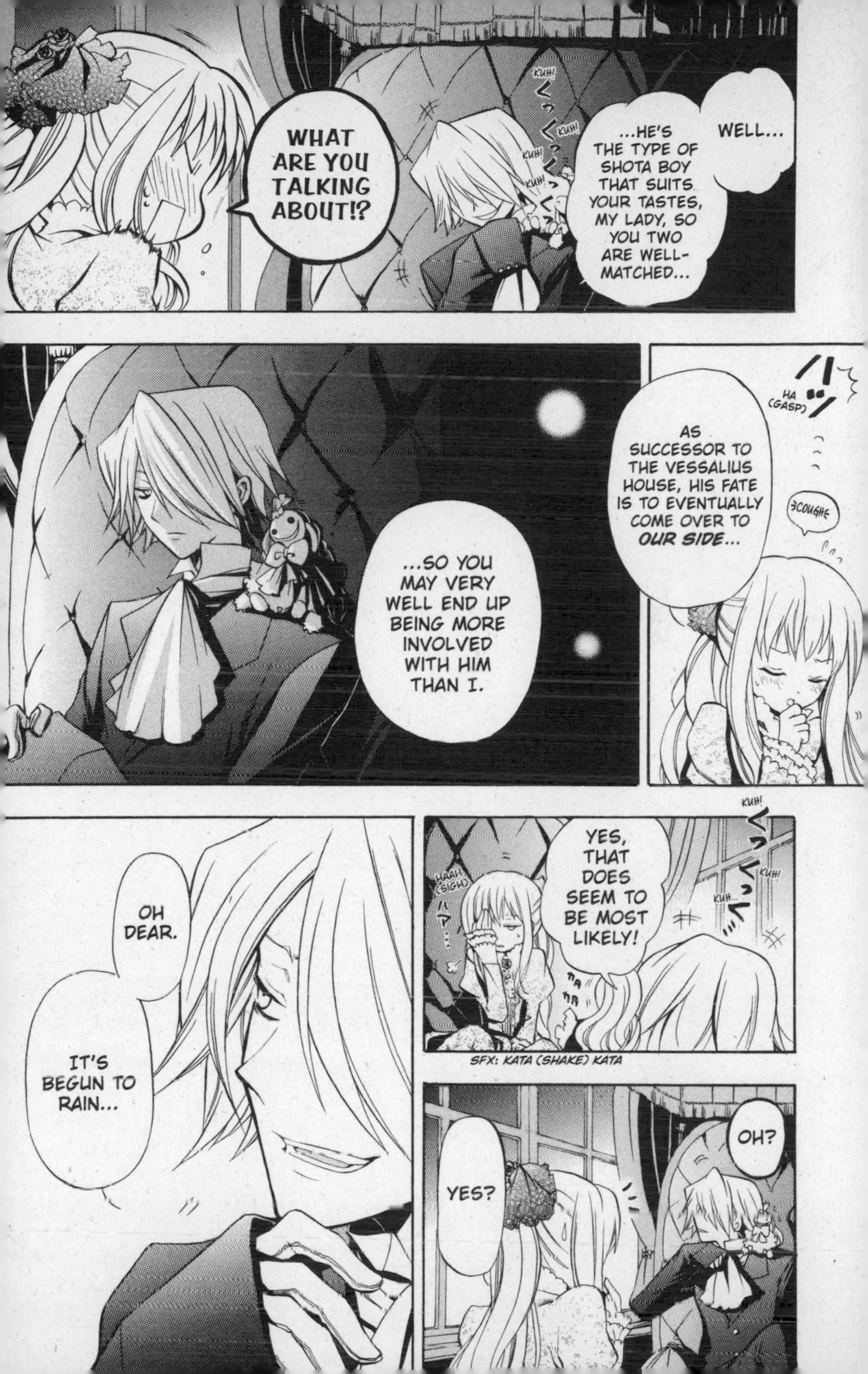
WELL...
...HE'S THE TYPE OF SHOTA BOY THAT SUITS YOUR TASTES, MY LADY, SO YOU TWO ARE WELL-MATCHED...
KUH! KUH! KUH! KUH!
WHAT ARE YOU TALKING ABOUT!?
HA (GASP)
AS SUCCESSOR TO THE VESSALIUS HOUSE, HIS FATE IS TO EVENTUALLY COME OVER TO ***OUR SIDE***...
COUGH
...SO YOU MAY VERY WELL END UP BEING MORE INVOLVED WITH HIM THAN I.
KUH! KUH! KUH...
YES, THAT DOES SEEM TO BE MOST LIKELY!
HAAH (SIGH)
SFX: KATA (SHAKE) KATA
OH?
YES?
OH DEAR.
IT'S BEGUN TO RAIN...

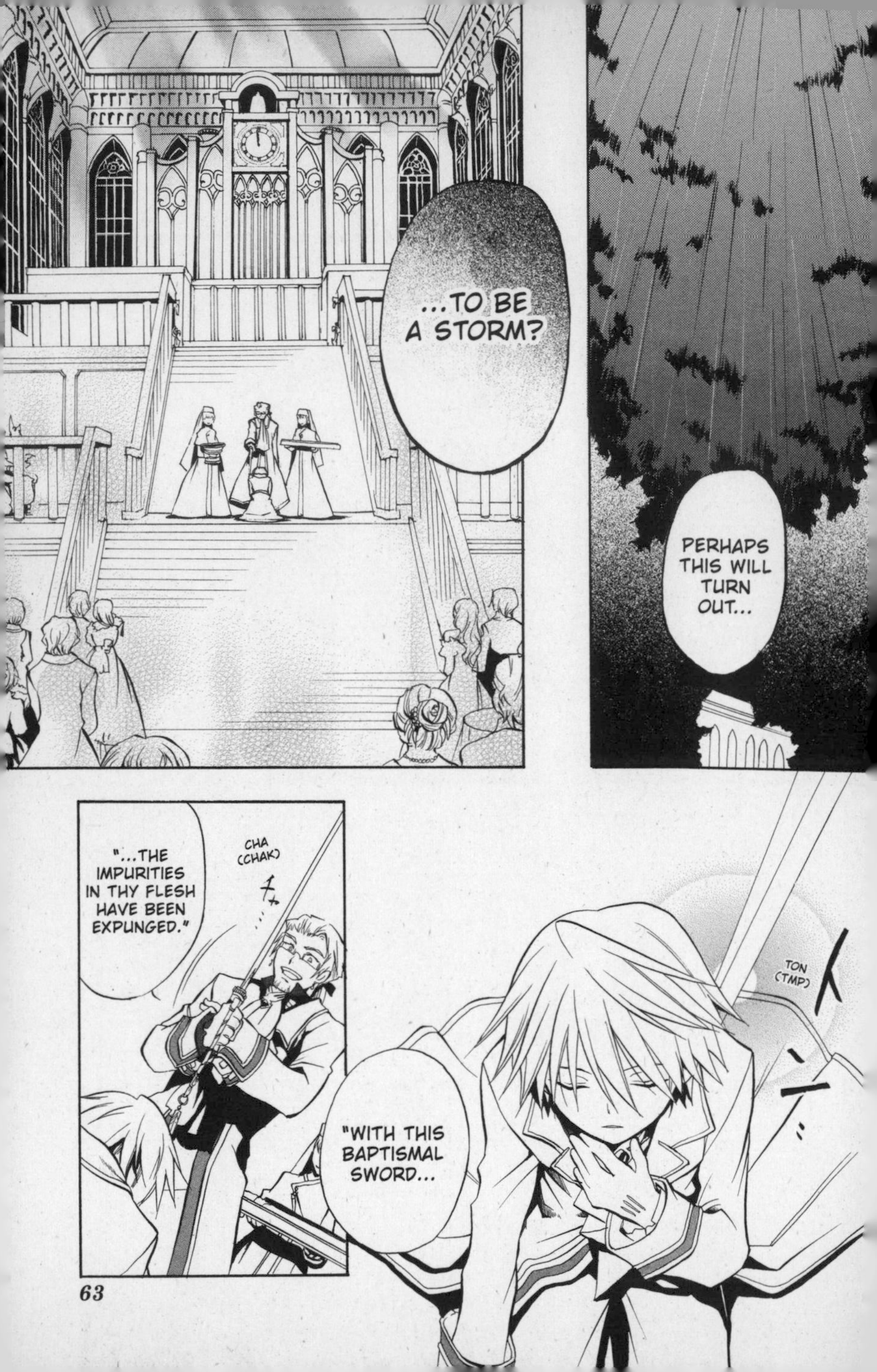
PERHAPS THIS WILL TURN OUT...
...TO BE A STORM?
TON (TMP)
"WITH THIS BAPTISMAL SWORD...
CHA (CHAK)
"...THE IMPURITIES IN THY FLESH HAVE BEEN EXPUNGED."

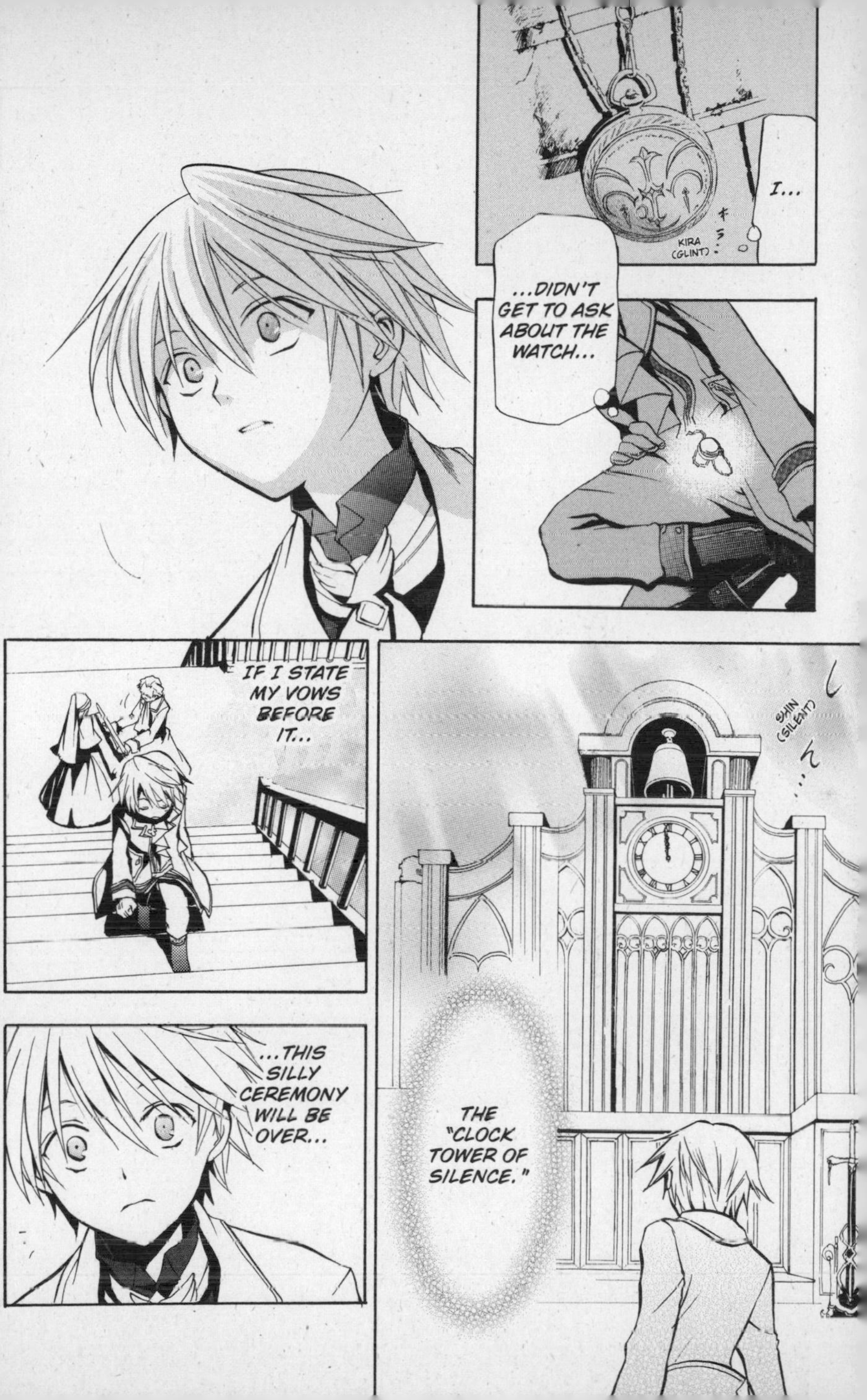
I...
キラ
KIRA (GLINT)
...DIDN'T GET TO ASK ABOUT THE WATCH...
しん…
SHIN (SILENT)
THE "CLOCK TOWER OF SILENCE."
IF I STATE MY VOWS BEFORE IT...
...THIS SILLY CEREMONY WILL BE OVER...

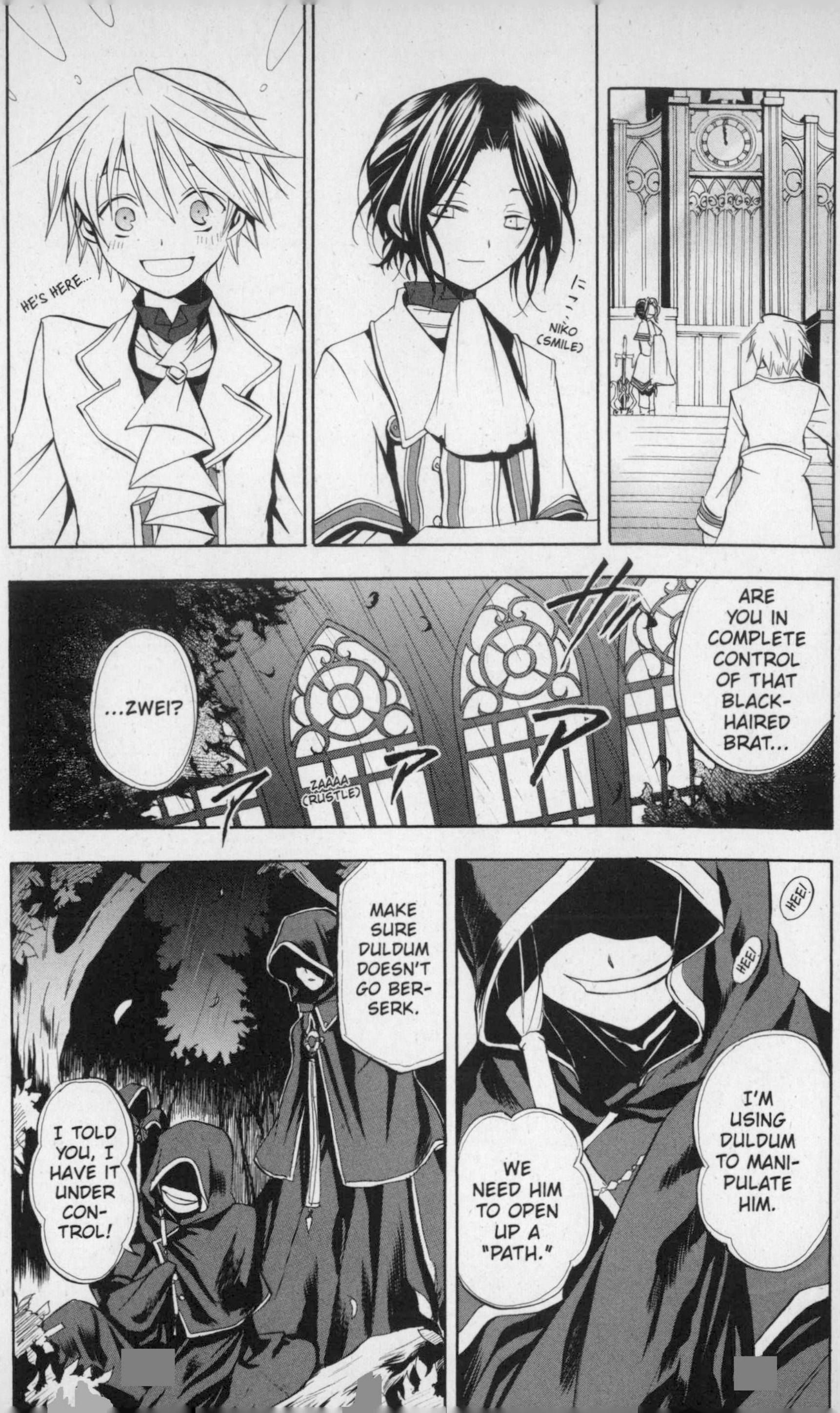
NIKO (SMILE)
HE'S HERE...
ARE YOU IN COMPLETE CONTROL OF THAT BLACK-HAIRED BRAT...
ZAAAA (RUSTLE)
...ZWEI?
HEE!
HEE!
I'M USING DULDUM TO MANIPULATE HIM.
WE NEED HIM TO OPEN UP A "PATH."
MAKE SURE DULDUM DOESN'T GO BERSERK.
I TOLD YOU, I HAVE IT UNDER CONTROL!

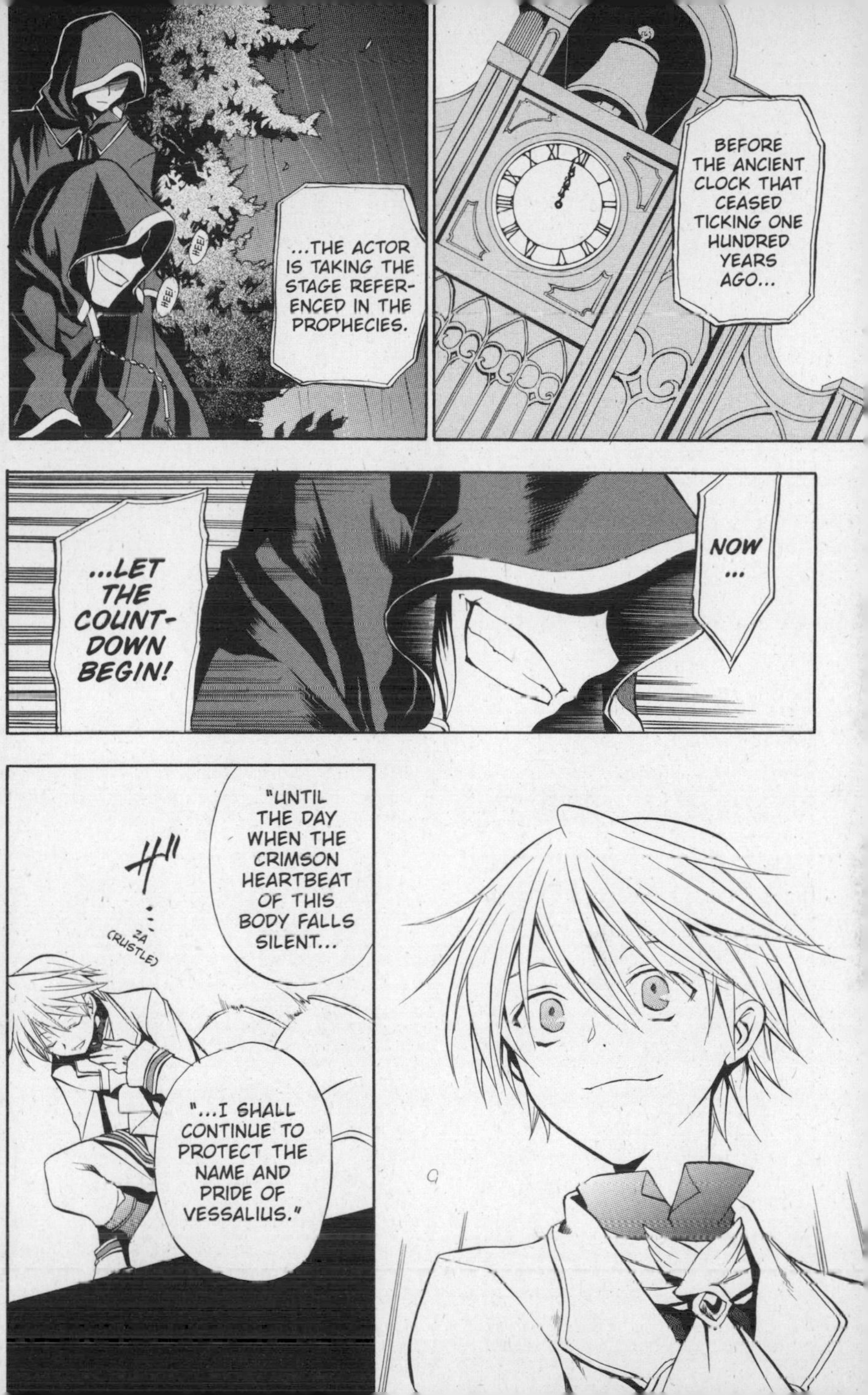
BEFORE THE ANCIENT CLOCK THAT CEASED TICKING ONE HUNDRED YEARS AGO...
...THE ACTOR IS TAKING THE STAGE REFERENCED IN THE PROPHECIES.
HEE!
HEE!
NOW...
...LET THE COUNT-DOWN BEGIN!
"UNTIL THE DAY WHEN THE CRIMSON HEARTBEAT OF THIS BODY FALLS SILENT...
ZA (RUSTLE)
"...I SHALL CONTINUE TO PROTECT THE NAME AND PRIDE OF VESSALIUS."

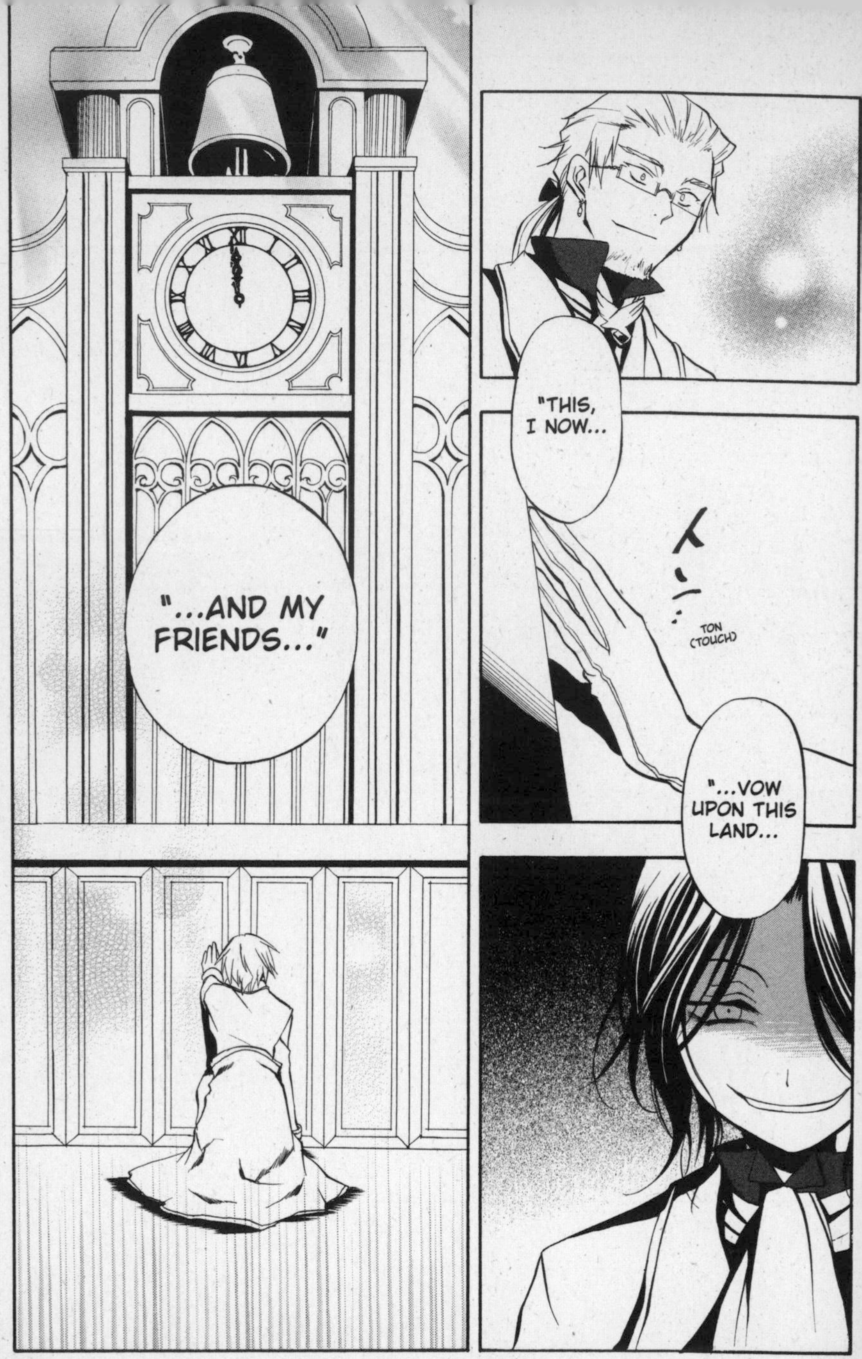
"THIS, I NOW...
TON (TOUCH)
"...VOW UPON THIS LAND...
"...AND MY FRIENDS..."

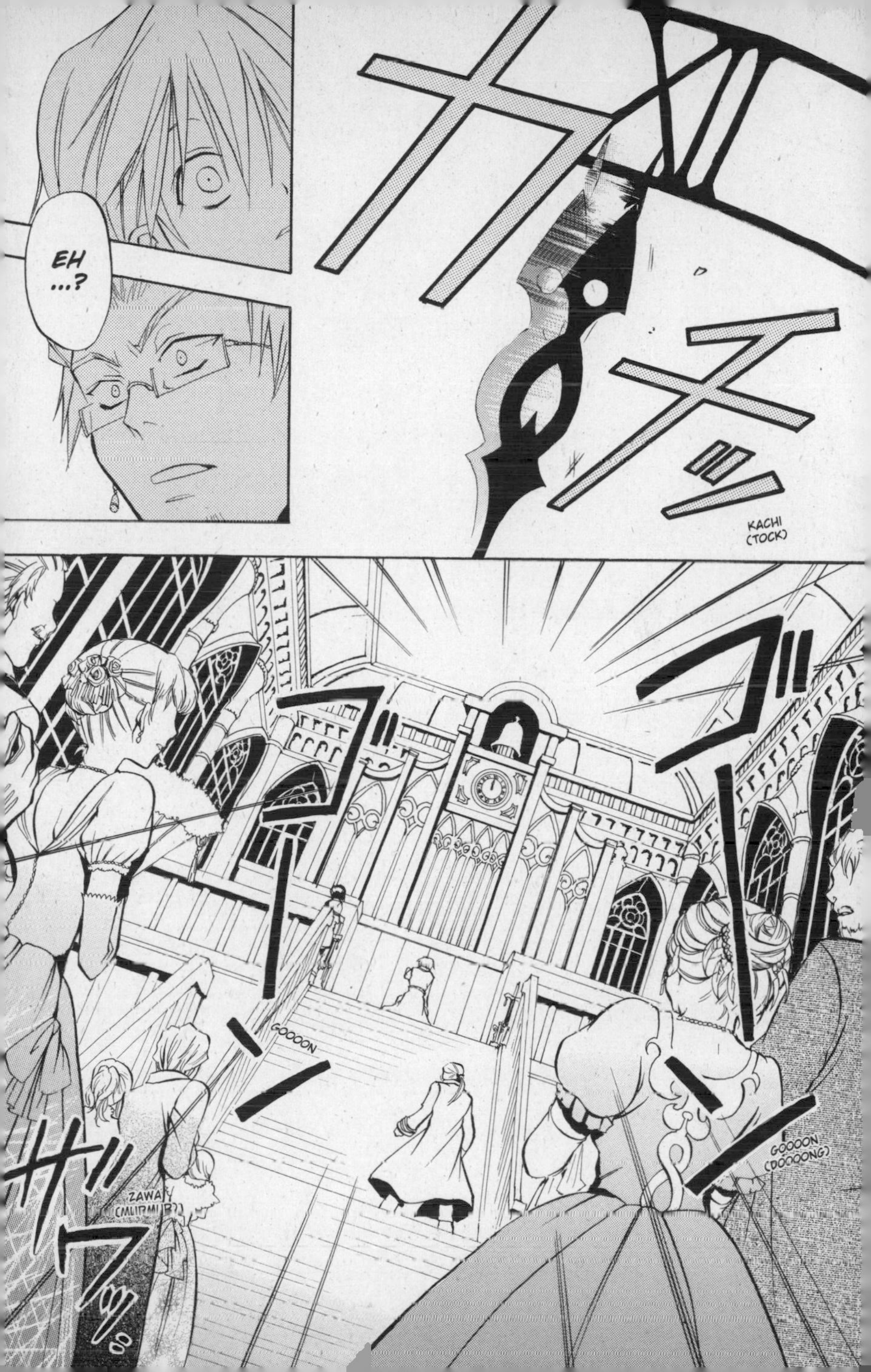
KACHI (TOCK)
EH ...?
GOOOON
GOOOON (DOOOONG)
ZAWA (MURMUR)

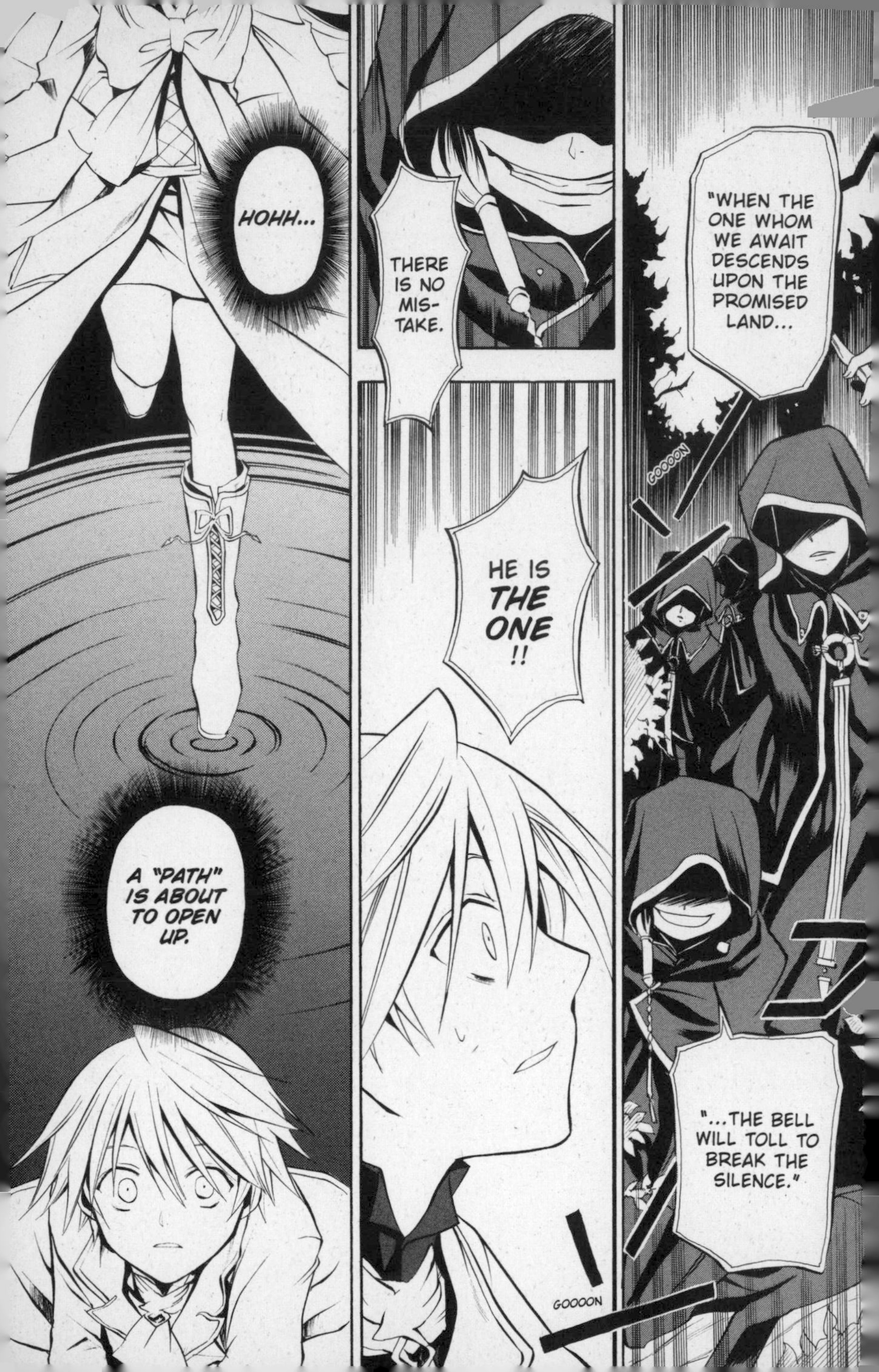
"WHEN THE ONE WHOM WE AWAIT DESCENDS UPON THE PROMISED LAND...
GOOOON
"...THE BELL WILL TOLL TO BREAK THE SILENCE."
THERE IS NO MIS-TAKE.
HE IS THE ONE !!
GOOOON
HOHH...
A "PATH" IS ABOUT TO OPEN UP.

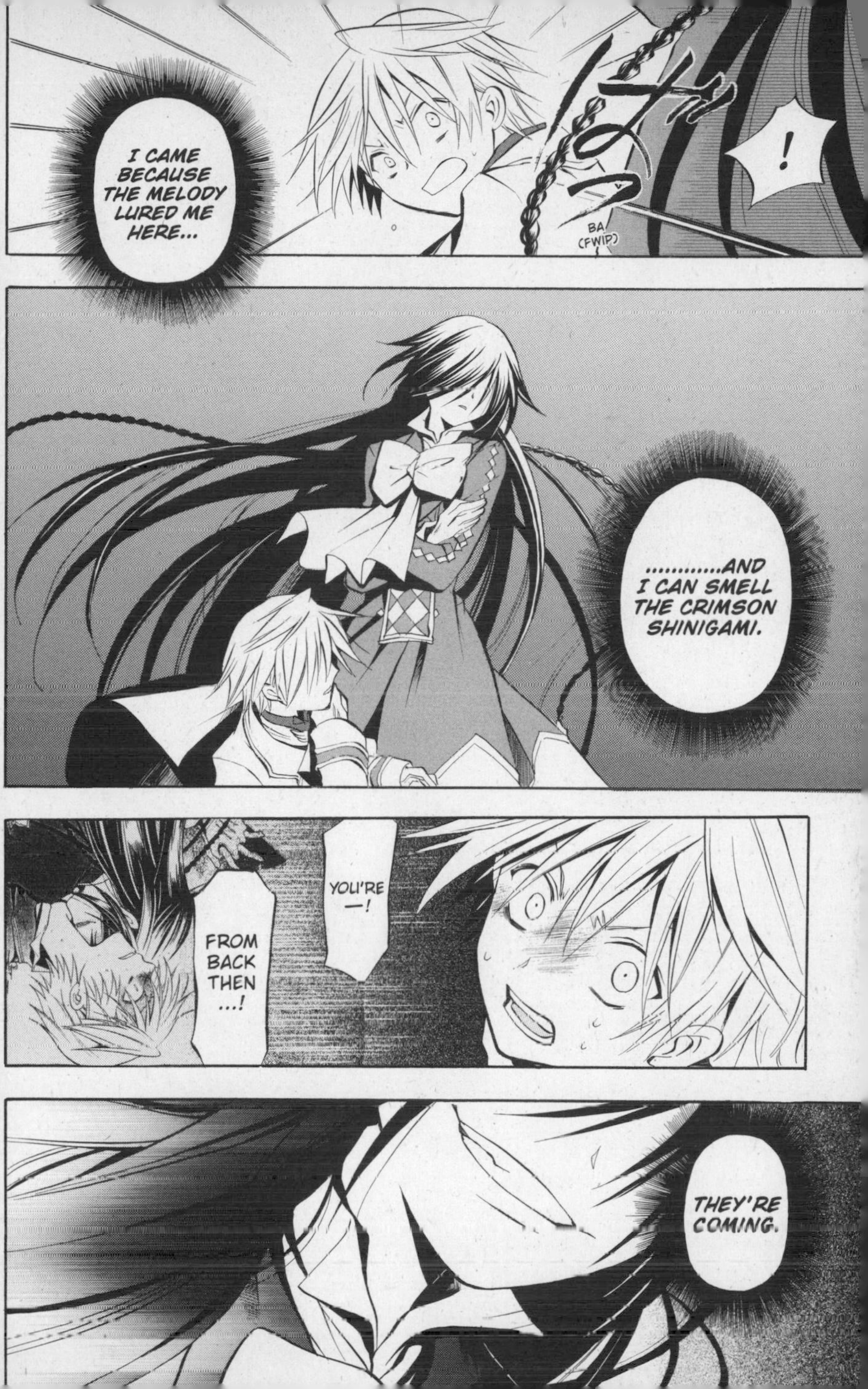
!
BA
(FWIP)
I CAME BECAUSE THE MELODY LURED ME HERE...
............AND I CAN SMELL THE CRIMSON SHINIGAMI.
YOU'RE—!
FROM BACK THEN ...!
THEY'RE COMING.

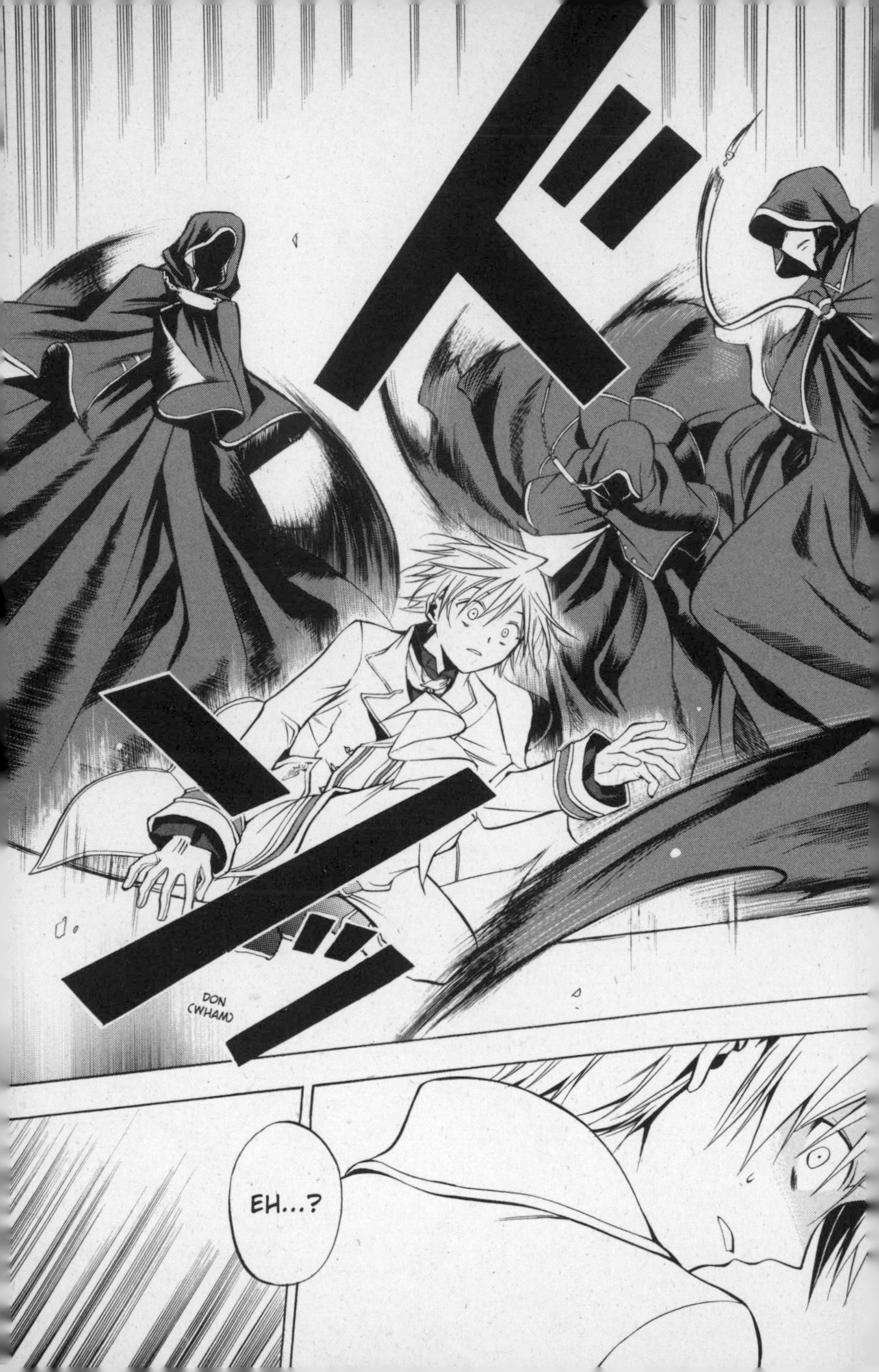
DON (WHAM)
EH...?

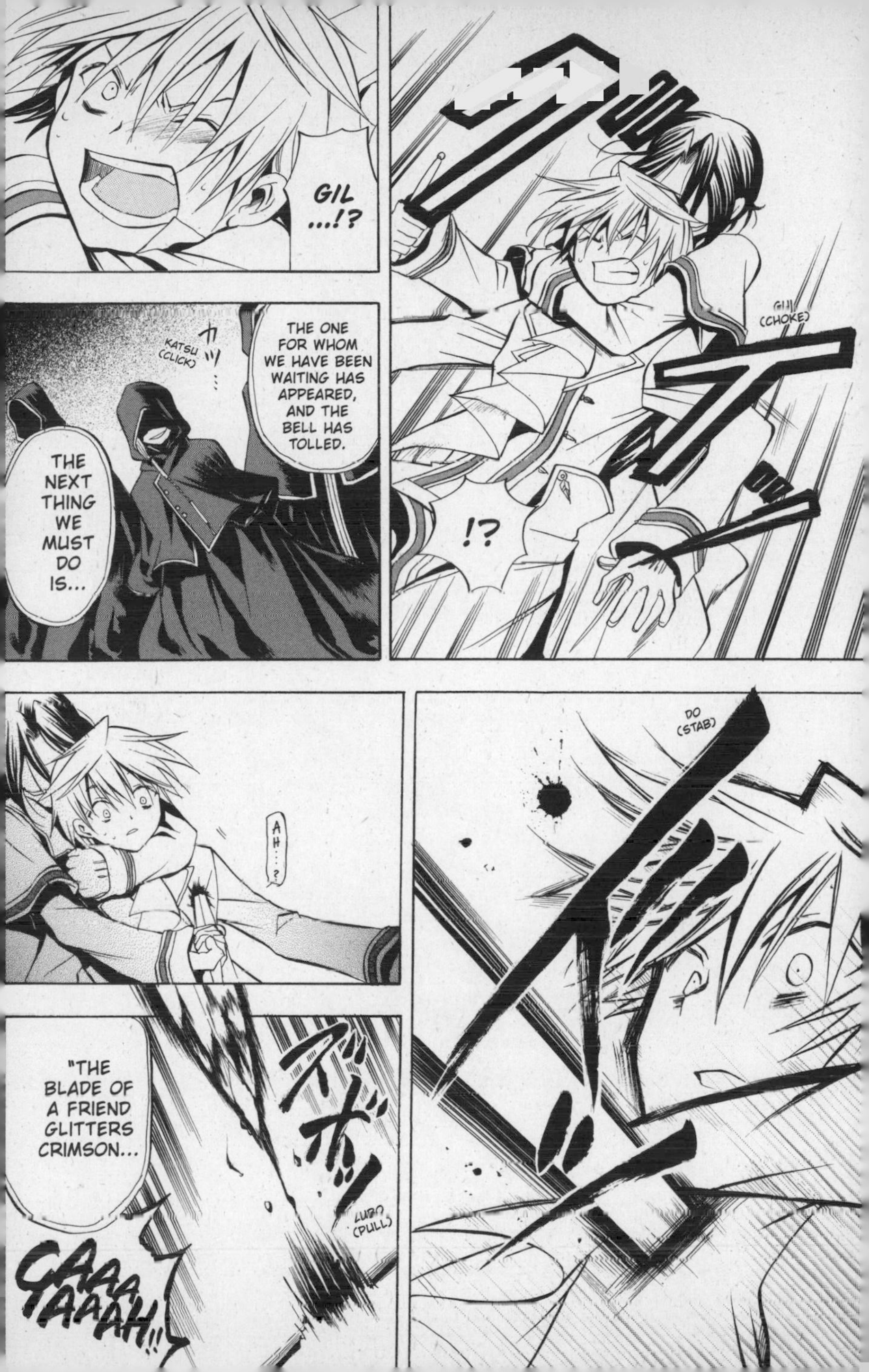
(CHOKE)
!?
GIL ...!?
KATSU (CLICK)
THE ONE FOR WHOM WE HAVE BEEN WAITING HAS APPEARED, AND THE BELL HAS TOLLED.
THE NEXT THING WE MUST DO IS...
DO (STAB)
AH...?
"THE BLADE OF A FRIEND GLITTERS CRIMSON...
(PULL)
GAAAAAAAH!!

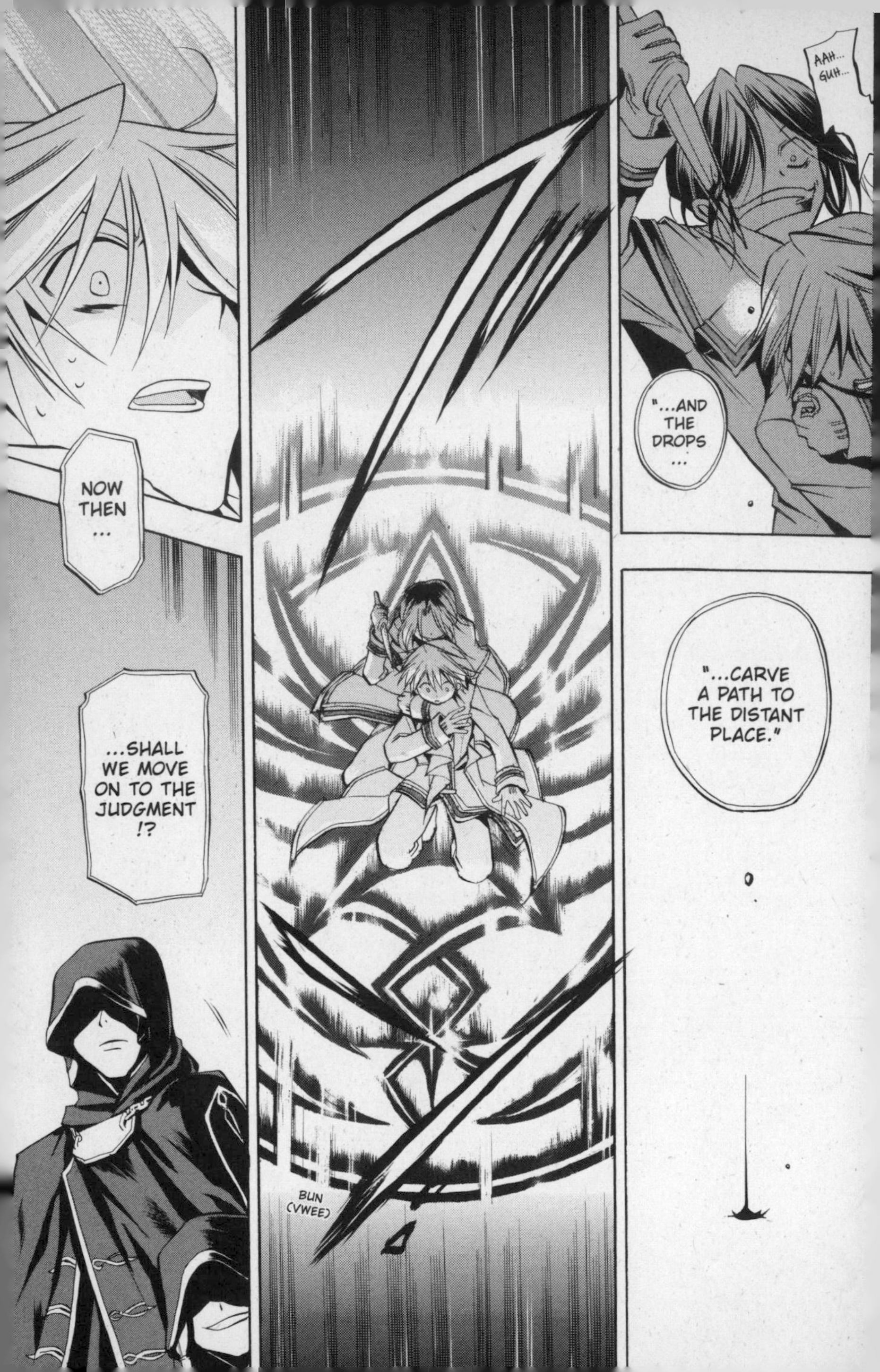
AAH... GUH...
"...AND THE DROPS ..."
"...CARVE A PATH TO THE DISTANT PLACE."
BUN (VWEE)
NOW THEN ...
...SHALL WE MOVE ON TO THE JUDGMENT !?

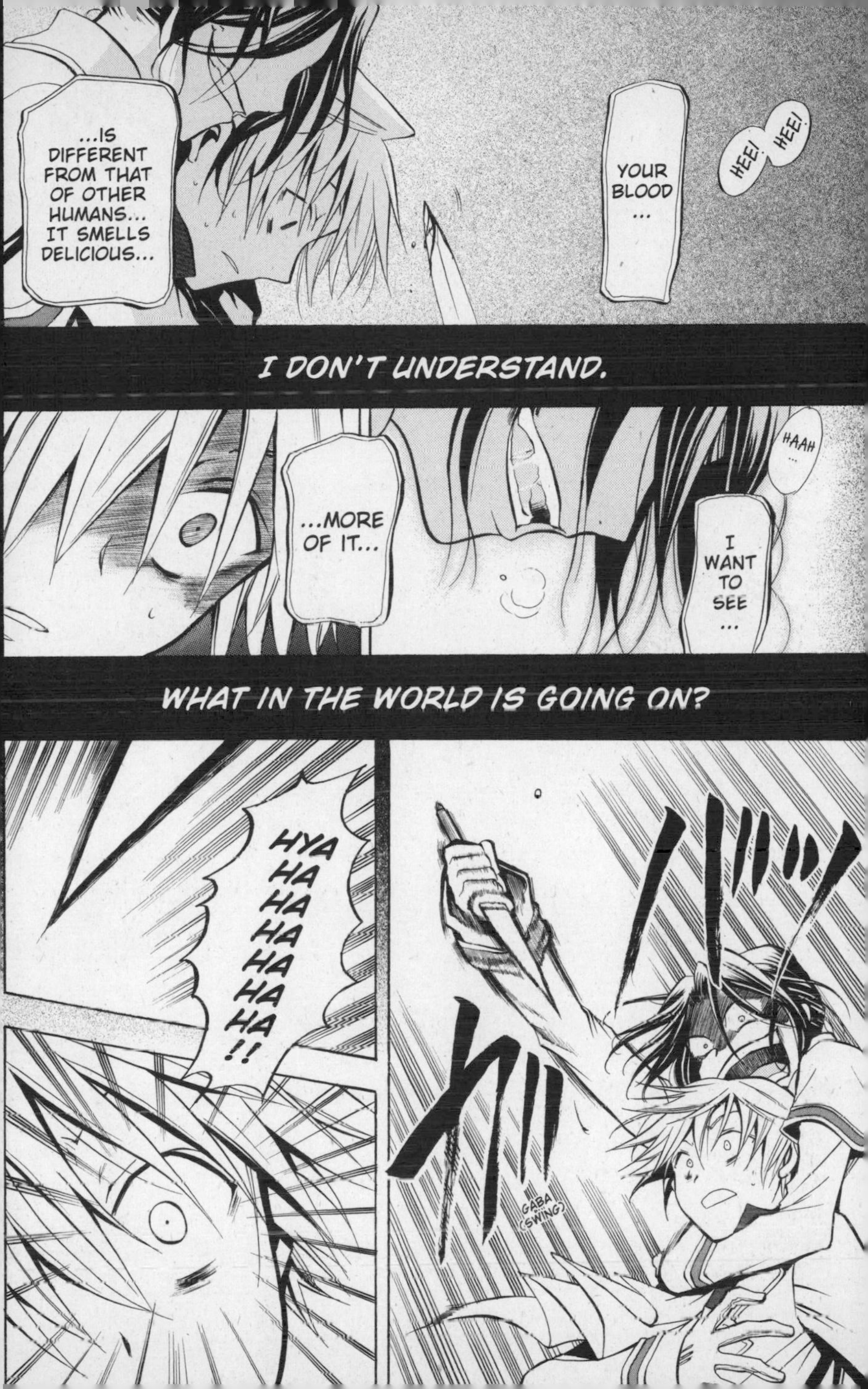
HEE! HEE!
YOUR BLOOD ...
...IS DIFFERENT FROM THAT OF OTHER HUMANS... IT SMELLS DELICIOUS...
I DON'T UNDERSTAND.
HAAH ...
I WANT TO SEE ...
...MORE OF IT...
WHAT IN THE WORLD IS GOING ON?
バッ
GABA (SWING)
HYA HA HA HA HA HA HA!!

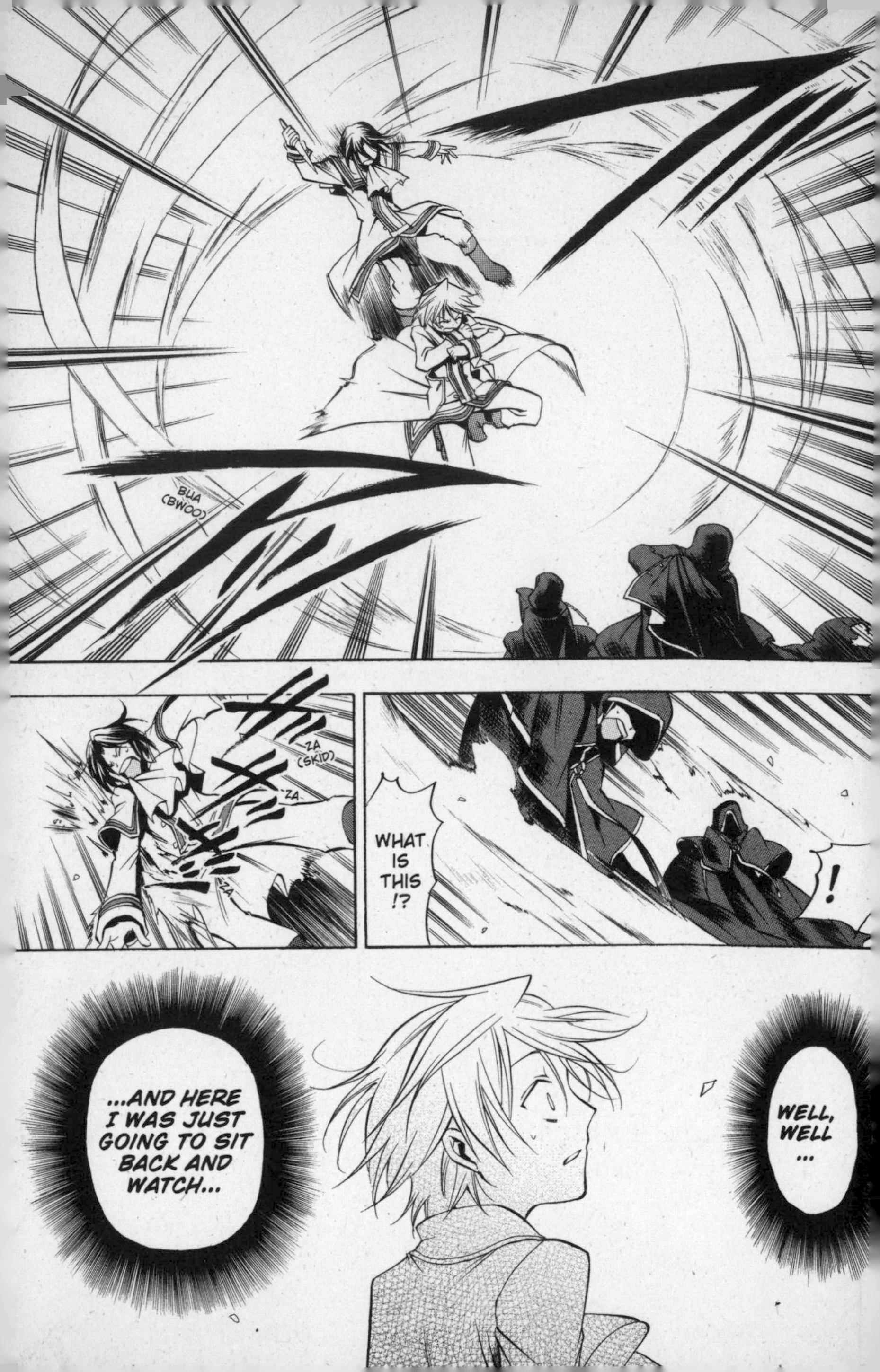
BUA (BWOO)
!
WHAT IS THIS !?
ZA (SKID)
ZA
ZA
WELL, WELL ...
...AND HERE I WAS JUST GOING TO SIT BACK AND WATCH...

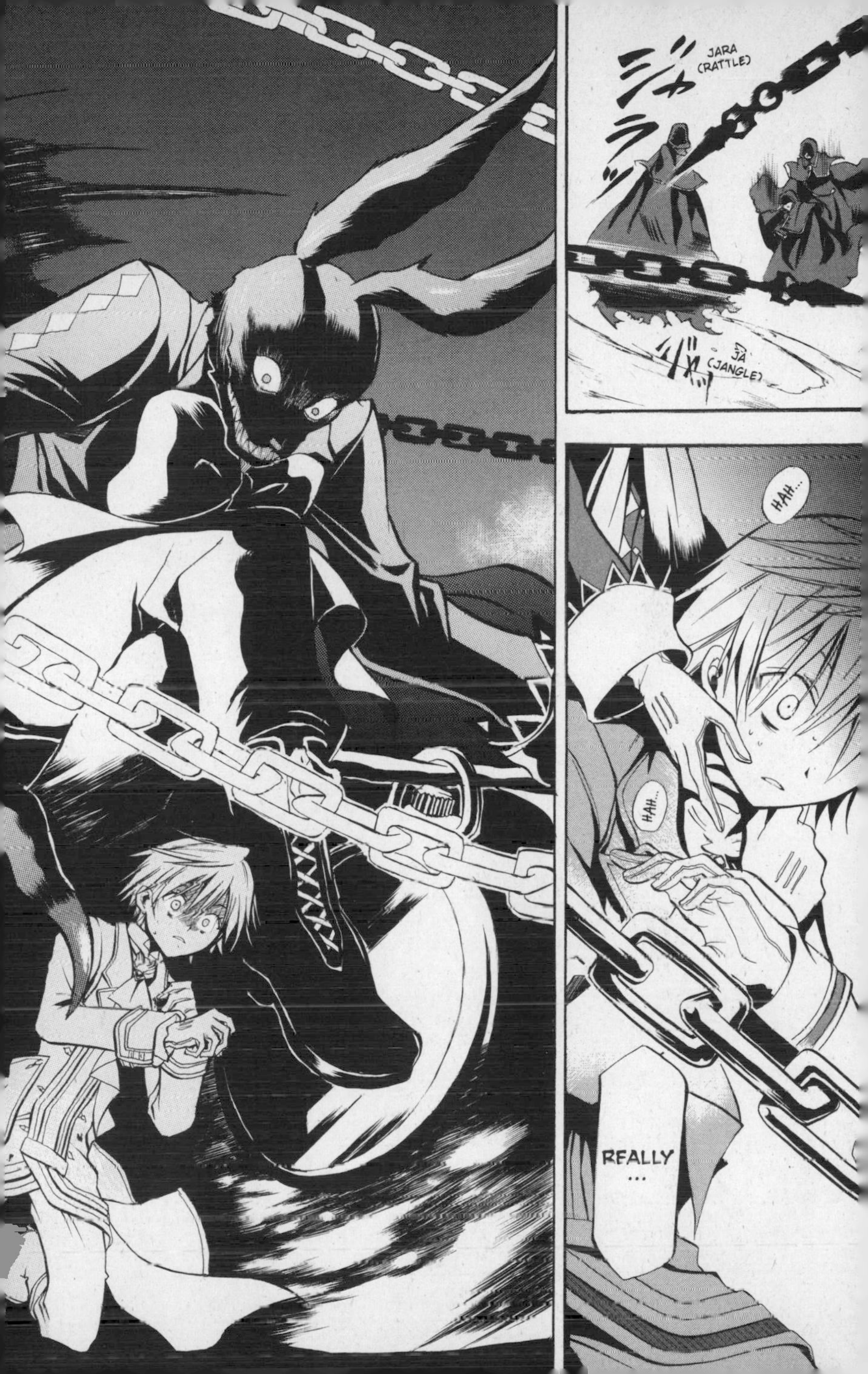
JARA (RATTLE)
JA (JANGLE)
HAH...
HAH...
REALLY ...

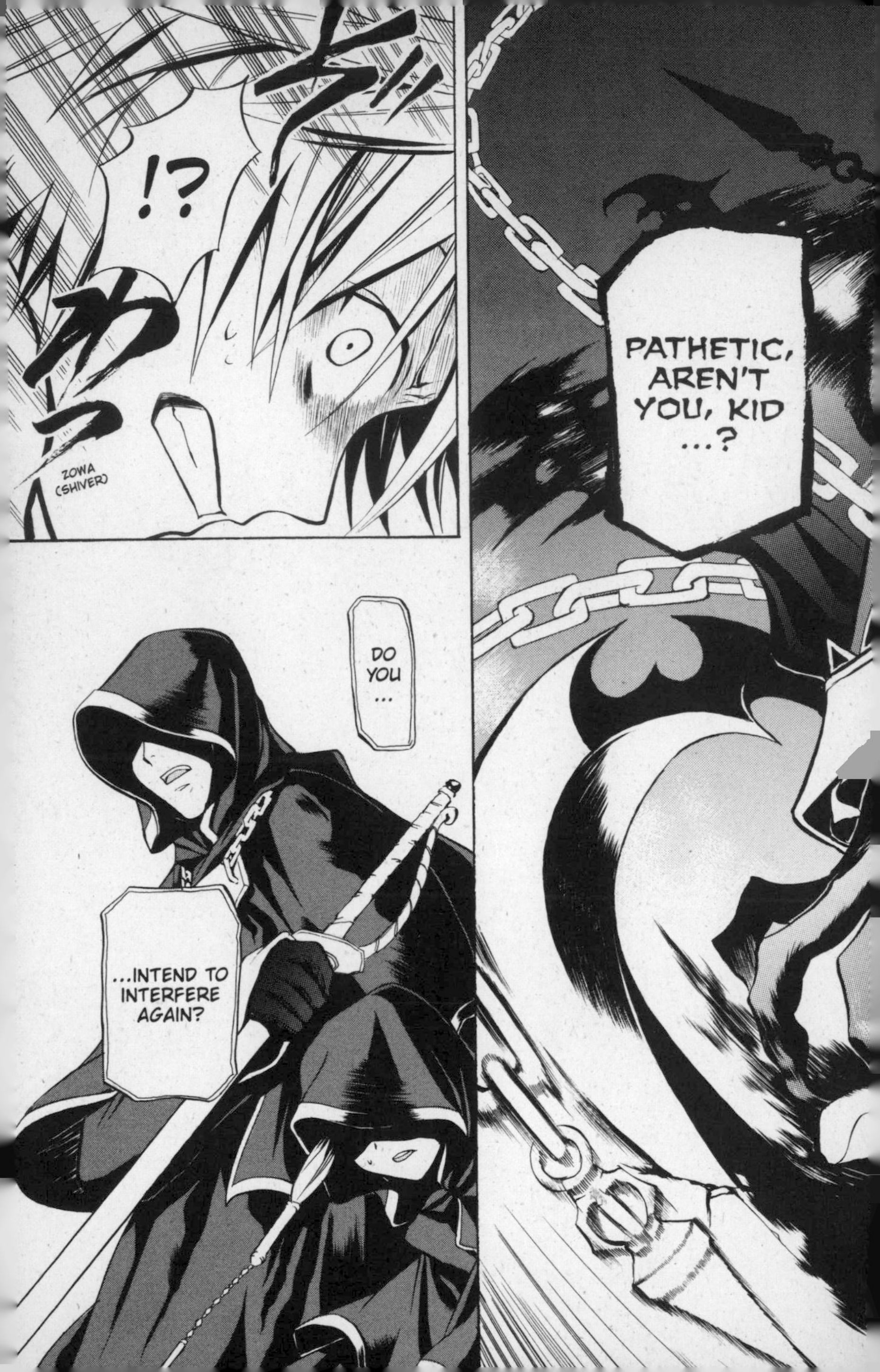
PATHETIC, AREN'T YOU, KID ...?
!?
ZOWA (SHIVER)
DO YOU ...
...INTEND TO INTERFERE AGAIN?

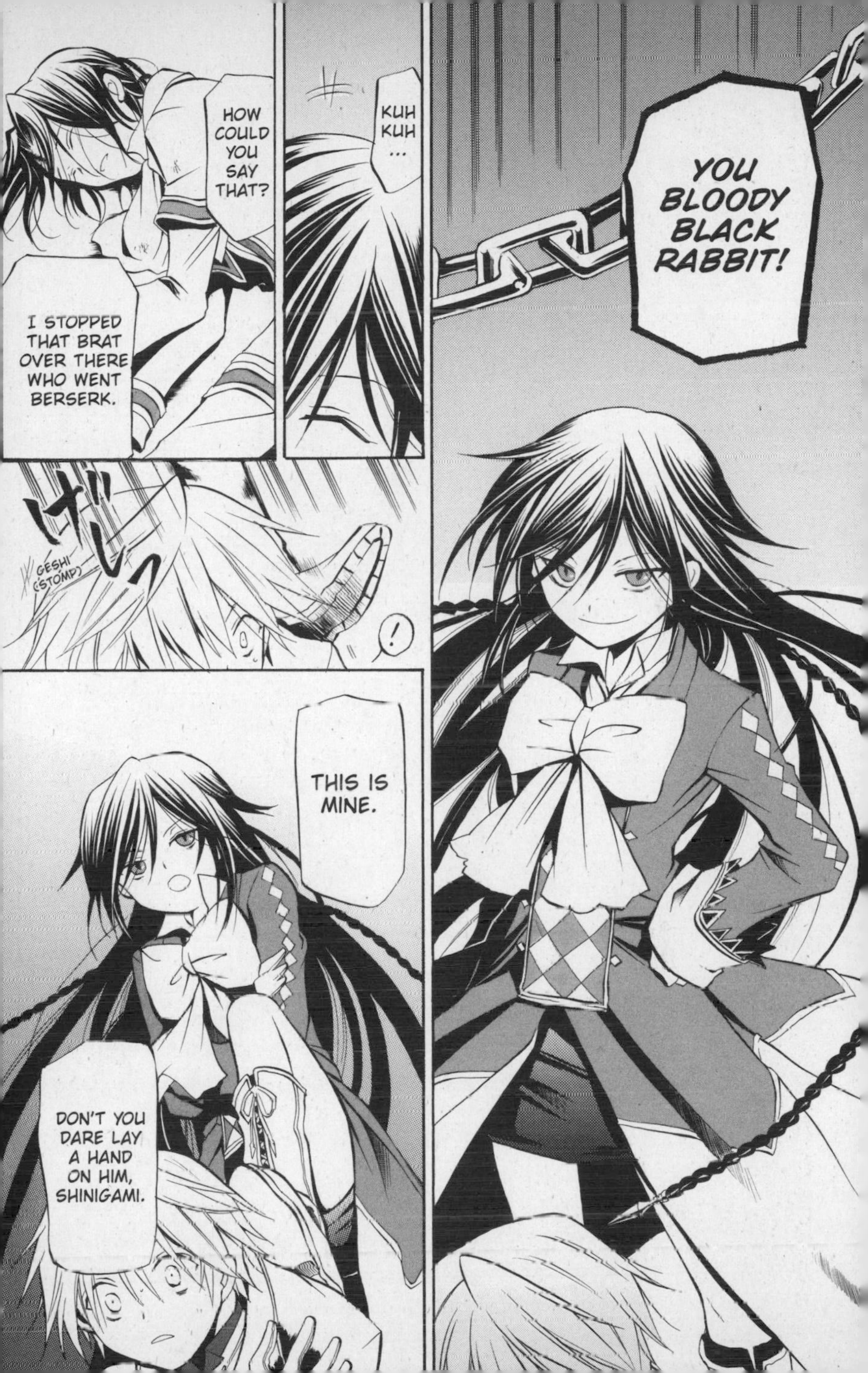
YOU BLOODY BLACK RABBIT!
KUH KUH ...
HOW COULD YOU SAY THAT?
I STOPPED THAT BRAT OVER THERE WHO WENT BERSERK.
GESHI (STOMP)
!
THIS IS MINE.
DON'T YOU DARE LAY A HAND ON HIM, SHINIGAMI.

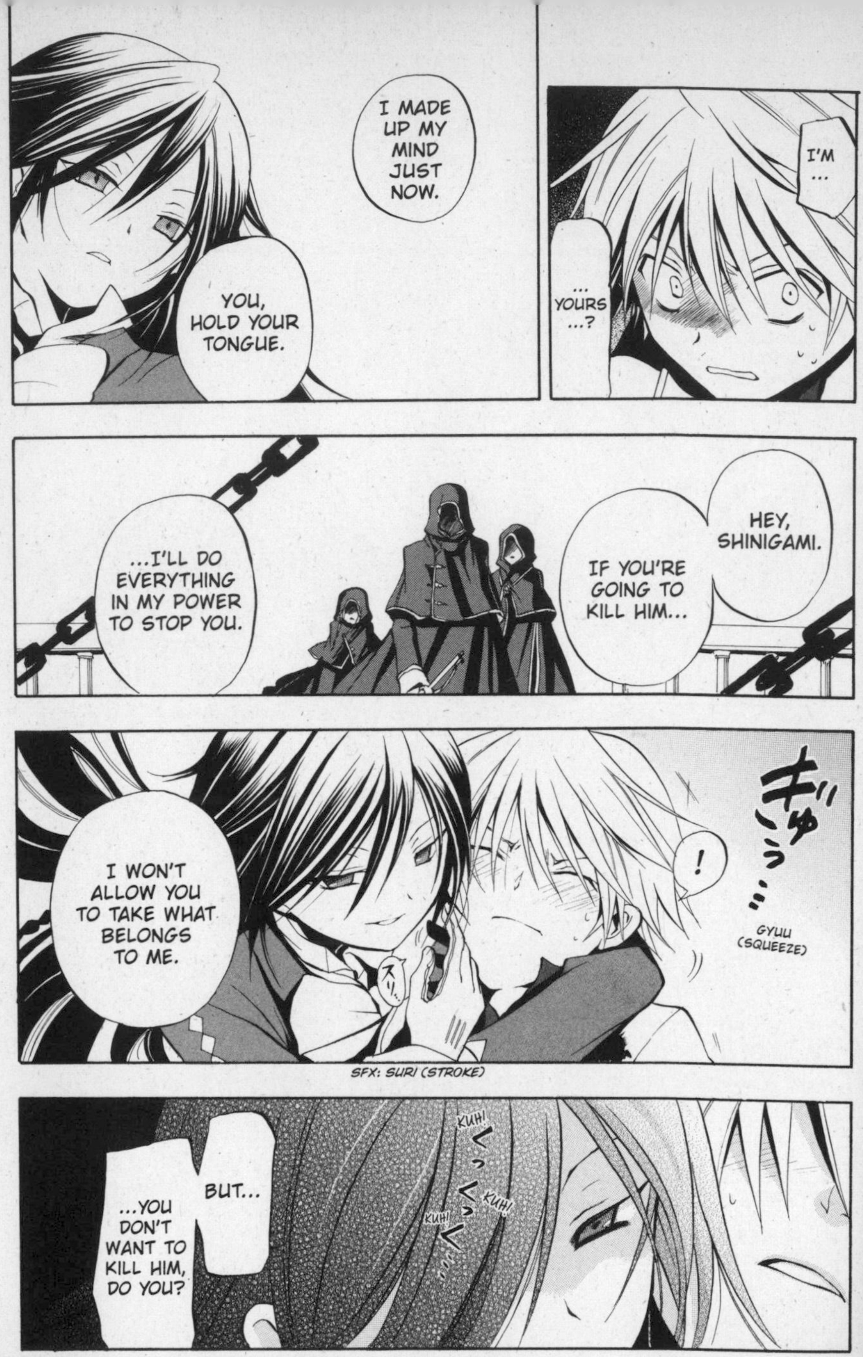
I'M ...
... YOURS ...?
I MADE UP MY MIND JUST NOW.
YOU, HOLD YOUR TONGUE.
HEY, SHINIGAMI.
IF YOU'RE GOING TO KILL HIM...
...I'LL DO EVERYTHING IN MY POWER TO STOP YOU.
GYUU (SQUEEZE)
!
I WON'T ALLOW YOU TO TAKE WHAT BELONGS TO ME.
SFX: SURI (STROKE)
KUH!
KUH!
KUH!
BUT...
...YOU DON'T WANT TO KILL HIM, DO YOU?

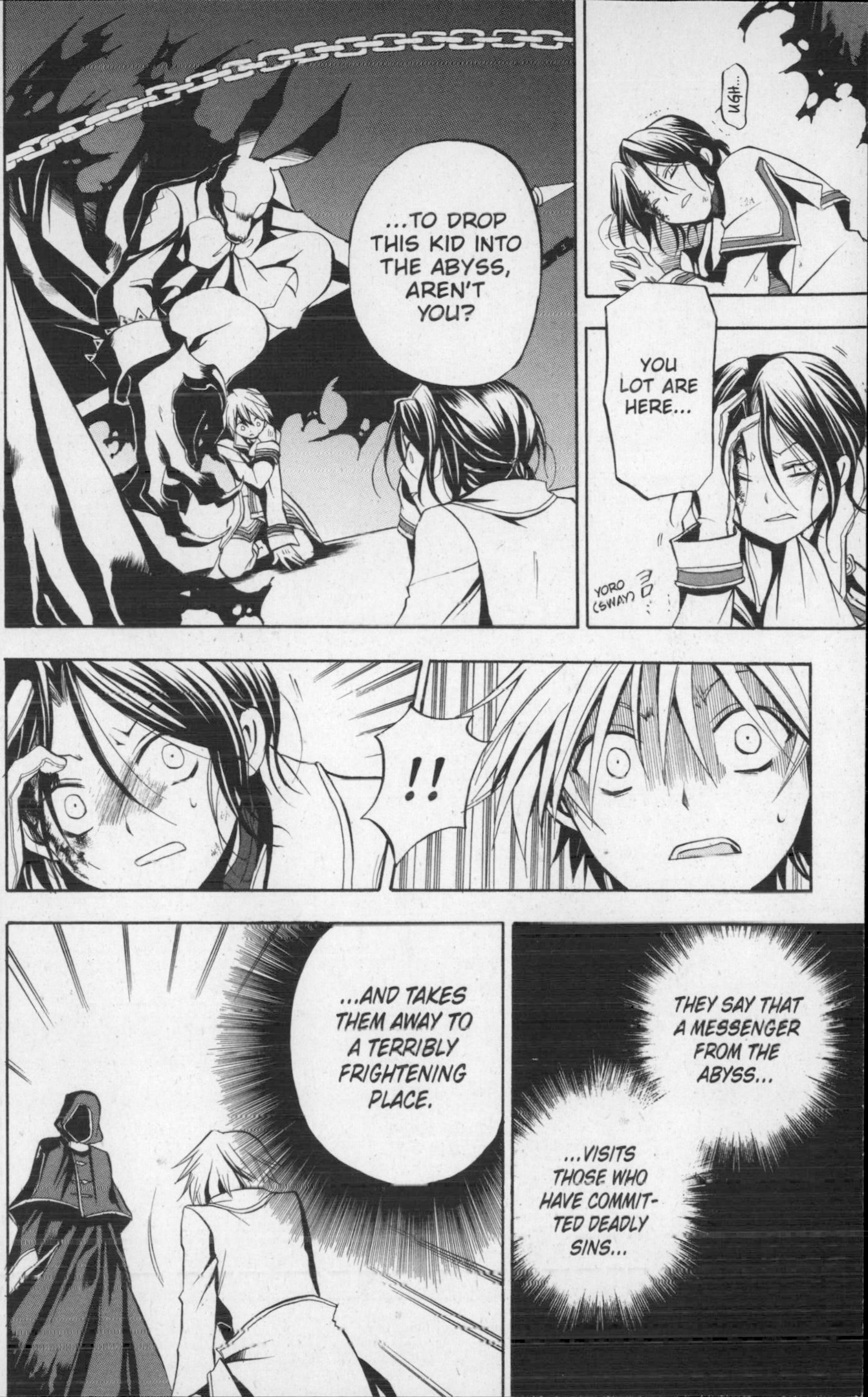
UGH...
YOU LOT ARE HERE...
YORO (SWAY)
...TO DROP THIS KID INTO THE ABYSS, AREN'T YOU?
!!
THEY SAY THAT A MESSENGER FROM THE ABYSS...
...VISITS THOSE WHO HAVE COMMIT-TED DEADLY SINS...
...AND TAKES THEM AWAY TO A TERRIBLY FRIGHTENING PLACE.

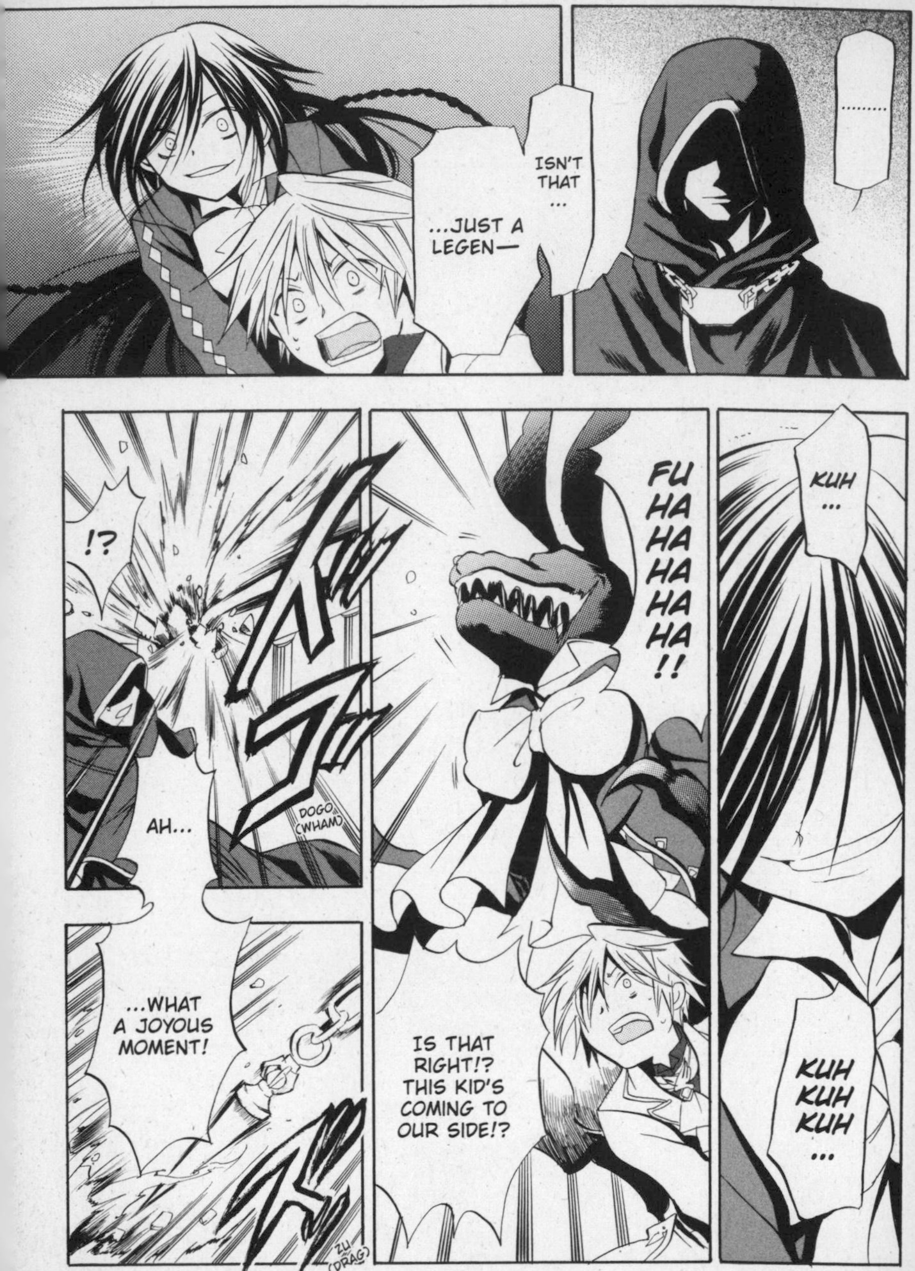
.........
ISN'T THAT ...
...JUST A LEGEN—
KUH ...
KUH KUH KUH ...
FU HA HA HA HA HA HA !!
IS THAT RIGHT!? THIS KID'S COMING TO OUR SIDE!?
!?
DOGO (WHAM)
AH...
...WHAT A JOYOUS MOMENT!
ZU (DRAG)

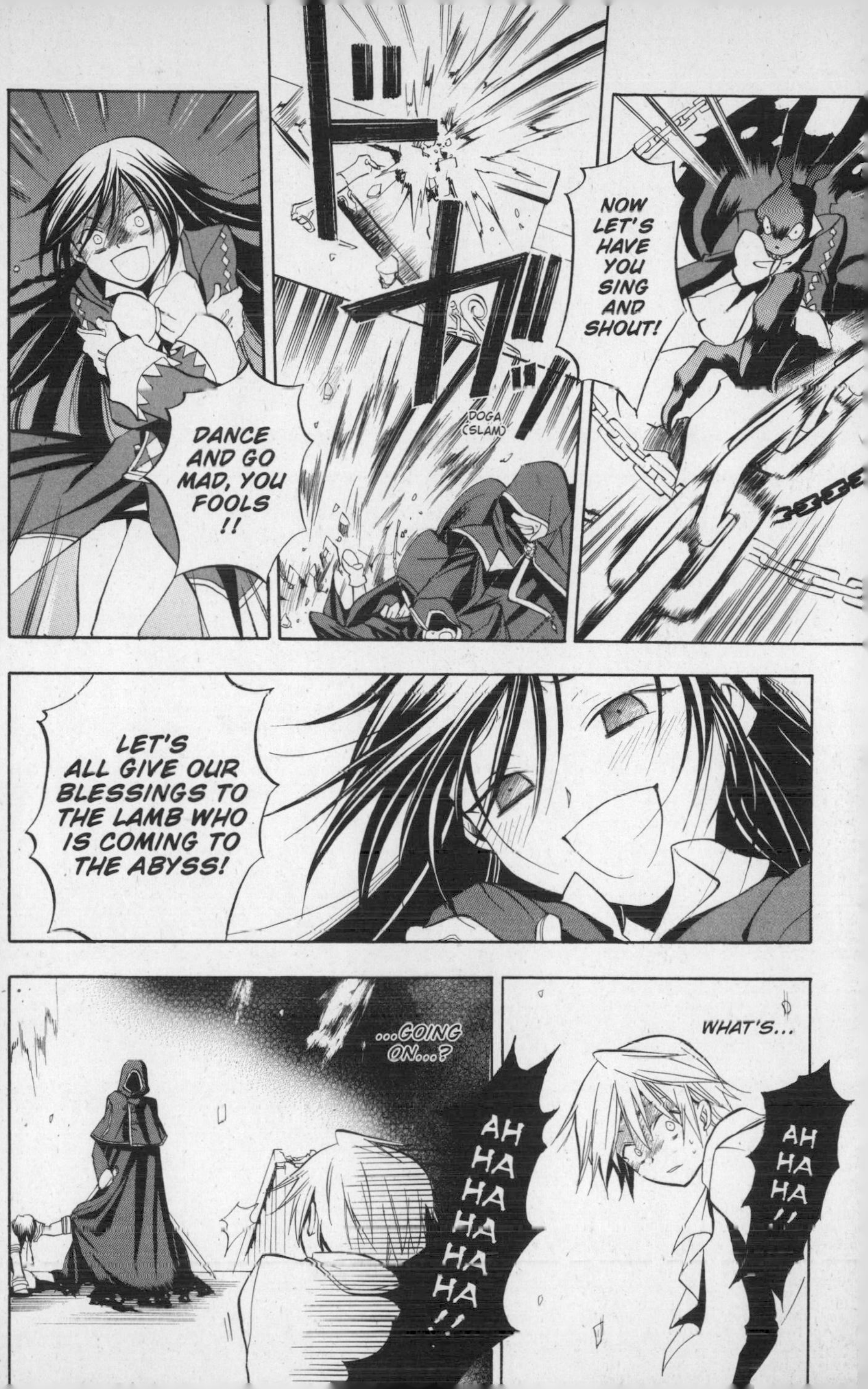
NOW LET'S HAVE YOU SING AND SHOUT!
DOGA (SLAM)
DANCE AND GO MAD, YOU FOOLS !!
LET'S ALL GIVE OUR BLESSINGS TO THE LAMB WHO IS COMING TO THE ABYSS!
WHAT'S...
AH HA HA !!
AH HA HA HA HA HA HA !!
...GOING ON...?

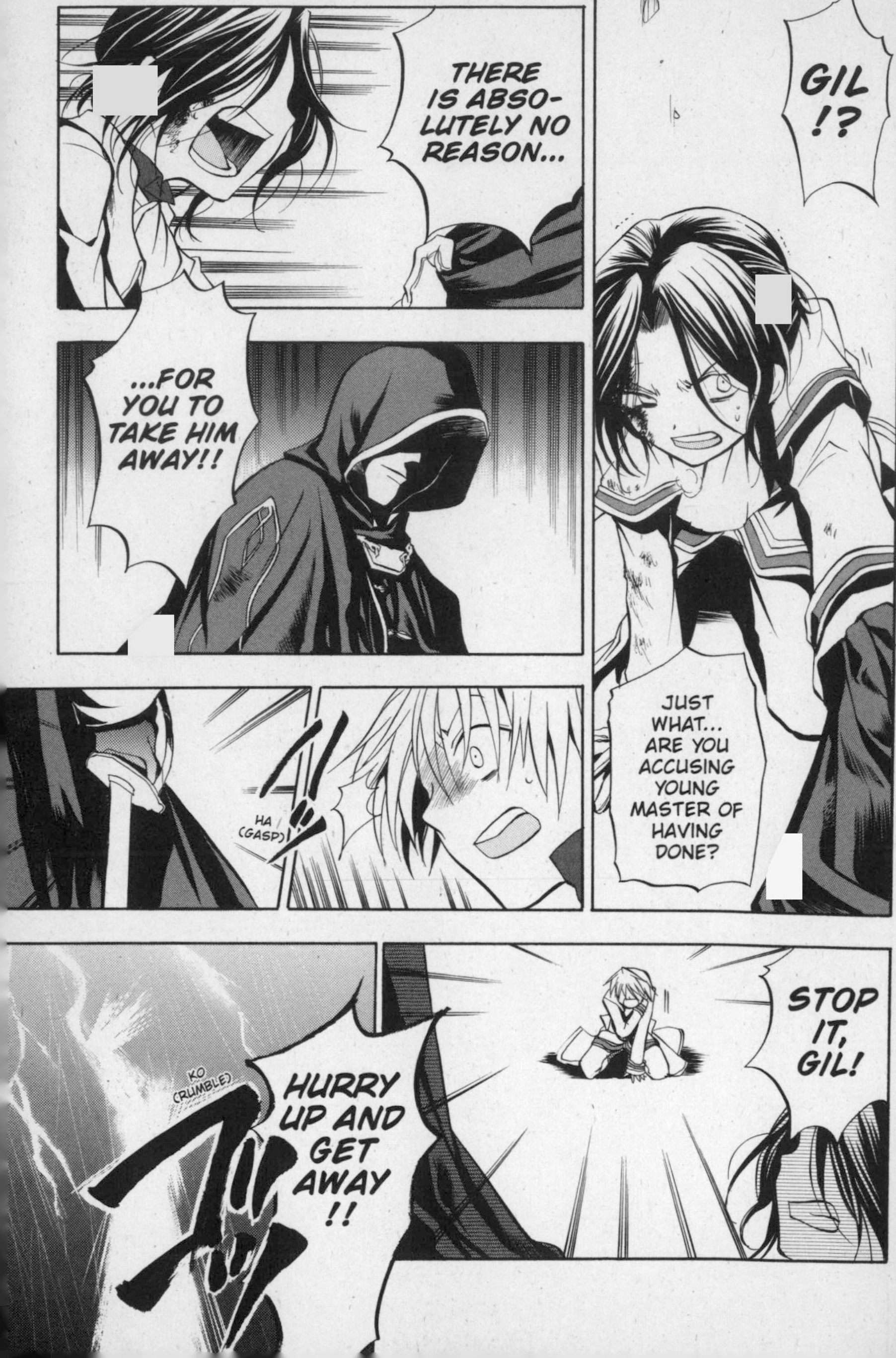
GIL !?
JUST WHAT... ARE YOU ACCUSING YOUNG MASTER OF HAVING DONE?
THERE IS ABSO- LUTELY NO REASON...
...FOR YOU TO TAKE HIM AWAY!!
HA (GASP)
STOP IT, GIL!
HURRY UP AND GET AWAY !!
KO (RUMBLE)

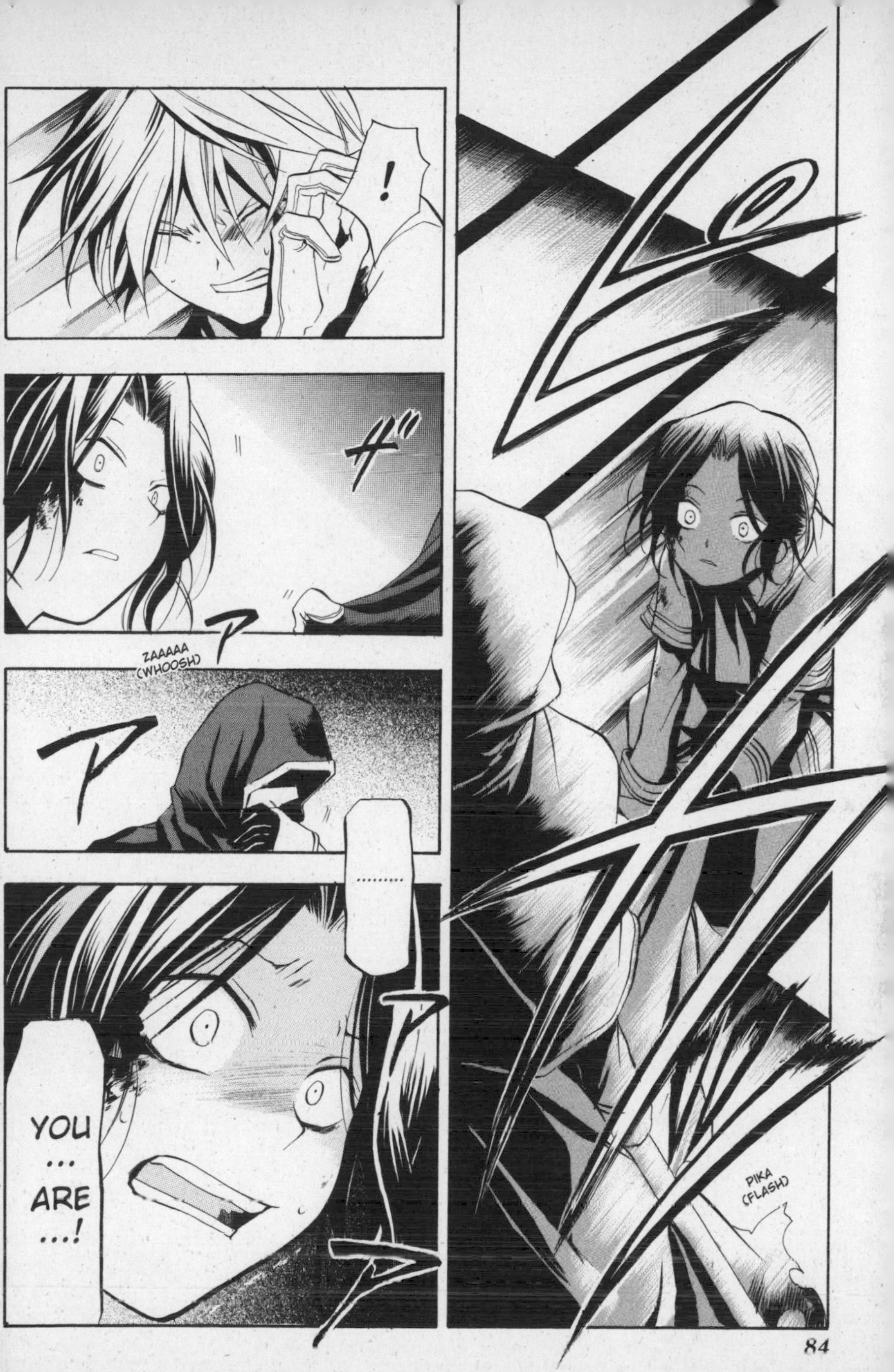
PIKA (FLASH)
!
ZAAAAA (WHOOSH)
.........
YOU ... ARE ...!

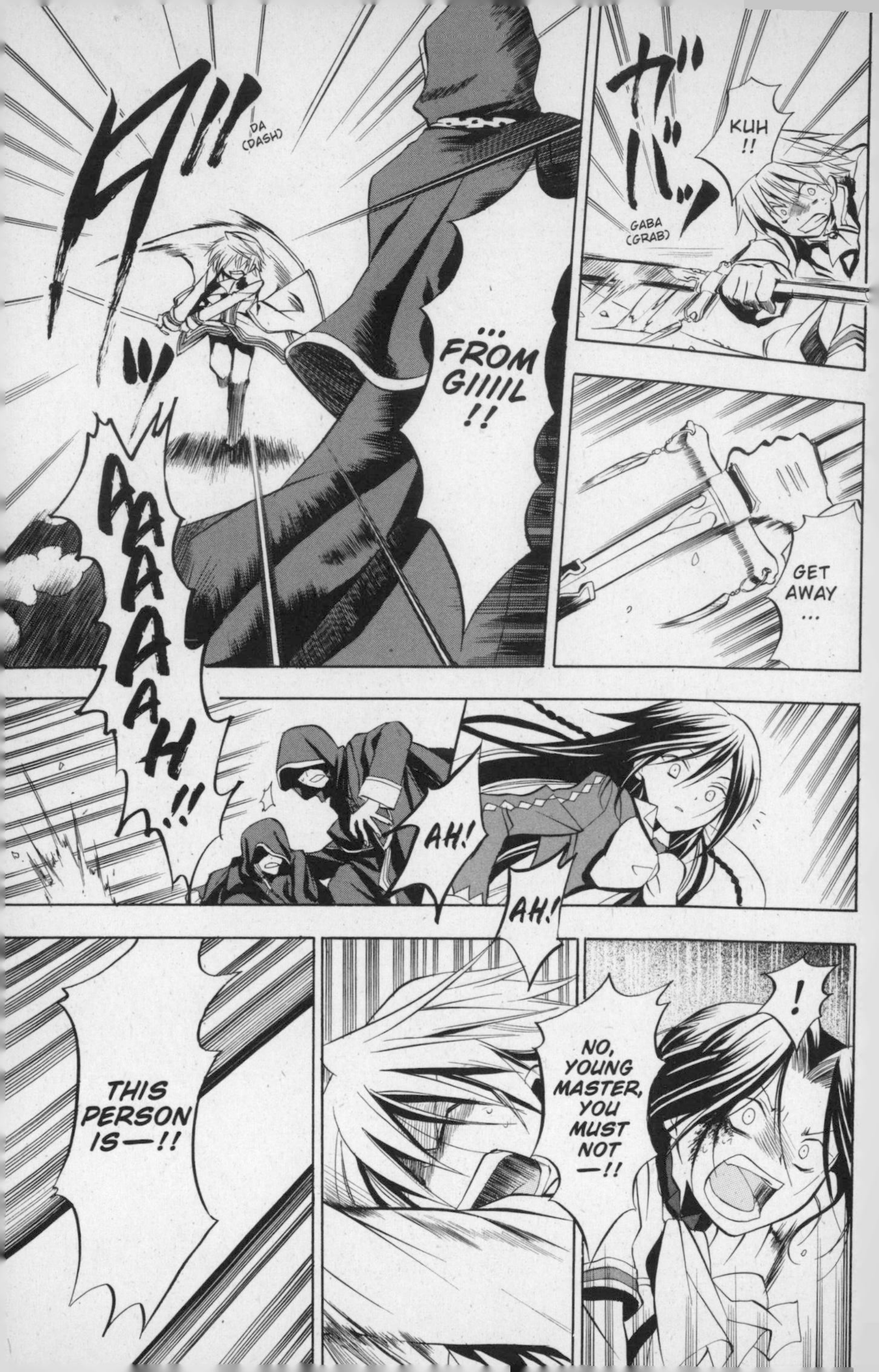
ガバッ
GABA (GRAB)
KUH !!
GET AWAY ...
ダッ
DA (DASH)
... FROM GIIIIL !!
AAAAAAAH!!
AH!
AH!
!
NO, YOUNG MASTER, YOU MUST NOT —!!
THIS PERSON IS—!!

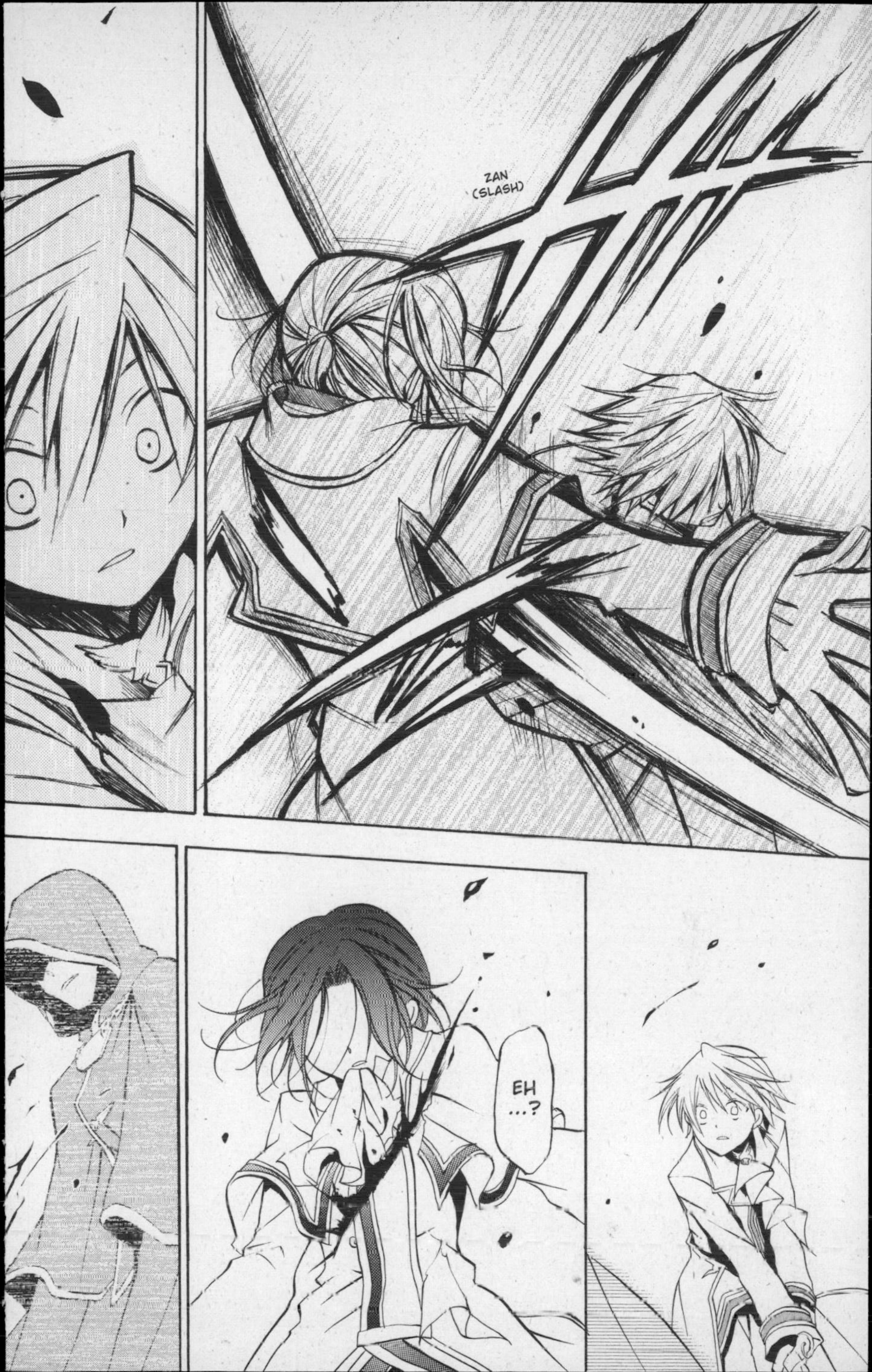
ZAN
(SLASH)
EH
...?

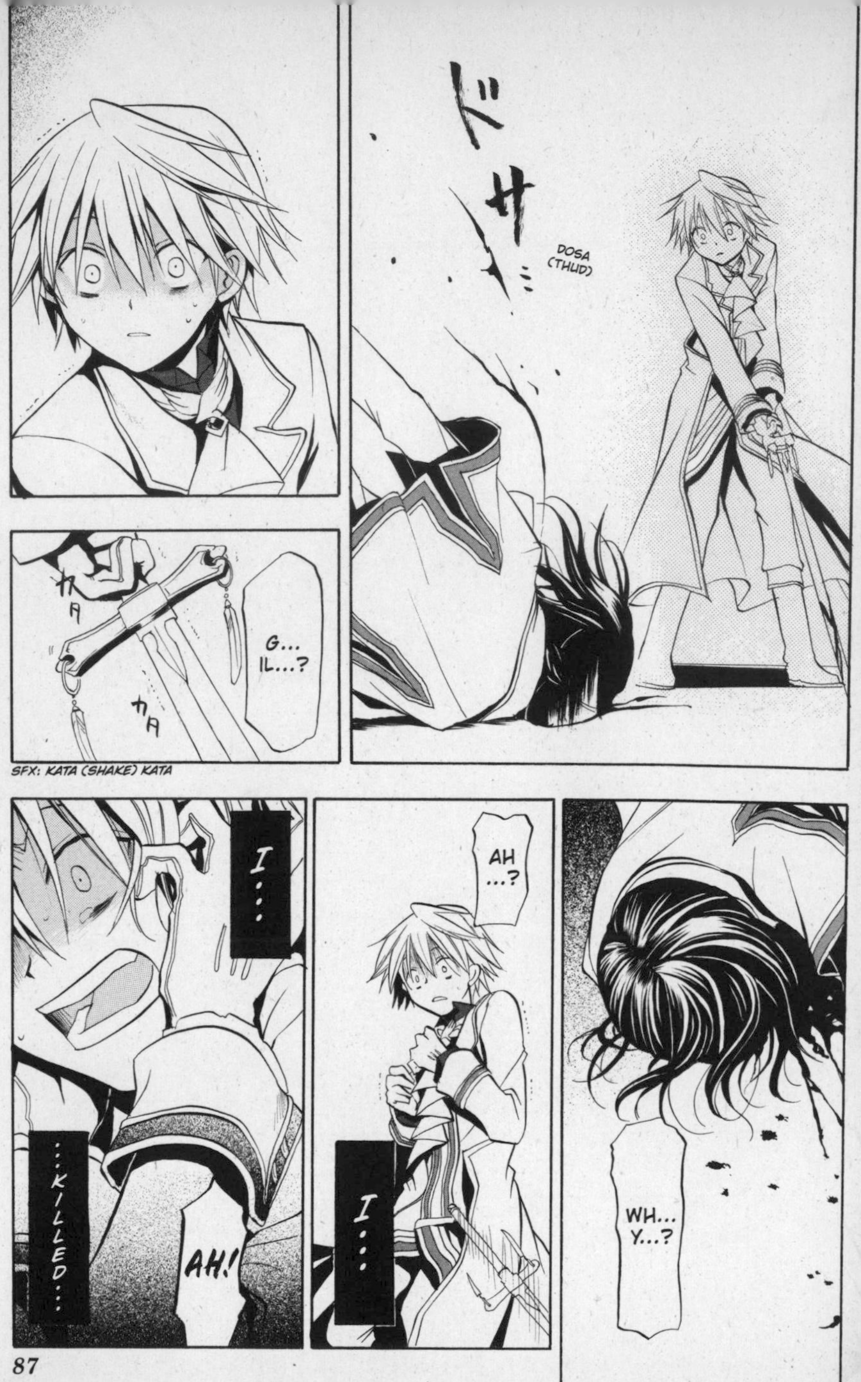
ドサ
DOSA (THUD)
G... IL...?
SFX: KATA (SHAKE) KATA
WH... Y...?
AH ...?
I...
I...
...KILLED...
AH!

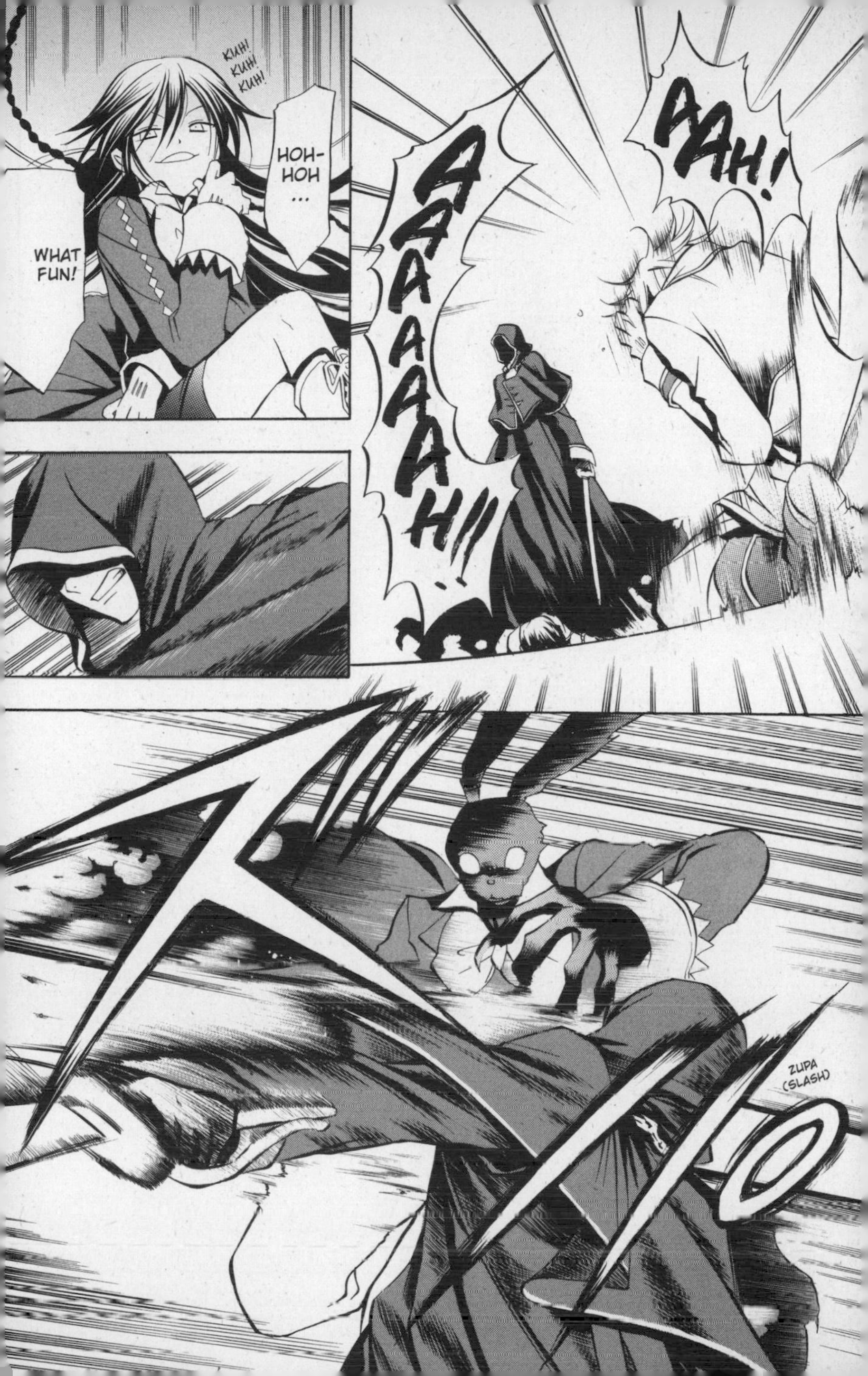
AAH!
AAAAAAAH!!
KUH! KUH! KUH!
HOH-HOH ...
WHAT FUN!
ZUPA (SLASH)

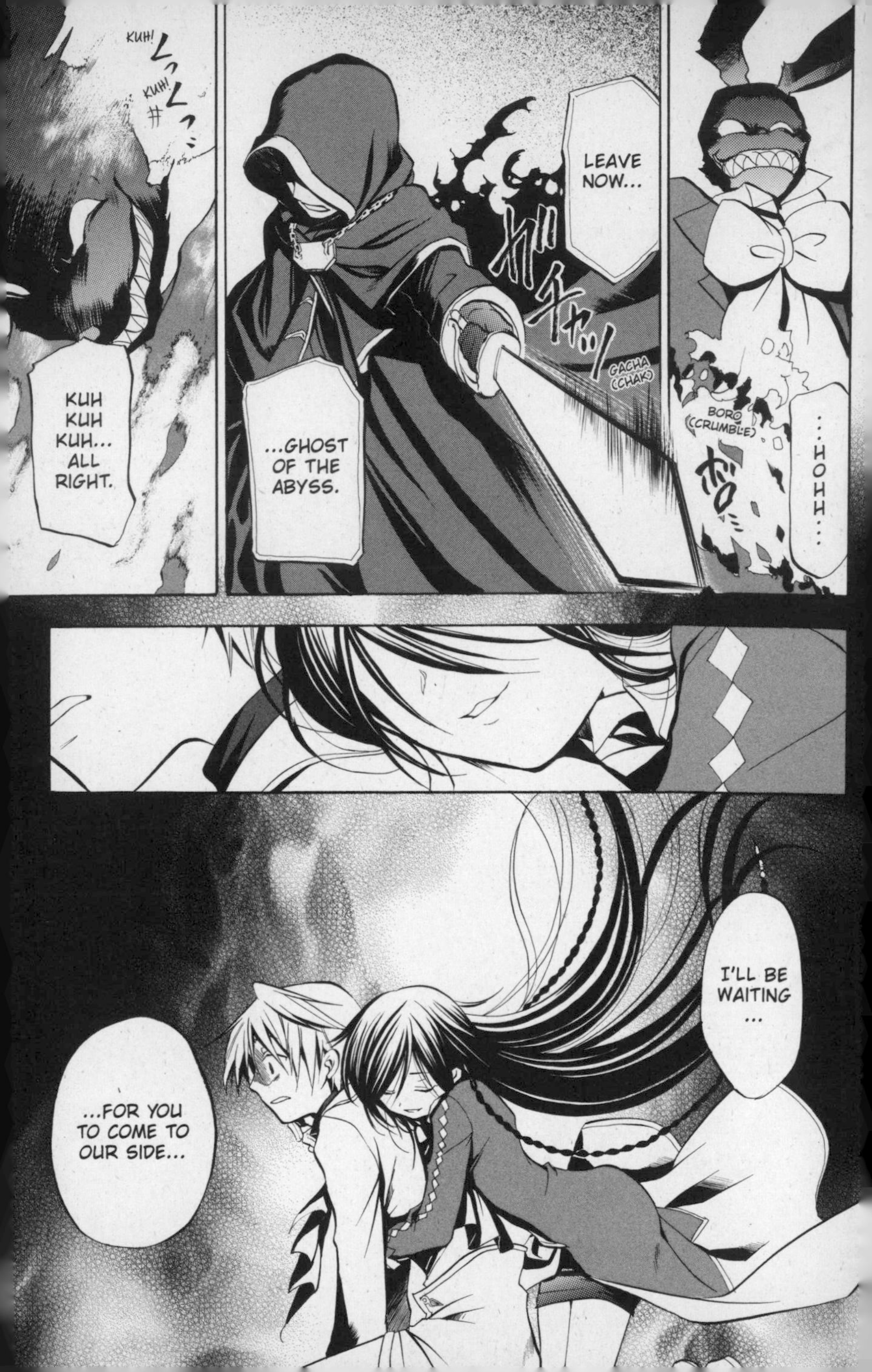
...HOHH...
BORO (CRUMBLE)
LEAVE NOW...
GACHA (CHAK)
...GHOST OF THE ABYSS.
KUH!
KUH!
KUH KUH KUH... ALL RIGHT.
I'LL BE WAITING ...
...FOR YOU TO COME TO OUR SIDE...

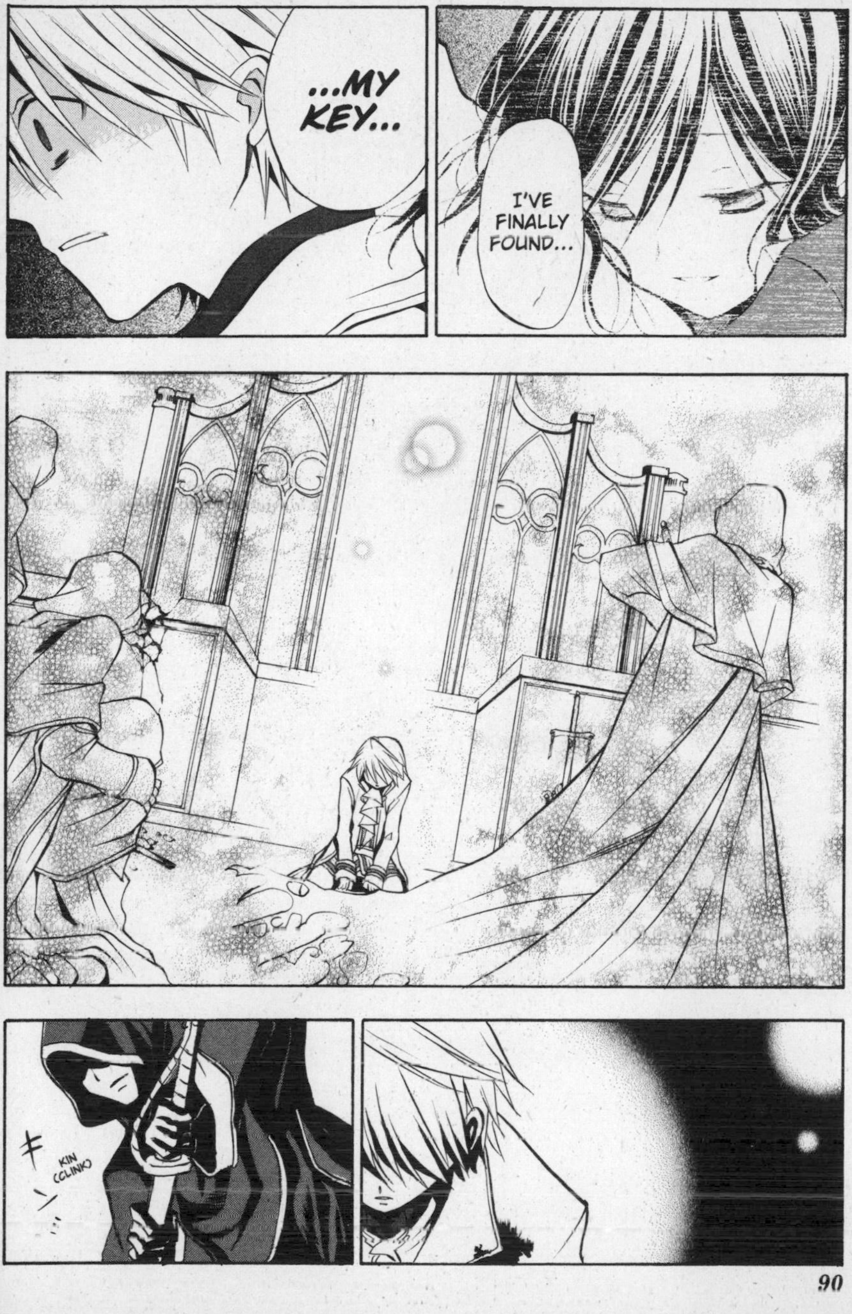
I'VE FINALLY FOUND...
...MY KEY...
KIN (CLINK)

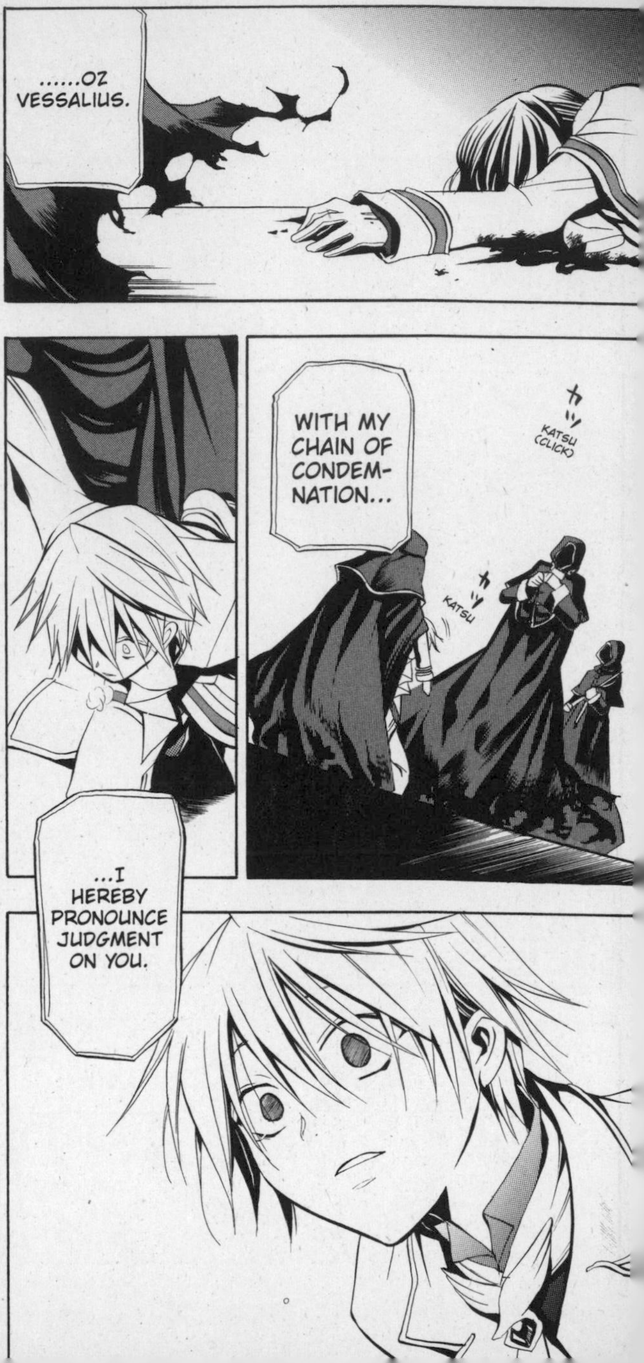
......OZ VESSALIUS.
WITH MY CHAIN OF CONDEM-NATION...
カッ
KATSU (CLICK)
カッ
KATSU
...I HEREBY PRONOUNCE JUDGMENT ON YOU.

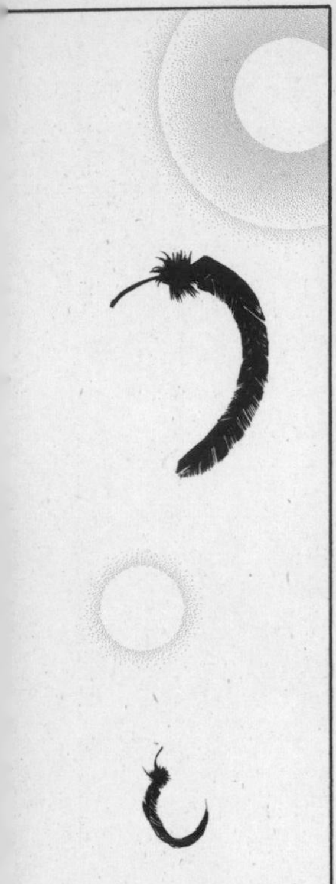
YOUR SIN IS...

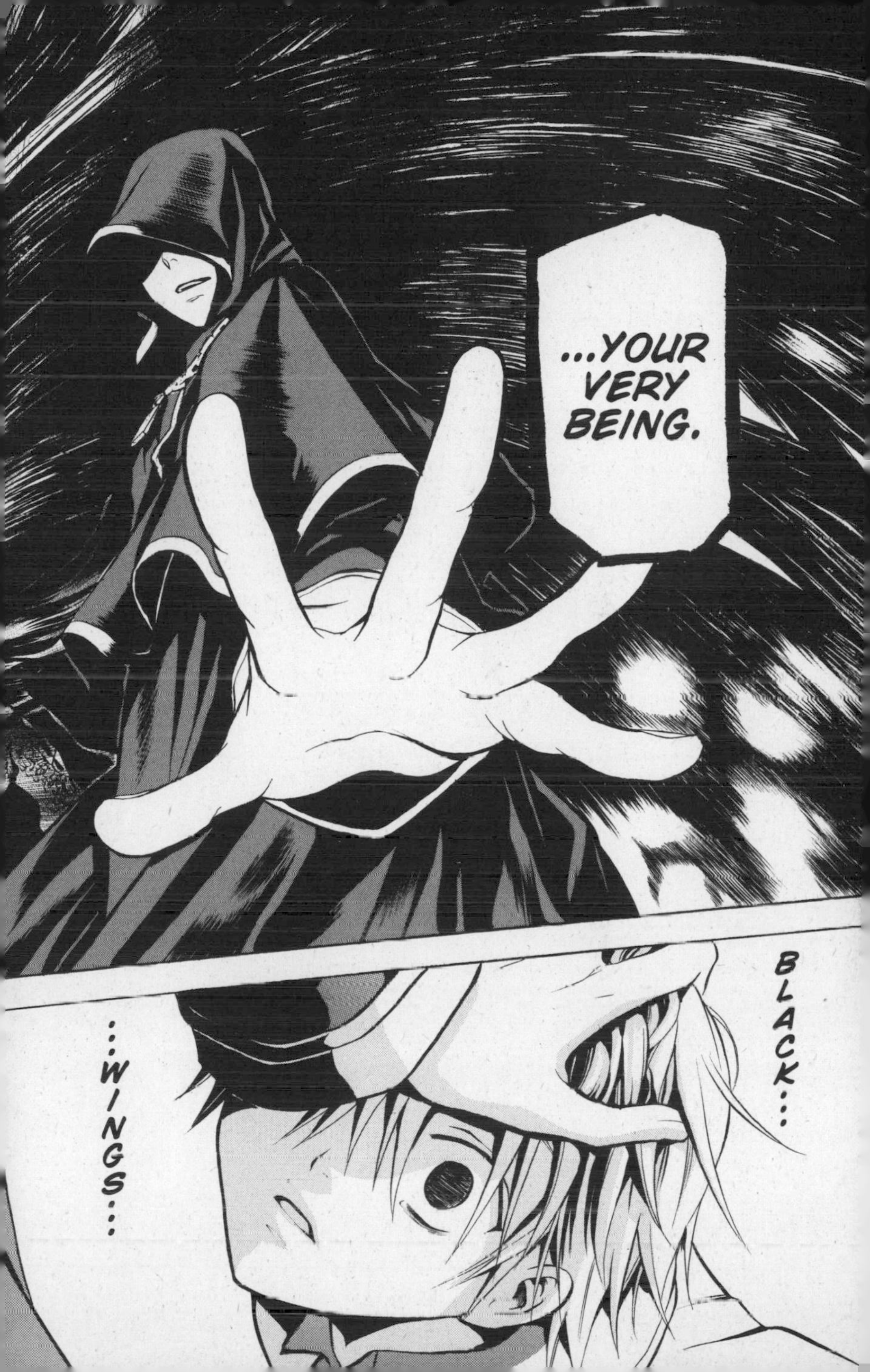
...YOUR VERY BEING.
BLACK...
...WINGS...

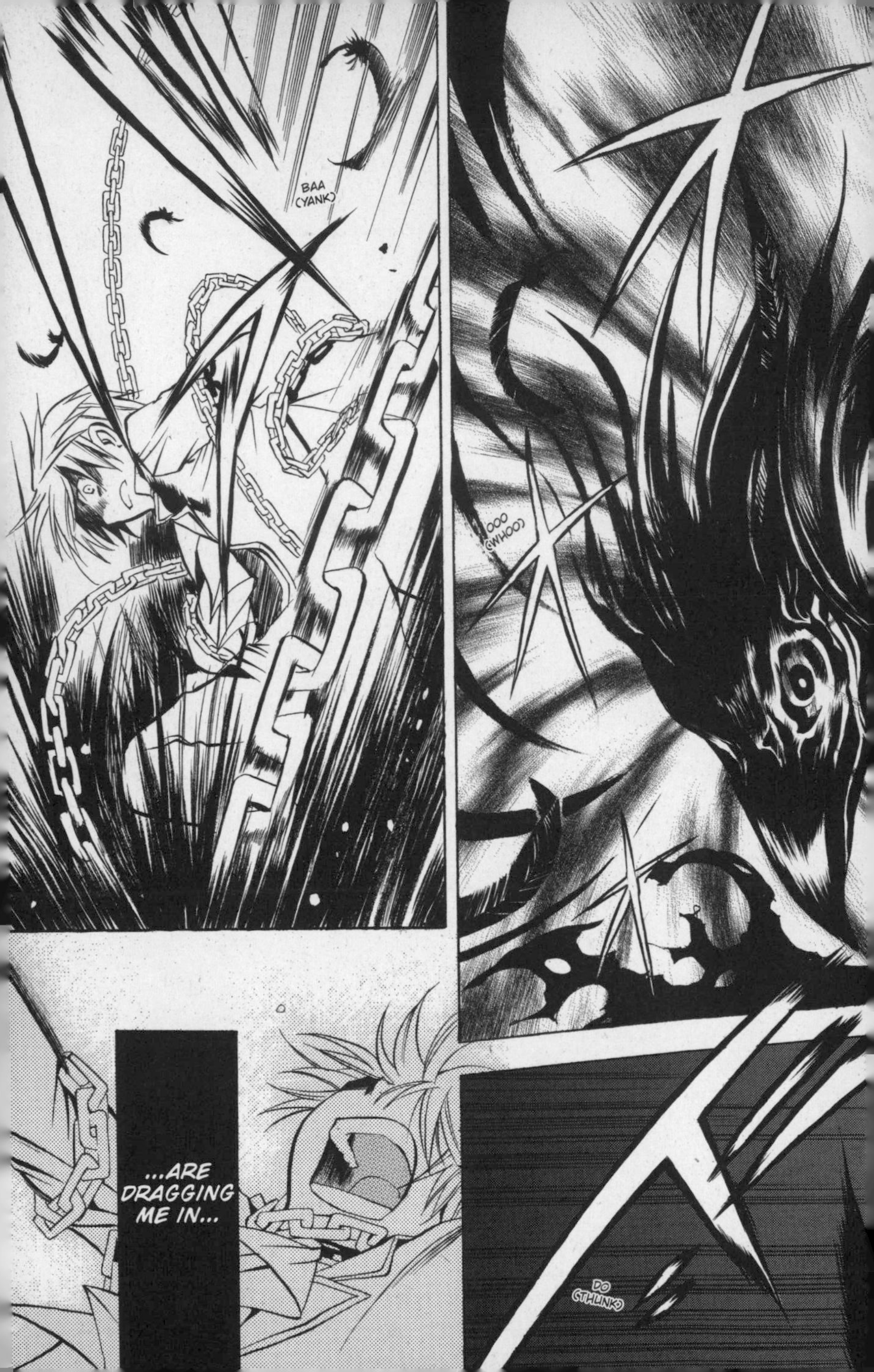
OOO
(WHOOO)
BAA
(YANK)
DO
(THUNK)
...ARE DRAGGING ME IN...

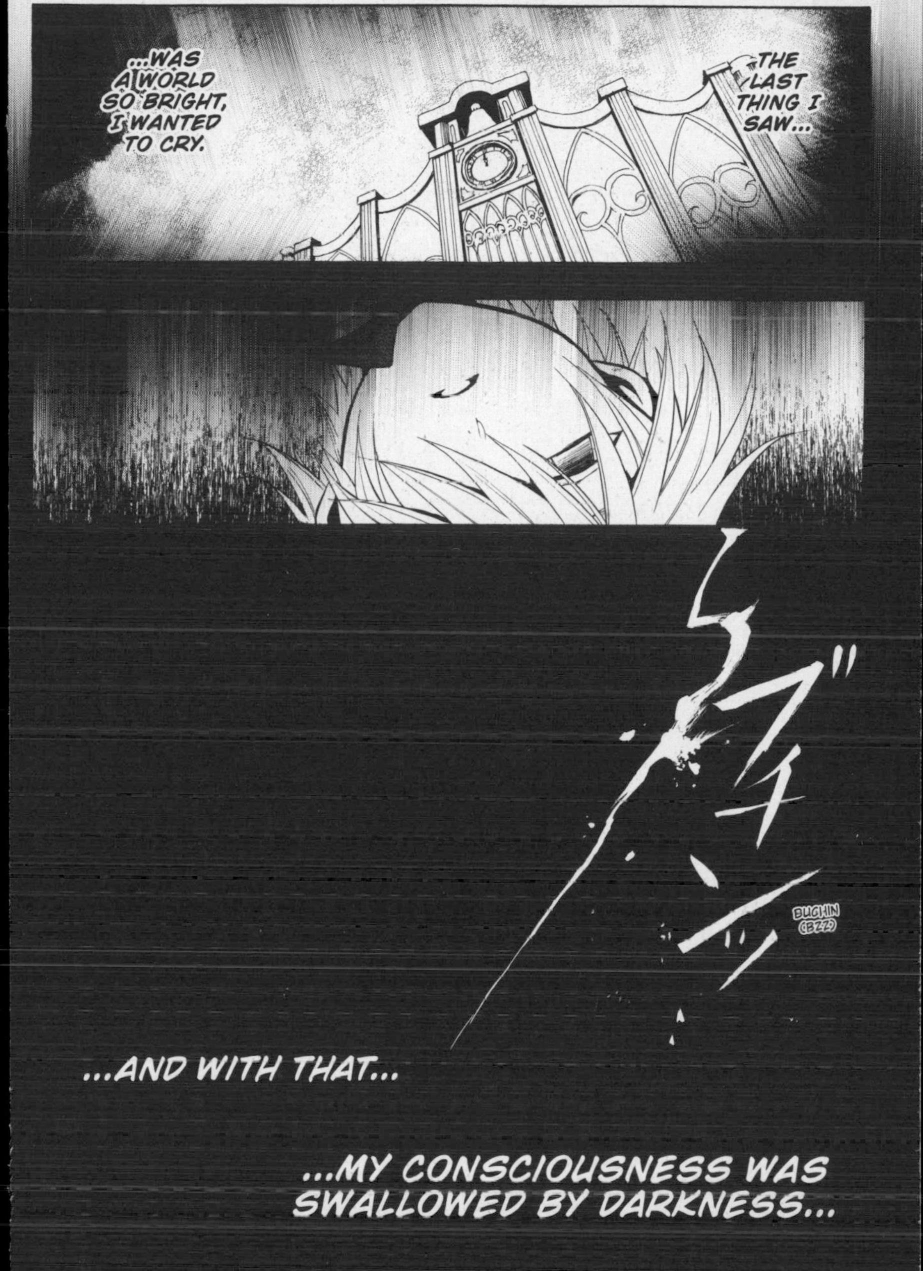

THE LAST THING I SAW...
...WAS A WORLD SO BRIGHT, I WANTED TO CRY.
ブチッ
BUCHIN (BZZ)
...AND WITH THAT...
...MY CONSCIOUSNESS WAS SWALLOWED BY DARKNESS...

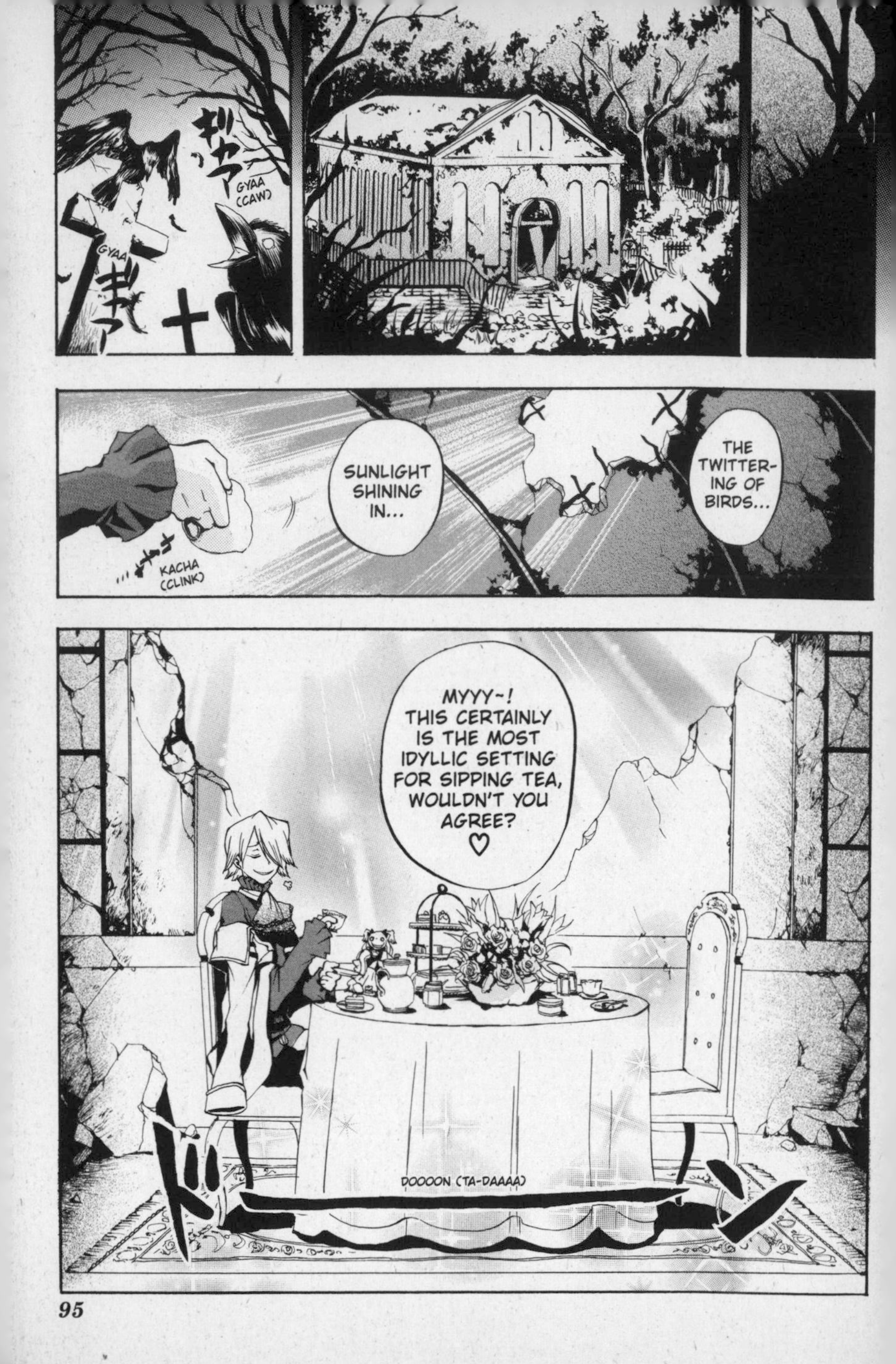
GYAA (CAW)
GYAA
THE TWITTER-ING OF BIRDS...
SUNLIGHT SHINING IN...
KACHA (CLINK)
MYYY~! THIS CERTAINLY IS THE MOST IDYLLIC SETTING FOR SIPPING TEA, WOULDN'T YOU AGREE? ♡
DOOOON (TA-DAAAA)

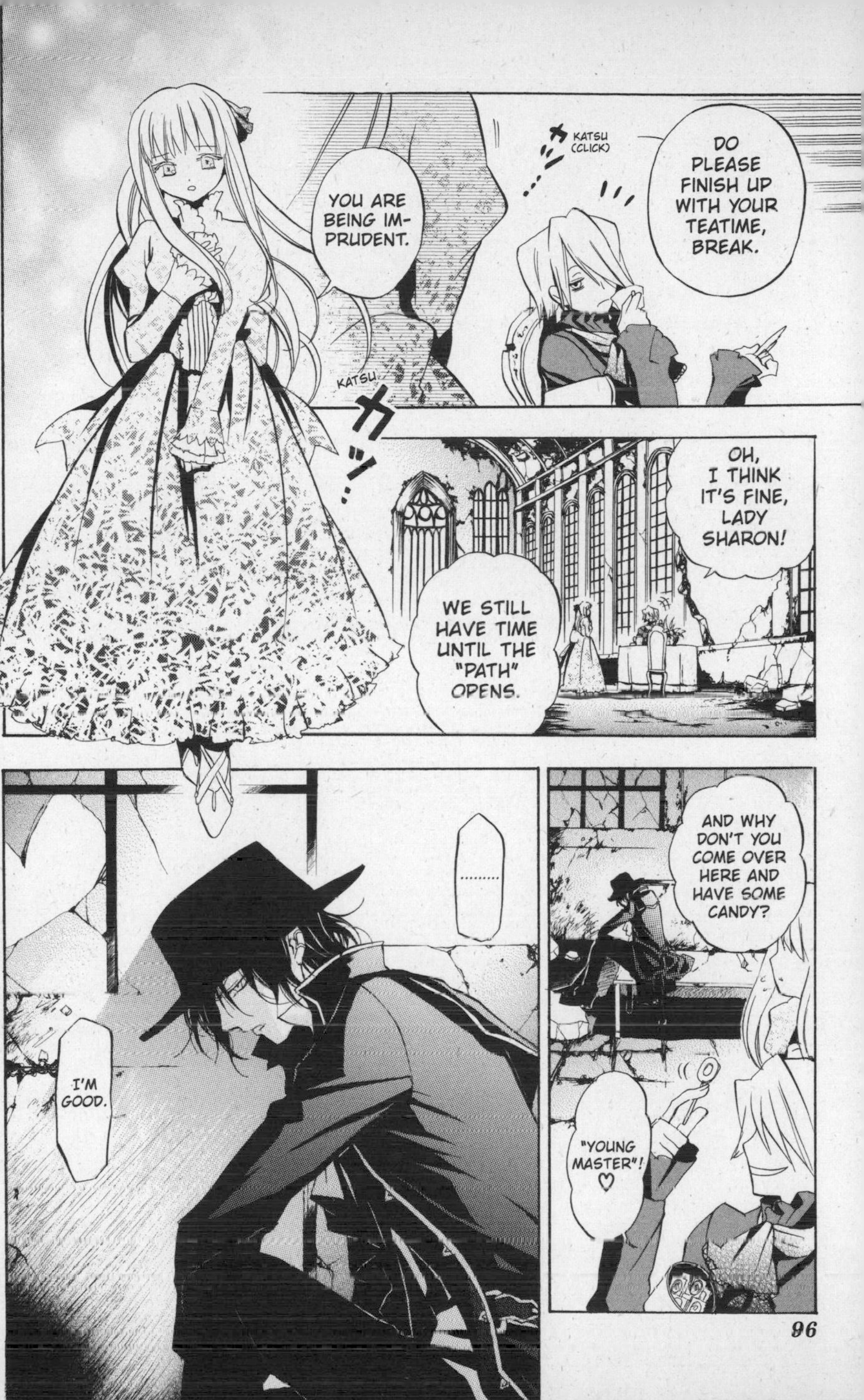
DO PLEASE FINISH UP WITH YOUR TEATIME, BREAK.
KATSU (CLICK)
YOU ARE BEING IM-PRUDENT.
KATSU
OH, I THINK IT'S FINE, LADY SHARON!
WE STILL HAVE TIME UNTIL THE "PATH" OPENS.
AND WHY DON'T YOU COME OVER HERE AND HAVE SOME CANDY?
"YOUNG MASTER"! ♡
.........
I'M GOOD.

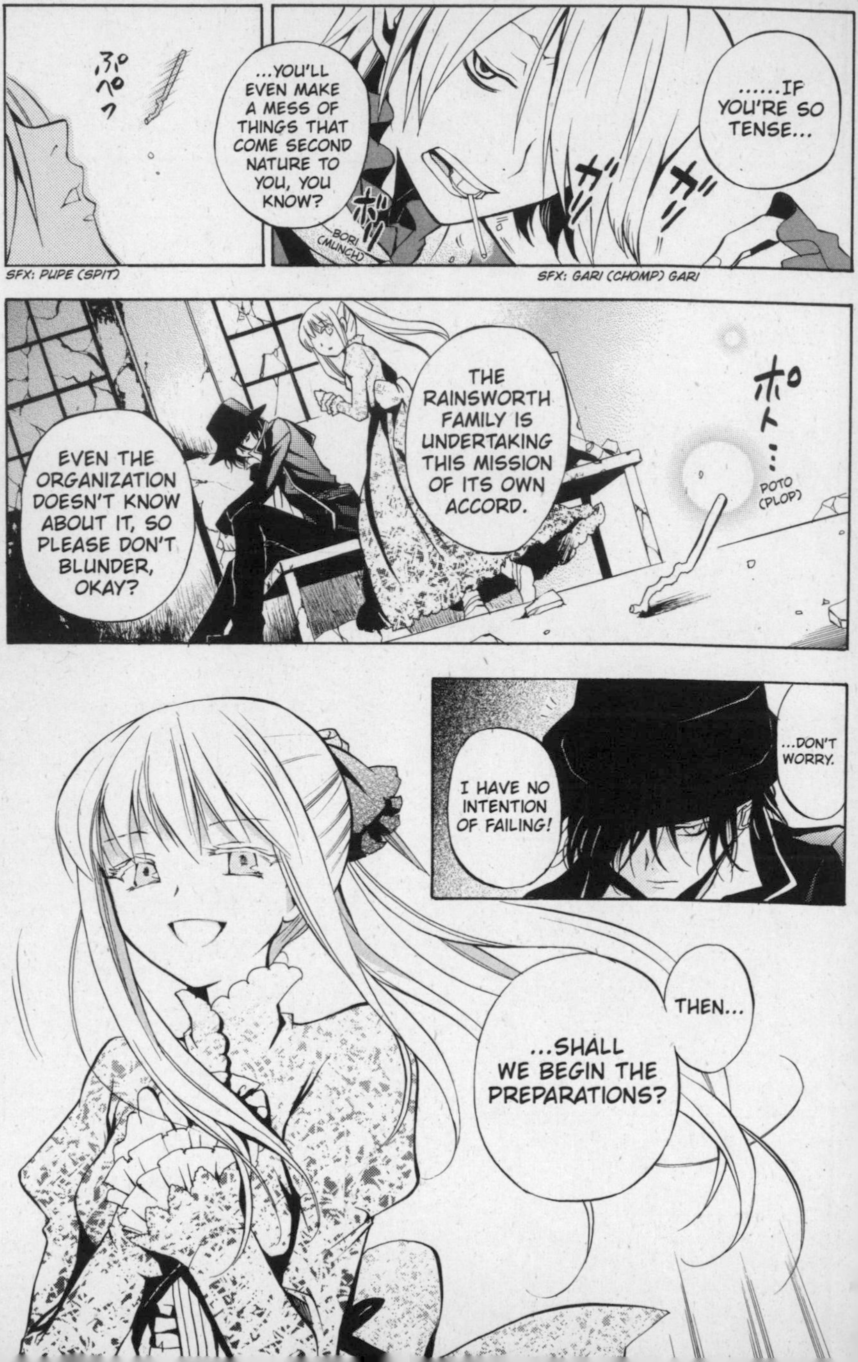
......IF YOU'RE SO TENSE...
...YOU'LL EVEN MAKE A MESS OF THINGS THAT COME SECOND NATURE TO YOU, YOU KNOW?
BORI (MUNCH)
SFX: GARI (CHOMP) GARI
SFX: PUPE (SPIT)
ポト…
POTO (PLOP)
THE RAINSWORTH FAMILY IS UNDERTAKING THIS MISSION OF ITS OWN ACCORD.
EVEN THE ORGANIZATION DOESN'T KNOW ABOUT IT, SO PLEASE DON'T BLUNDER, OKAY?
...DON'T WORRY.
I HAVE NO INTENTION OF FAILING!
THEN...
...SHALL WE BEGIN THE PREPARATIONS?

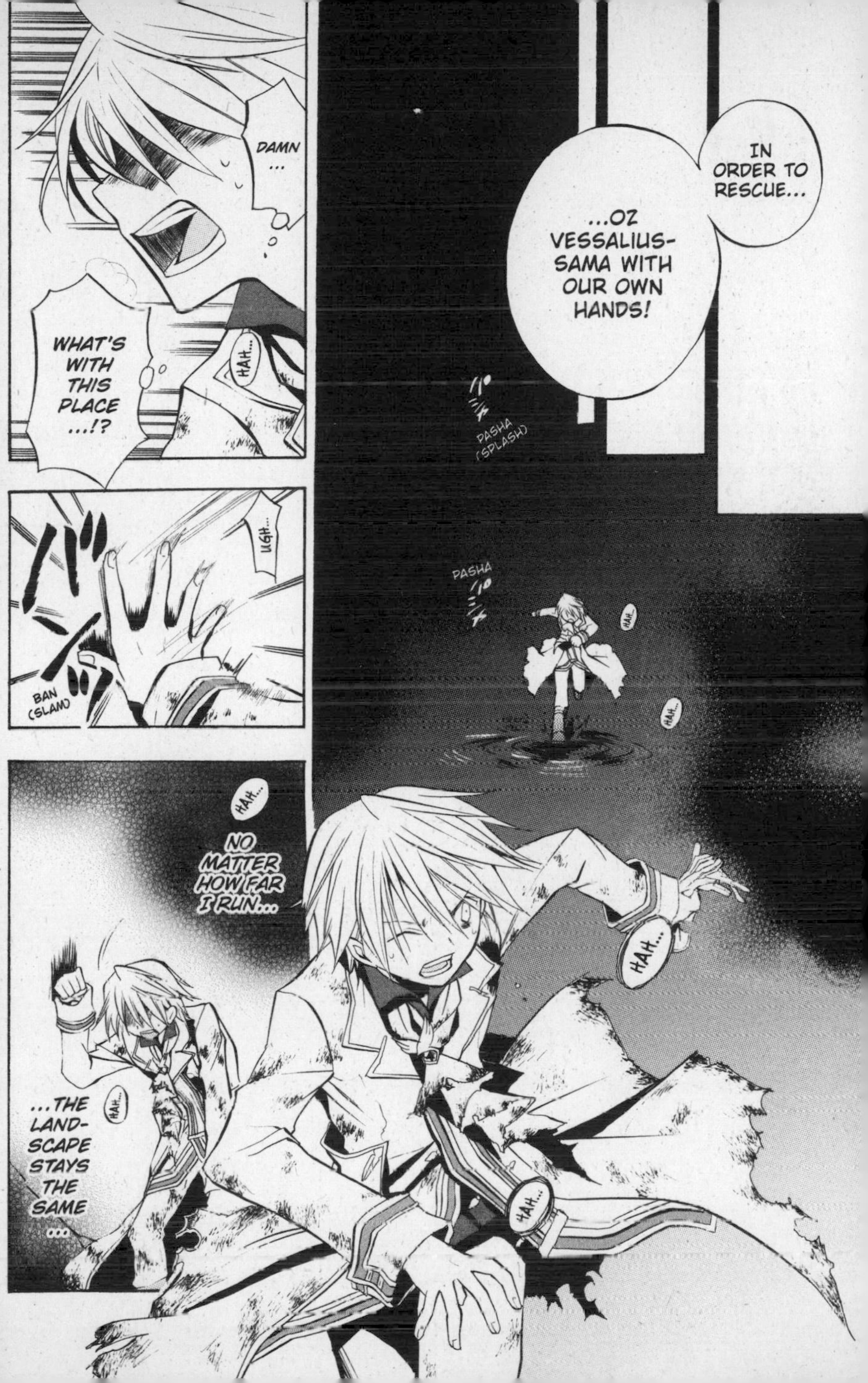
IN ORDER TO RESCUE...
...OZ VESSALIUS-SAMA WITH OUR OWN HANDS!
PASHA (SPLASH)
PASHA
HAH...
HAH...
DAMN ...
HAH...
WHAT'S WITH THIS PLACE ...!?
UGH...
BAN (SLAM)
HAH...
NO MATTER HOW FAR I RUN...
HAH...
HAH...
HAH...
...THE LAND-SCAPE STAYS THE SAME ...

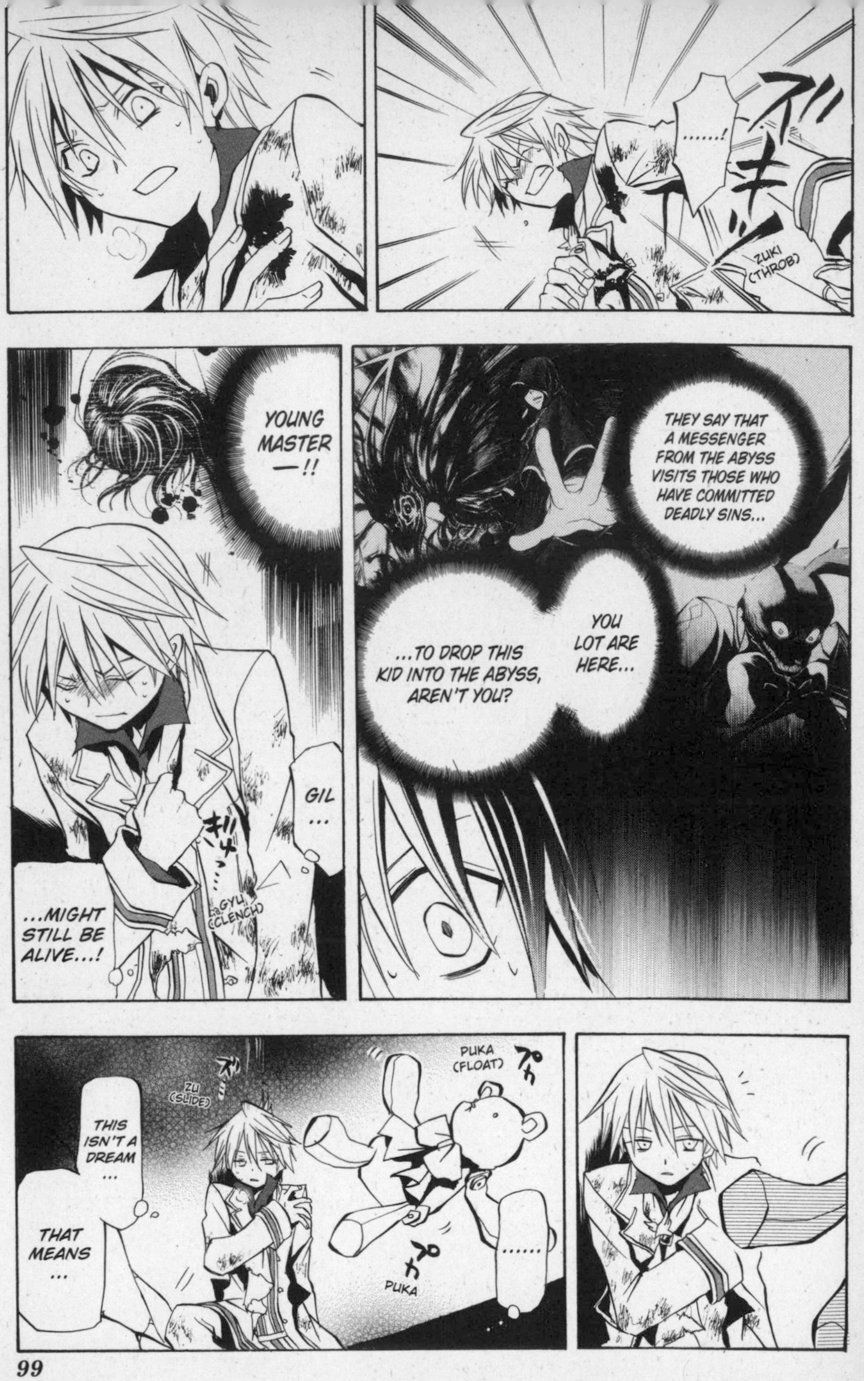
......!
ZUKI (THROB)
THEY SAY THAT A MESSENGER FROM THE ABYSS VISITS THOSE WHO HAVE COMMITTED DEADLY SINS...
YOU LOT ARE HERE...
...TO DROP THIS KID INTO THE ABYSS, AREN'T YOU?
YOUNG MASTER—!!
GIL...
GYU (CLENCH)
...MIGHT STILL BE ALIVE...!
PUKA (FLOAT)
ZU (SLIDE)
THIS ISN'T A DREAM...
......
THAT MEANS...
PUKA

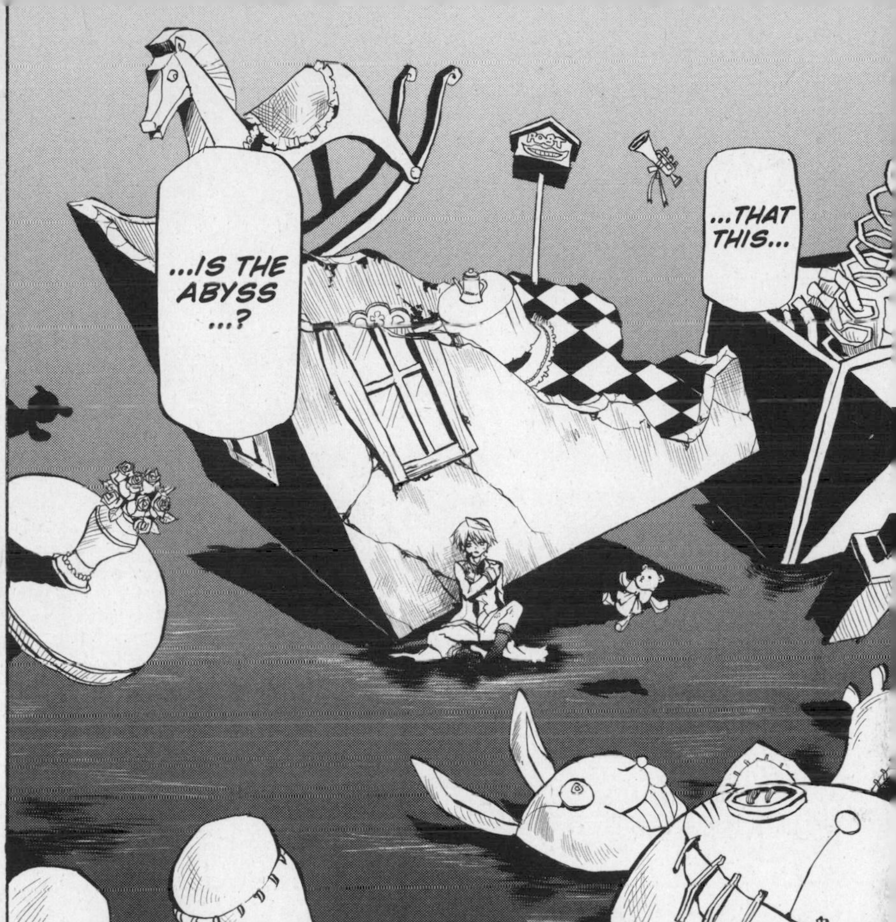
...THAT THIS...
...IS THE ABYSS ...?
Retrace: III Prisoner & Alichino

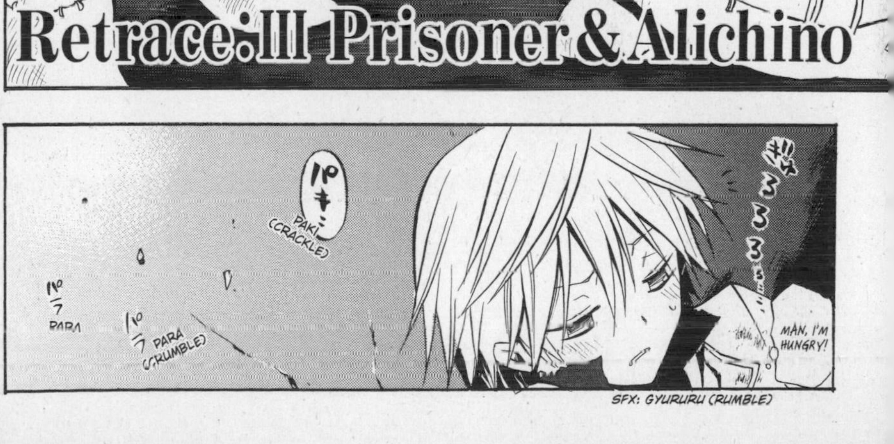
MAN, I'M HUNGRY!
パキ
PAKI (CRACKLE)
パラ
PARA
パラ
PARA (CRUMBLE)

SFX: GYURURU (RUMBLE)

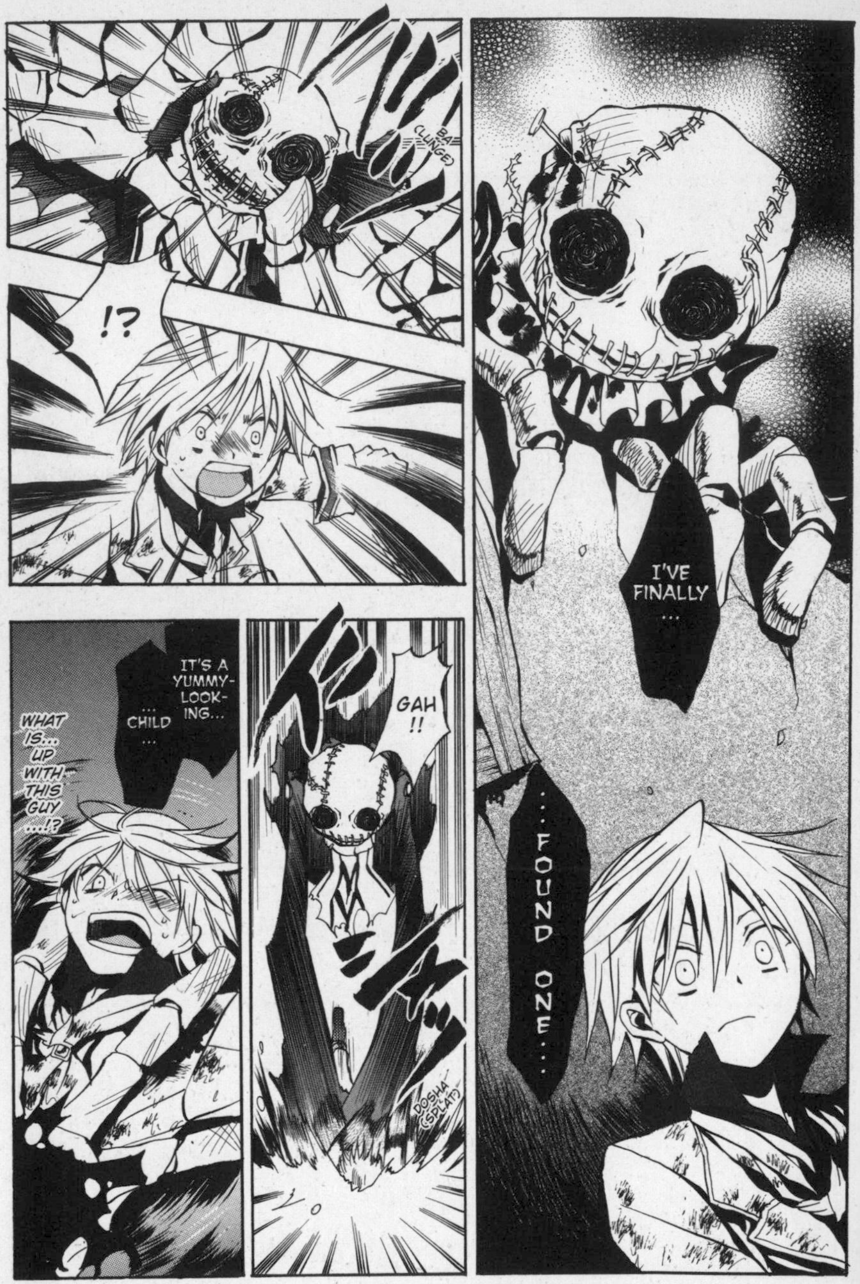
I'VE FINALLY ...
...FOUND ONE...
BA (LUNGE)
!?
GAH !!
DOSHA (SPLAT)
IT'S A YUMMY-LOOKING... ...CHILD ...
WHAT IS... UP WITH THIS GUY ...!?

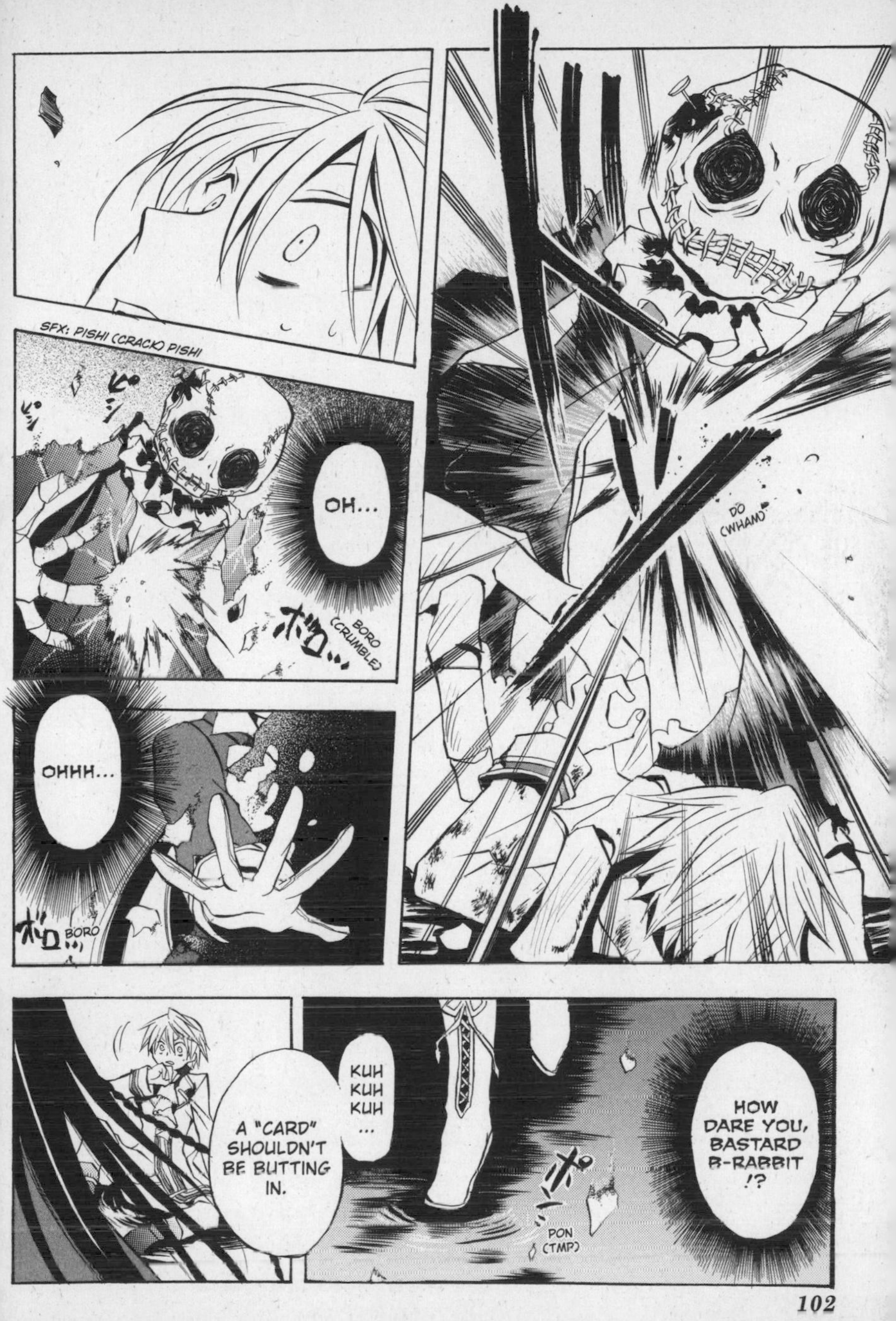
DO (WHAM)
SFX: PISHI (CRACK) PISHI
OH...
BORO (CRUMBLE)
OHHH...
BORO
HOW DARE YOU, BASTARD B-RABBIT !?
KUH KUH KUH ...
PON (TMP)
A "CARD" SHOULDN'T BE BUTTING IN.

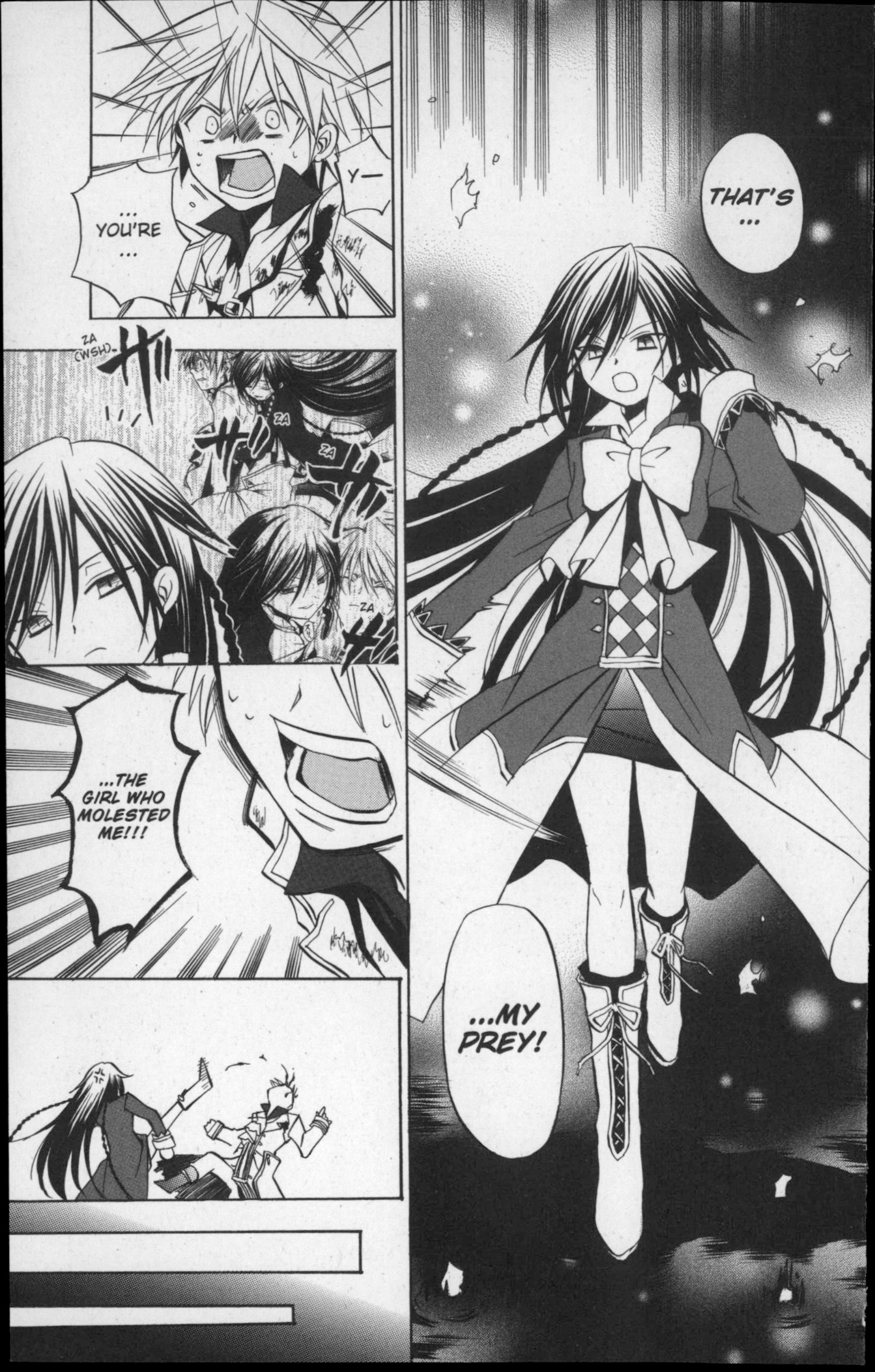
THAT'S ...
...MY PREY!
Y—
... YOU'RE ...
ZA (WSH)
ZA
ZA
ZA
...THE GIRL WHO MOLESTED ME!!!

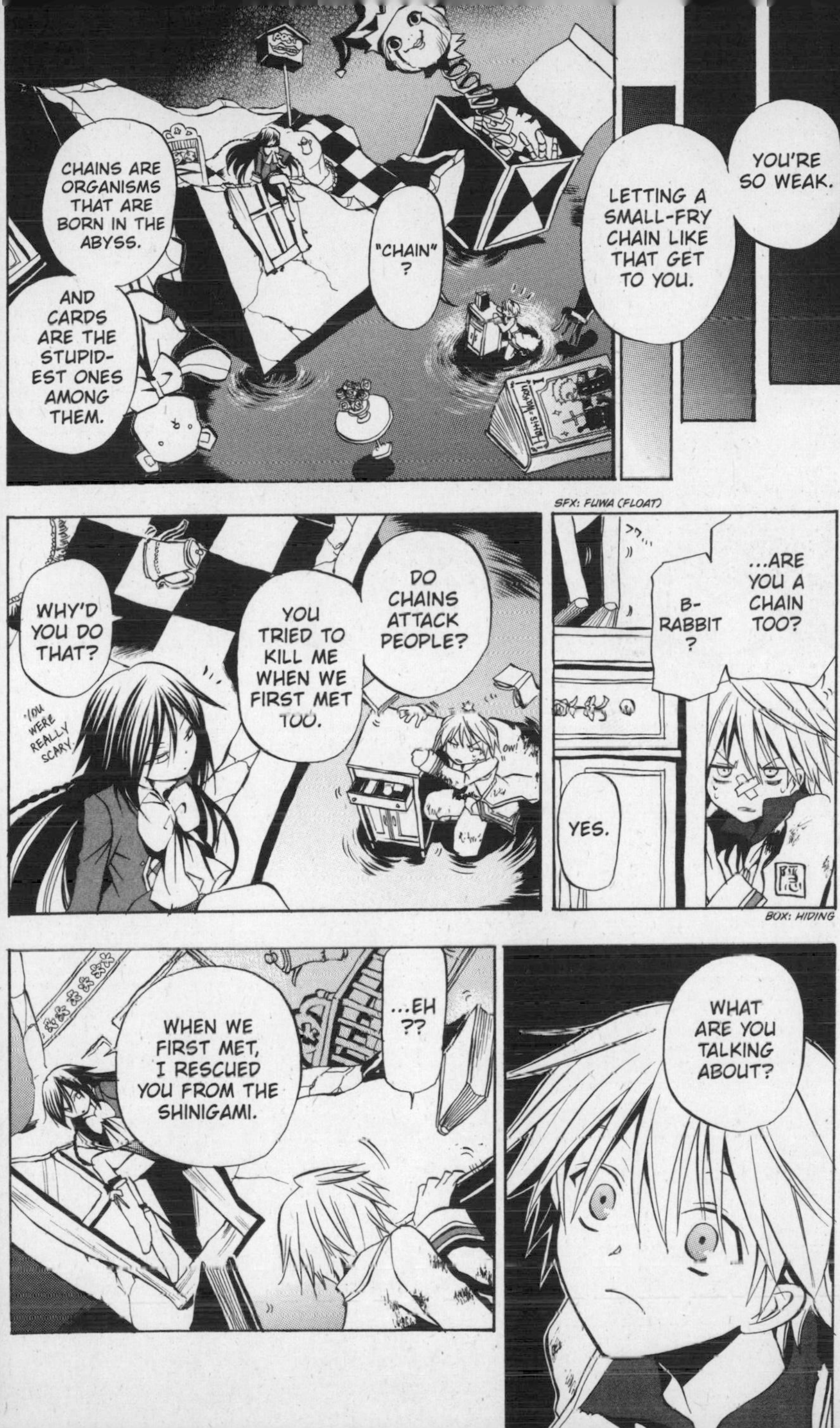
YOU'RE SO WEAK.
LETTING A SMALL-FRY CHAIN LIKE THAT GET TO YOU.
"CHAIN"?
CHAINS ARE ORGANISMS THAT ARE BORN IN THE ABYSS.
AND CARDS ARE THE STUPID-EST ONES AMONG THEM.
SFX: FUWA (FLOAT)
...ARE YOU A CHAIN TOO?
B-RABBIT?
YES.
BOX: HIDING
DO CHAINS ATTACK PEOPLE?
YOU TRIED TO KILL ME WHEN WE FIRST MET TOO.
OW!
WHY'D YOU DO THAT?
YOU WERE REALLY SCARY.
WHAT ARE YOU TALKING ABOUT?
...EH??
WHEN WE FIRST MET, I RESCUED YOU FROM THE SHINIGAMI.

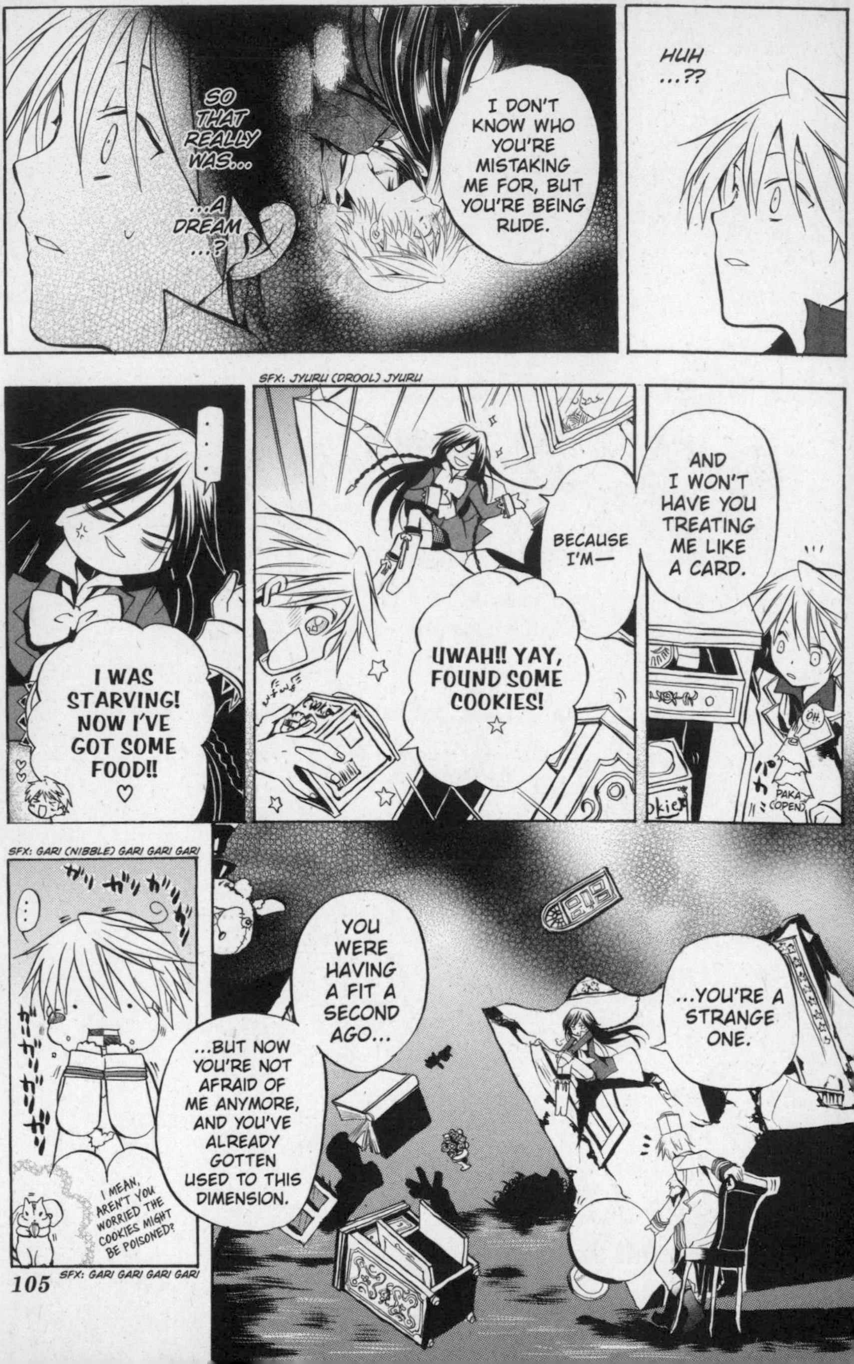
HUH ...??
I DON'T KNOW WHO YOU'RE MISTAKING ME FOR, BUT YOU'RE BEING RUDE.
SO THAT REALLY WAS...
...A DREAM ...?
AND I WON'T HAVE YOU TREATING ME LIKE A CARD.
BECAUSE I'M—
ÖH.
PAKA (OPEN)
SFX: JYURU (DROOL) JYURU
UWAH!! YAY, FOUND SOME COOKIES!
I WAS STARVING! NOW I'VE GOT SOME FOOD!!
...YOU'RE A STRANGE ONE.
YOU WERE HAVING A FIT A SECOND AGO...
...BUT NOW YOU'RE NOT AFRAID OF ME ANYMORE, AND YOU'VE ALREADY GOTTEN USED TO THIS DIMENSION.
SFX: GARI (NIBBLE) GARI GARI GARI
I MEAN, AREN'T YOU WORRIED THE COOKIES MIGHT BE POISONED?
SFX: GARI GARI GARI GARI

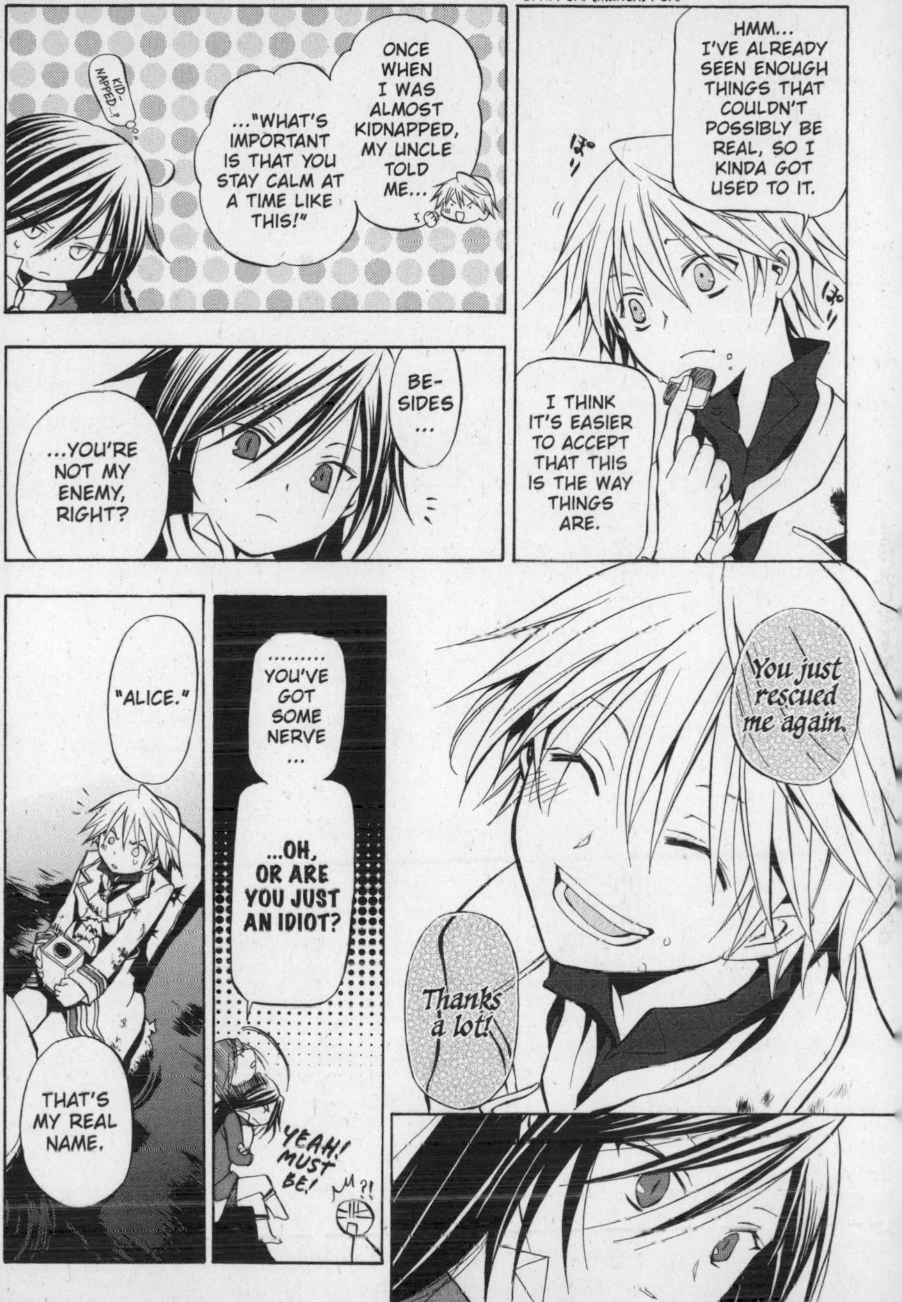
SFX: PORI (MUNCH) PORI
HMM... I'VE ALREADY SEEN ENOUGH THINGS THAT COULDN'T POSSIBLY BE REAL, SO I KINDA GOT USED TO IT.
I THINK IT'S EASIER TO ACCEPT THAT THIS IS THE WAY THINGS ARE.
ONCE WHEN I WAS ALMOST KIDNAPPED, MY UNCLE TOLD ME...
..."WHAT'S IMPORTANT IS THAT YOU STAY CALM AT A TIME LIKE THIS!"
KID-NAPPED...?
BE-SIDES...
...YOU'RE NOT MY ENEMY, RIGHT?
You just rescued me again.
Thanks a lot!
.........
YOU'VE GOT SOME NERVE...
...OH, OR ARE YOU JUST AN IDIOT?
YEAH! MUST BE!
"ALICE."
THAT'S MY REAL NAME.

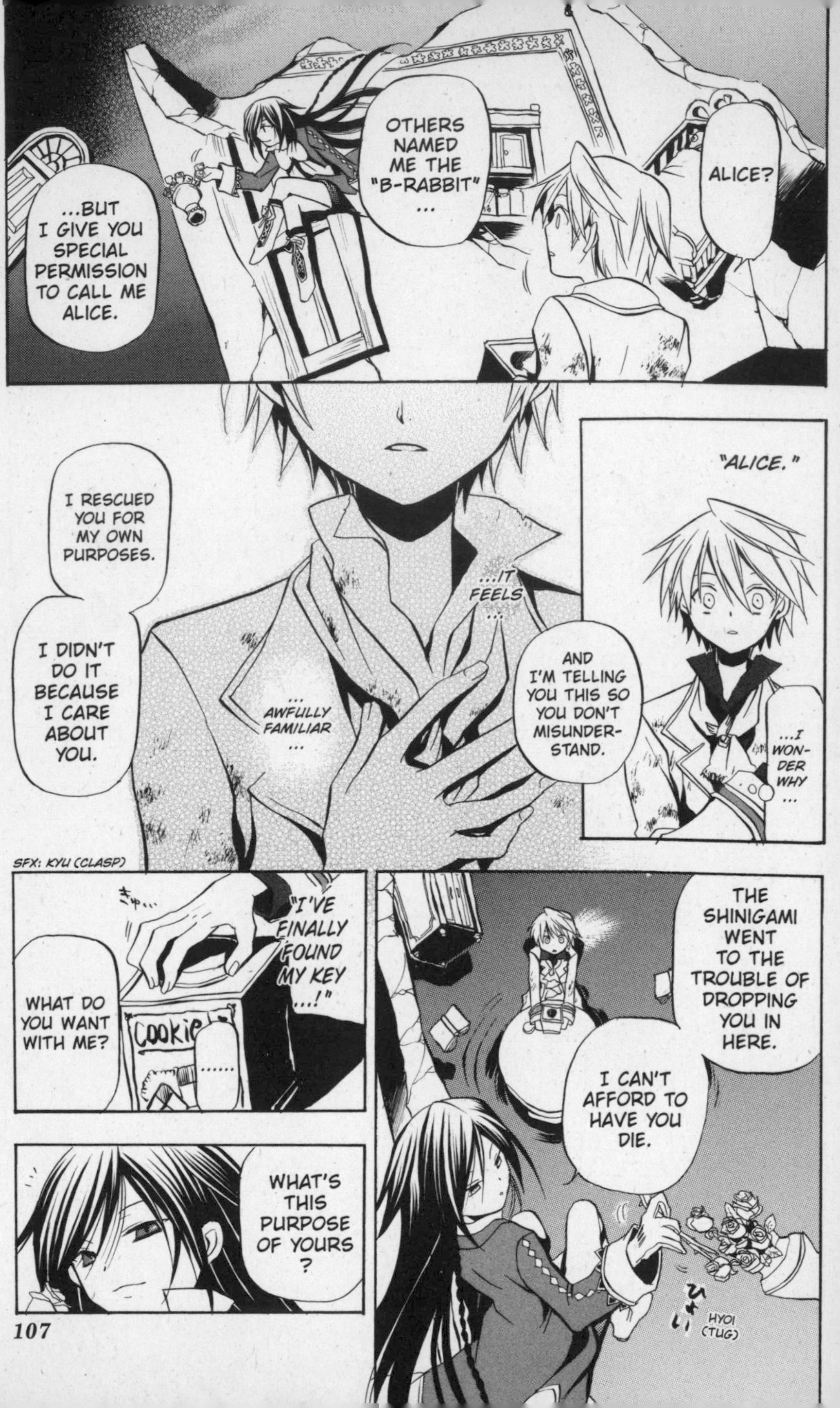
OTHERS NAMED ME THE "B-RABBIT" ...
...BUT I GIVE YOU SPECIAL PERMISSION TO CALL ME ALICE.
ALICE?
I RESCUED YOU FOR MY OWN PURPOSES.
I DIDN'T DO IT BECAUSE I CARE ABOUT YOU.
AND I'M TELLING YOU THIS SO YOU DON'T MISUNDER-STAND.
"ALICE."
...I WONDER WHY ...
...IT FEELS ...
... AWFULLY FAMILIAR ...
SFX: KYU (CLASP)
きゅ...
"I'VE FINALLY FOUND MY KEY ...!"
WHAT DO YOU WANT WITH ME?
......
WHAT'S THIS PURPOSE OF YOURS ?
THE SHINIGAMI WENT TO THE TROUBLE OF DROPPING YOU IN HERE.
I CAN'T AFFORD TO HAVE YOU DIE.
ひょい
HYOI (TUG)

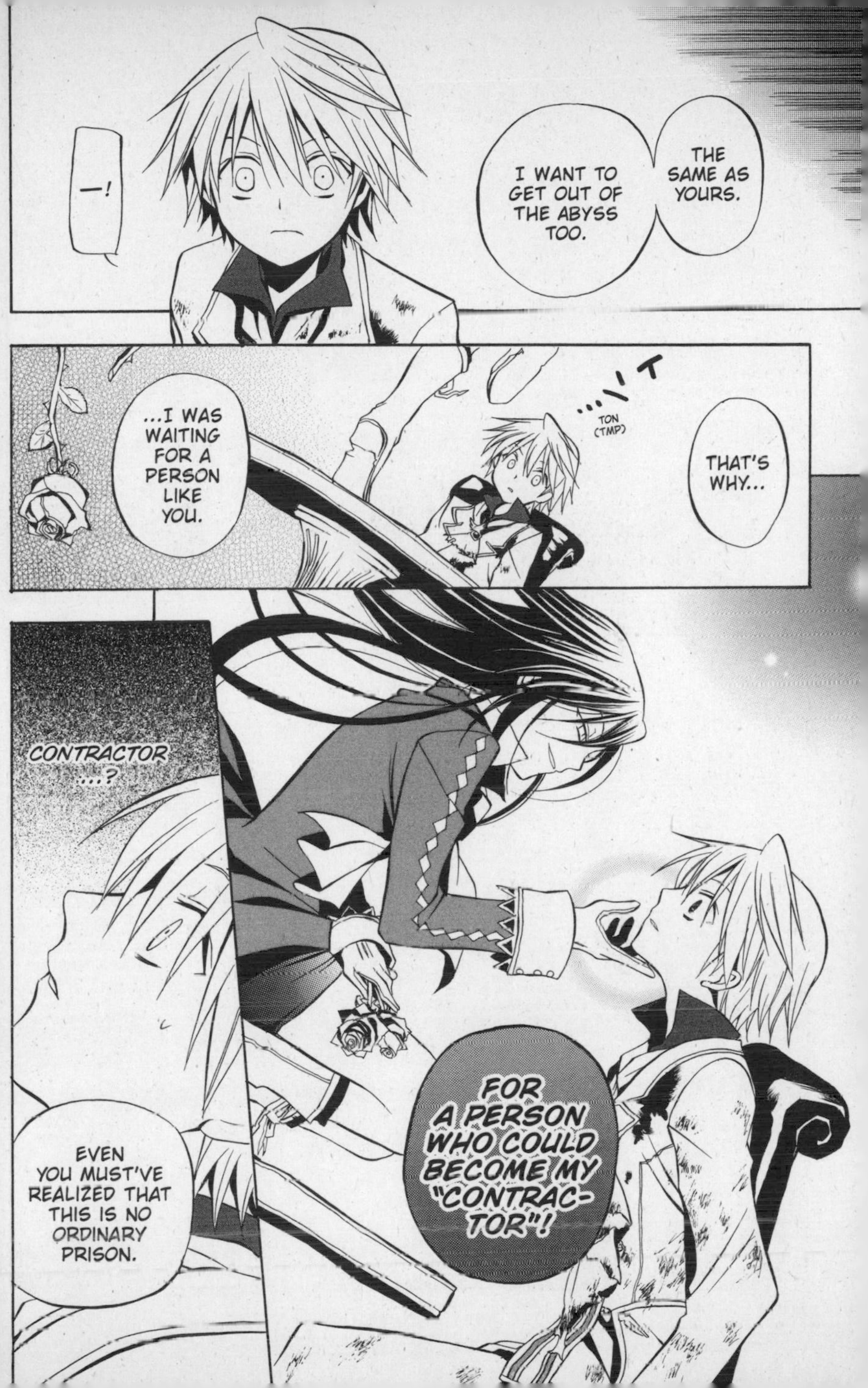
THE SAME AS YOURS.
I WANT TO GET OUT OF THE ABYSS TOO.
—!
THAT'S WHY...
TON (TMP)
...I WAS WAITING FOR A PERSON LIKE YOU.
FOR A PERSON WHO COULD BECOME MY "CONTRAC-TOR"!
CONTRACTOR ....?
EVEN YOU MUST'VE REALIZED THAT THIS IS NO ORDINARY PRISON.

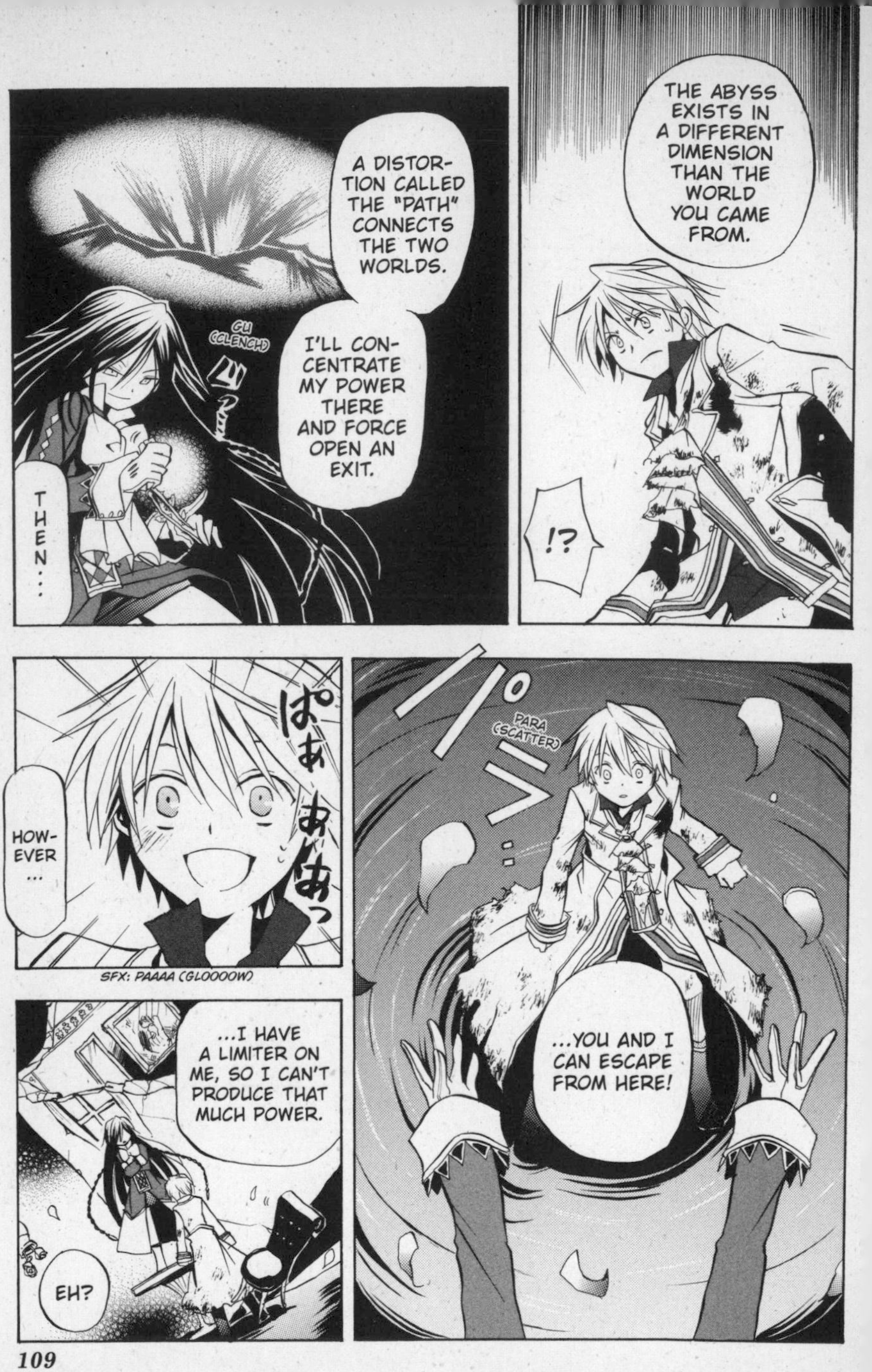
THE ABYSS EXISTS IN A DIFFERENT DIMENSION THAN THE WORLD YOU CAME FROM.
!?
A DISTORTION CALLED THE "PATH" CONNECTS THE TWO WORLDS.
GU (CLENCH)
I'LL CONCENTRATE MY POWER THERE AND FORCE OPEN AN EXIT.
THEN...
PARA (SCATTER)
...YOU AND I CAN ESCAPE FROM HERE!
HOWEVER...
SFX: PAAAA (GLOOOOW)
...I HAVE A LIMITER ON ME, SO I CAN'T PRODUCE THAT MUCH POWER.
EH?

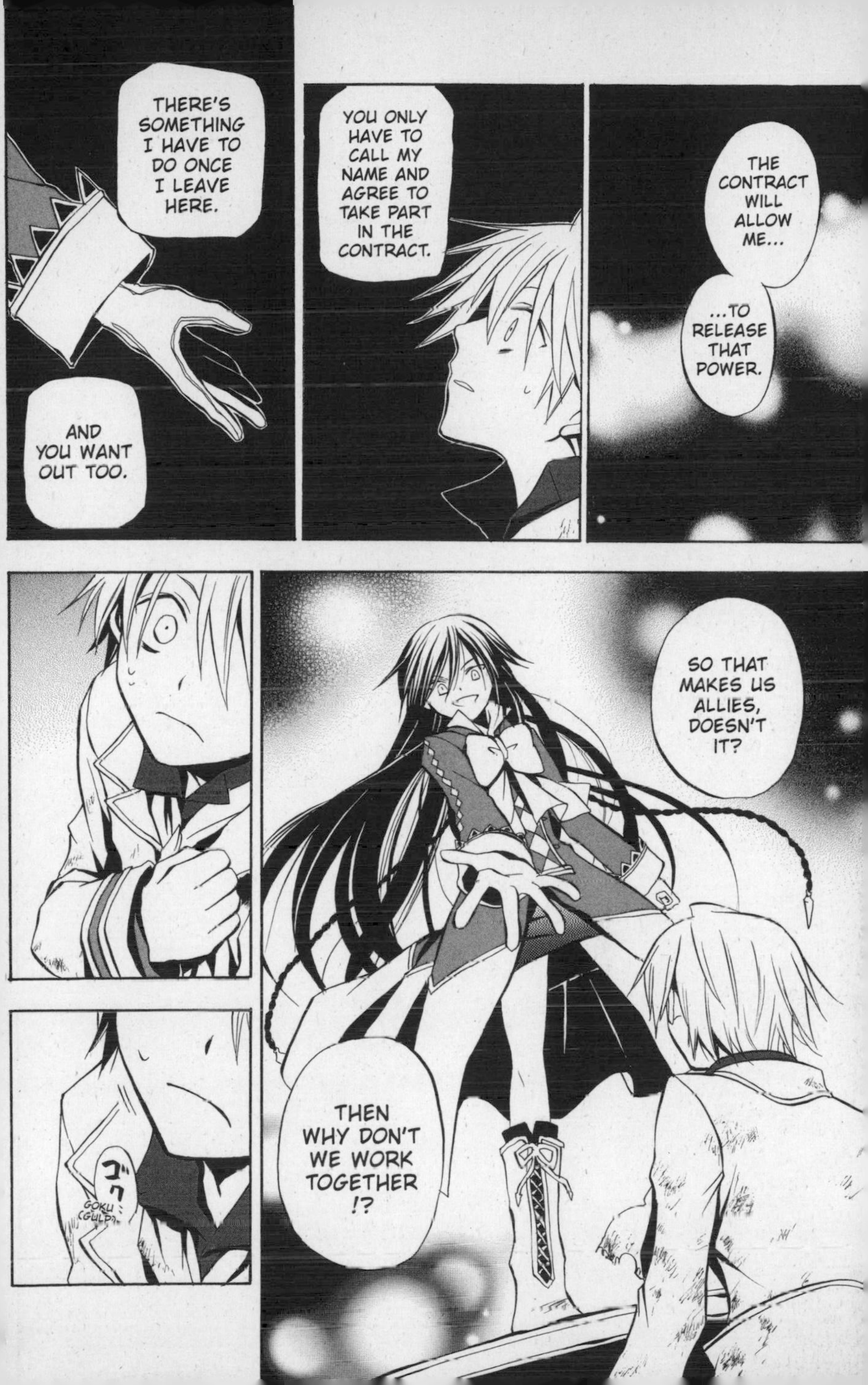
THE CONTRACT WILL ALLOW ME...
...TO RELEASE THAT POWER.
YOU ONLY HAVE TO CALL MY NAME AND AGREE TO TAKE PART IN THE CONTRACT.
THERE'S SOMETHING I HAVE TO DO ONCE I LEAVE HERE.
AND YOU WANT OUT TOO.
SO THAT MAKES US ALLIES, DOESN'T IT?
THEN WHY DON'T WE WORK TOGETHER!?
ゴク
GOKU (GULP)

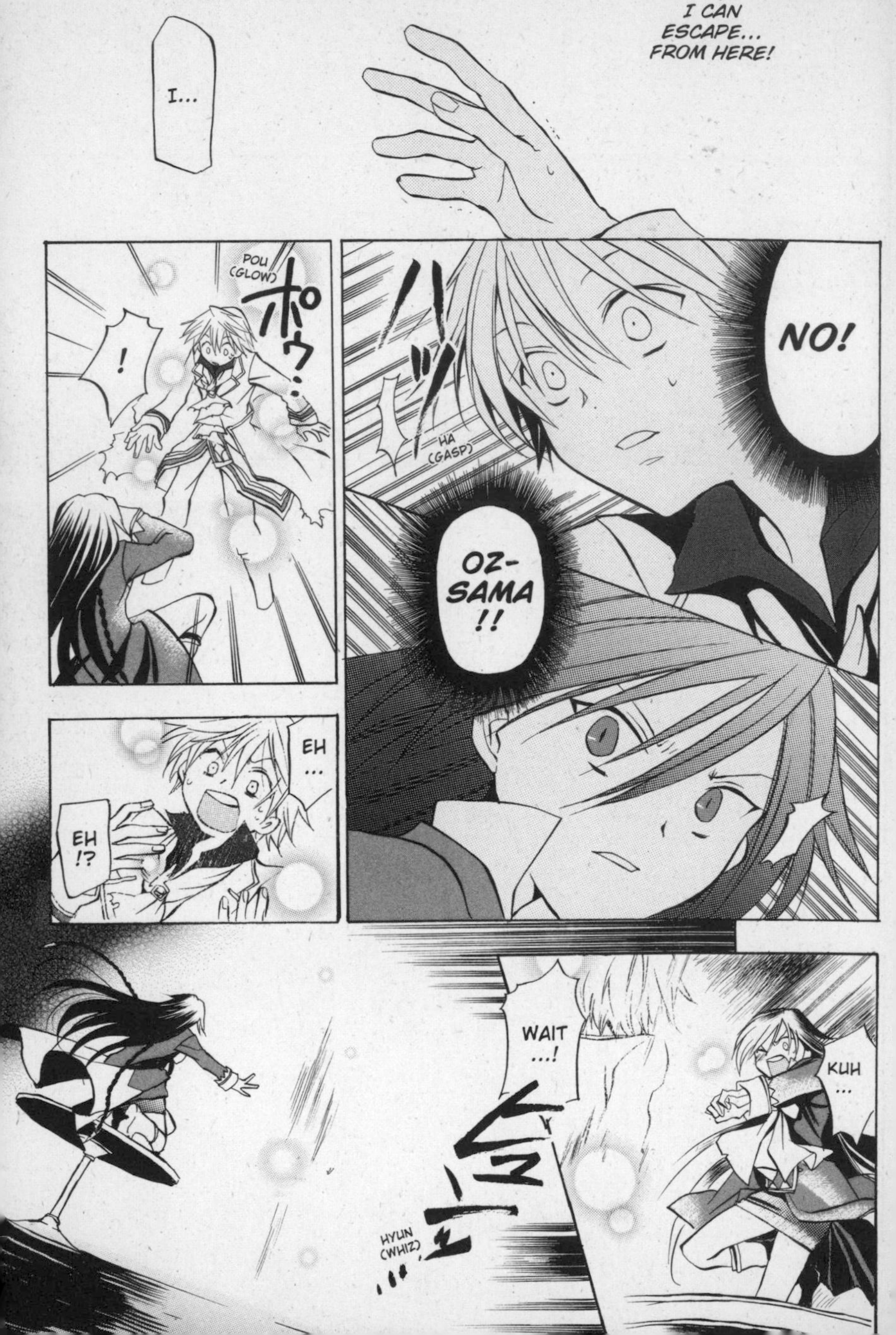
I CAN ESCAPE... FROM HERE!
I...
NO!
ハッ
HA (GASP)
OZ-SAMA!!
ポウ…
POU (GLOW)
!
EH ...
EH !?
KUH ...
WAIT ...!
HYUN (WHIZ)

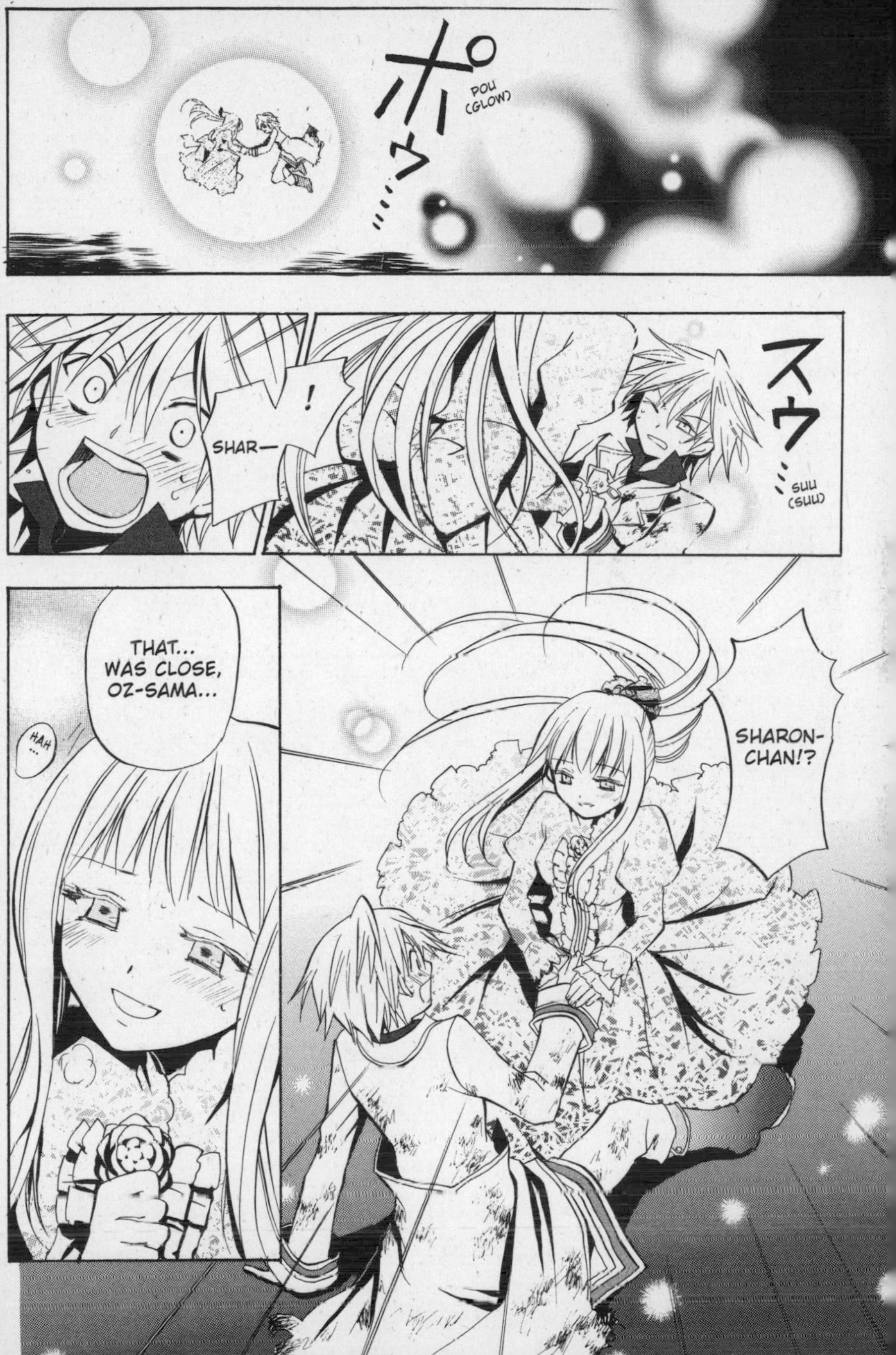
ポウ……
POU (GLOW)
スウ……
SUU (SUU)
!
SHAR—
SHARON-CHAN!?
THAT... WAS CLOSE, OZ-SAMA...
HAH...

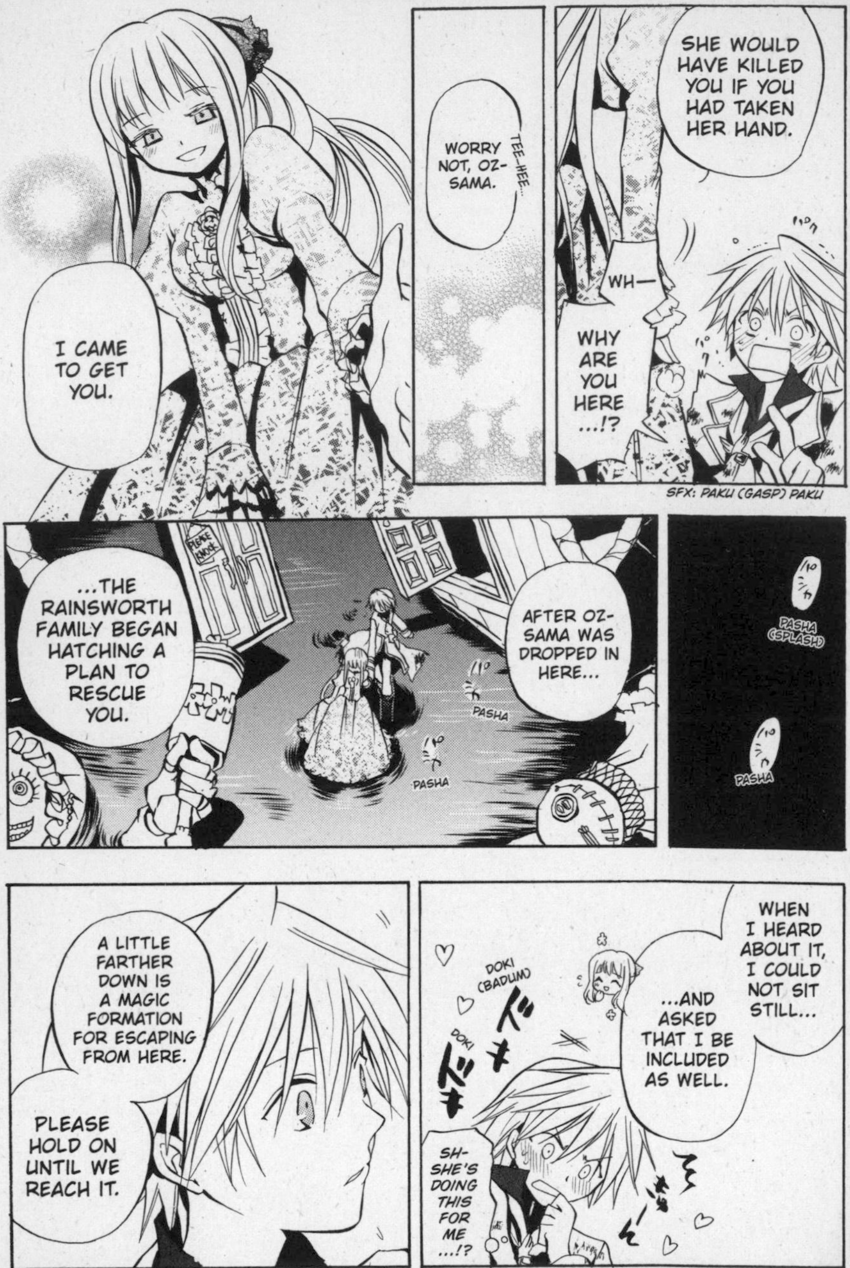
SHE WOULD HAVE KILLED YOU IF YOU HAD TAKEN HER HAND.
WH—
WHY ARE YOU HERE ...!?
WORRY NOT, OZ-SAMA.
TEE-HEE...
I CAME TO GET YOU.
PASHA (SPLASH)
PASHA
AFTER OZ-SAMA WAS DROPPED IN HERE...
PASHA
PASHA
PLEASE KNOCK
...THE RAINSWORTH FAMILY BEGAN HATCHING A PLAN TO RESCUE YOU.
WHEN I HEARD ABOUT IT, I COULD NOT SIT STILL...
...AND ASKED THAT I BE INCLUDED AS WELL.
DOKI (BADUM)
DOKI
SH-SHE'S DOING THIS FOR ME ...!?
A LITTLE FARTHER DOWN IS A MAGIC FORMATION FOR ESCAPING FROM HERE.
PLEASE HOLD ON UNTIL WE REACH IT.

SFX: PAKU (GASP) PAKU

SFX: KYUUN (TWINGE)

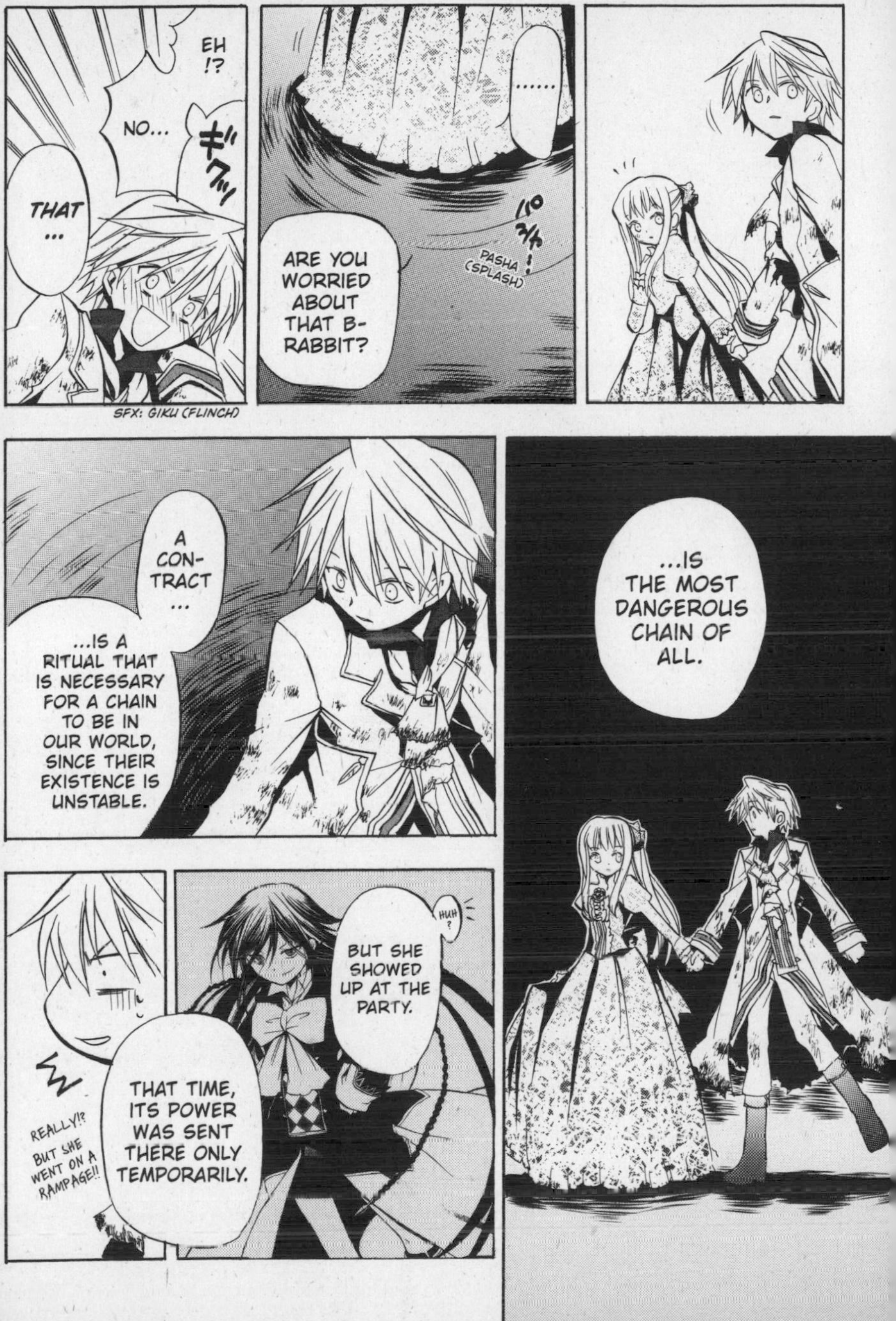
......
ARE YOU WORRIED ABOUT THAT B-RABBIT?
PASHA (SPLASH)
EH !?
NO...
THAT ...
SFX: GIKU (FLINCH)
...IS THE MOST DANGEROUS CHAIN OF ALL.
A CONTRACT ...
...IS A RITUAL THAT IS NECESSARY FOR A CHAIN TO BE IN OUR WORLD, SINCE THEIR EXISTENCE IS UNSTABLE.
HUH ?
BUT SHE SHOWED UP AT THE PARTY.
THAT TIME, ITS POWER WAS SENT THERE ONLY TEMPORARILY.
REALLY!? BUT SHE WENT ON A RAMPAGE!!

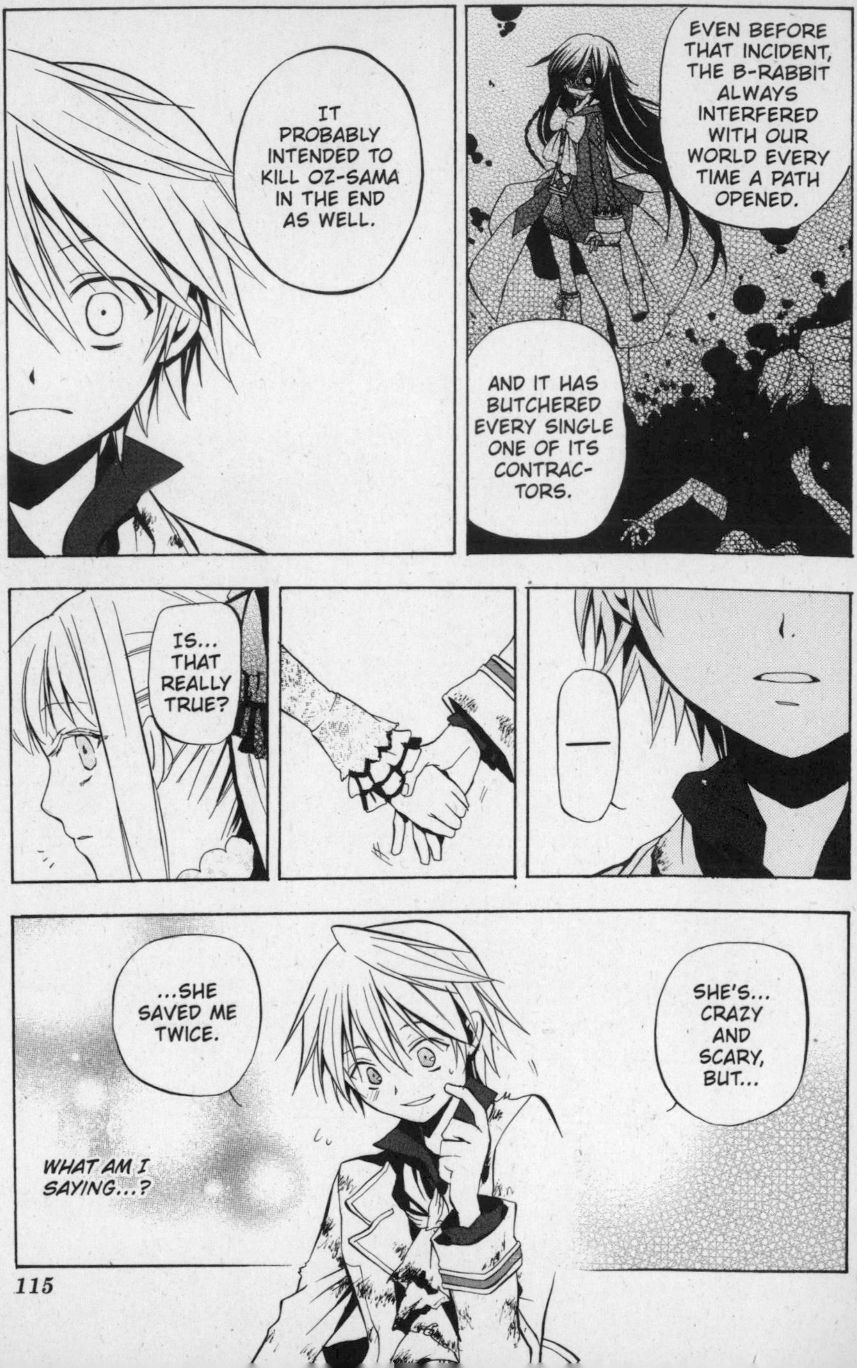
EVEN BEFORE THAT INCIDENT, THE B-RABBIT ALWAYS INTERFERED WITH OUR WORLD EVERY TIME A PATH OPENED.
AND IT HAS BUTCHERED EVERY SINGLE ONE OF ITS CONTRAC- TORS.
IT PROBABLY INTENDED TO KILL OZ-SAMA IN THE END AS WELL.
—
IS... THAT REALLY TRUE?
SHE'S... CRAZY AND SCARY, BUT...
...SHE SAVED ME TWICE.
WHAT AM I SAYING...?

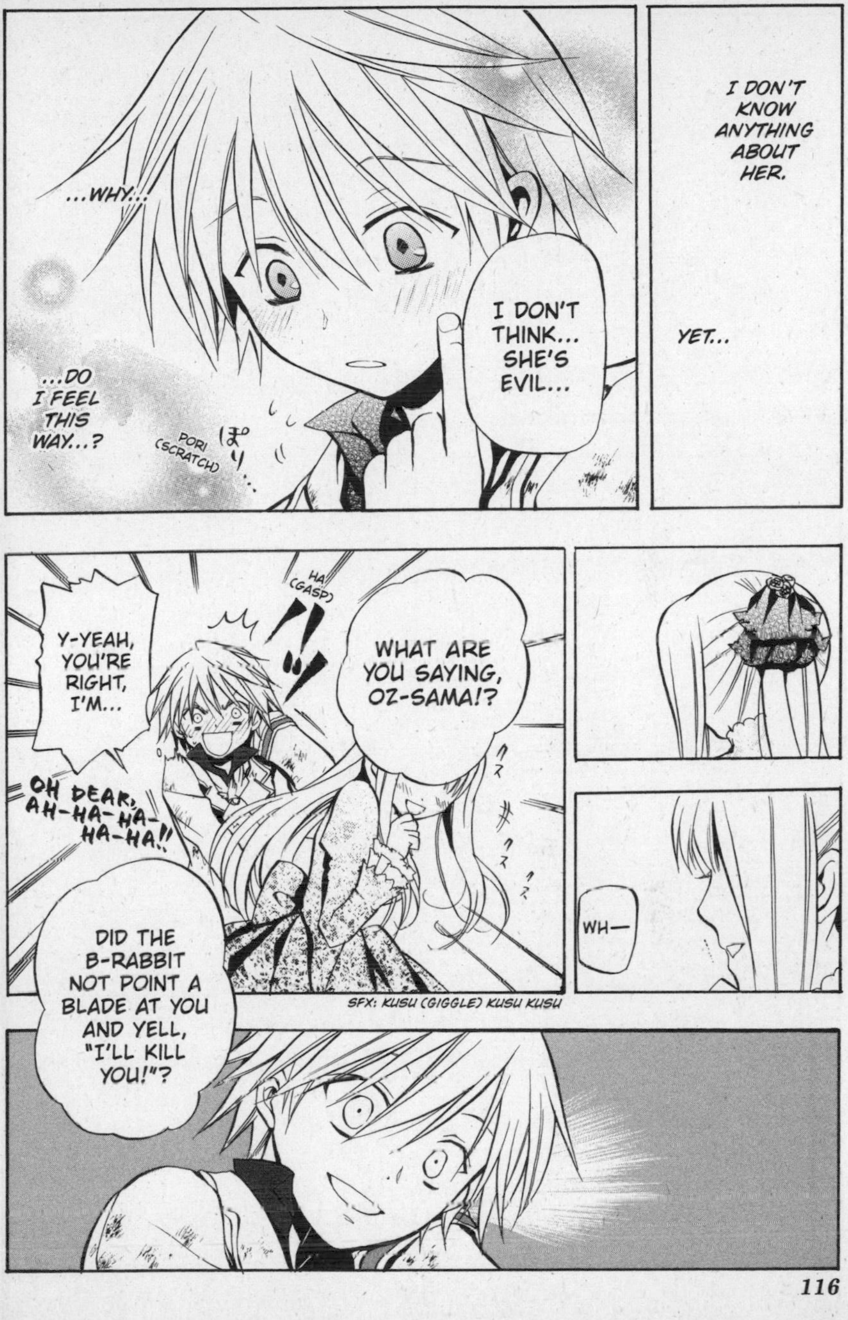
I DON'T KNOW ANYTHING ABOUT HER.
YET...
I DON'T THINK... SHE'S EVIL...
...WHY...
...DO I FEEL THIS WAY...?
ぽり...
PORI (SCRATCH)
WH—
HA (GASP)
WHAT ARE YOU SAYING, OZ-SAMA!?
Y-YEAH, YOU'RE RIGHT, I'M...
OH DEAR, AH-HA-HA-HA-HA!!
DID THE B-RABBIT NOT POINT A BLADE AT YOU AND YELL, "I'LL KILL YOU!"?
SFX: KUSU (GIGGLE) KUSU KUSU

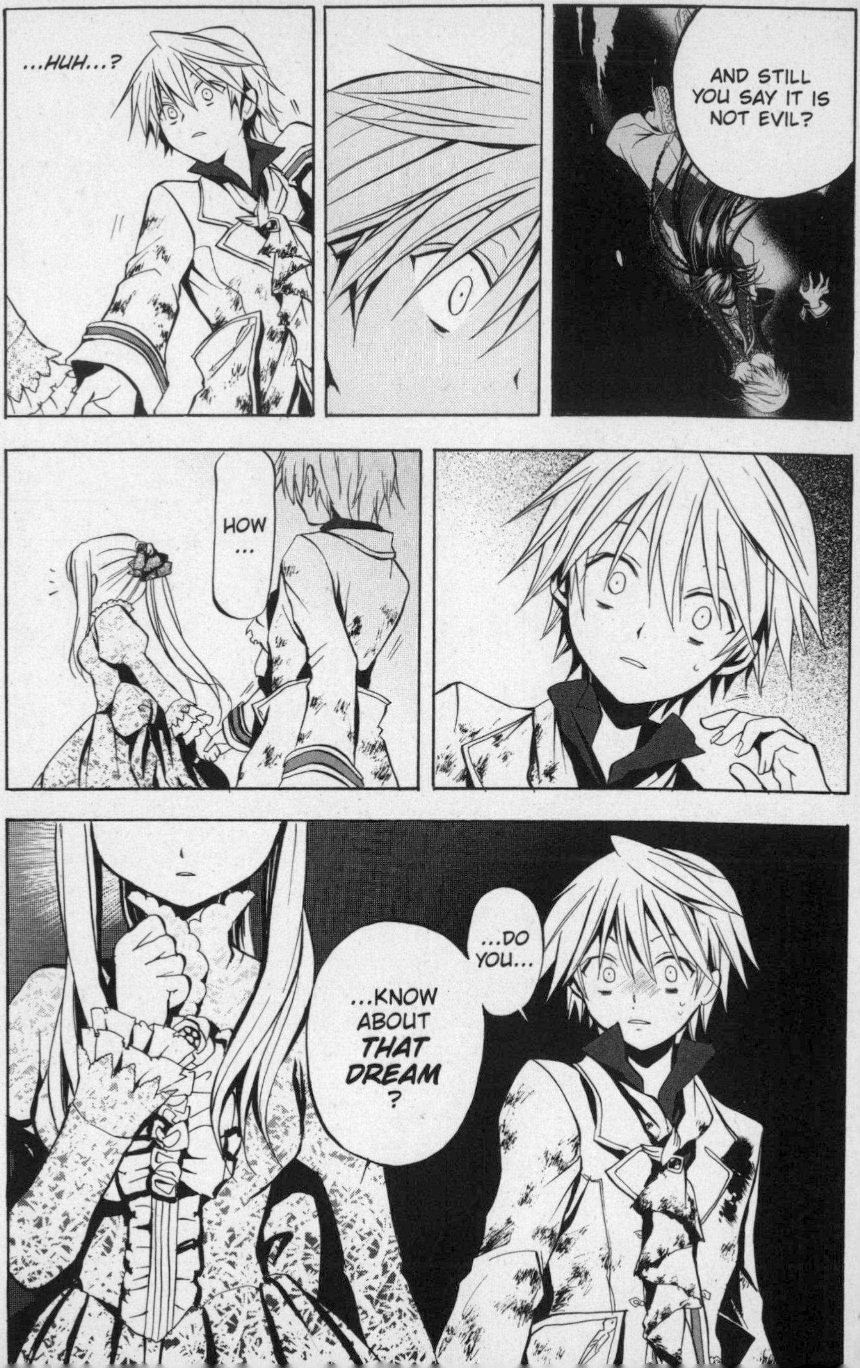
AND STILL YOU SAY IT IS NOT EVIL?
...HUH...?
HOW ...
...DO YOU...
...KNOW ABOUT *THAT DREAM* ?

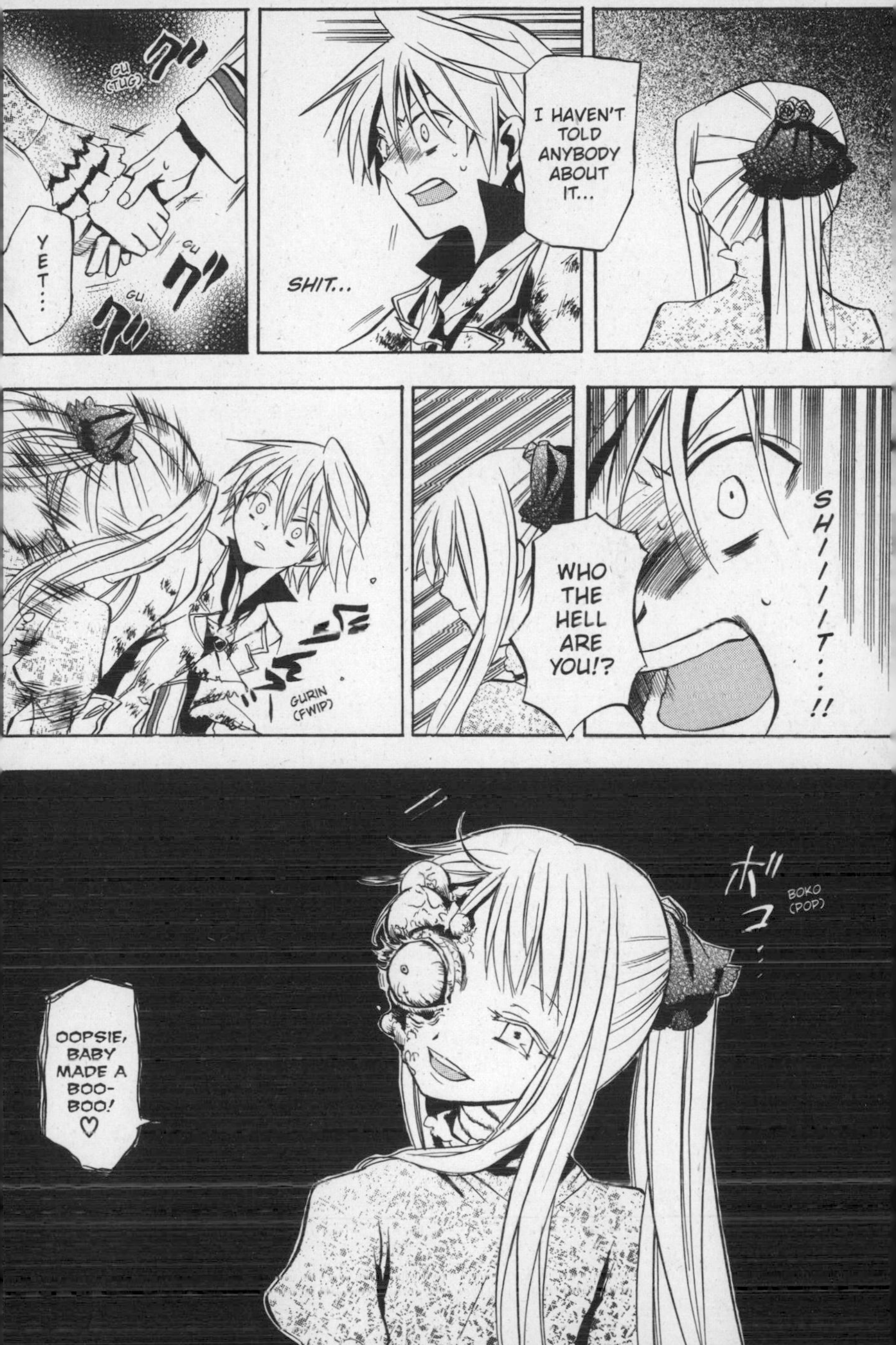
I HAVEN'T TOLD ANYBODY ABOUT IT...
SHIT...
GU (TUG)
GU
GU
YET...
SHI///T...!!
WHO THE HELL ARE YOU!?
GURIN (FWIP)
BOKO (POP)
OOPSIE, BABY MADE A BOO-BOO! ♡

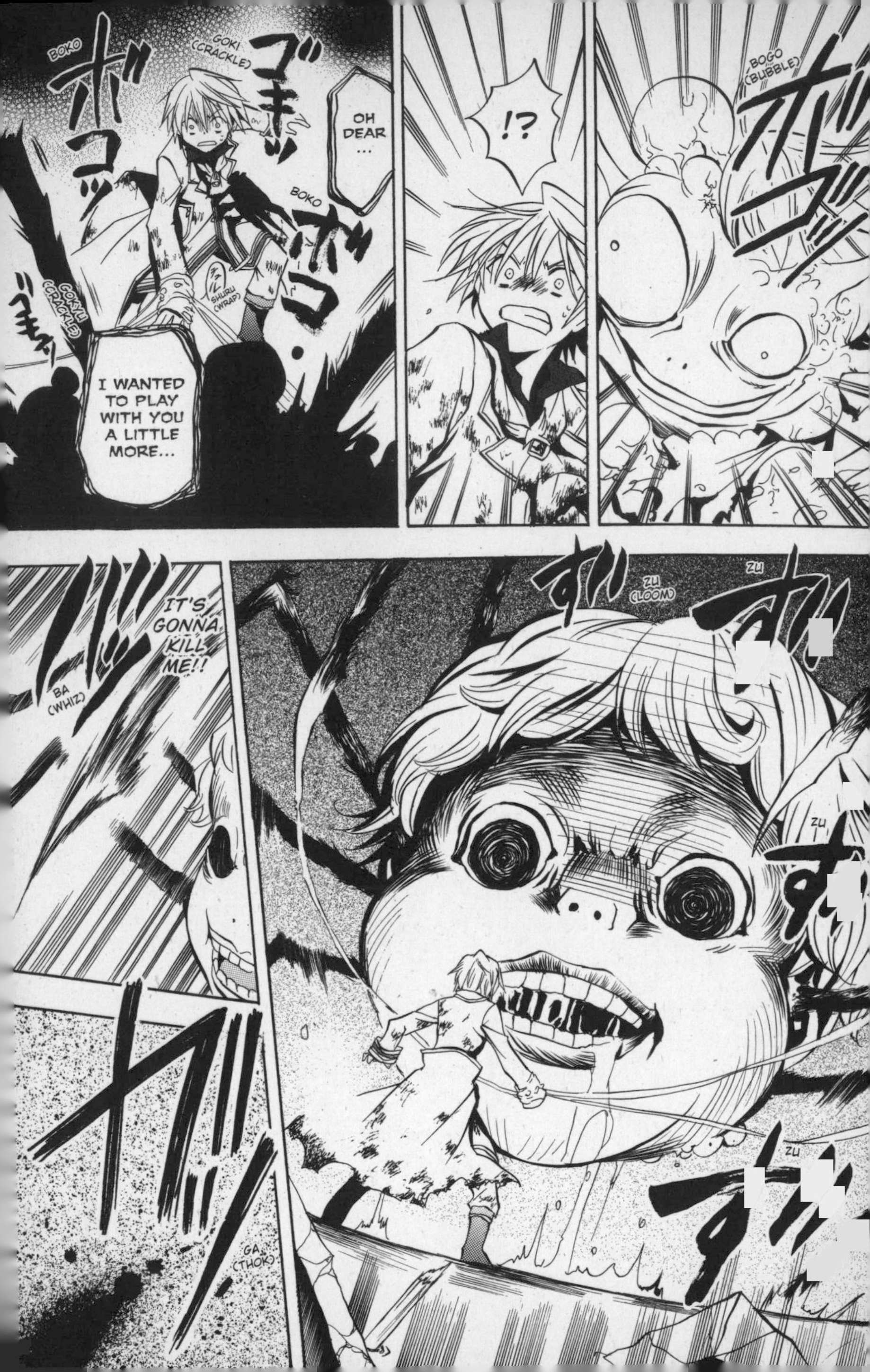
BOGO (BUBBLE)
!?
OH DEAR ...
GOKI (CRACKLE)
BOKO
BOKO
SHURU (WRAP)
GOKYU (CRACKLE)
I WANTED TO PLAY WITH YOU A LITTLE MORE...
ZU
ZU (LOOM)
ZU
ZU
IT'S GONNA KILL ME!!
BA (WHIZ)
GA (THOK)

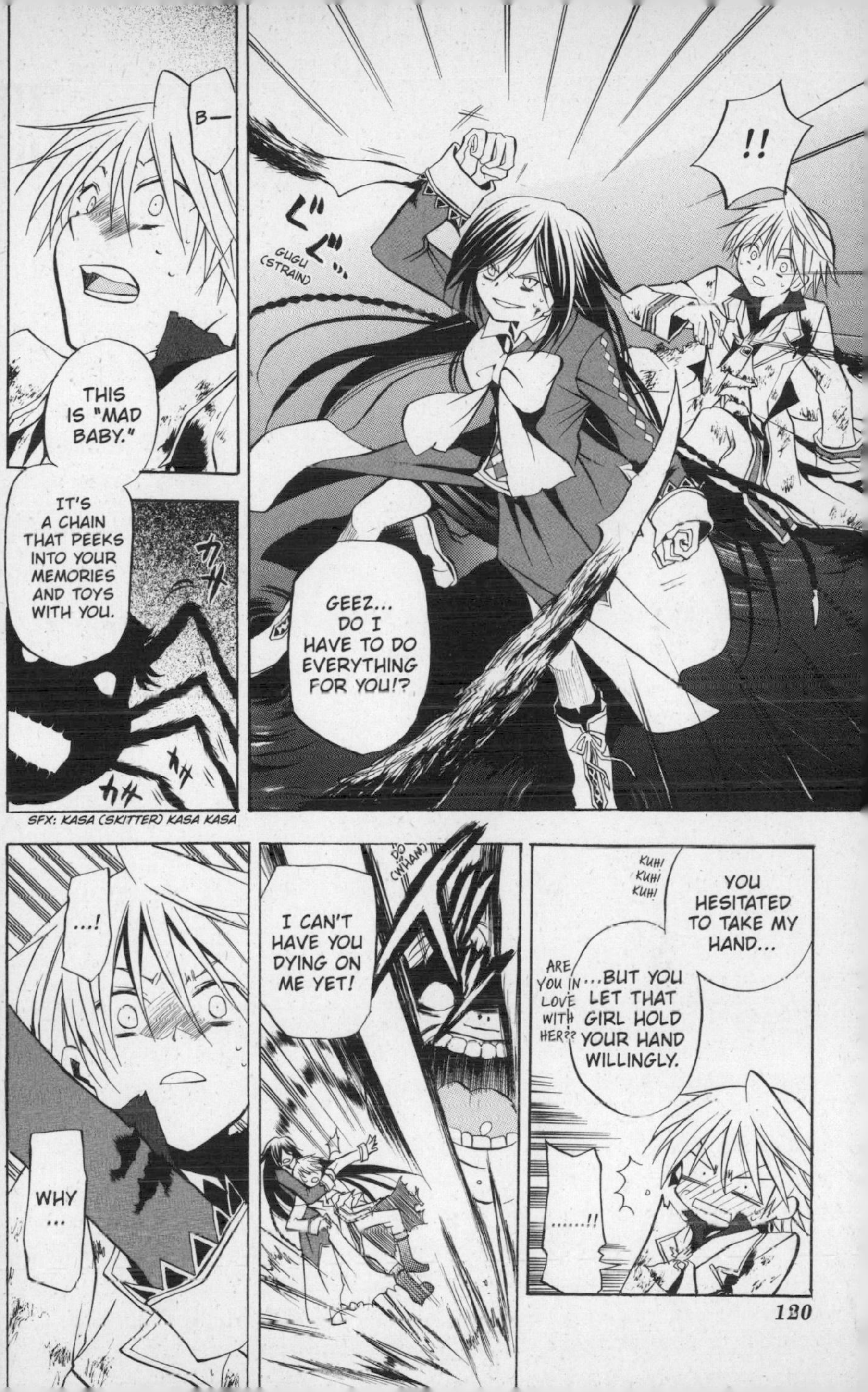
!!
GUGU (STRAIN)
GEEZ... DO I HAVE TO DO EVERYTHING FOR YOU!?
B—
THIS IS "MAD BABY."
IT'S A CHAIN THAT PEEKS INTO YOUR MEMORIES AND TOYS WITH YOU.
SFX: KASA (SKITTER) KASA KASA
KUHI KUHI KUHI
YOU HESITATED TO TAKE MY HAND...
...BUT YOU LET THAT GIRL HOLD YOUR HAND WILLINGLY.
ARE YOU IN LOVE WITH HER??
......!!
DO (WHAM)
I CAN'T HAVE YOU DYING ON ME YET!
...!
WHY ...

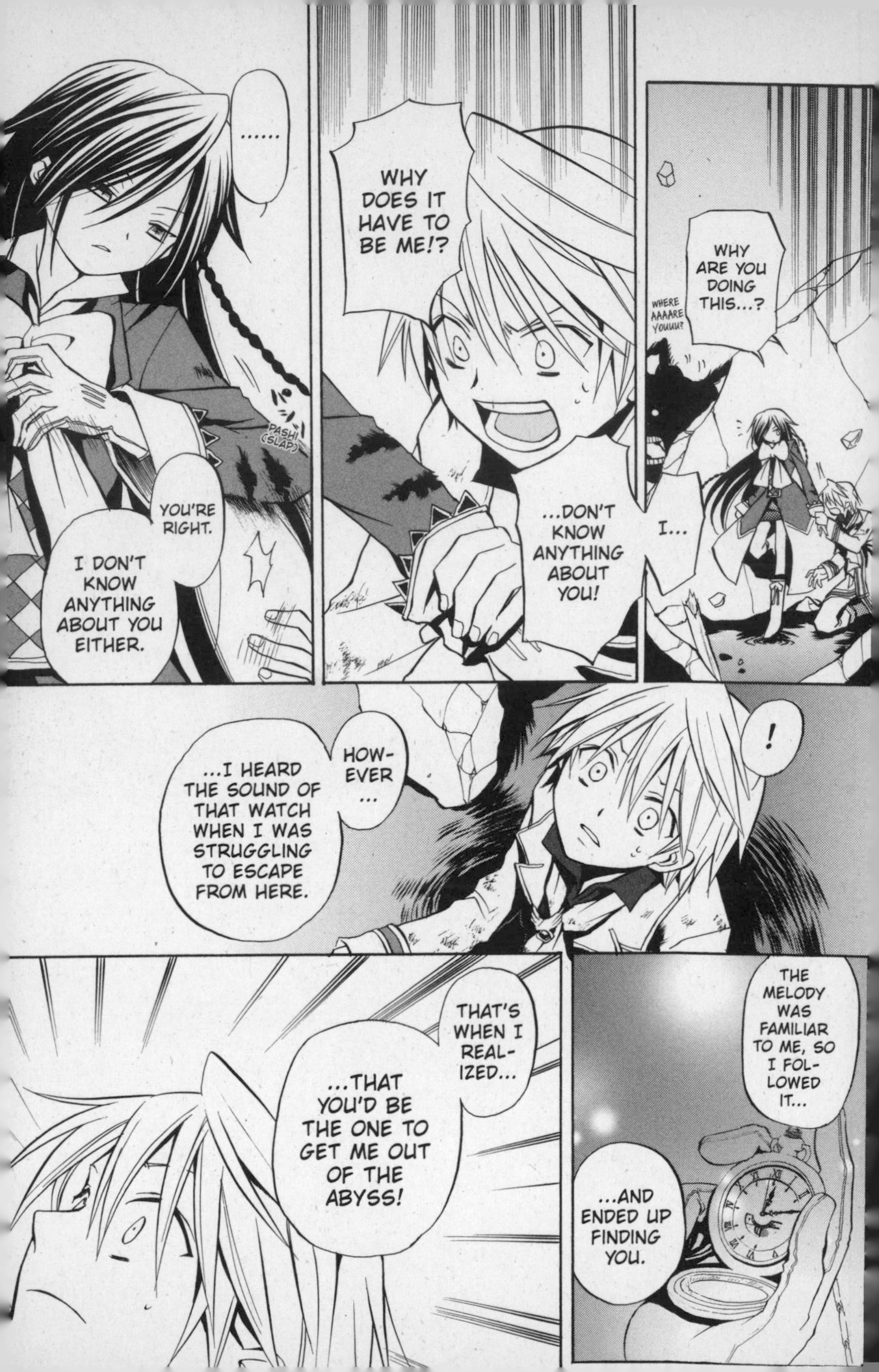
WHY ARE YOU DOING THIS...?
WHERE AAAARE YOUUU?
I...
WHY DOES IT HAVE TO BE ME!?
...DON'T KNOW ANYTHING ABOUT YOU!
......
PASHI (SLAP)
YOU'RE RIGHT.
I DON'T KNOW ANYTHING ABOUT YOU EITHER.
!
HOWEVER...
...I HEARD THE SOUND OF THAT WATCH WHEN I WAS STRUGGLING TO ESCAPE FROM HERE.
THE MELODY WAS FAMILIAR TO ME, SO I FOLLOWED IT...
...AND ENDED UP FINDING YOU.
THAT'S WHEN I REALIZED...
...THAT YOU'D BE THE ONE TO GET ME OUT OF THE ABYSS!

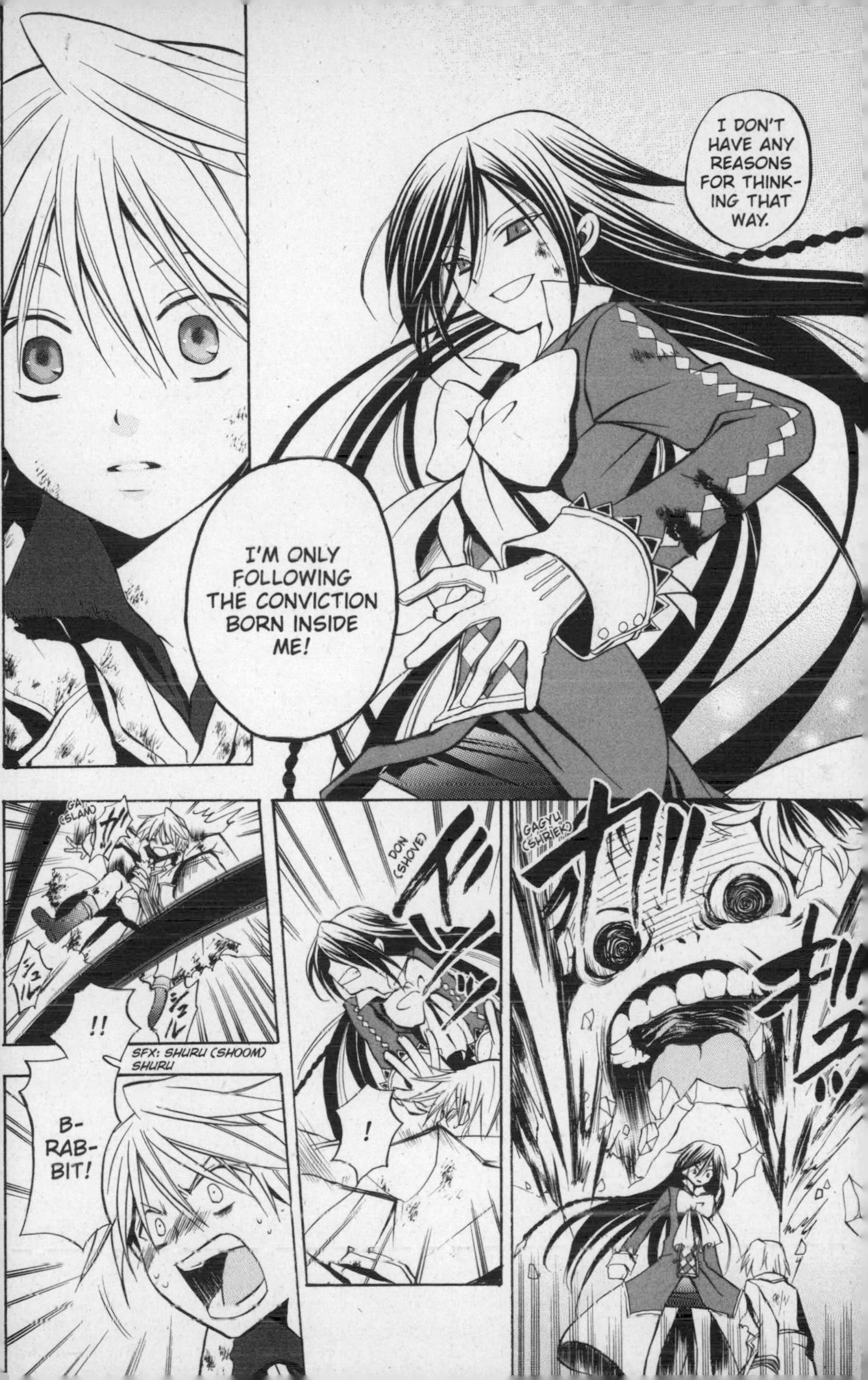
I DON'T HAVE ANY REASONS FOR THINKING THAT WAY.
I'M ONLY FOLLOWING THE CONVICTION BORN INSIDE ME!
GAGYU (SHRIEK)
DON (SHOVE)
!
GA (SLAM)
SFX: SHURU (SHOOM) SHURU
!!
B-RAB-BIT!

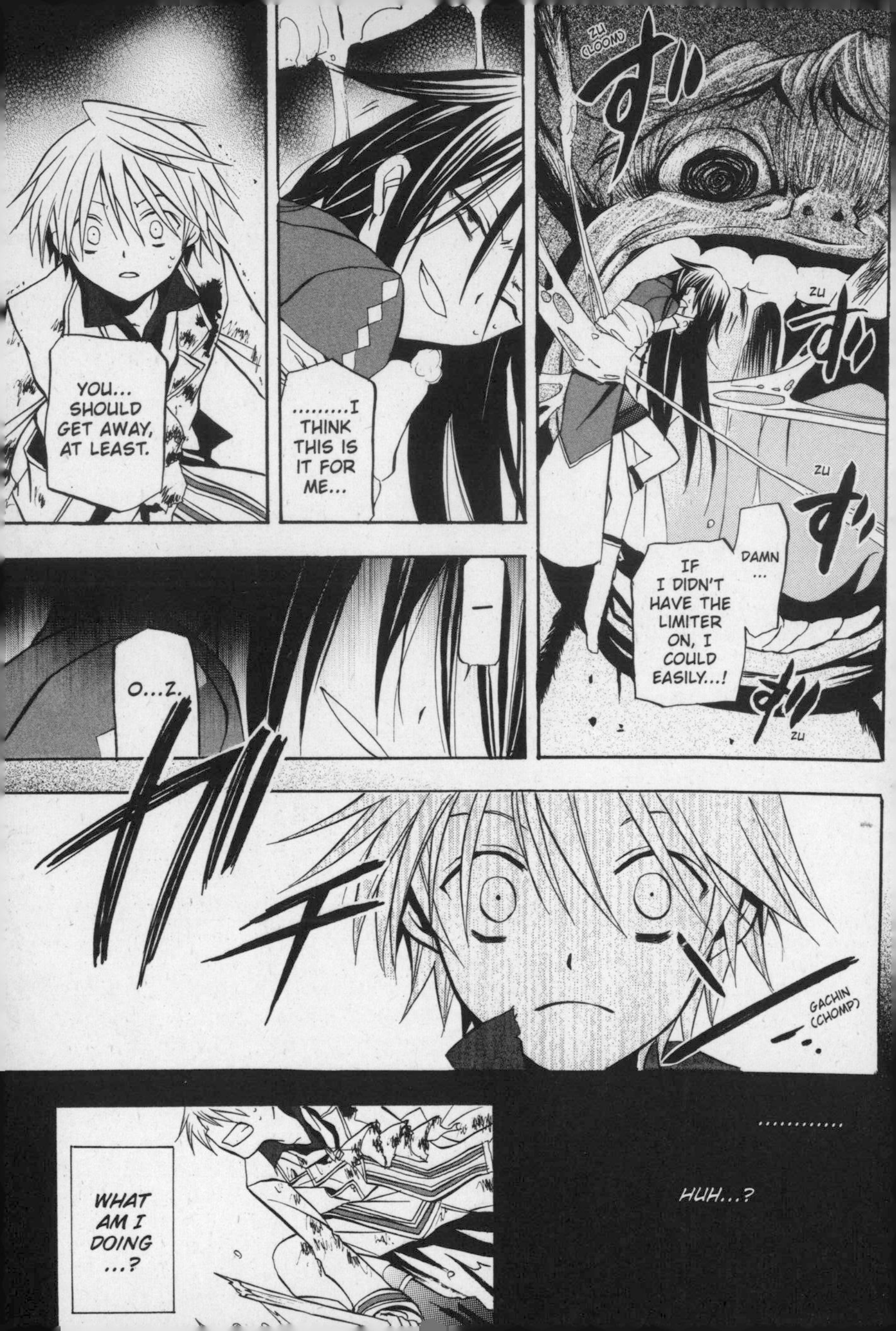
ZU (LOOON)
ZU
ZU
DAMN...
IF I DIDN'T HAVE THE LIMITER ON, I COULD EASILY...!
ZU
.........I THINK THIS IS IT FOR ME...
YOU... SHOULD GET AWAY, AT LEAST.
O...Z.
GACHIN (CHOMP)
............
HUH...?
WHAT AM I DOING ...?

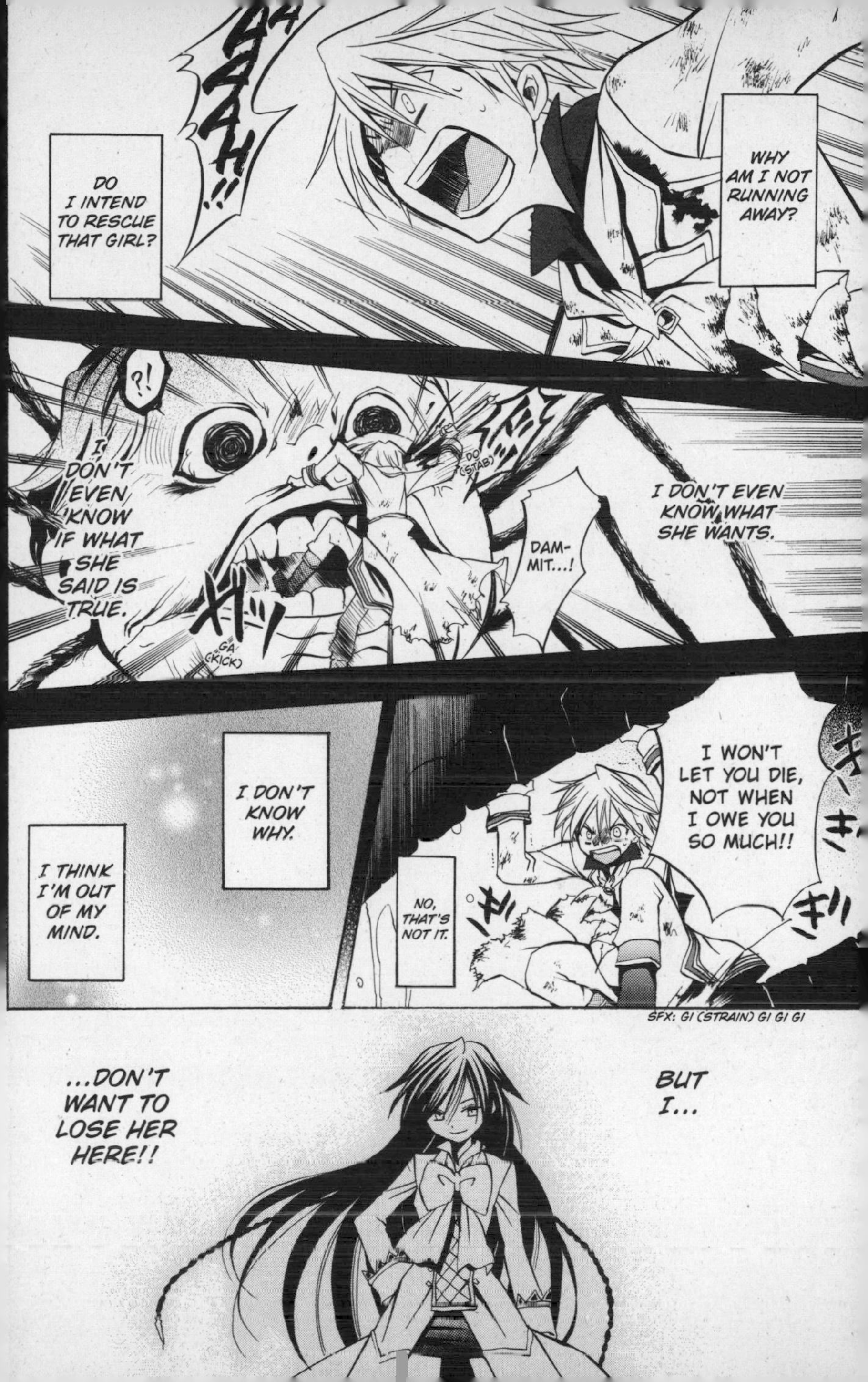
WHY AM I NOT RUNNING AWAY?
WAAAH!!
DO I INTEND TO RESCUE THAT GIRL?
I DON'T EVEN KNOW WHAT SHE WANTS.
DAM-MIT...!
DO (STAB)
?!
I DON'T EVEN KNOW IF WHAT SHE SAID IS TRUE.
GA (KICK)
I WON'T LET YOU DIE, NOT WHEN I OWE YOU SO MUCH!!
NO, THAT'S NOT IT.
I DON'T KNOW WHY.
I THINK I'M OUT OF MY MIND.
SFX: GI (STRAIN) GI GI GI
BUT I...
...DON'T WANT TO LOSE HER HERE!!

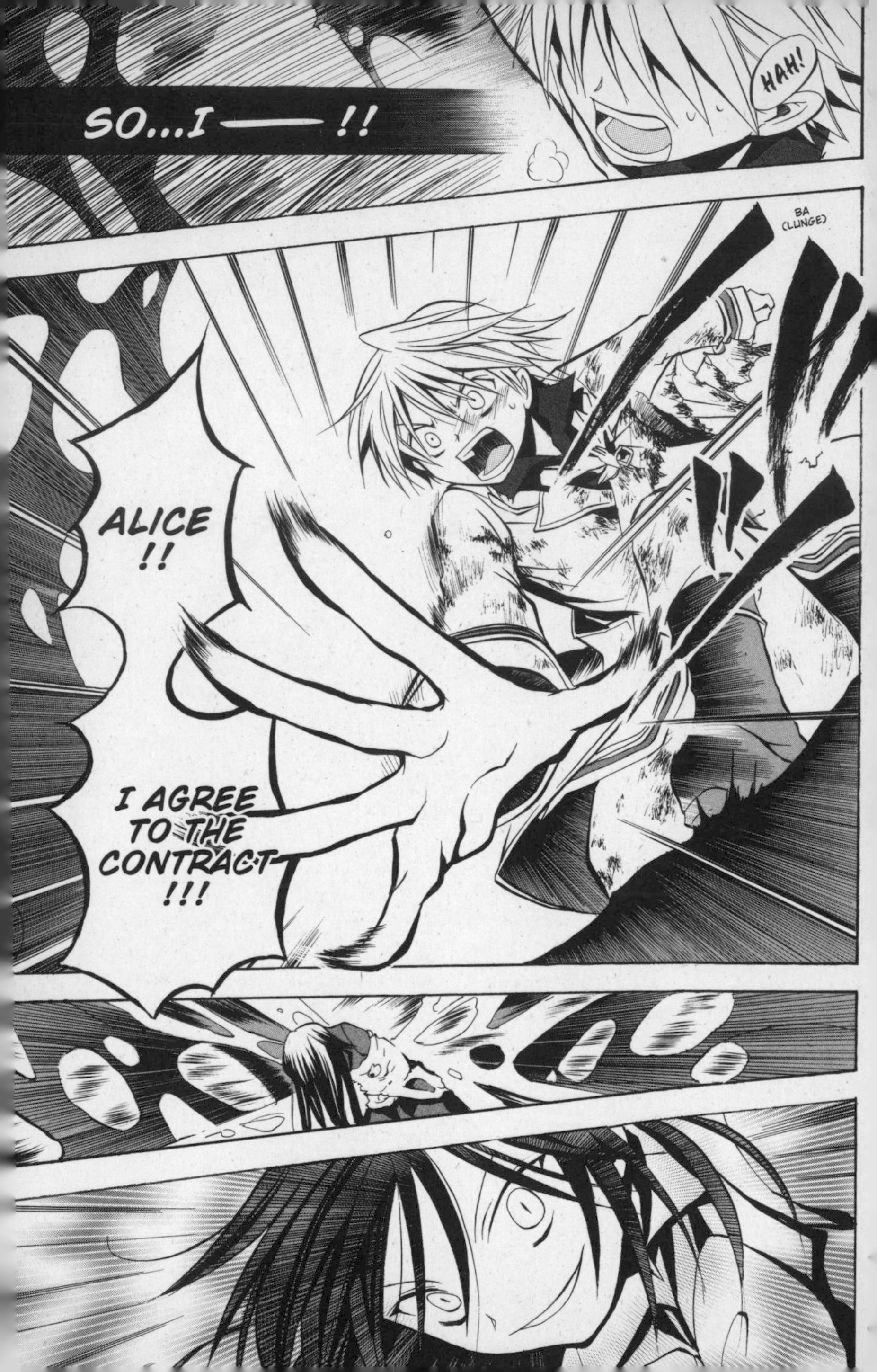
HAH!
SO...I——!!
BA (LUNGE)
ALICE !!
I AGREE TO THE CONTRACT !!!

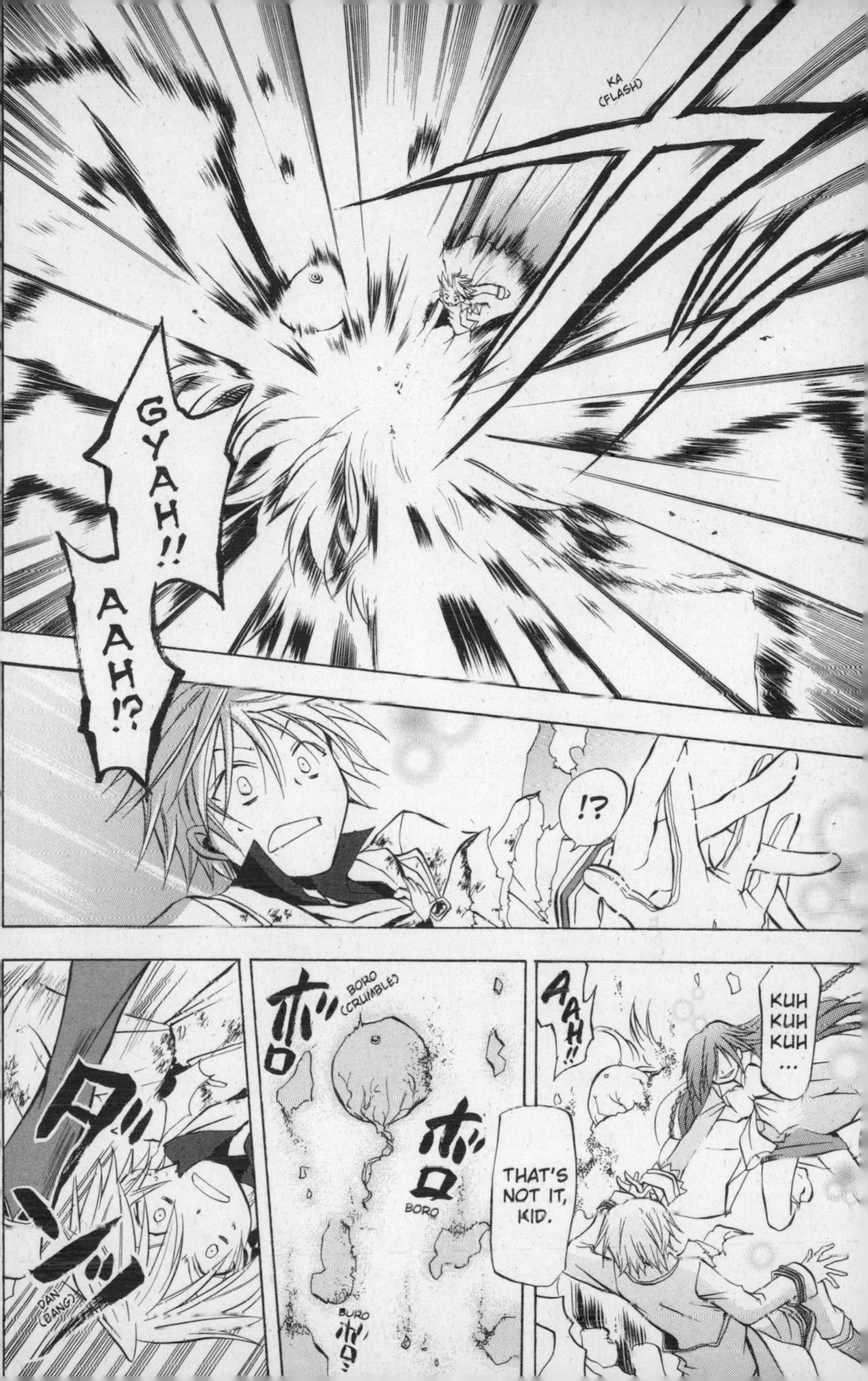
KA (FLASH)
GYAH!! AAH!?
!?
KUH KUH KUH ...
AAH!!
THAT'S NOT IT, KID.
BORO (CRUMBLE)
BORO
BURO
DAN (BANG)

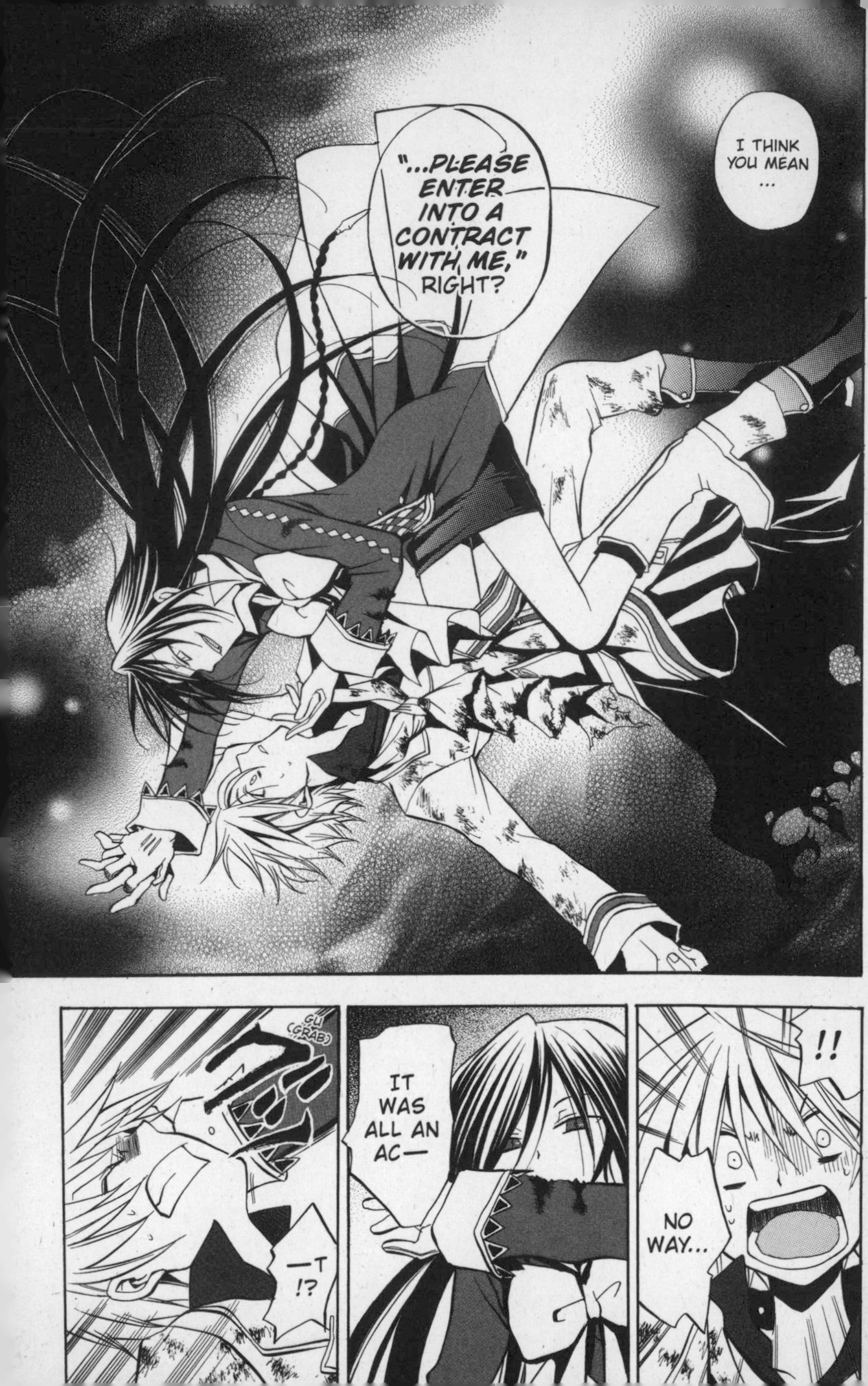
I THINK YOU MEAN ...
"...PLEASE ENTER INTO A CONTRACT WITH ME," RIGHT?
!!
NO WAY...
IT WAS ALL AN AC—
GU (GRAB)
—T !?

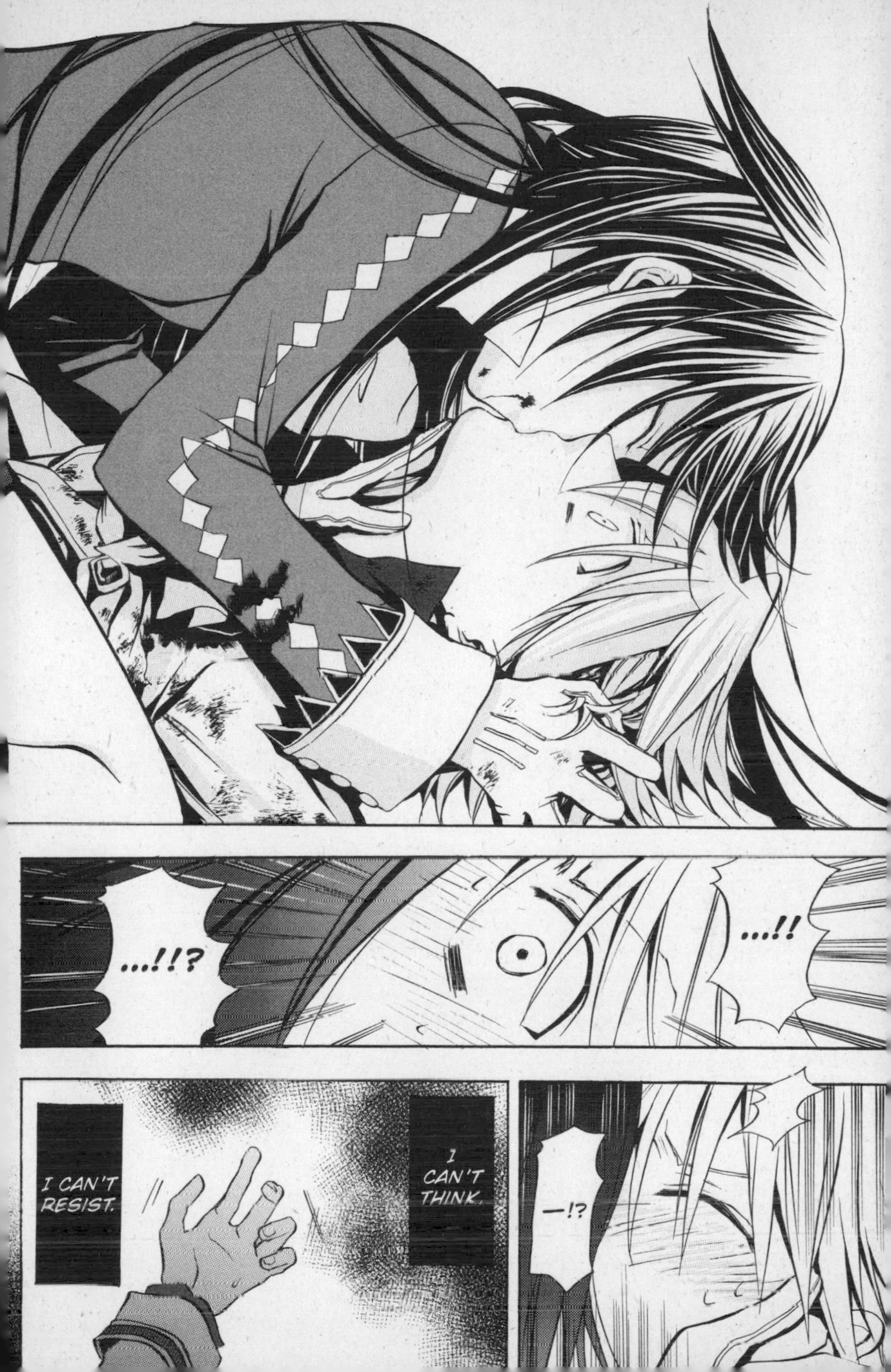
...!!
...!!?
—!?
I CAN'T THINK.
I CAN'T RESIST.

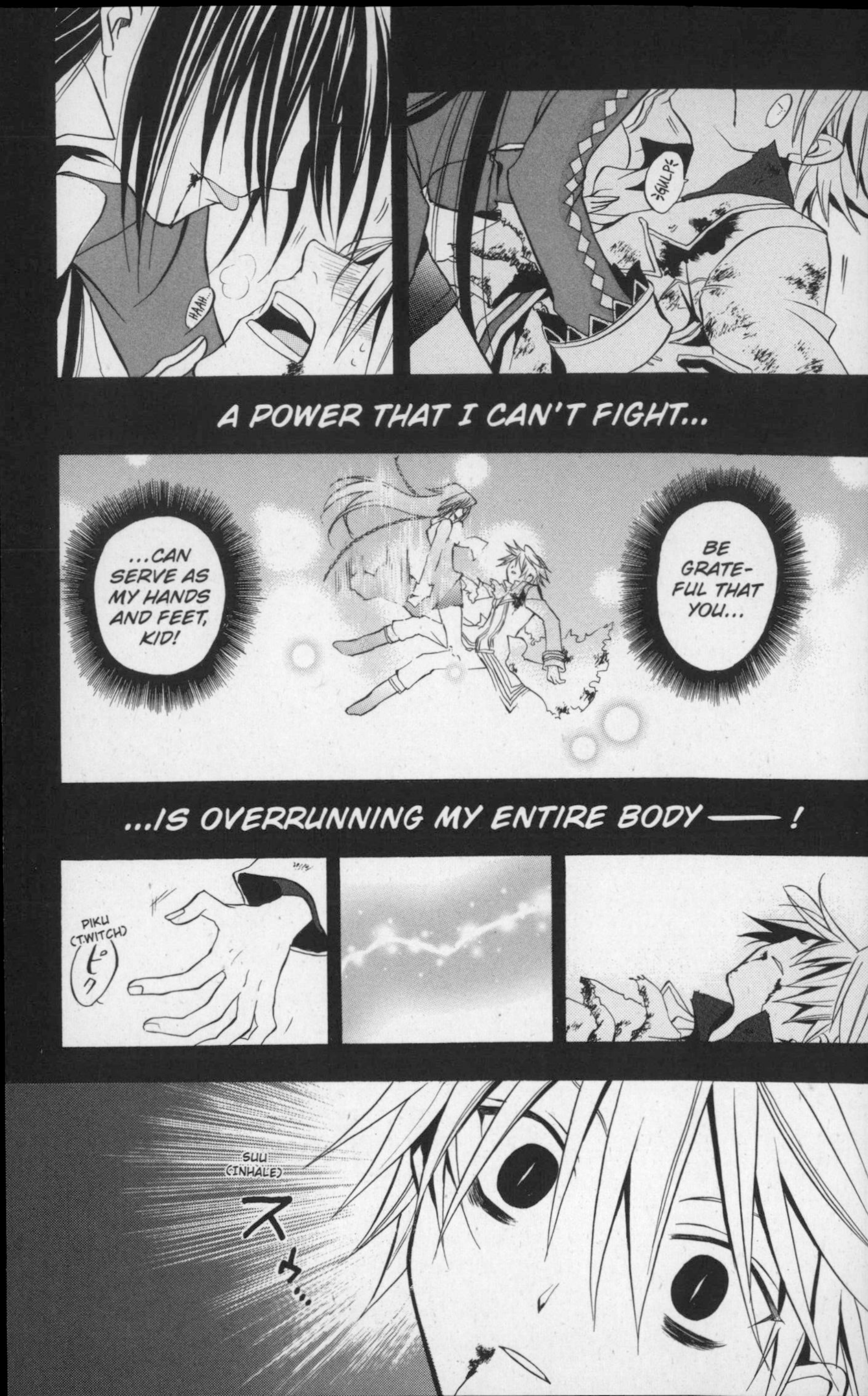
GULP
HAAH...
A POWER THAT I CAN'T FIGHT...
BE GRATE-FUL THAT YOU...
...CAN SERVE AS MY HANDS AND FEET, KID!
...IS OVERRUNNING MY ENTIRE BODY——!
PIKU (TWITCH)
SUU (INHALE)

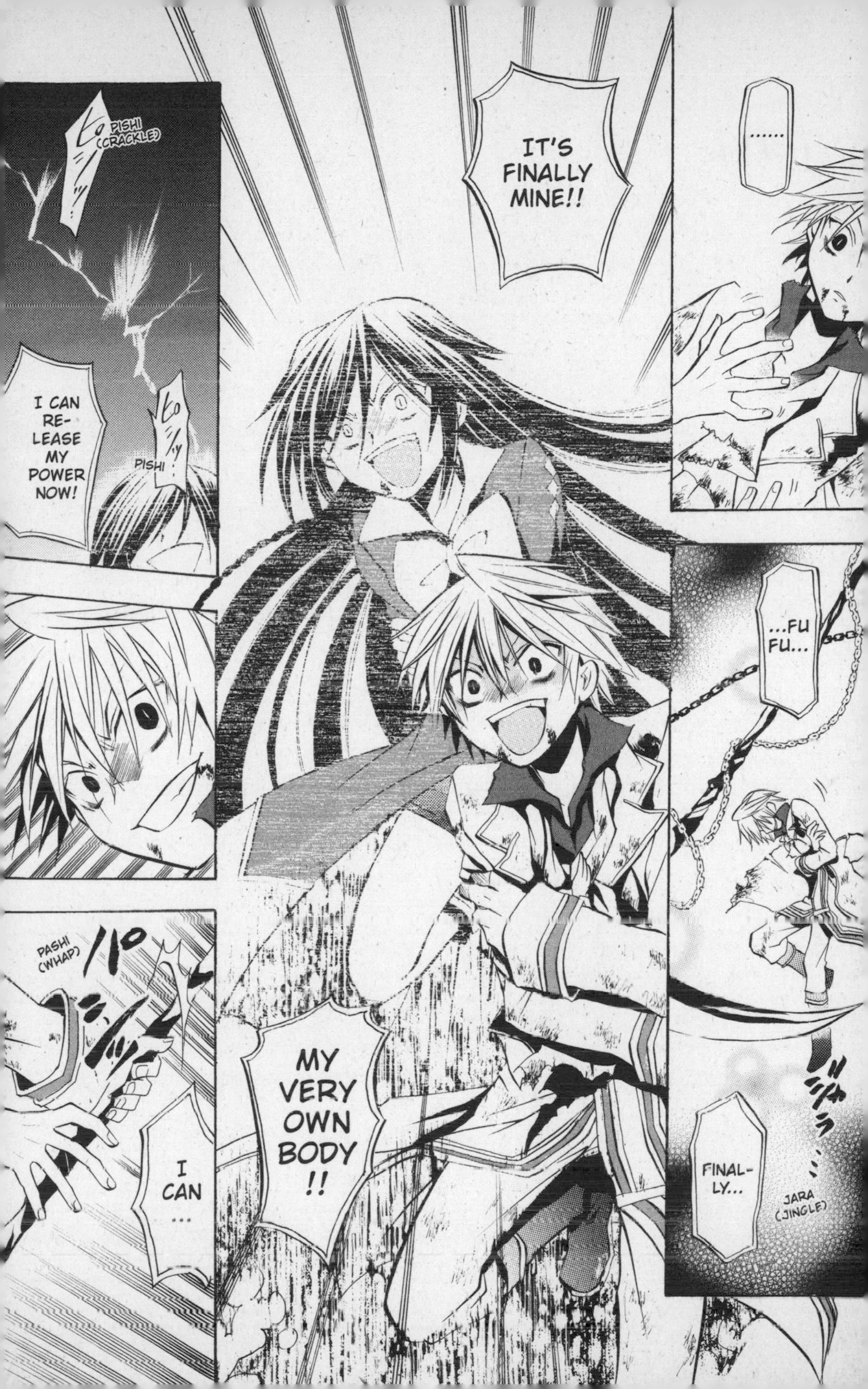
......
...FU FU...
FINAL-LY...
JARA (JINGLE)
IT'S FINALLY MINE!!
MY VERY OWN BODY !!
PISHI (CRACKLE)
I CAN RE-LEASE MY POWER NOW!
PISHI
PASHI (WHAP)
I CAN ...

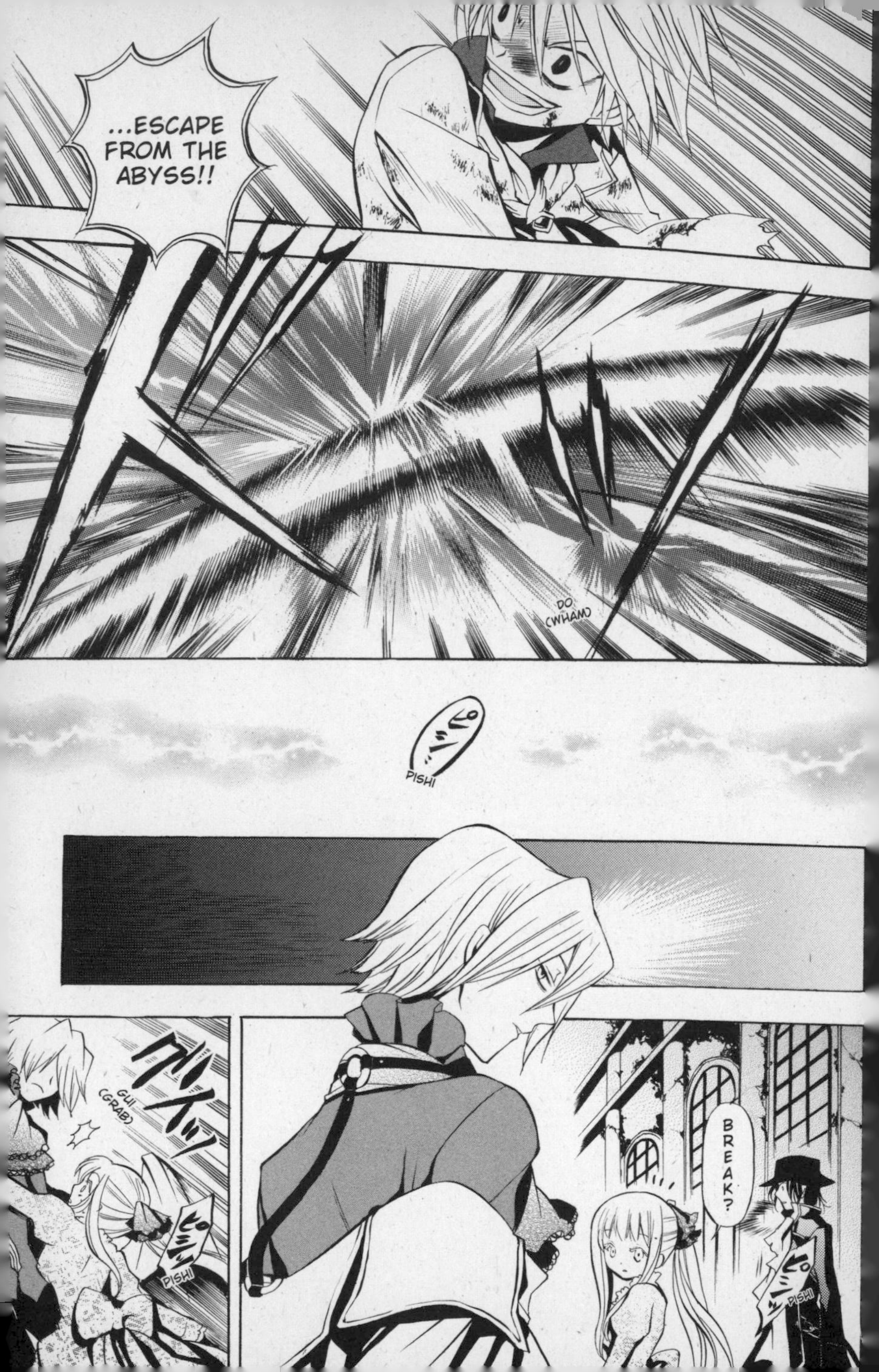
...ESCAPE FROM THE ABYSS!!
DO (WHAM)
PISHI
BREAK?
PISHI
GUI (GRAB)
PISHI

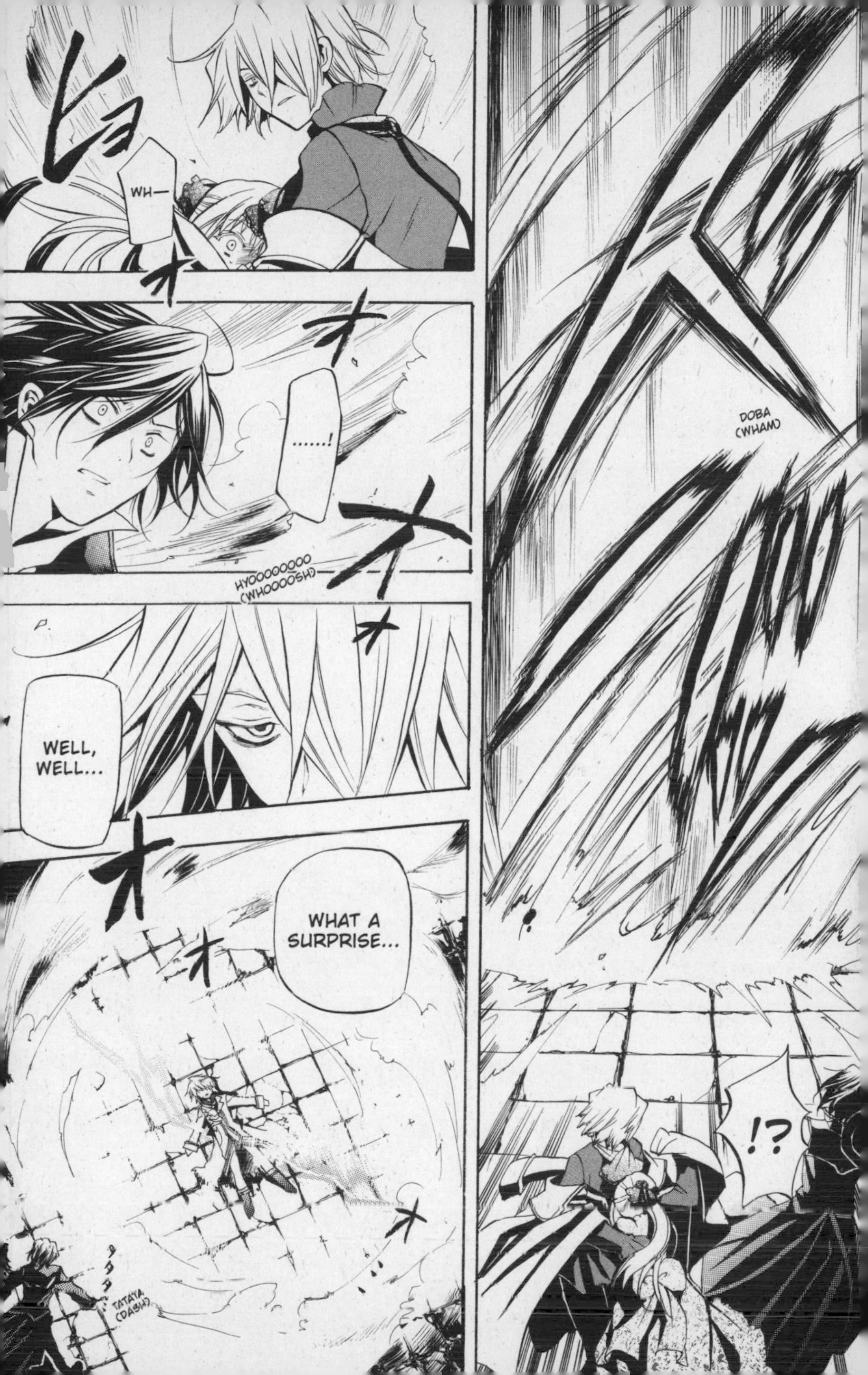
DOBA (WHAM)
!?
WH—
......!
HYOOOOOOOO (WHOOOOSH)
WELL, WELL...
WHAT A SURPRISE...
TATATA (DASH)

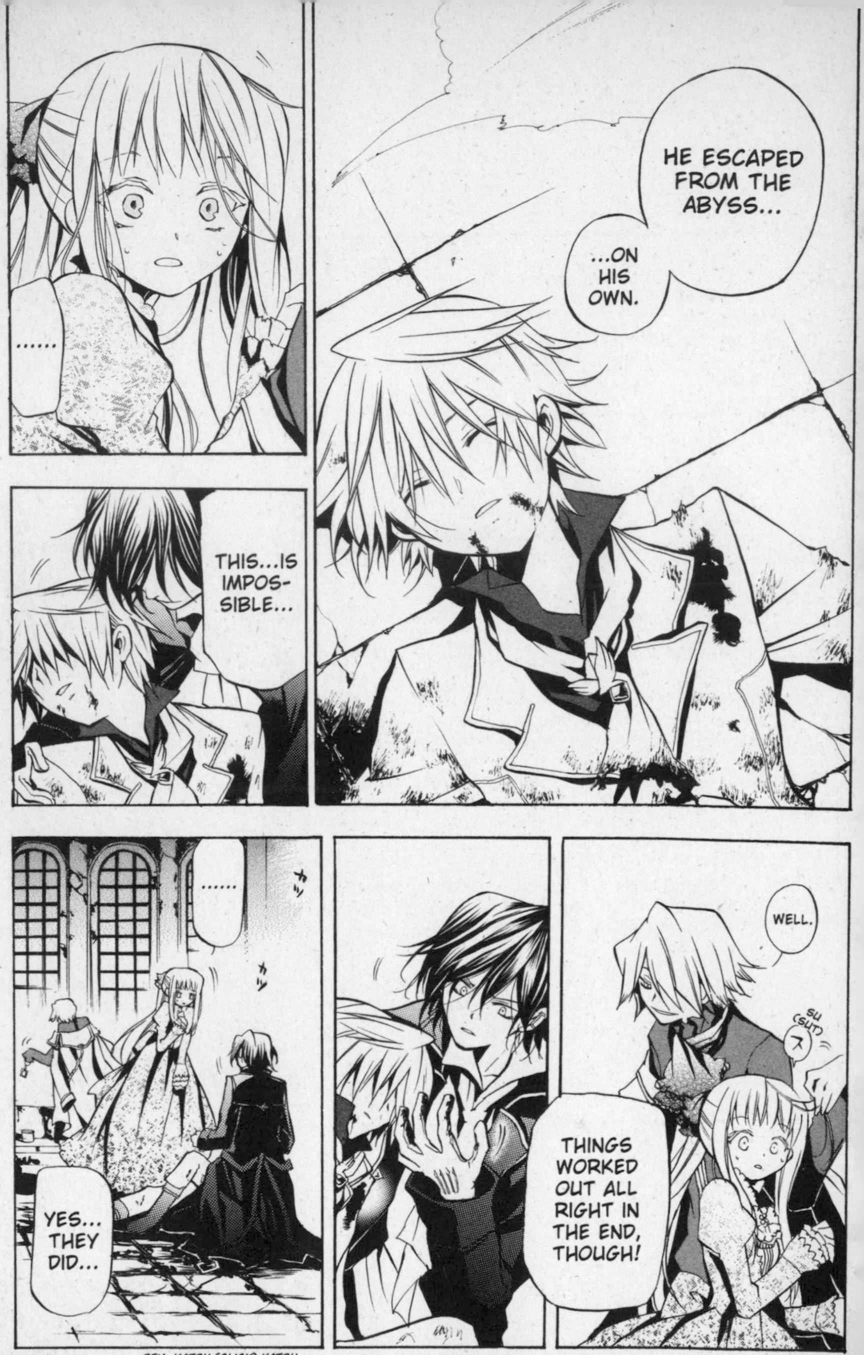
HE ESCAPED FROM THE ABYSS...
...ON HIS OWN.
......
THIS...IS IMPOSSIBLE...
WELL.
SU (SUT)
ス
THINGS WORKED OUT ALL RIGHT IN THE END, THOUGH!
カツ
......
カツ
YES... THEY DID...


SFX: KATSU (CLICK) KATSU

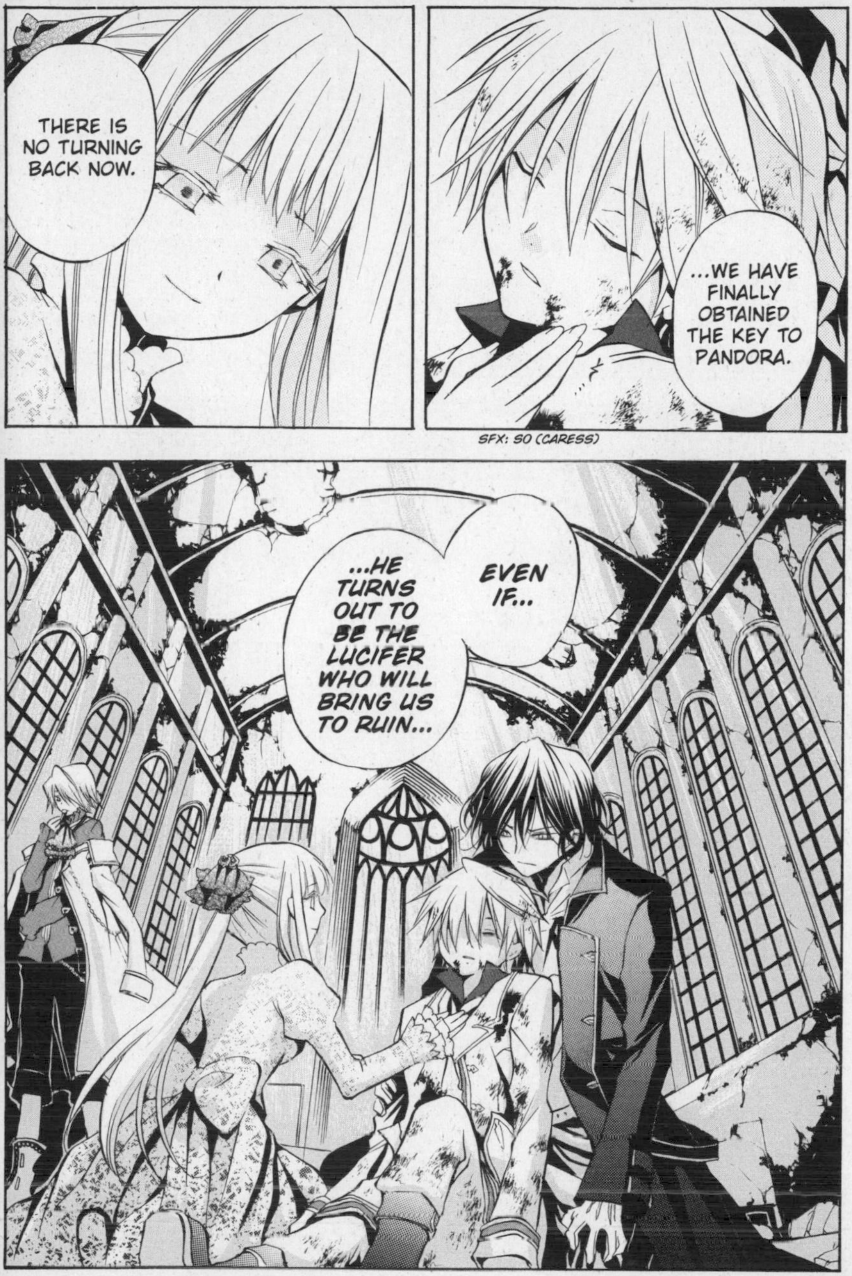
...WE HAVE FINALLY OBTAINED THE KEY TO PANDORA.
THERE IS NO TURNING BACK NOW.
SFX: SO (CARESS)
EVEN IF...
...HE TURNS OUT TO BE THE LUCIFER WHO WILL BRING US TO RUIN...

# Retrace:IV Rendezvous

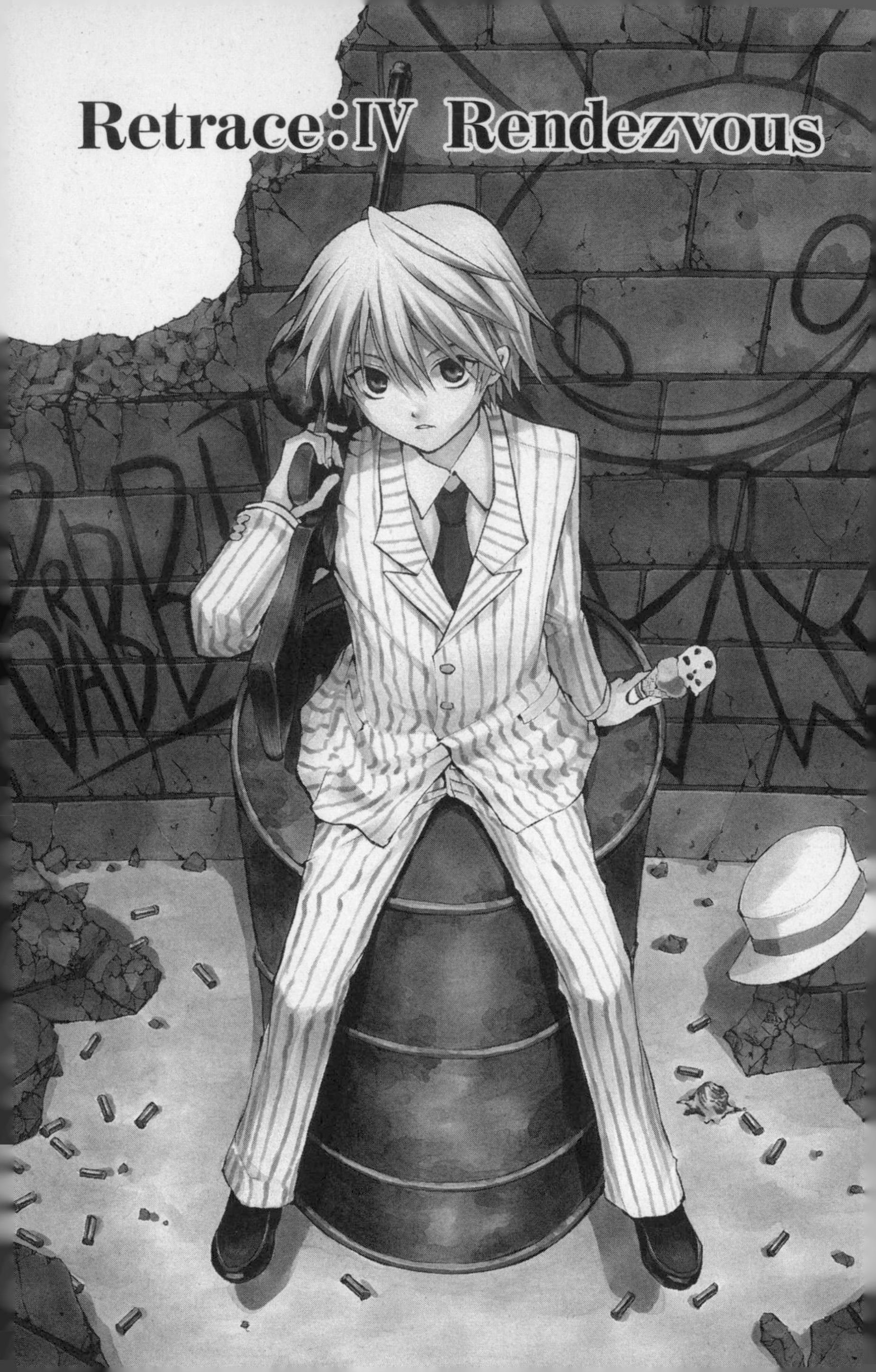

KIRA
(GLINT)

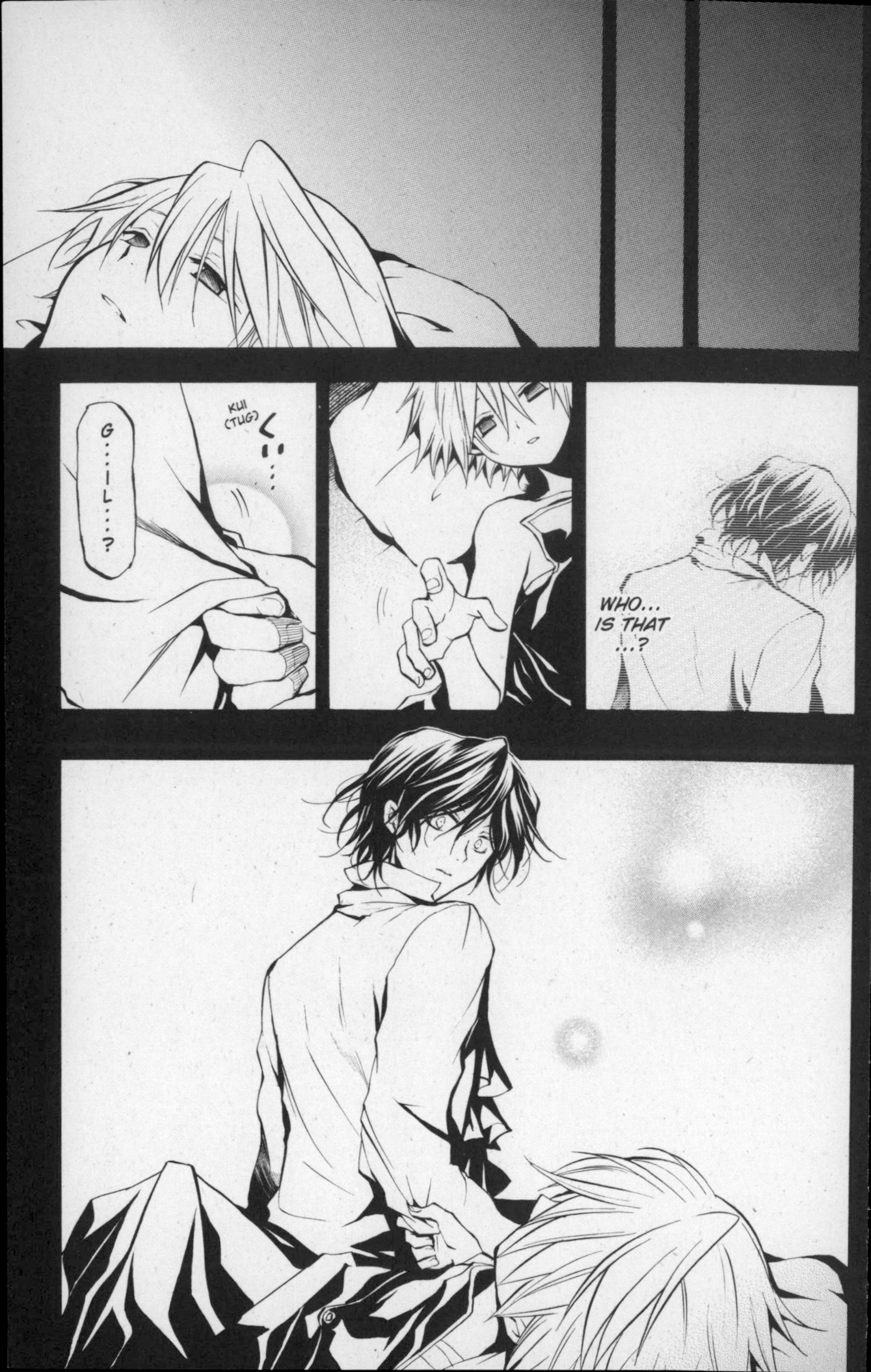
WHO... IS THAT ...?
KUI (TUG)
くい…
G...I...L...?

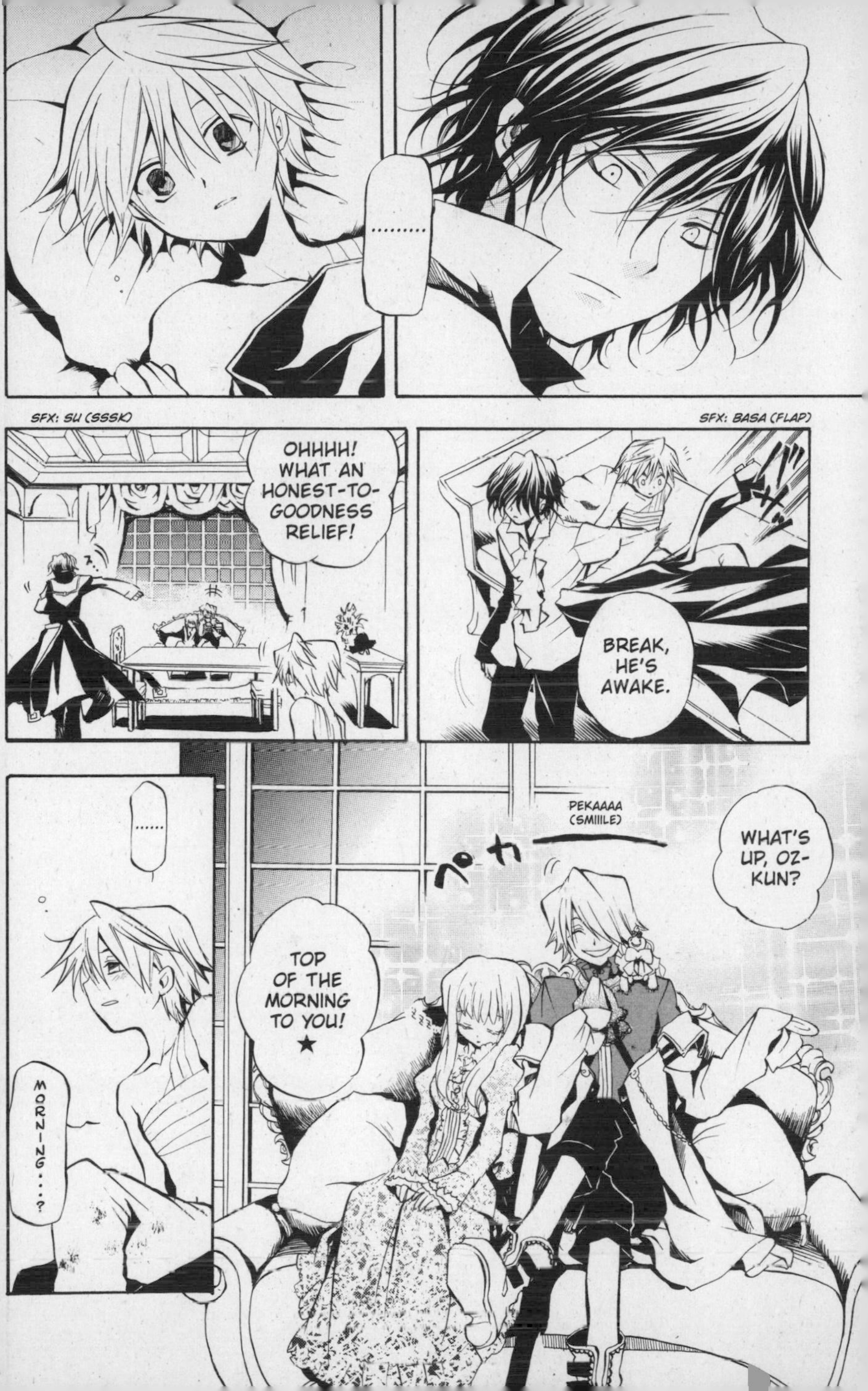
........
SFX: BASA (FLAP)
SFX: SU (SSSK)
BREAK, HE'S AWAKE.
OHHHH! WHAT AN HONEST-TO-GOODNESS RELIEF!
WHAT'S UP, OZ-KUN?
PEKAAAA (SMIIILE)
TOP OF THE MORNING TO YOU! ★
......
MORNING...?

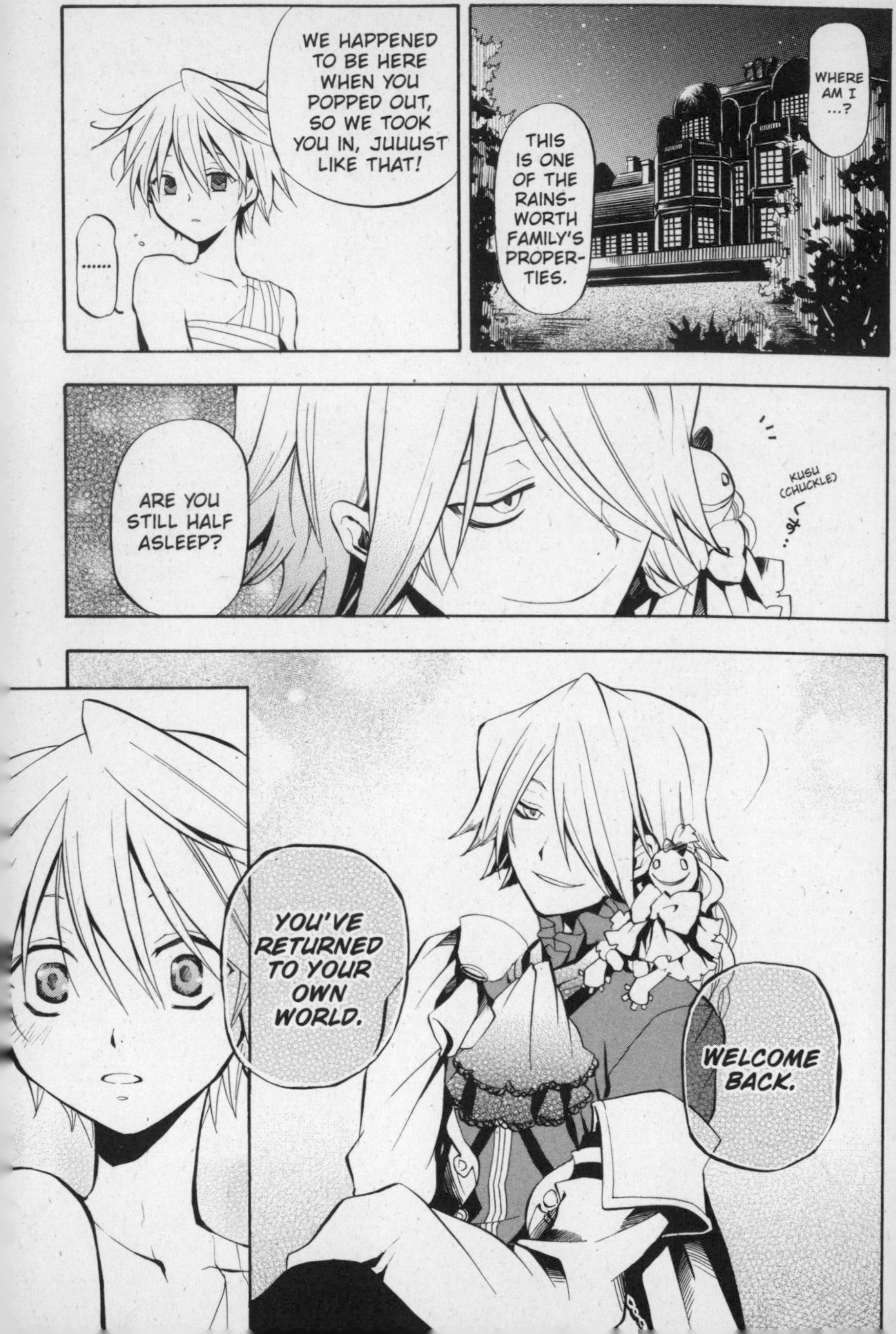
WHERE AM I ...?
THIS IS ONE OF THE RAINSWORTH FAMILY'S PROPERTIES.
WE HAPPENED TO BE HERE WHEN YOU POPPED OUT, SO WE TOOK YOU IN, JUUUST LIKE THAT!
......
KUSU (CHUCKLE)
ARE YOU STILL HALF ASLEEP?
WELCOME BACK.
YOU'VE RETURNED TO YOUR OWN WORLD.

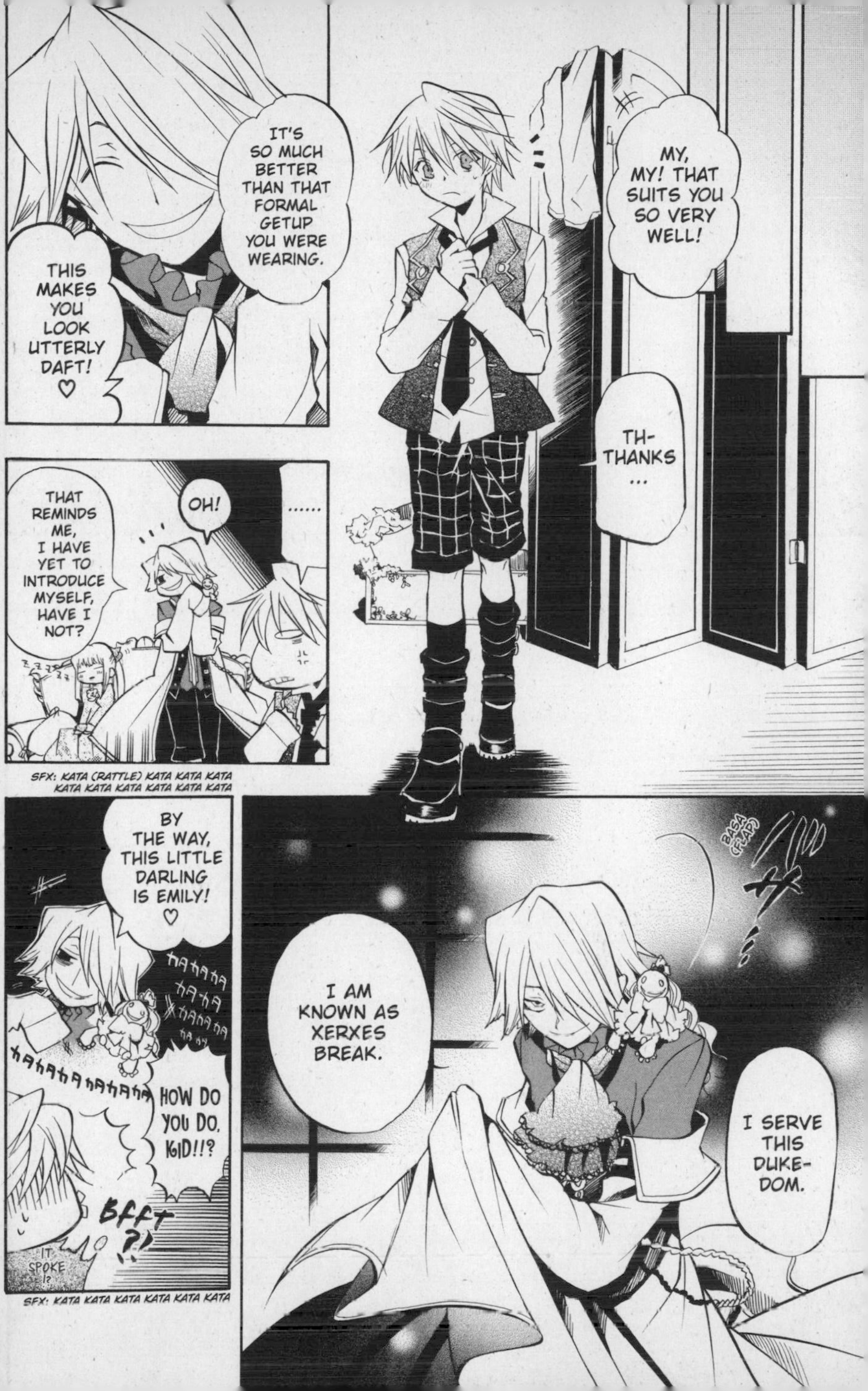
MY, MY! THAT SUITS YOU SO VERY WELL!
TH-THANKS...
IT'S SO MUCH BETTER THAN THAT FORMAL GETUP YOU WERE WEARING.
THIS MAKES YOU LOOK UTTERLY DAFT! ♡
......
OH!
THAT REMINDS ME, I HAVE YET TO INTRODUCE MYSELF, HAVE I NOT?
SFX: KATA (RATTLE) KATA KATA KATA KATA KATA KATA KATA KATA KATA KATA
BASA (FLAP)
I AM KNOWN AS XERXES BREAK.
I SERVE THIS DUKEDOM.
BY THE WAY, THIS LITTLE DARLING IS EMILY! ♡
HOW DO YOU DO, KID!!?
Bfft ?!
IT SPOKE!?
SFX: KATA KATA KATA KATA KATA KATA

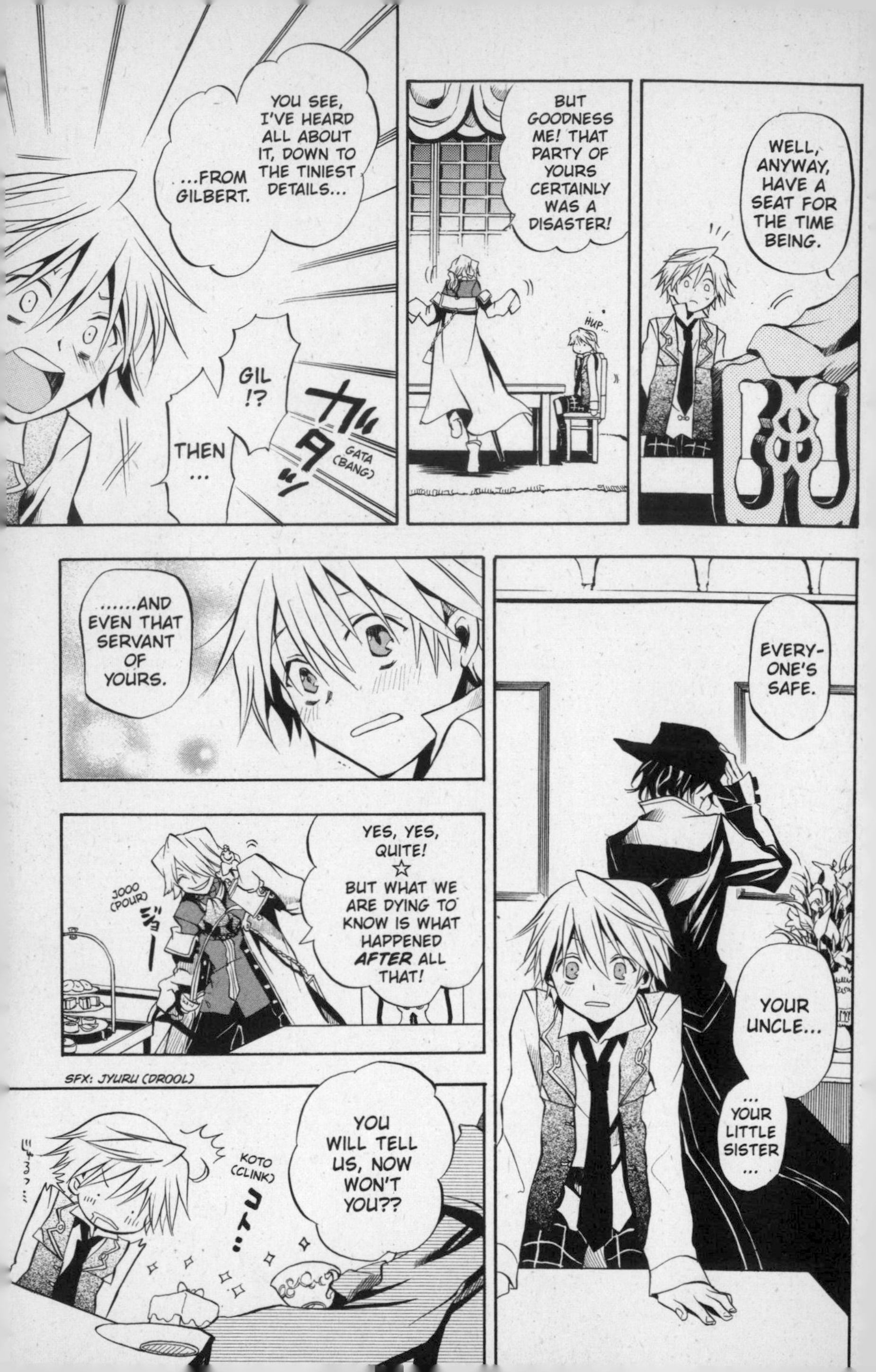
WELL, ANYWAY, HAVE A SEAT FOR THE TIME BEING.
BUT GOODNESS ME! THAT PARTY OF YOURS CERTAINLY WAS A DISASTER!
HUP...
YOU SEE, I'VE HEARD ALL ABOUT IT, DOWN TO THE TINIEST DETAILS...
...FROM GILBERT.
GIL !?
GATA (BANG)
THEN ...
EVERY-ONE'S SAFE.
YOUR UNCLE...
... YOUR LITTLE SISTER ...
......AND EVEN THAT SERVANT OF YOURS.
YES, YES, QUITE! ☆ BUT WHAT WE ARE DYING TO KNOW IS WHAT HAPPENED AFTER ALL THAT!
JOOO (POUR)
YOU WILL TELL US, NOW WON'T YOU??
KOTO (CLINK)
SFX: JYURU (DROOL)

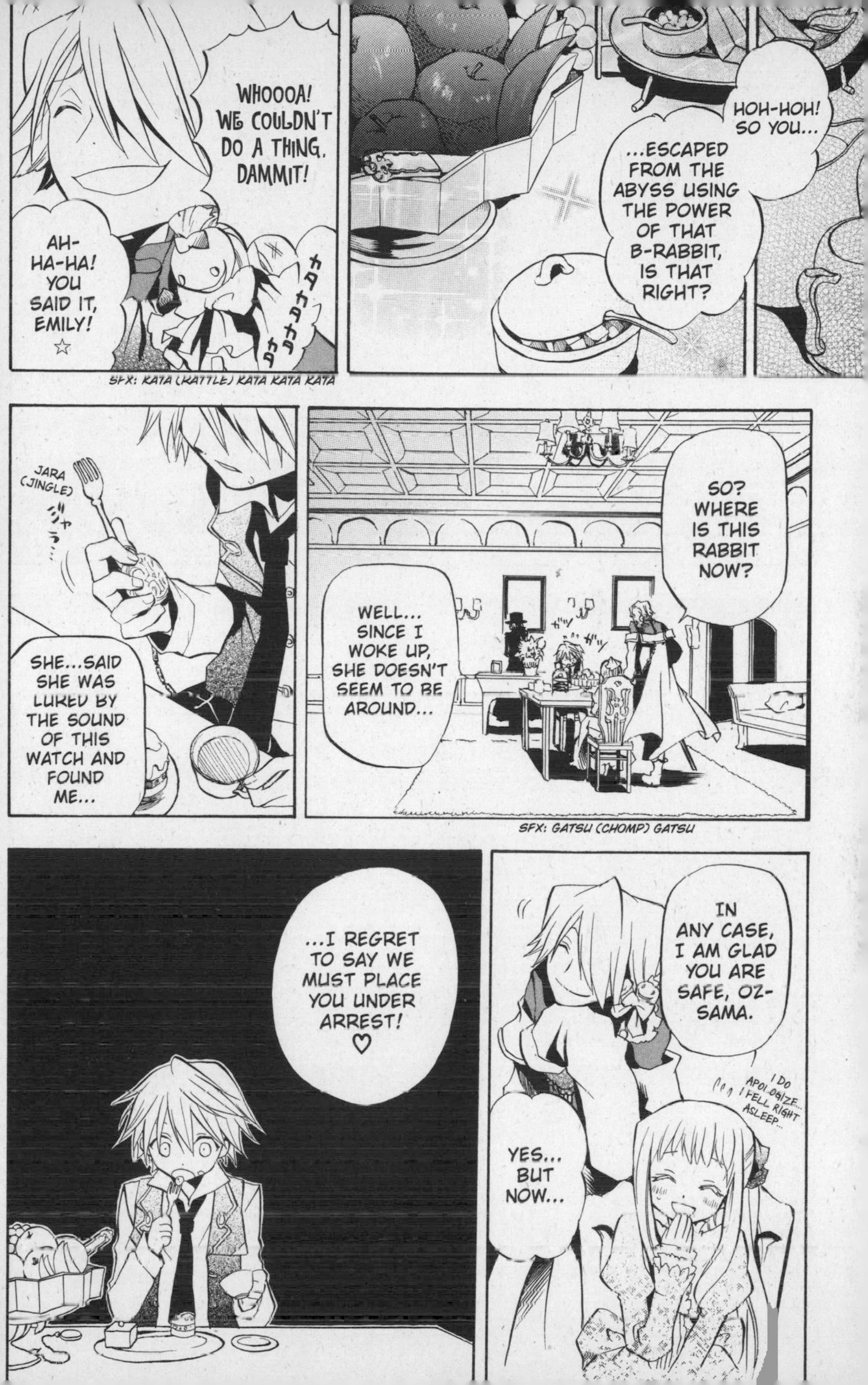
HOH-HOH! SO YOU...
...ESCAPED FROM THE ABYSS USING THE POWER OF THAT B-RABBIT, IS THAT RIGHT?
WHOOOA! WE COULDN'T DO A THING, DAMMIT!
AH-HA-HA! YOU SAID IT, EMILY! ☆
カタカタカタカタ
SFX: KATA (RATTLE) KATA KATA KATA
SO? WHERE IS THIS RABBIT NOW?
WELL... SINCE I WOKE UP, SHE DOESN'T SEEM TO BE AROUND...
SFX: GATSU (CHOMP) GATSU
JARA (JINGLE)
SHE...SAID SHE WAS LURED BY THE SOUND OF THIS WATCH AND FOUND ME...
IN ANY CASE, I AM GLAD YOU ARE SAFE, OZ-SAMA.
I DO APOLOGIZE... I FELL RIGHT ASLEEP...
YES... BUT NOW...
...I REGRET TO SAY WE MUST PLACE YOU UNDER ARREST! ♡

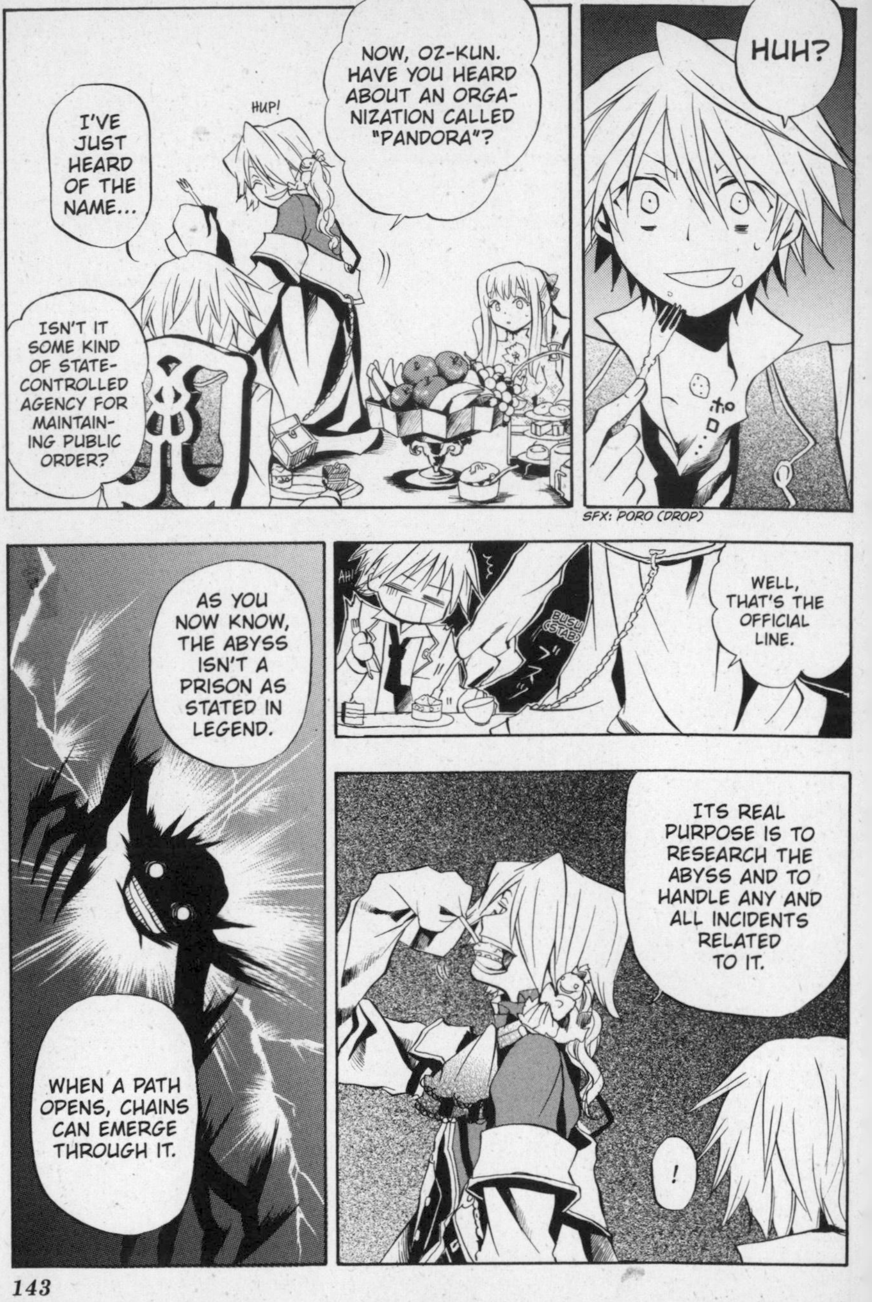
HUH?
SFX: PORO (DROP)
NOW, OZ-KUN. HAVE YOU HEARD ABOUT AN ORGA-NIZATION CALLED "PANDORA"?
HUP!
I'VE JUST HEARD OF THE NAME...
ISN'T IT SOME KIND OF STATE-CONTROLLED AGENCY FOR MAINTAIN-ING PUBLIC ORDER?
WELL, THAT'S THE OFFICIAL LINE.
AH!
BUSU (STAB)
ITS REAL PURPOSE IS TO RESEARCH THE ABYSS AND TO HANDLE ANY AND ALL INCIDENTS RELATED TO IT.
!
AS YOU NOW KNOW, THE ABYSS ISN'T A PRISON AS STATED IN LEGEND.
WHEN A PATH OPENS, CHAINS CAN EMERGE THROUGH IT.

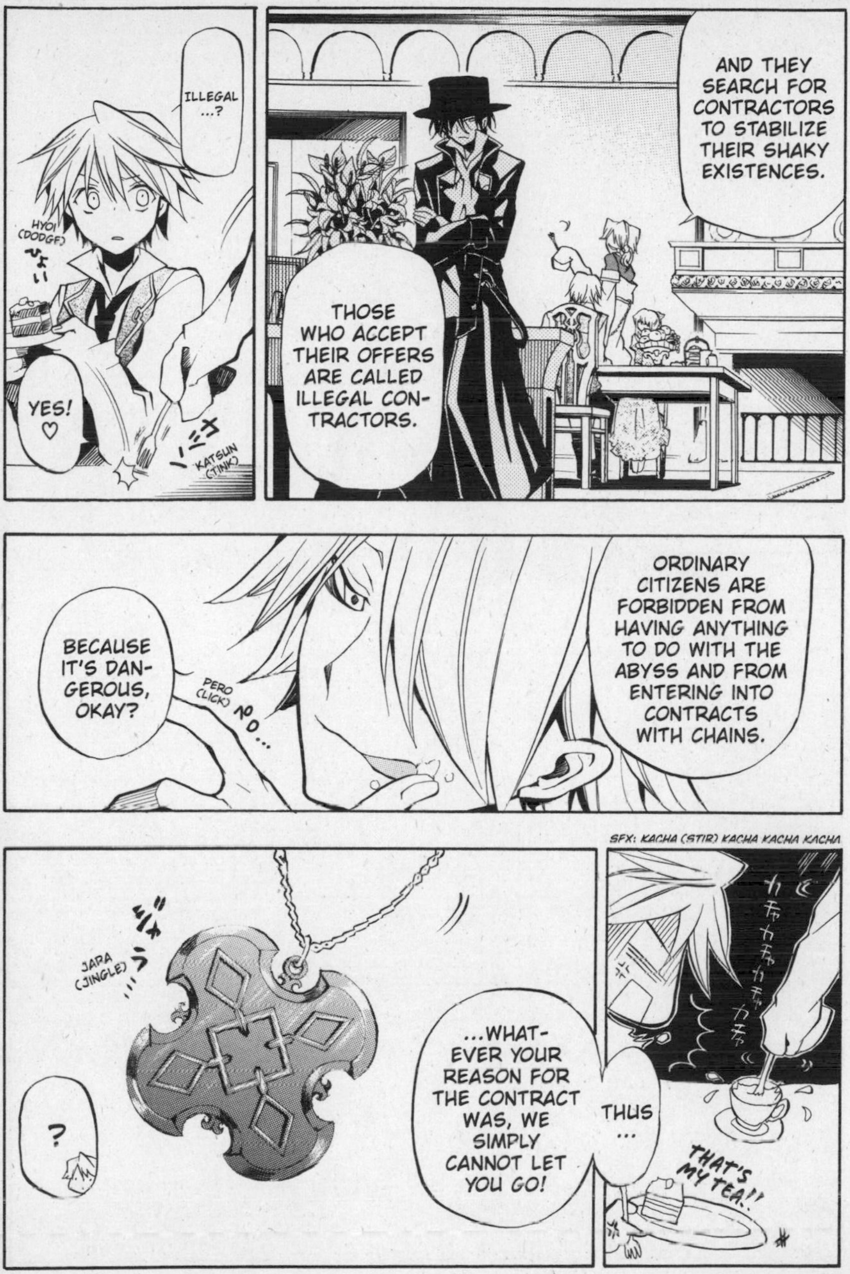
AND THEY SEARCH FOR CONTRACTORS TO STABILIZE THEIR SHAKY EXISTENCES.
THOSE WHO ACCEPT THEIR OFFERS ARE CALLED ILLEGAL CON-TRACTORS.
ILLEGAL ...?
HYOI (DODGE)
YES! ♡
KATSUN (TINK)
ORDINARY CITIZENS ARE FORBIDDEN FROM HAVING ANYTHING TO DO WITH THE ABYSS AND FROM ENTERING INTO CONTRACTS WITH CHAINS.
PERO (LICK)
BECAUSE IT'S DAN-GEROUS, OKAY?
SFX: KACHA (STIR) KACHA KACHA KACHA
THAT'S MY TEA!!
THUS ...
...WHAT-EVER YOUR REASON FOR THE CONTRACT WAS, WE SIMPLY CANNOT LET YOU GO!
JAPA (JINGLE)
?

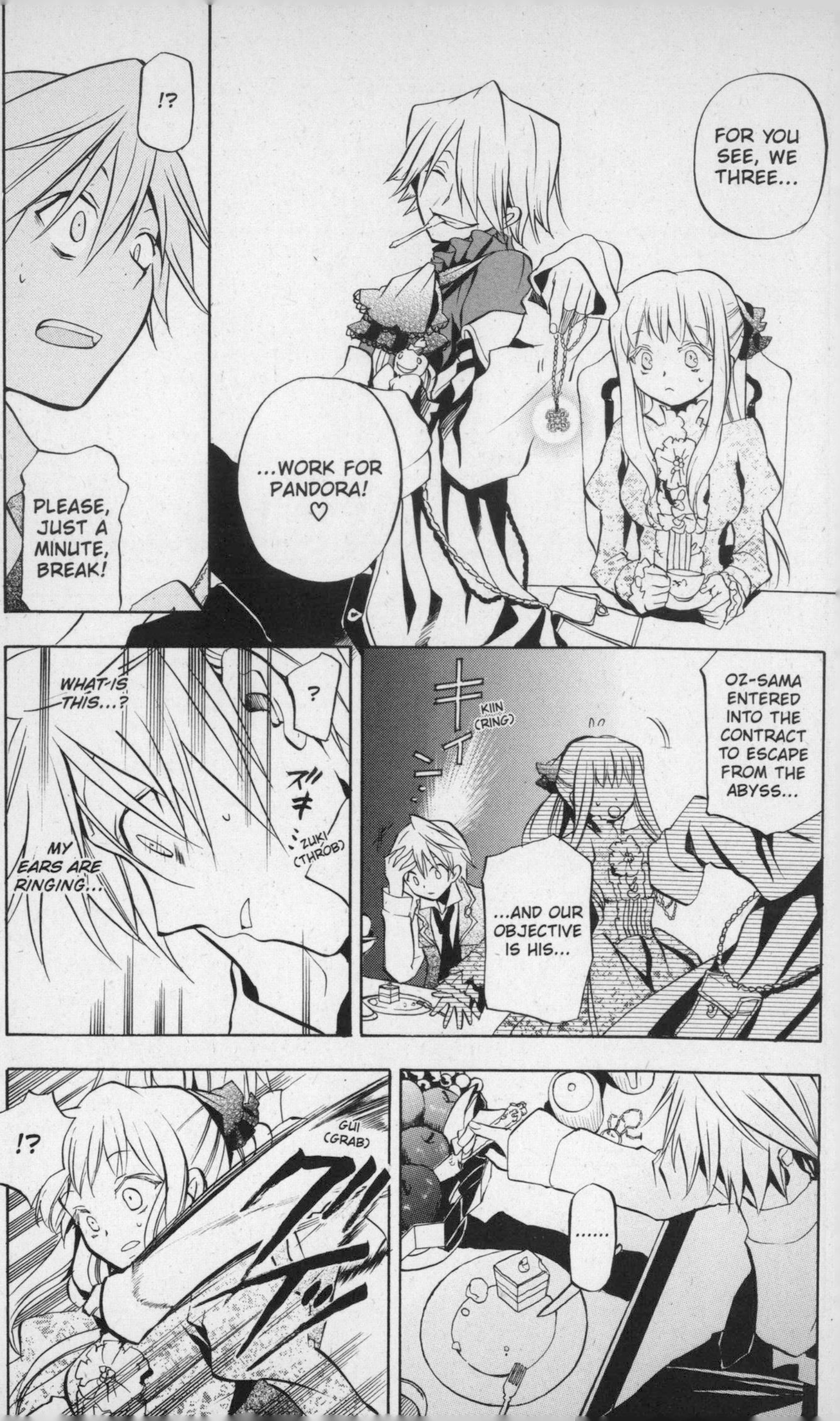
FOR YOU SEE, WE THREE...
...WORK FOR PANDORA! ♡
!?
PLEASE, JUST A MINUTE, BREAK!
OZ-SAMA ENTERED INTO THE CONTRACT TO ESCAPE FROM THE ABYSS...
KIIN (RING)
...AND OUR OBJECTIVE IS HIS...
WHAT IS THIS...?
?
ZUKI (THROB)
MY EARS ARE RINGING...
......
GUI (GRAB)
!?

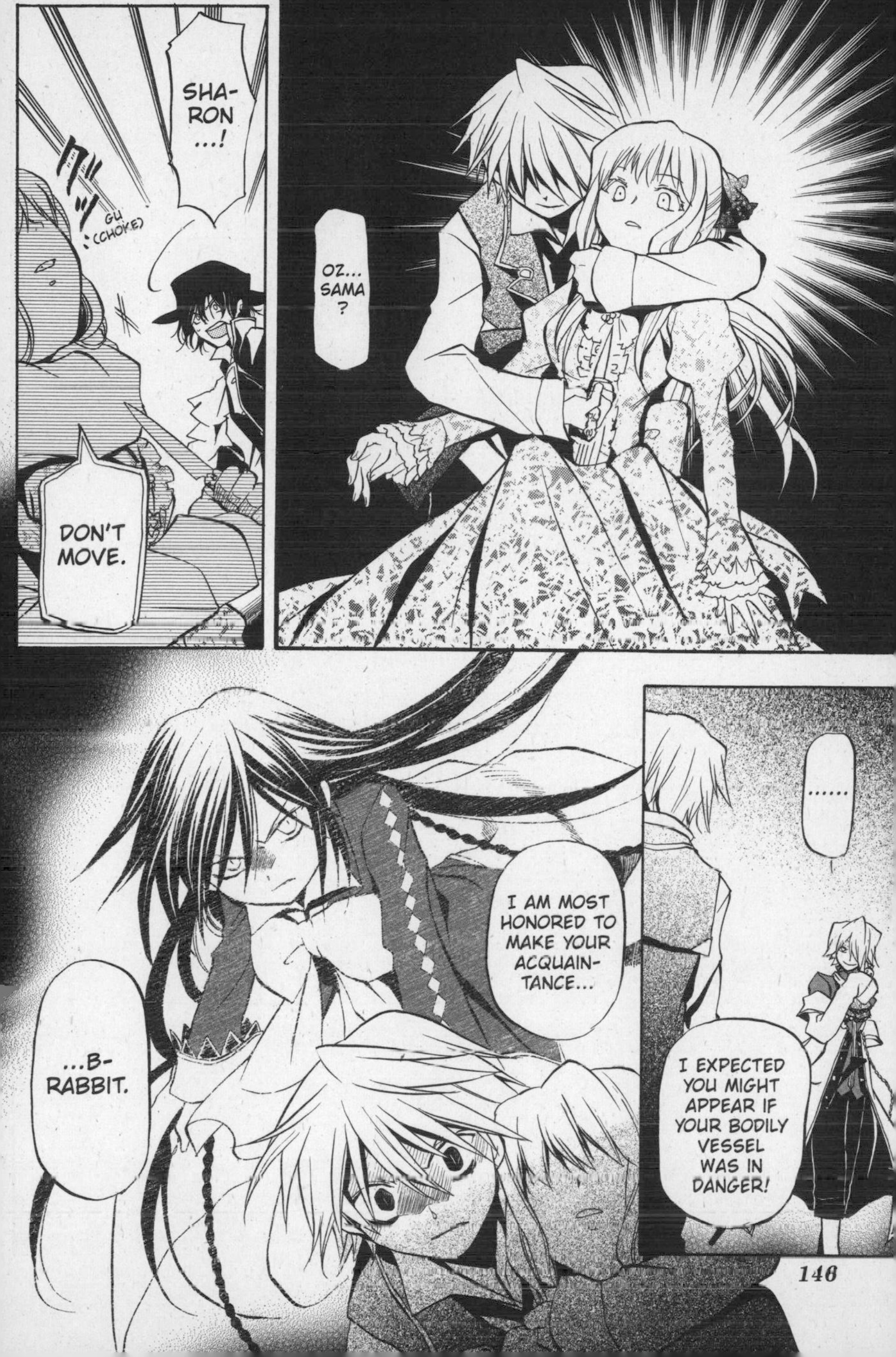
OZ... SAMA ?
SHA-RON ...!
GU (CHOKE)
DON'T MOVE.
......
I EXPECTED YOU MIGHT APPEAR IF YOUR BODILY VESSEL WAS IN DANGER!
I AM MOST HONORED TO MAKE YOUR ACQUAIN-TANCE...
...B-RABBIT.

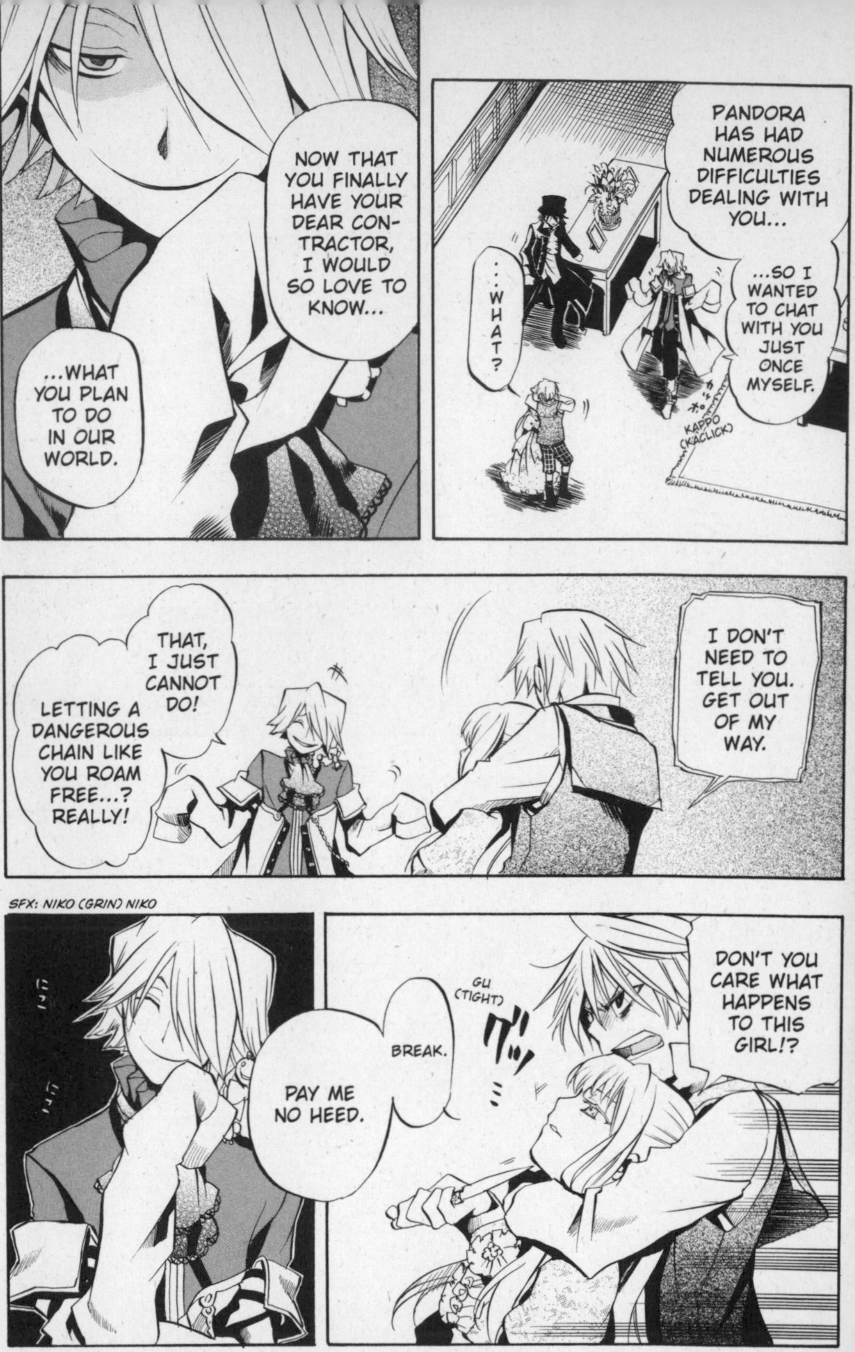
PANDORA HAS HAD NUMEROUS DIFFICULTIES DEALING WITH YOU...
...SO I WANTED TO CHAT WITH YOU JUST ONCE MYSELF.
KAPPO (KACLICK)
...WHAT?
NOW THAT YOU FINALLY HAVE YOUR DEAR CONTRACTOR, I WOULD SO LOVE TO KNOW...
...WHAT YOU PLAN TO DO IN OUR WORLD.
I DON'T NEED TO TELL YOU. GET OUT OF MY WAY.
THAT, I JUST CANNOT DO!
LETTING A DANGEROUS CHAIN LIKE YOU ROAM FREE...? REALLY!
SFX: NIKO (GRIN) NIKO
DON'T YOU CARE WHAT HAPPENS TO THIS GIRL!?
GU (TIGHT)
BREAK.
PAY ME NO HEED.

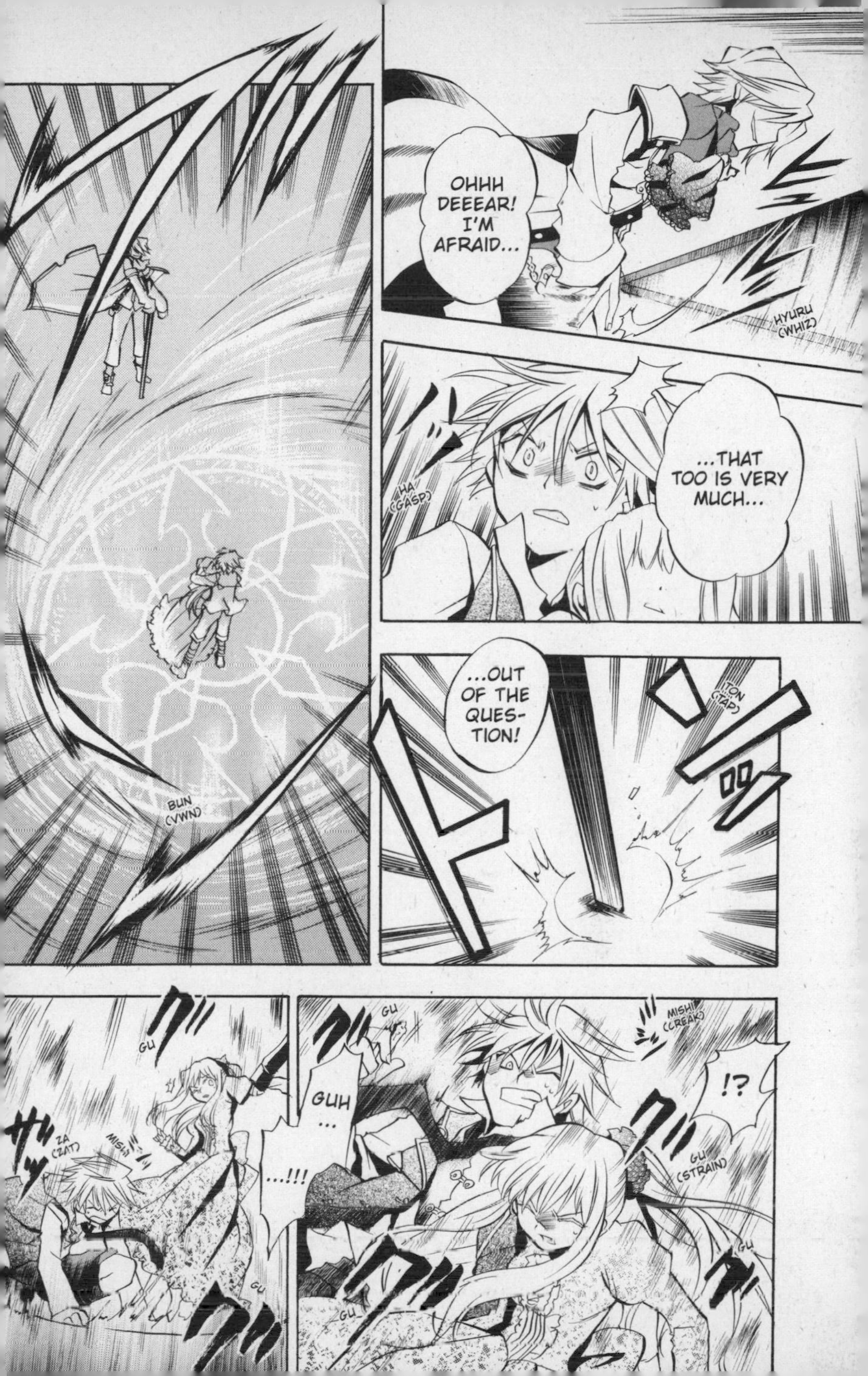
OHHH DEEEAR! I'M AFRAID...
HYURU (WHIZ)
...THAT TOO IS VERY MUCH...
HA (GASP)
TON (TAP)
...OUT OF THE QUES- TION!
BUN (VWN)
MISHI (CREAK)
!?
GU
GU (STRAIN)
GU
GUH ...
...!!!
GU
GU
MISHI
ZA (ZAT)
GU

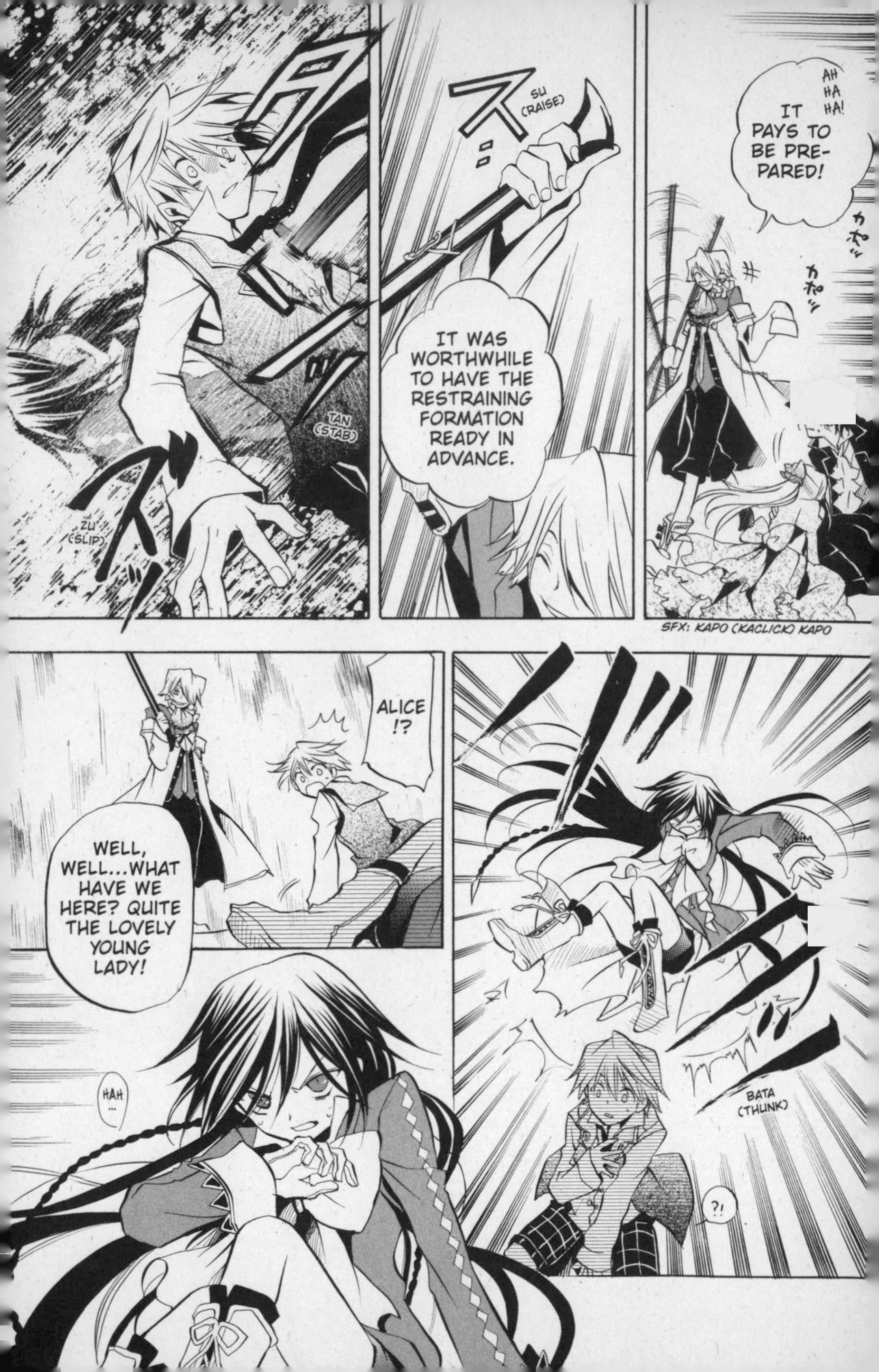
AH HA HA!
IT PAYS TO BE PRE-PARED!
カポッ
カポッ
SFX: KAPO (KACLICK) KAPO
SU (RAISE)
IT WAS WORTHWHILE TO HAVE THE RESTRAINING FORMATION READY IN ADVANCE.
TAN (STAB)
ZU (SLIP)
BATA (THUNK)
?!
ALICE !?
WELL, WELL...WHAT HAVE WE HERE? QUITE THE LOVELY YOUNG LADY!
HAH...

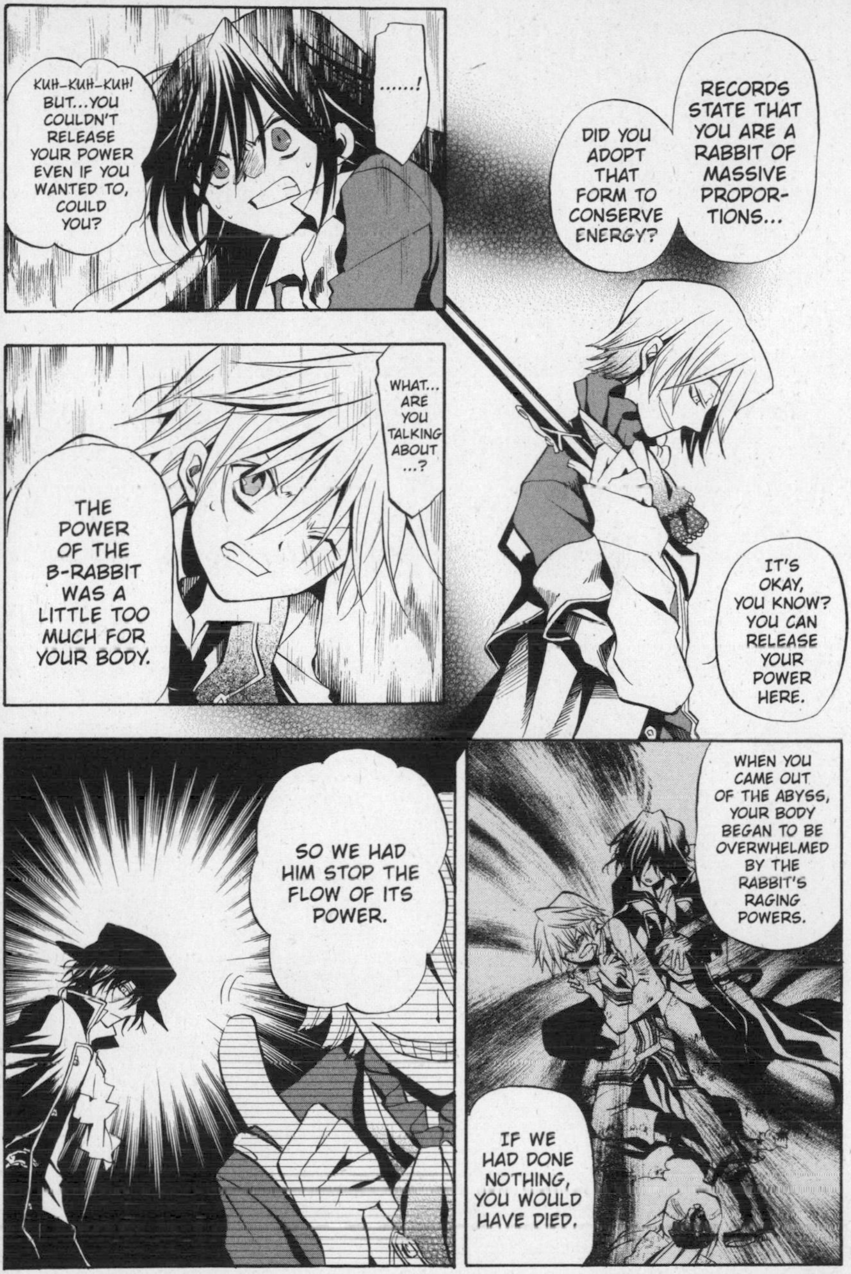
RECORDS STATE THAT YOU ARE A RABBIT OF MASSIVE PROPORTIONS...
DID YOU ADOPT THAT FORM TO CONSERVE ENERGY?
IT'S OKAY, YOU KNOW? YOU CAN RELEASE YOUR POWER HERE.
......!
KUH-KUH-KUH! BUT...YOU COULDN'T RELEASE YOUR POWER EVEN IF YOU WANTED TO, COULD YOU?
WHAT... ARE YOU TALKING ABOUT ...?
THE POWER OF THE B-RABBIT WAS A LITTLE TOO MUCH FOR YOUR BODY.
WHEN YOU CAME OUT OF THE ABYSS, YOUR BODY BEGAN TO BE OVERWHELMED BY THE RABBIT'S RAGING POWERS.
IF WE HAD DONE NOTHING, YOU WOULD HAVE DIED.
SO WE HAD HIM STOP THE FLOW OF ITS POWER.

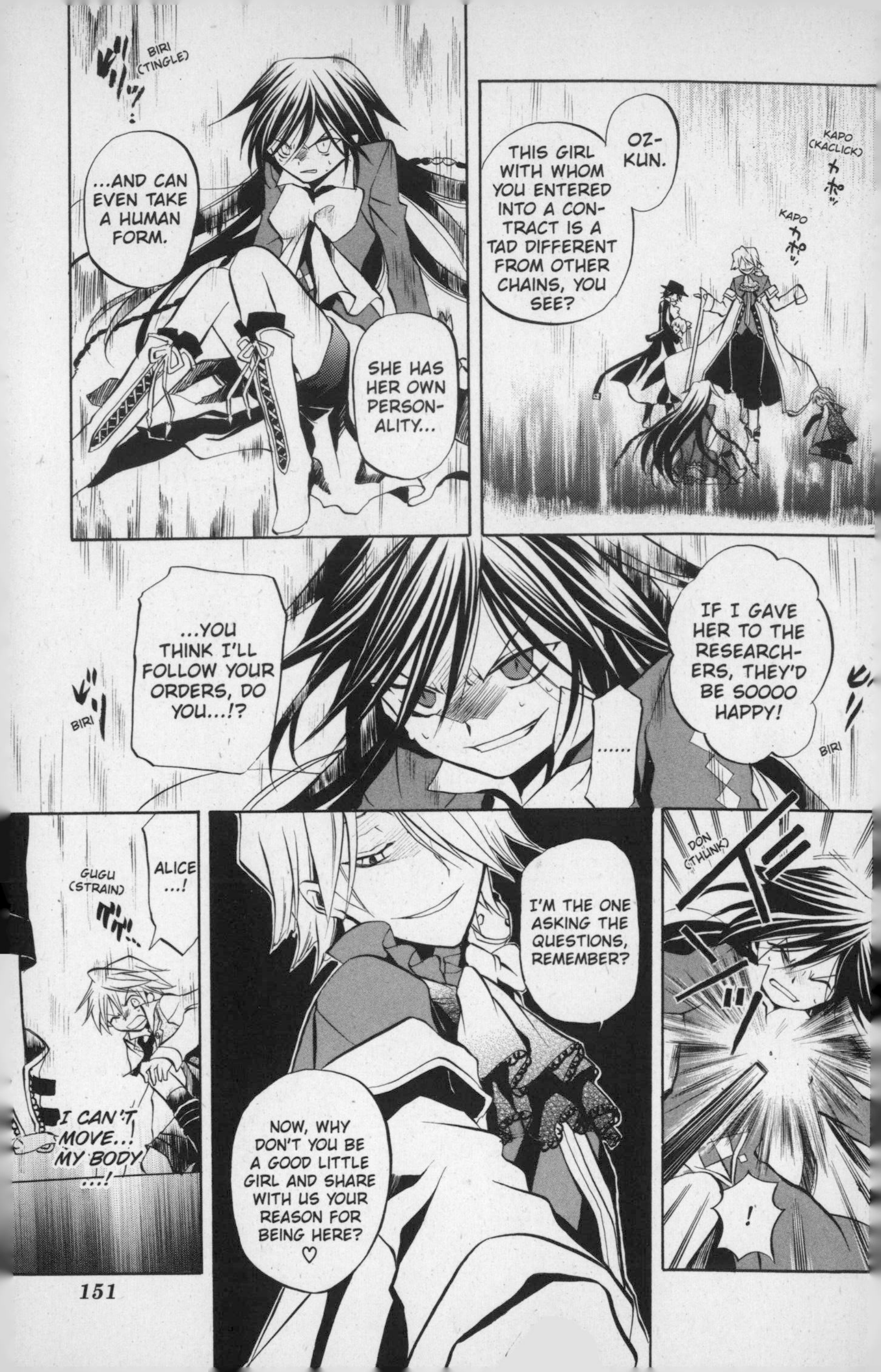
OZ-KUN.
THIS GIRL WITH WHOM YOU ENTERED INTO A CONTRACT IS A TAD DIFFERENT FROM OTHER CHAINS, YOU SEE?
KAPO (KACLICK)
KAPO
BIRI (TINGLE)
SHE HAS HER OWN PERSONALITY...
...AND CAN EVEN TAKE A HUMAN FORM.
IF I GAVE HER TO THE RESEARCHERS, THEY'D BE SOOOO HAPPY!
BIRI
......
...YOU THINK I'LL FOLLOW YOUR ORDERS, DO YOU...!?
BIRI
DON (THUNK)
!
I'M THE ONE ASKING THE QUESTIONS, REMEMBER?
NOW, WHY DON'T YOU BE A GOOD LITTLE GIRL AND SHARE WITH US YOUR REASON FOR BEING HERE? ♡
ALICE ...!
GUGU (STRAIN)
I CAN'T MOVE... MY BODY ...!

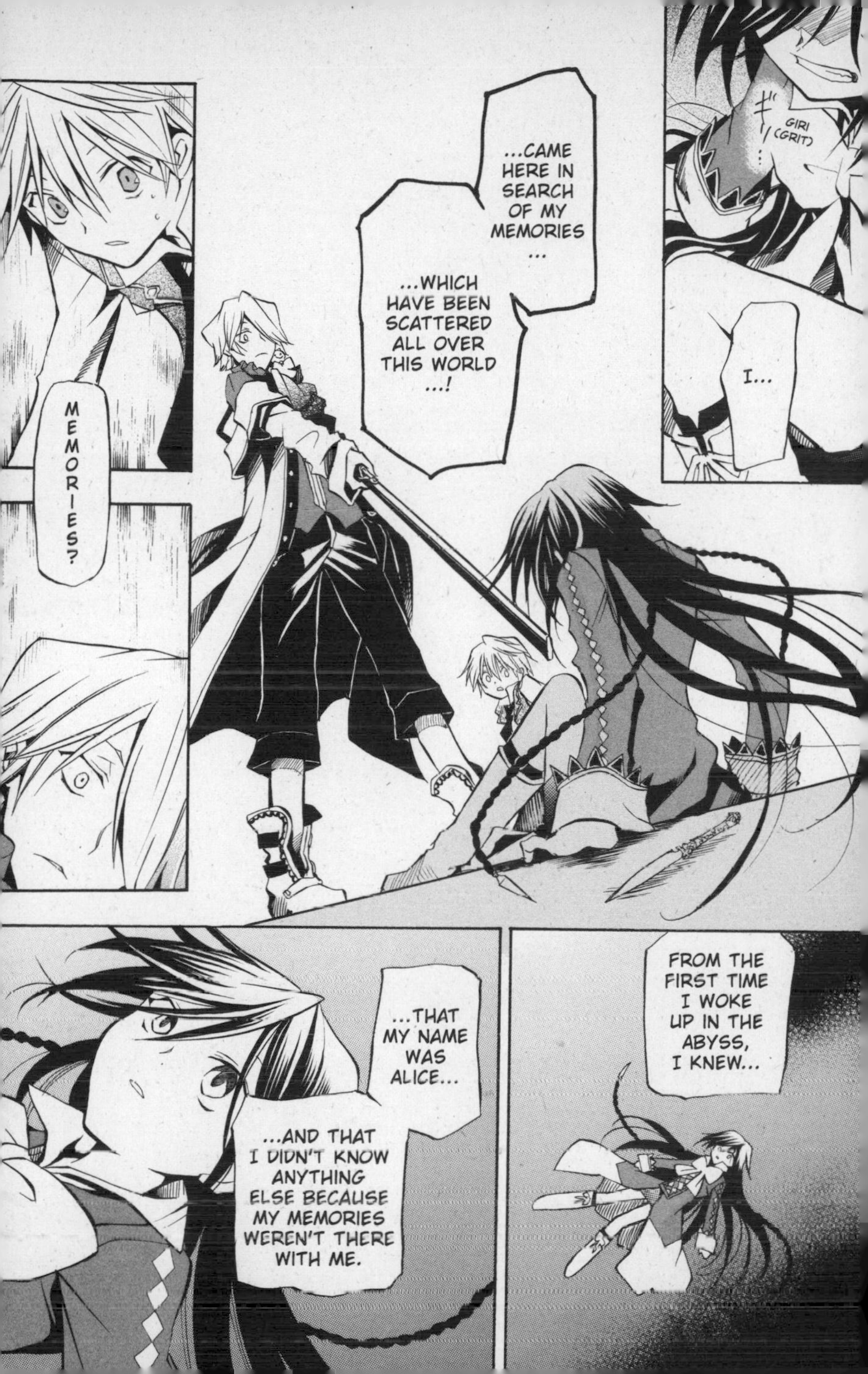
GIRI (GRIT)
I...
...CAME HERE IN SEARCH OF MY MEMORIES ...
...WHICH HAVE BEEN SCATTERED ALL OVER THIS WORLD ...!
MEMORIES?
FROM THE FIRST TIME I WOKE UP IN THE ABYSS, I KNEW...
...THAT MY NAME WAS ALICE...
...AND THAT I DIDN'T KNOW ANYTHING ELSE BECAUSE MY MEMORIES WEREN'T THERE WITH ME.

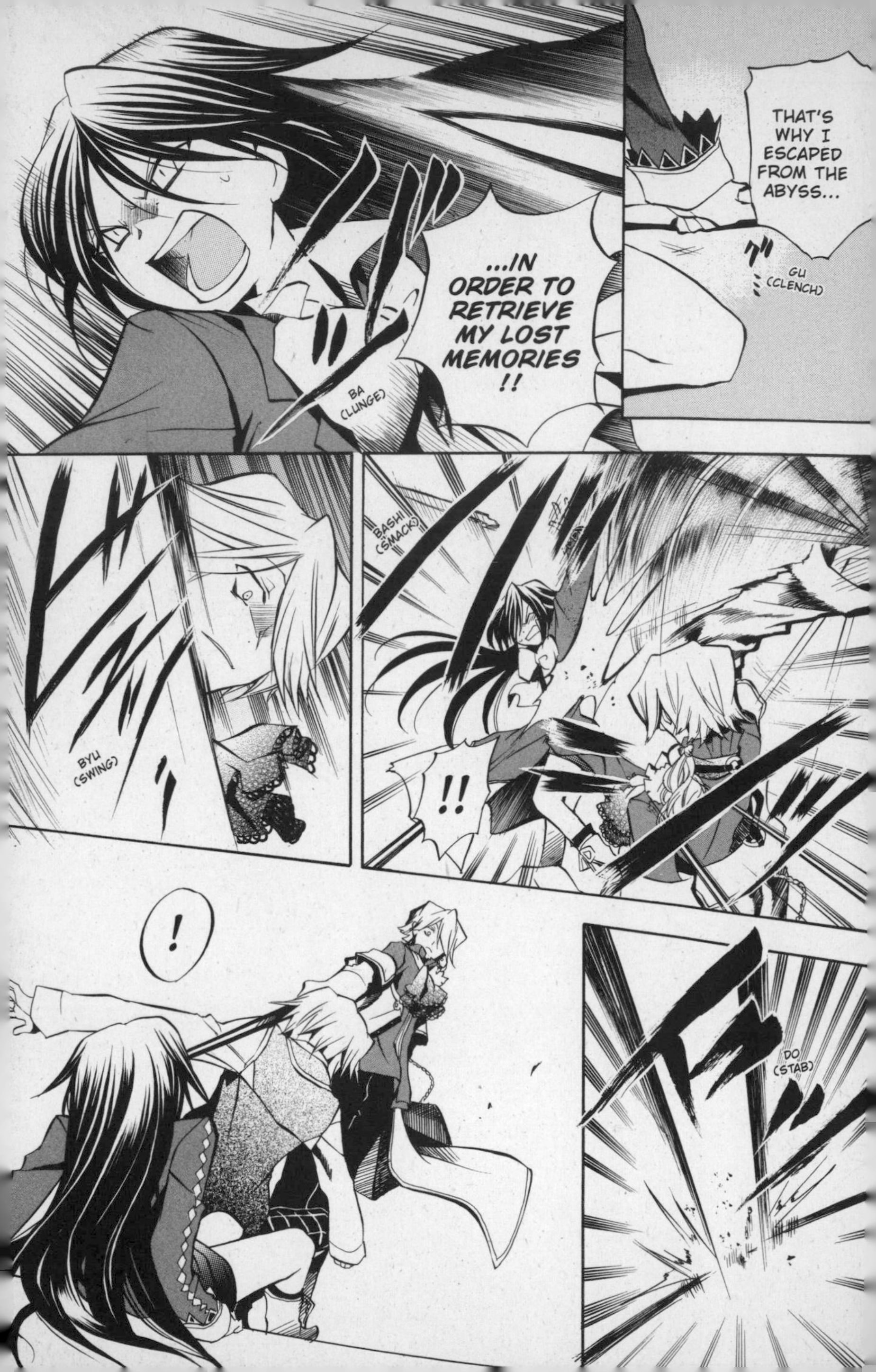
THAT'S WHY I ESCAPED FROM THE ABYSS...
GU (CLENCH)
...IN ORDER TO RETRIEVE MY LOST MEMORIES !!
BA (LUNGE)
BASHI (SMACK)
!!
BYU (SWING)
DO (STAB)
!

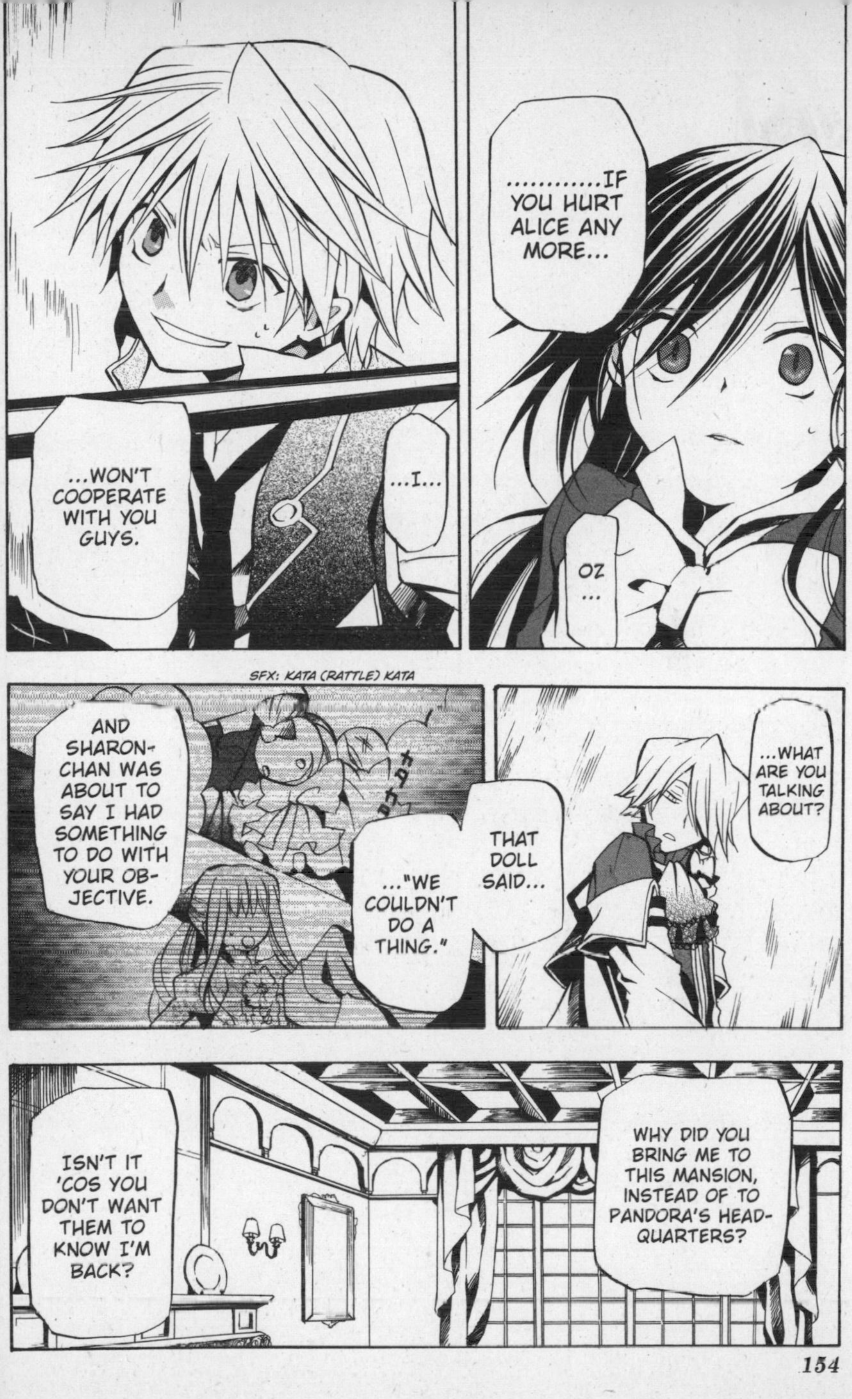
............IF YOU HURT ALICE ANY MORE...
OZ ...
...I...
...WON'T COOPERATE WITH YOU GUYS.
SFX: KATA (RATTLE) KATA
...WHAT ARE YOU TALKING ABOUT?
THAT DOLL SAID...
..."WE COULDN'T DO A THING."
AND SHARON-CHAN WAS ABOUT TO SAY I HAD SOMETHING TO DO WITH YOUR OBJECTIVE.
WHY DID YOU BRING ME TO THIS MANSION, INSTEAD OF TO PANDORA'S HEADQUARTERS?
ISN'T IT 'COS YOU DON'T WANT THEM TO KNOW I'M BACK?

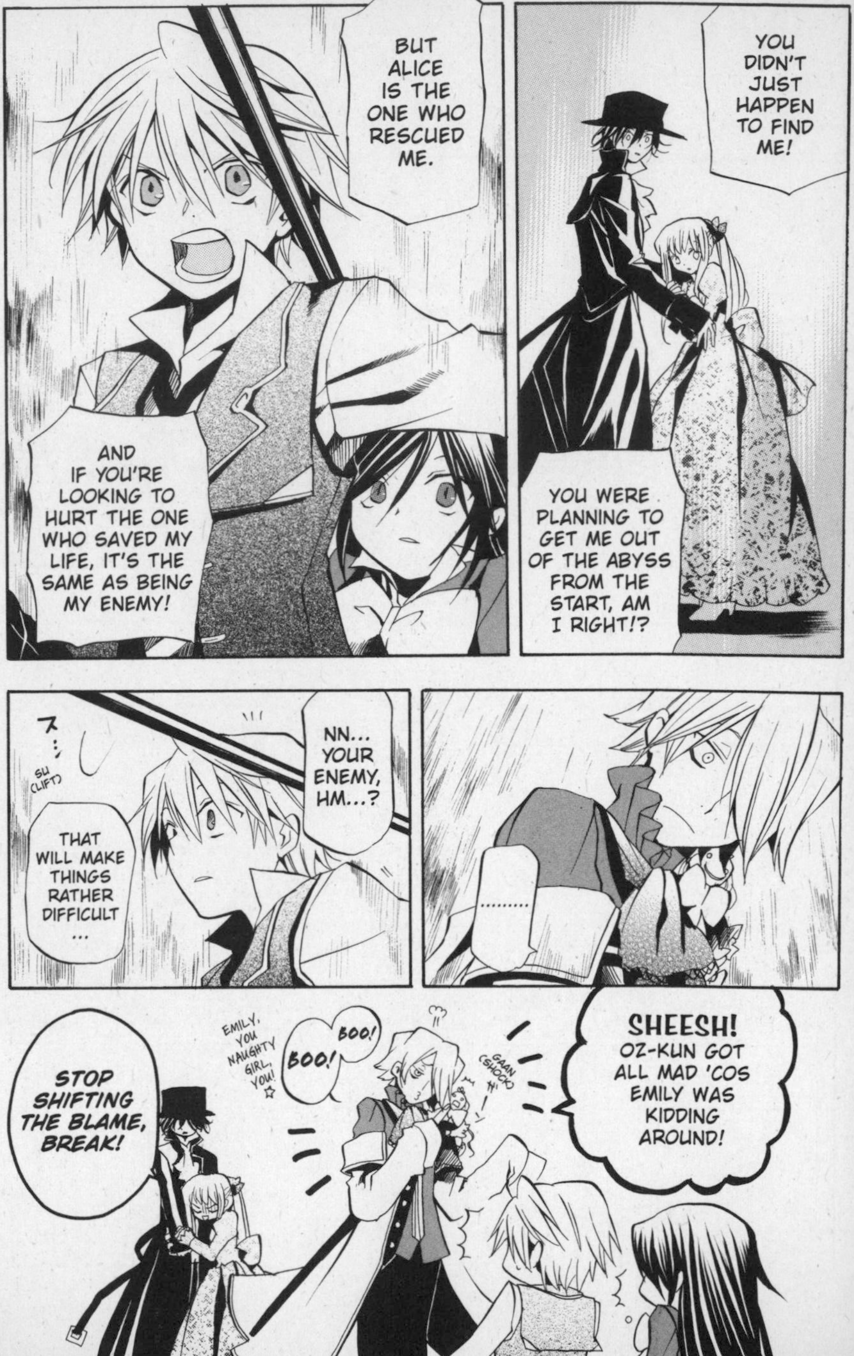
YOU DIDN'T JUST HAPPEN TO FIND ME!
YOU WERE PLANNING TO GET ME OUT OF THE ABYSS FROM THE START, AM I RIGHT!?
BUT ALICE IS THE ONE WHO RESCUED ME.
AND IF YOU'RE LOOKING TO HURT THE ONE WHO SAVED MY LIFE, IT'S THE SAME AS BEING MY ENEMY!
.........
NN... YOUR ENEMY, HM...?
SU (LIFT)
THAT WILL MAKE THINGS RATHER DIFFICULT ...
SHEESH! OZ-KUN GOT ALL MAD 'COS EMILY WAS KIDDING AROUND!
GAAN (SHOCK)
BOO!
BOO!
EMILY, YOU NAUGHTY GIRL, YOU!
STOP SHIFTING THE BLAME, BREAK!

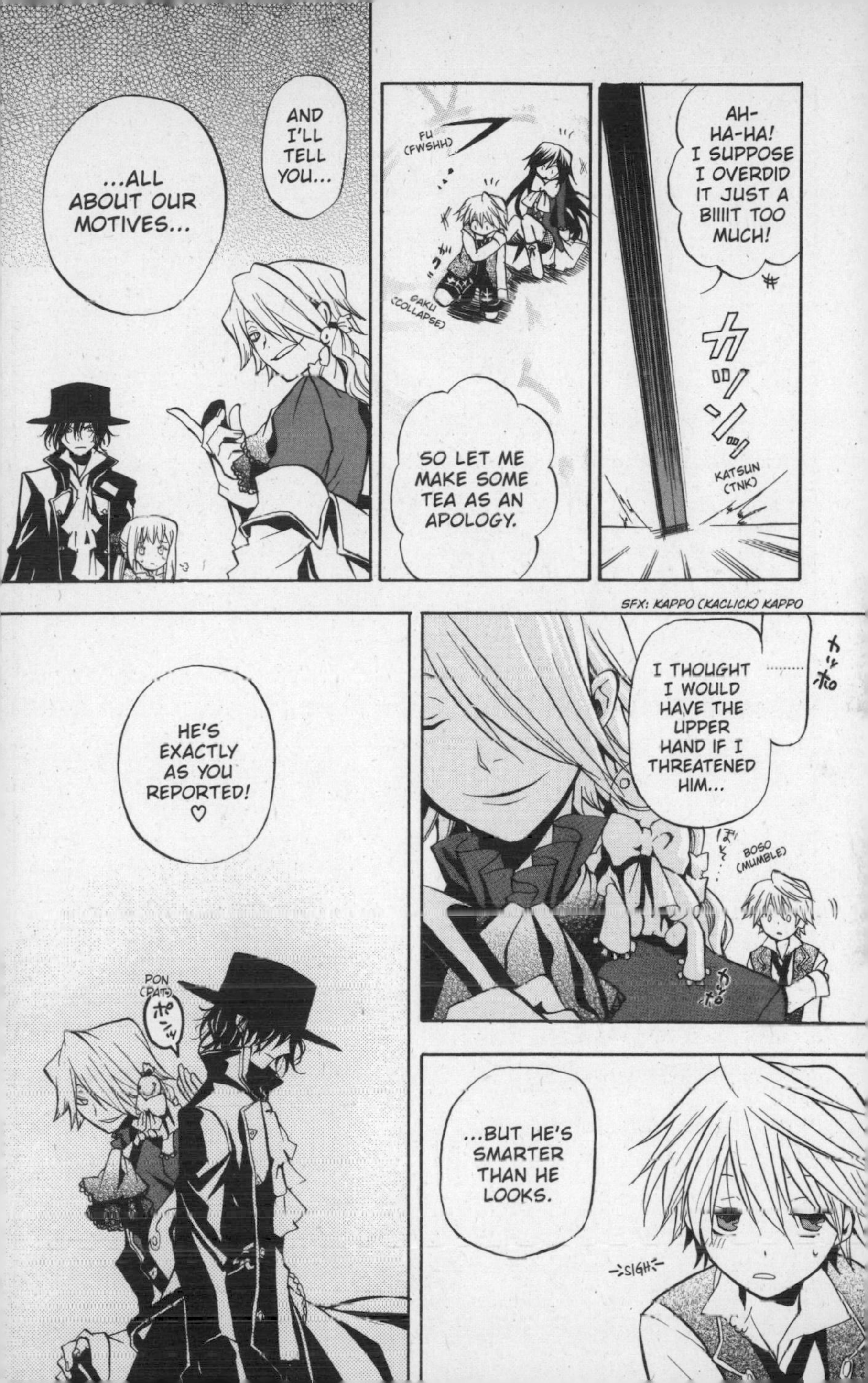
AH-HA-HA! I SUPPOSE I OVERDID IT JUST A BIIIIT TOO MUCH!
KATSUN (TNK)
FU (FWSHH)
GAKU (COLLAPSE)
SO LET ME MAKE SOME TEA AS AN APOLOGY.
AND I'LL TELL YOU...
...ALL ABOUT OUR MOTIVES...
SFX: KAPPO (KACLICK) KAPPO
I THOUGHT I WOULD HAVE THE UPPER HAND IF I THREATENED HIM...
BOSO (MUMBLE)
...BUT HE'S SMARTER THAN HE LOOKS.
SIGH
HE'S EXACTLY AS YOU REPORTED! ♡
PON (PAT)

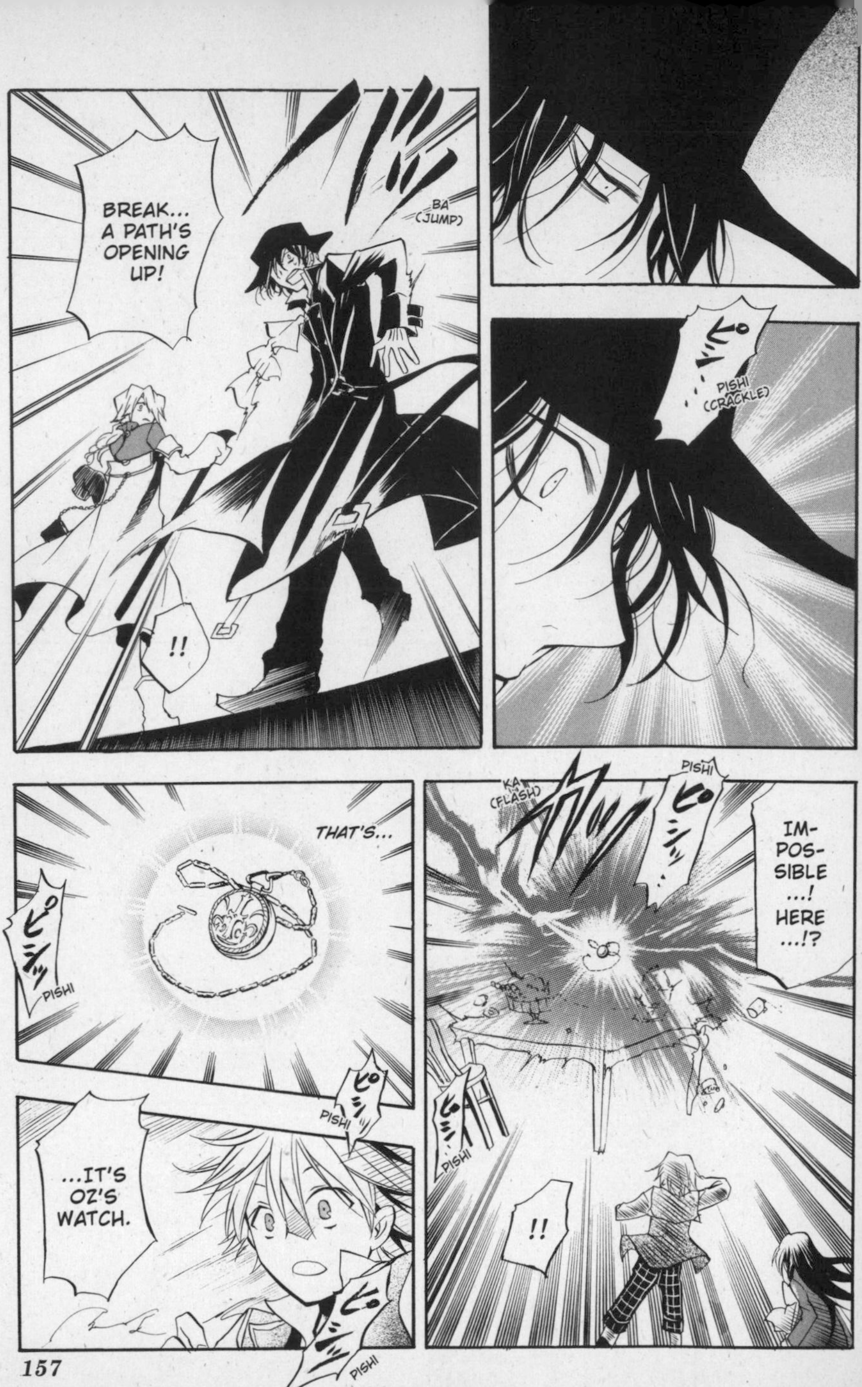
PISHI (CRACKLE)
BA (JUMP)
BREAK... A PATH'S OPENING UP!
!!
KA (FLASH)
PISHI
IMPOSSIBLE ...! HERE ...!?
PISHI
!!
THAT'S...
PISHI
PISHI
...IT'S OZ'S WATCH.
PISHI

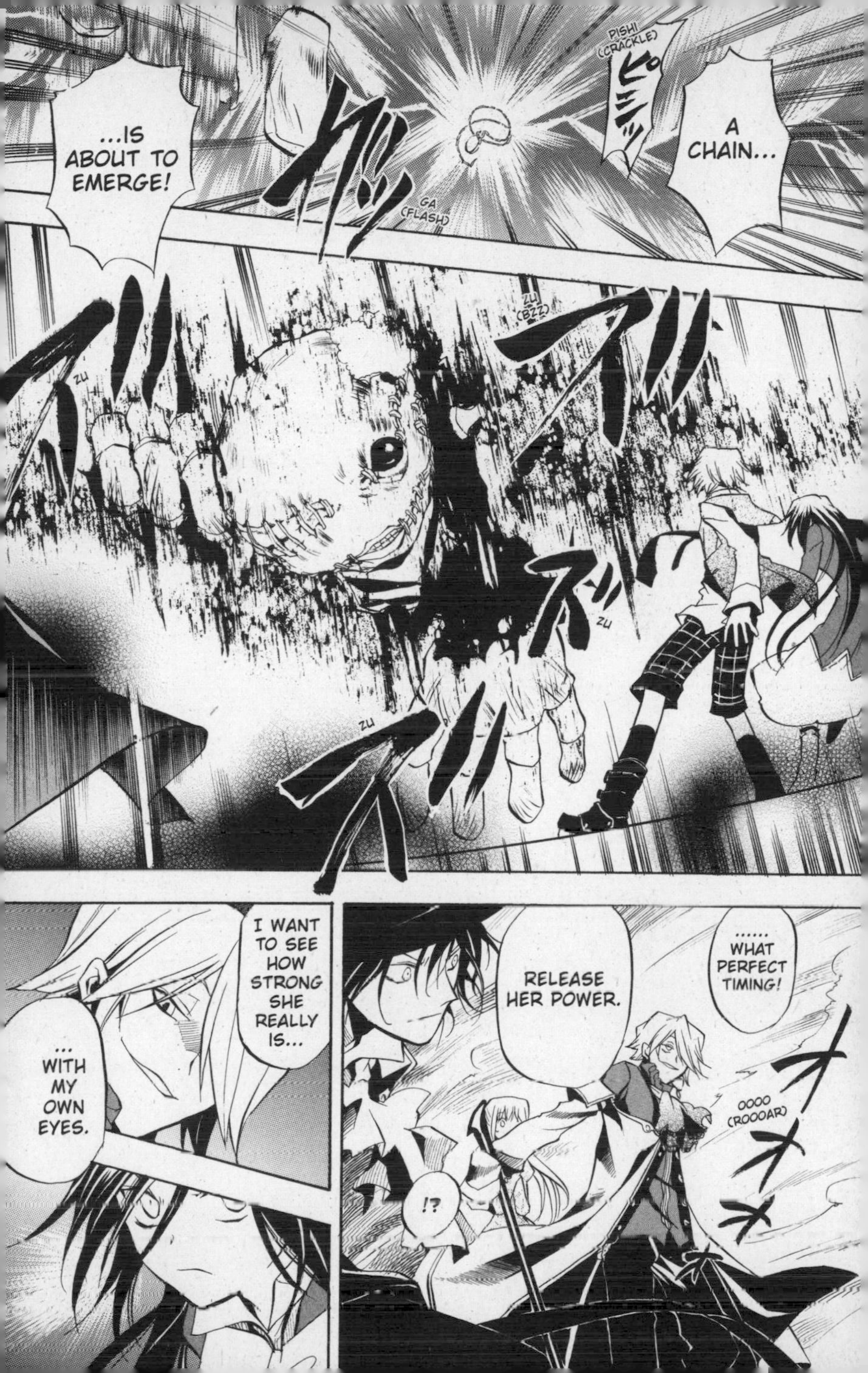
PISHI (CRACKLE)
A CHAIN...
GA (FLASH)
...IS ABOUT TO EMERGE!
ZU (BZZ)
ZU
ZU
ZU
...... WHAT PERFECT TIMING!
RELEASE HER POWER.
OOOO (ROOOAR)
!?
I WANT TO SEE HOW STRONG SHE REALLY IS...
... WITH MY OWN EYES.

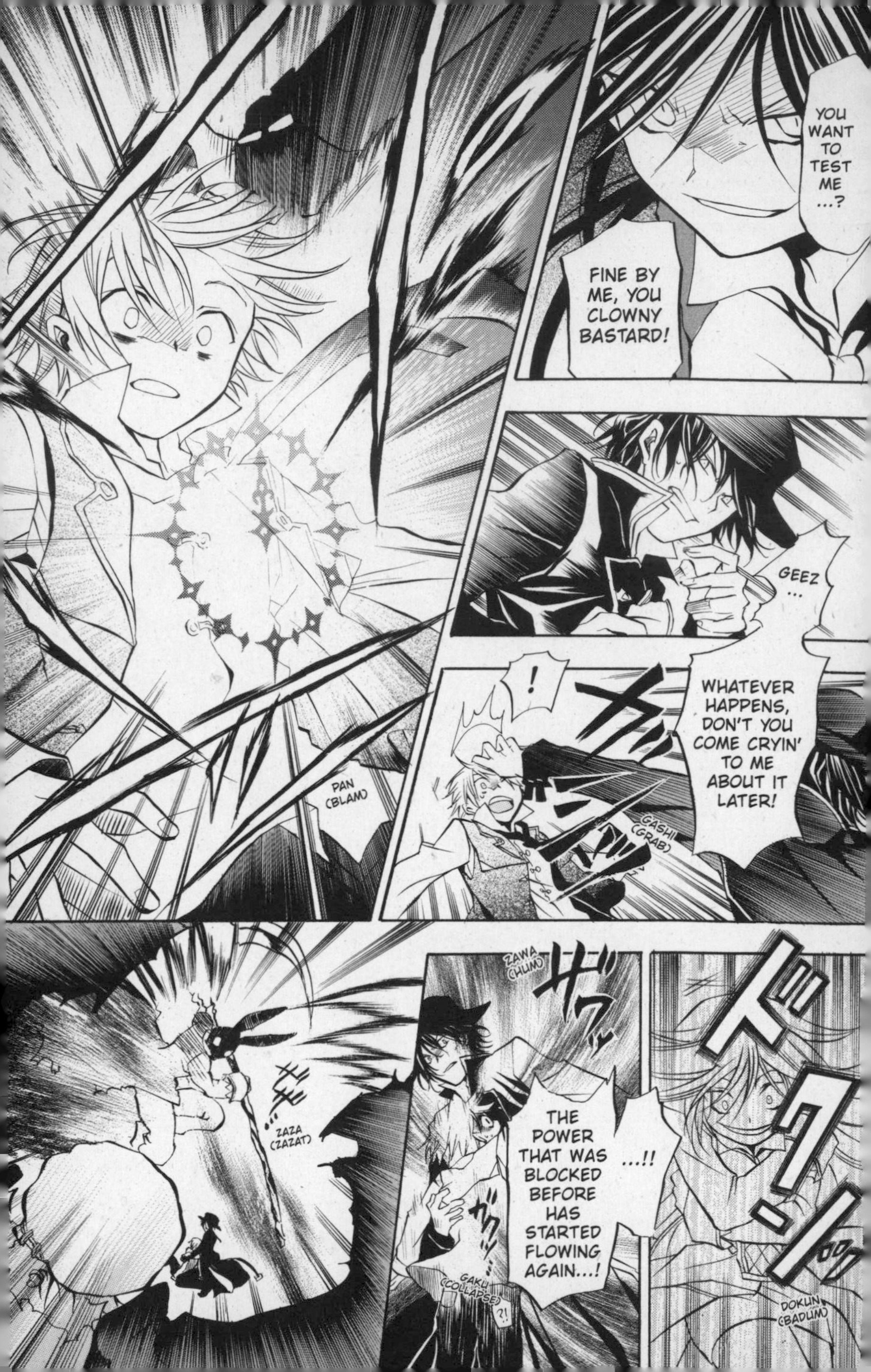
YOU WANT TO TEST ME ...?
FINE BY ME, YOU CLOWNY BASTARD!
GEEZ ...
!
WHATEVER HAPPENS, DON'T YOU COME CRYIN' TO ME ABOUT IT LATER!
GASHI (GRAB)
PAN (BLAM)
DOKUN (BADUM)
ZAWA (HUM)
THE POWER THAT WAS BLOCKED BEFORE HAS STARTED FLOWING AGAIN...!
...!!
GAKU (COLLAPSE)
?!
ZAZA (ZAZAT)

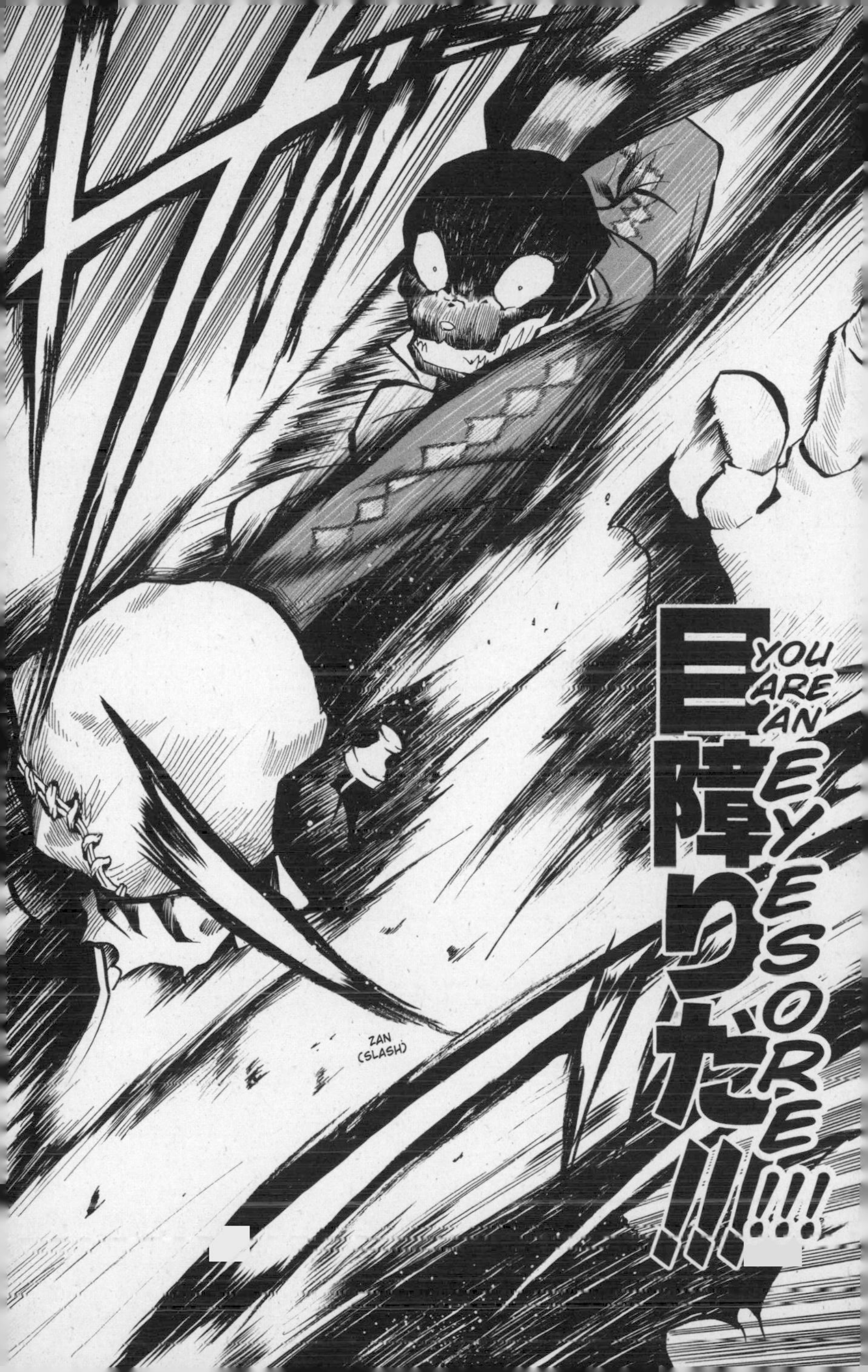
目障りだ!!!
YOU ARE AN EYESORE!!!
ZAN (SLASH)

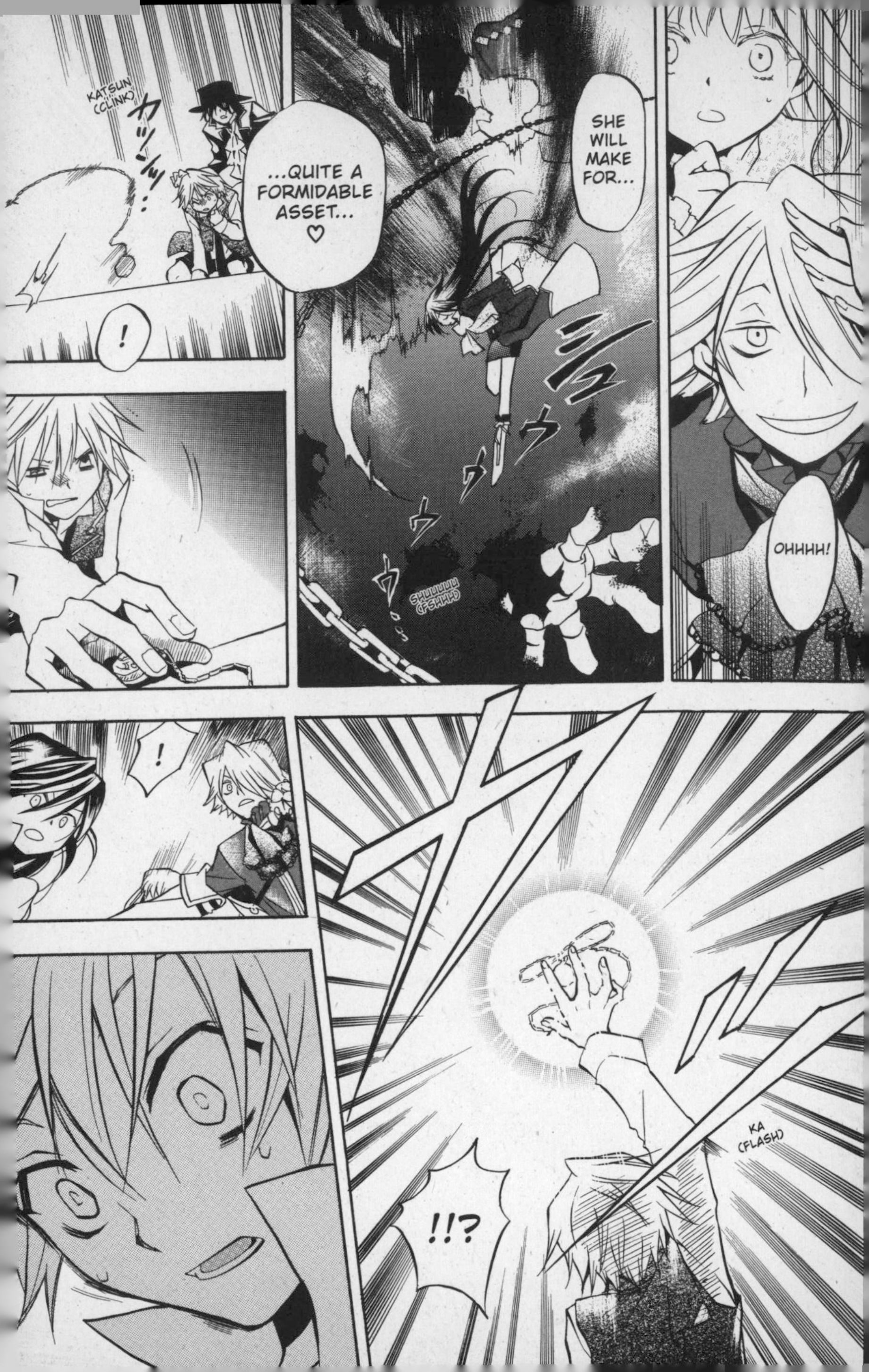
OHHHH!
SHE WILL MAKE FOR...
...QUITE A FORMIDABLE ASSET... ♡
SHUUUUU (FSHHH)
KATSUN (CLINK)
!
KA (FLASH)
!!?
!

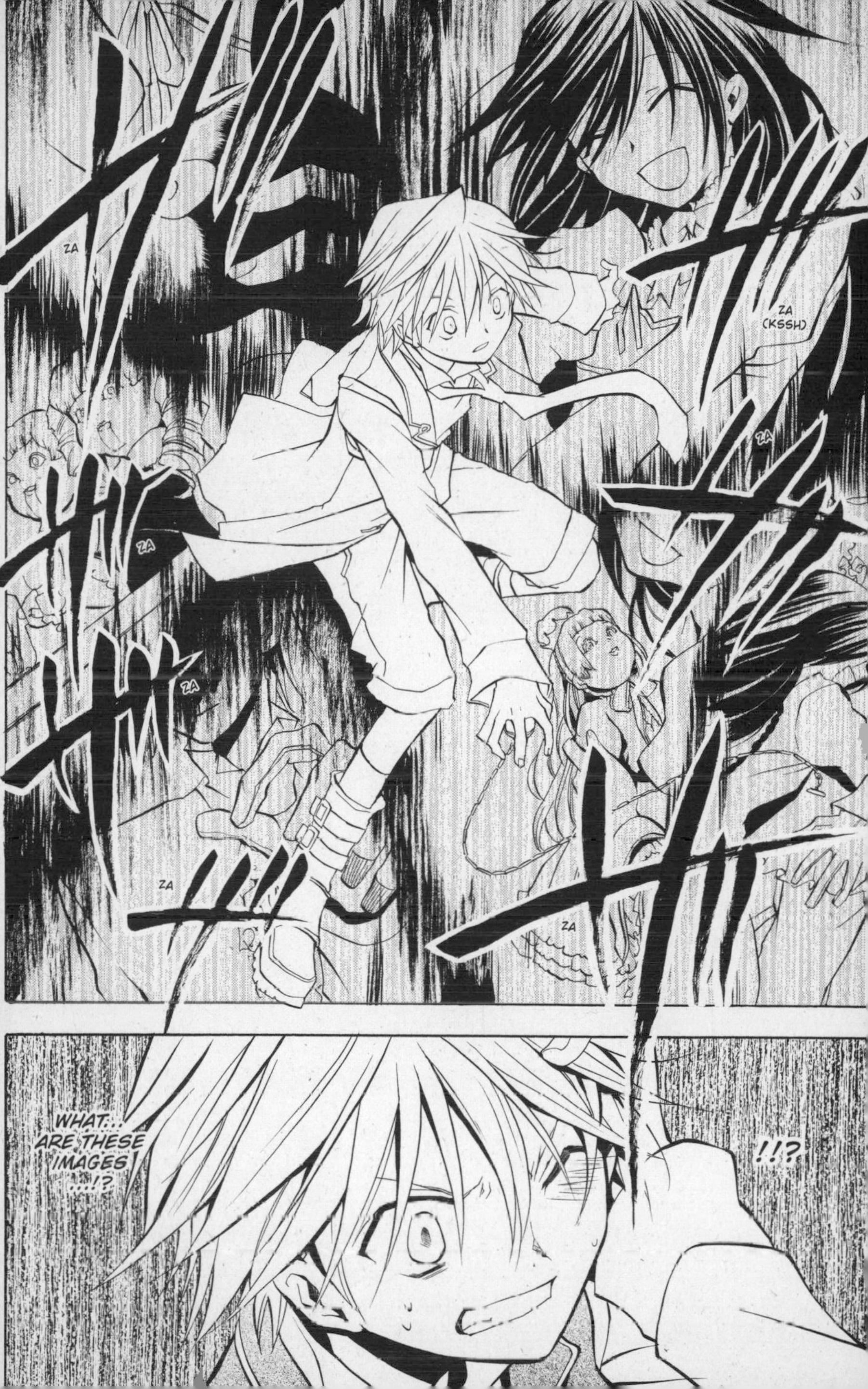
ZA (KSSH)
ZA
ZA
ZA
ZA
ZA
ZA
!!?
WHAT... ARE THESE IMAGES ...!?

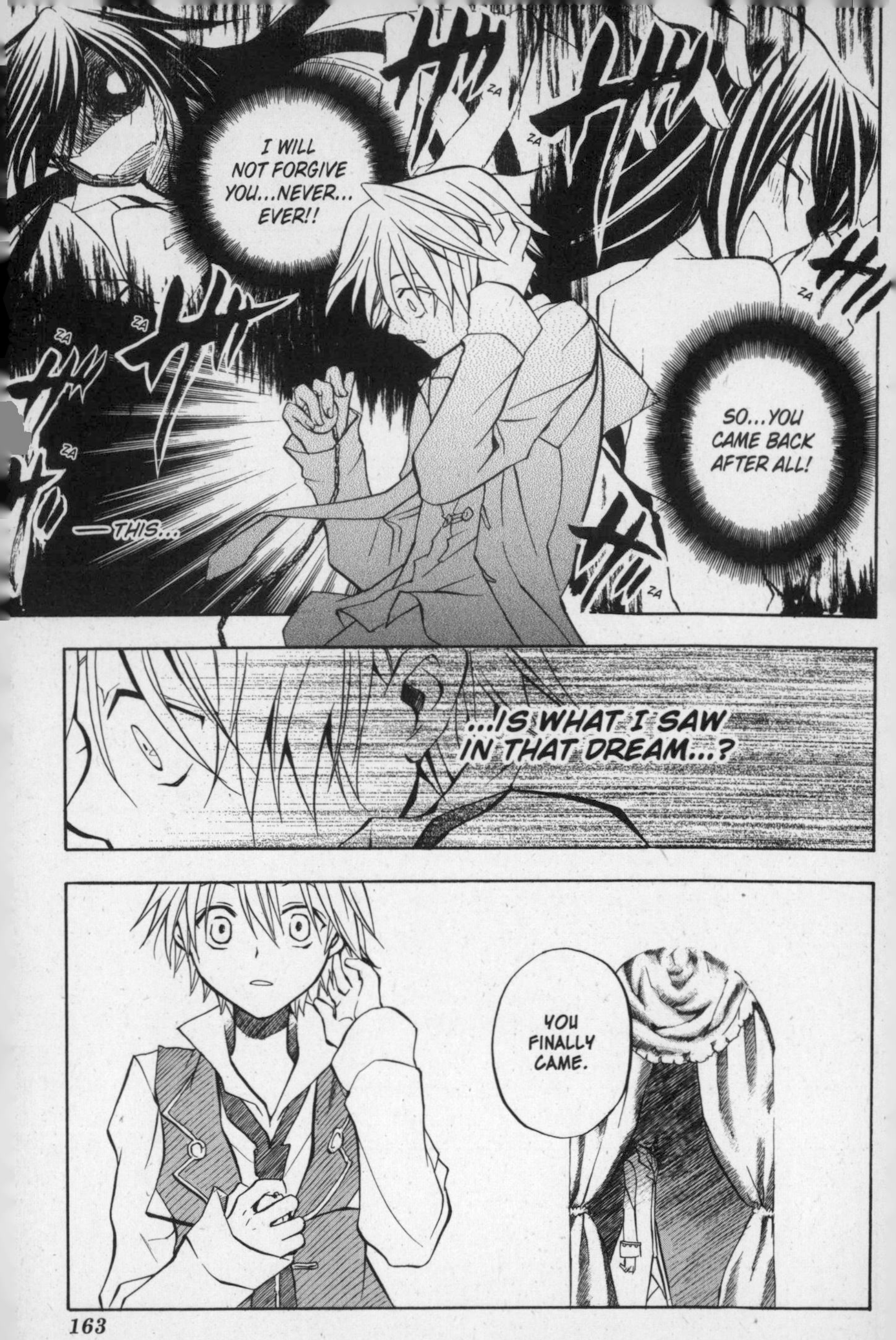
ZA
ZA
ZA
SO...YOU CAME BACK AFTER ALL!
ZA
I WILL NOT FORGIVE YOU...NEVER... EVER!!
ZA
ZA
ZA
—THIS...
...IS WHAT I SAW IN THAT DREAM...?
YOU FINALLY CAME.

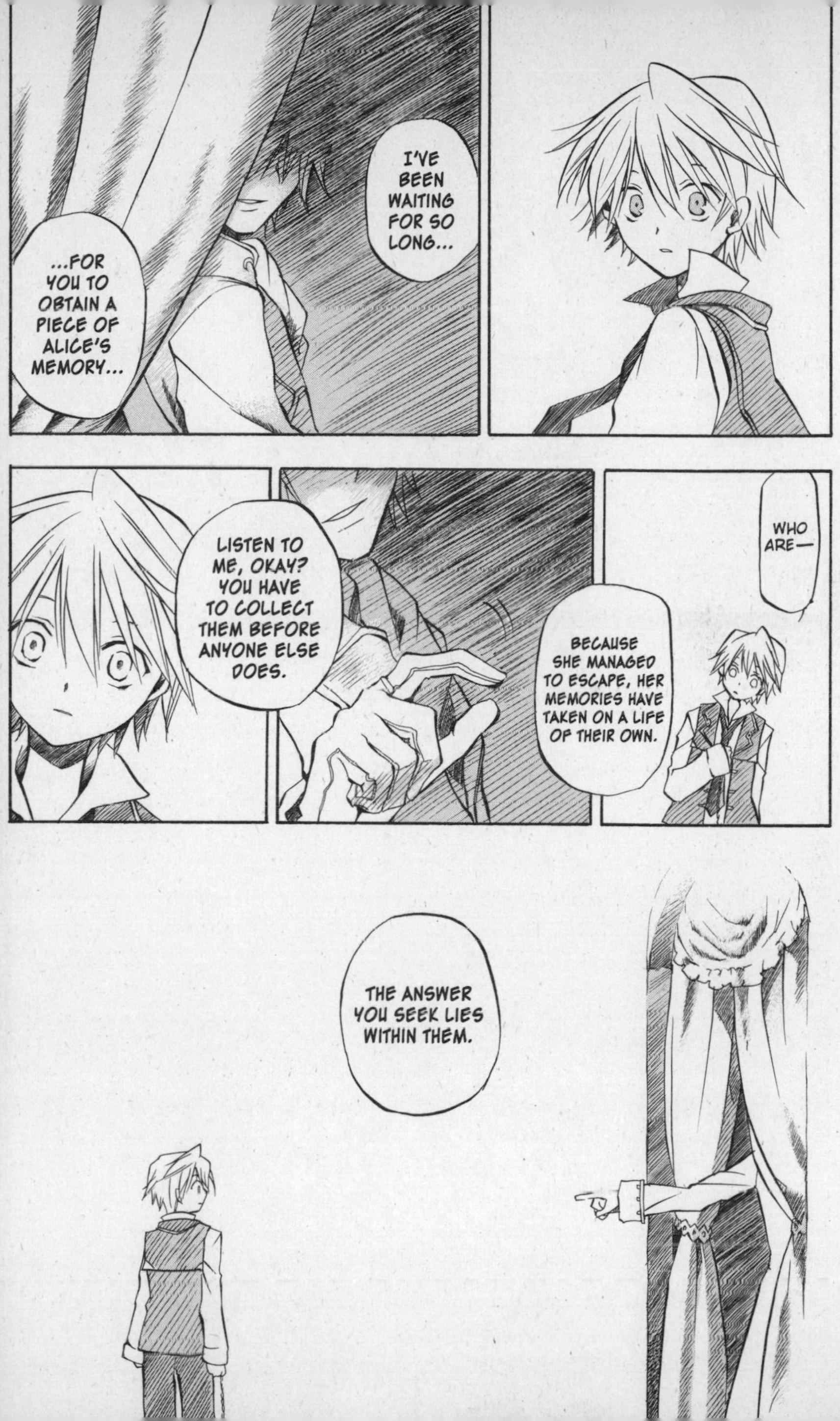
I'VE BEEN WAITING FOR SO LONG...
...FOR YOU TO OBTAIN A PIECE OF ALICE'S MEMORY...
WHO ARE—
BECAUSE SHE MANAGED TO ESCAPE, HER MEMORIES HAVE TAKEN ON A LIFE OF THEIR OWN.
LISTEN TO ME, OKAY? YOU HAVE TO COLLECT THEM BEFORE ANYONE ELSE DOES.
THE ANSWER YOU SEEK LIES WITHIN THEM.

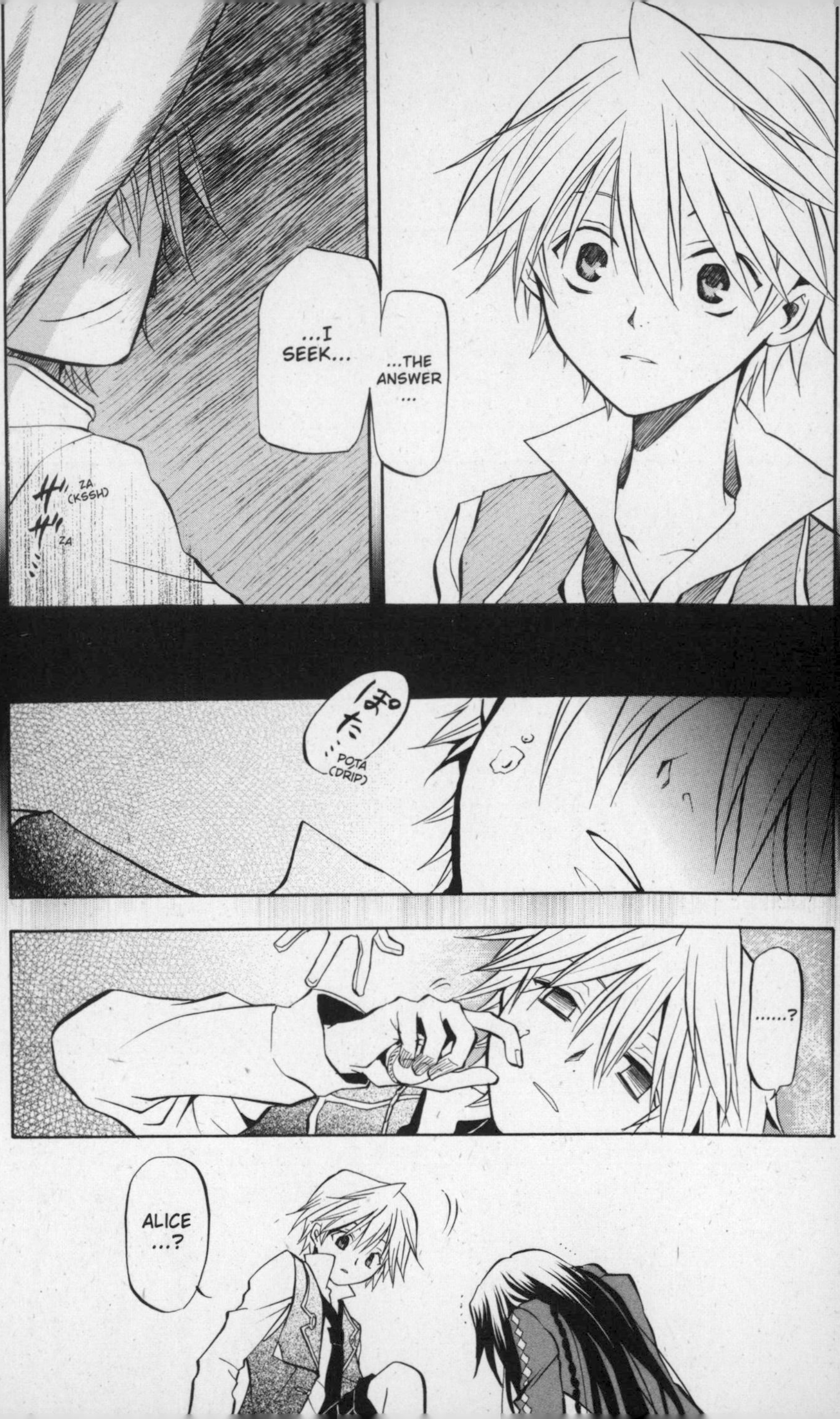
...I SEEK...
...THE ANSWER...
ザ ZA (KSSH)
ザ ZA
ぽた POTA (DRIP)
......?
ALICE ...?

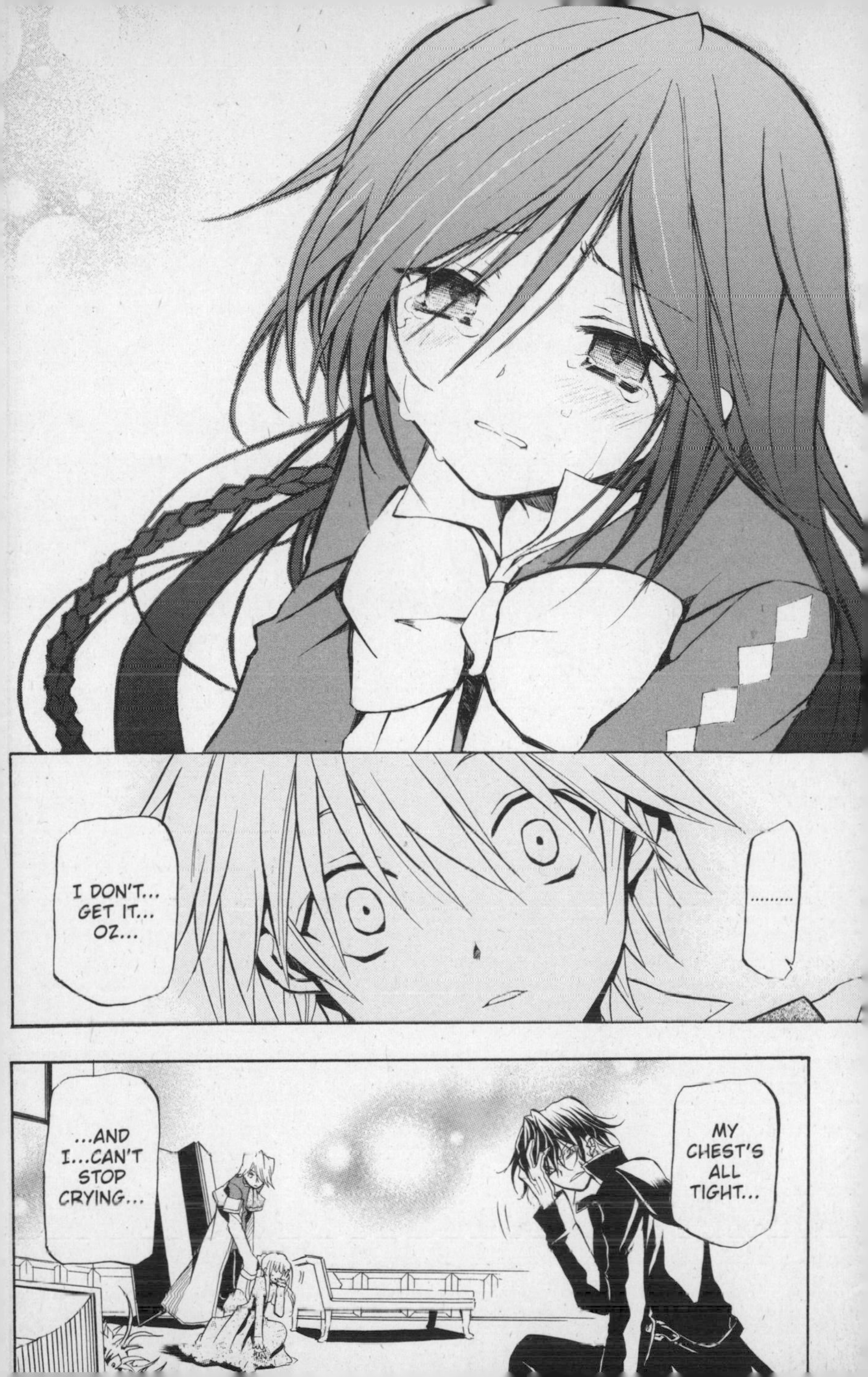
.........
I DON'T... GET IT... OZ...
MY CHEST'S ALL TIGHT...
...AND I...CAN'T STOP CRYING...

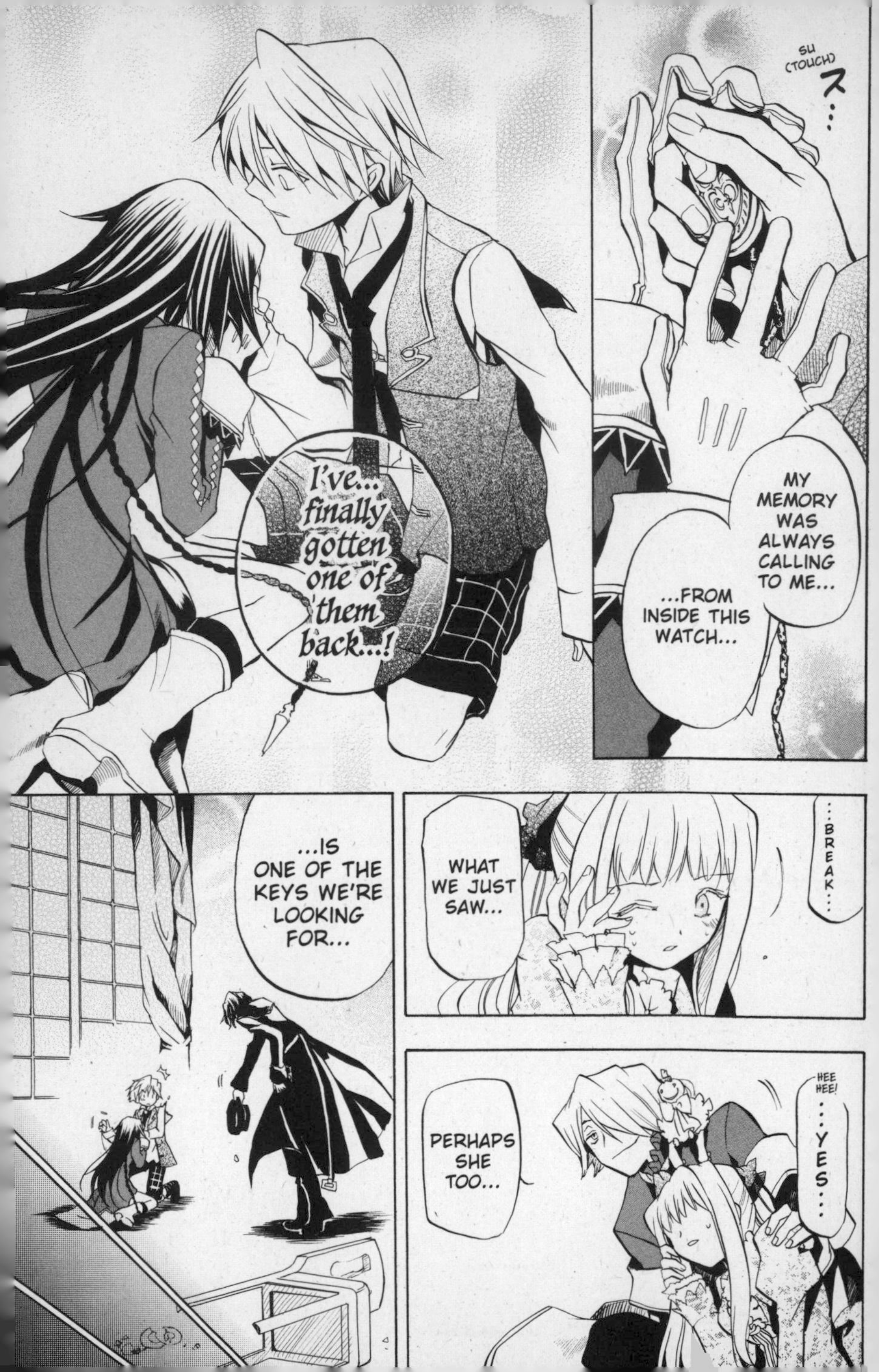
SU (TOUCH)
ス…
MY MEMORY WAS ALWAYS CALLING TO ME...
...FROM INSIDE THIS WATCH...
I've... finally gotten one of them back...!
...BREAK...
WHAT WE JUST SAW...
HEE HEE!
...YES...
PERHAPS SHE TOO...
...IS ONE OF THE KEYS WE'RE LOOKING FOR...

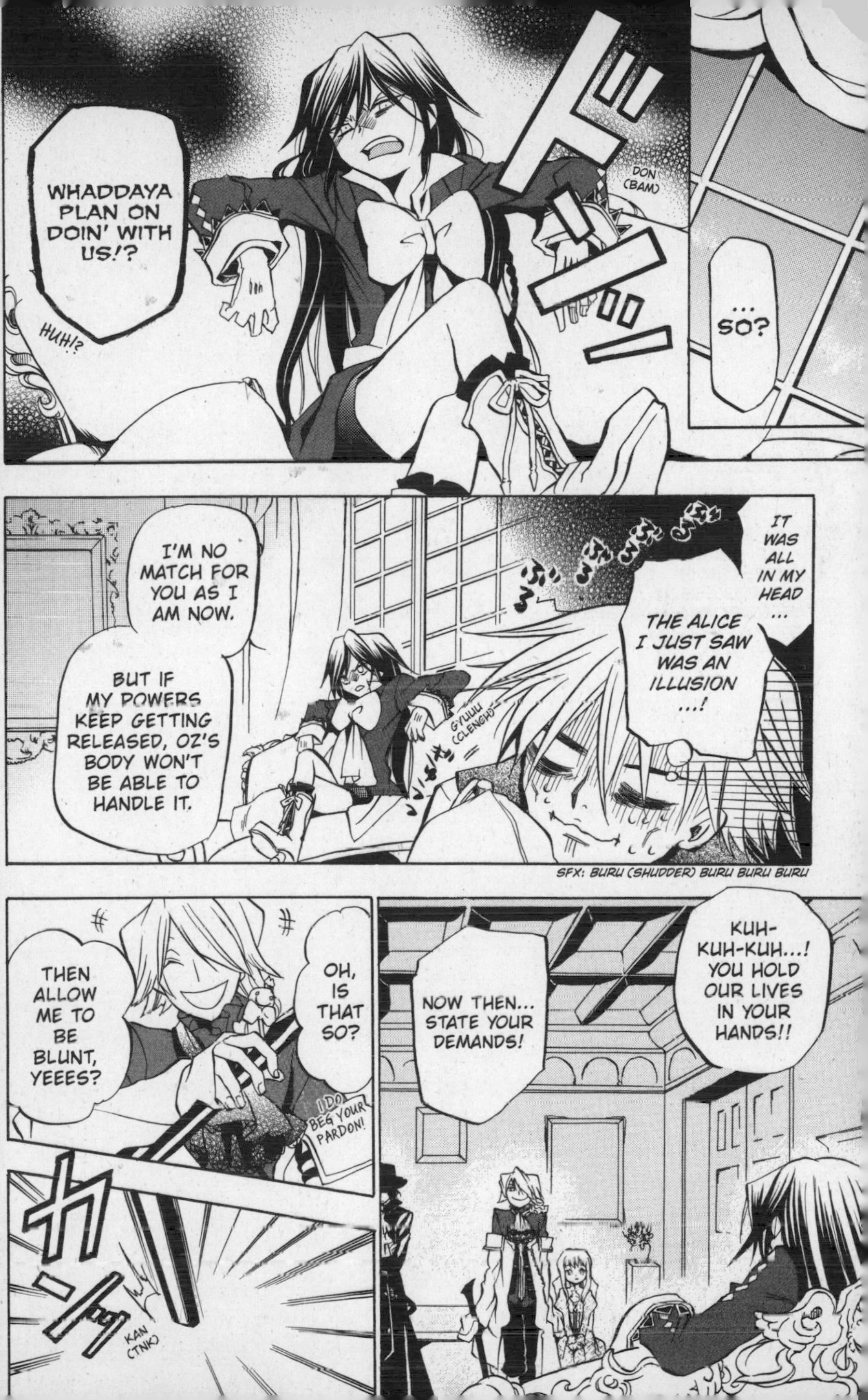
... SO?
WHADDAYA PLAN ON DOIN' WITH US!?
DON (BAM)
HUH!?
IT WAS ALL IN MY HEAD...
THE ALICE I JUST SAW WAS AN ILLUSION...!
GYUUU (CLENCH)
I'M NO MATCH FOR YOU AS I AM NOW.
BUT IF MY POWERS KEEP GETTING RELEASED, OZ'S BODY WON'T BE ABLE TO HANDLE IT.
SFX: BURU (SHUDDER) BURU BURU BURU
KUH-KUH-KUH...! YOU HOLD OUR LIVES IN YOUR HANDS!!
NOW THEN... STATE YOUR DEMANDS!
OH, IS THAT SO?
THEN ALLOW ME TO BE BLUNT, YEEES?
I DO BEG YOUR PARDON!
KAN (TNK)

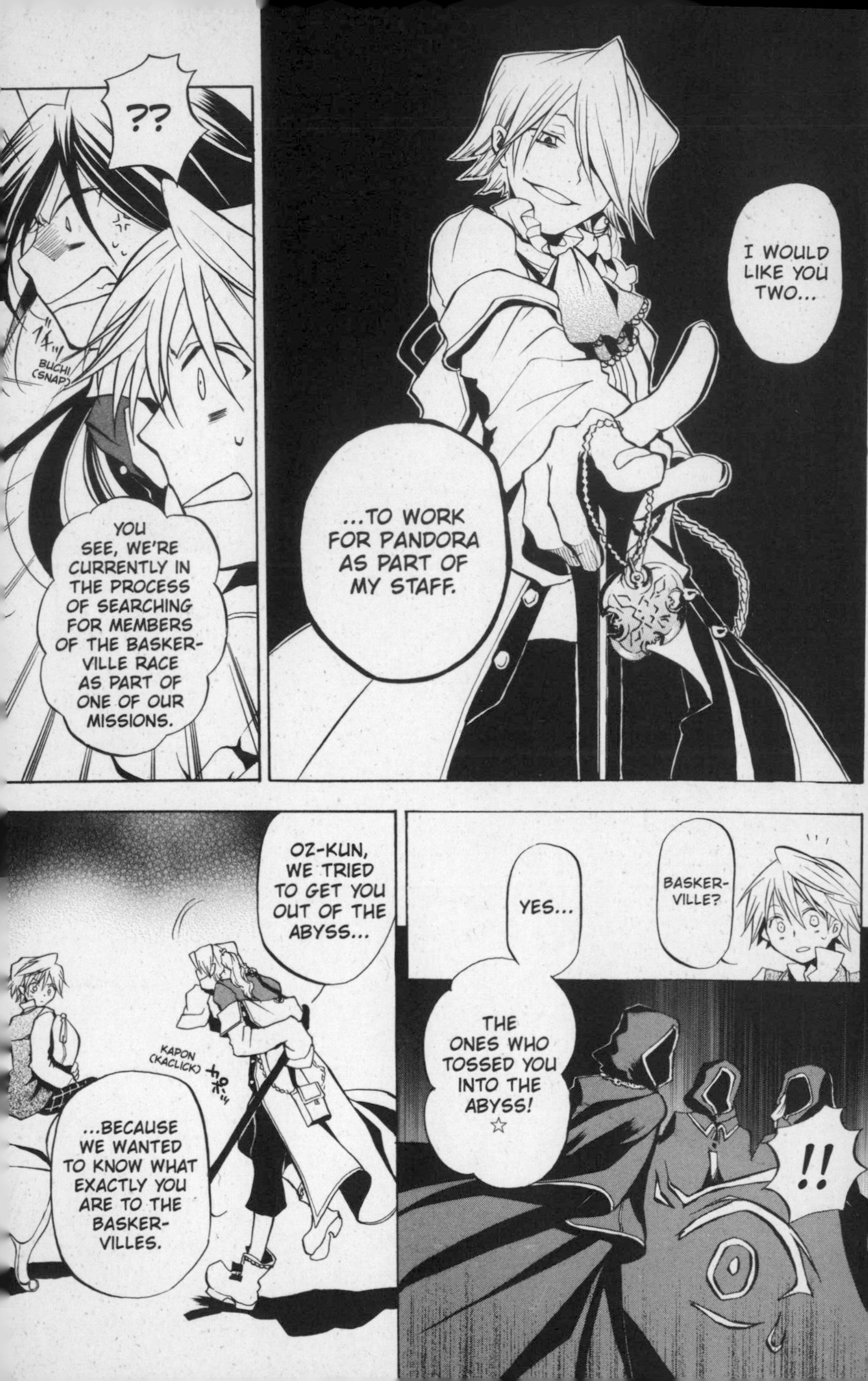
I WOULD LIKE YOU TWO...
...TO WORK FOR PANDORA AS PART OF MY STAFF.
??
BUCHI (SNAP)
YOU SEE, WE'RE CURRENTLY IN THE PROCESS OF SEARCHING FOR MEMBERS OF THE BASKER-VILLE RACE AS PART OF ONE OF OUR MISSIONS.
BASKER-VILLE?
YES...
THE ONES WHO TOSSED YOU INTO THE ABYSS! ☆
!!
OZ-KUN, WE TRIED TO GET YOU OUT OF THE ABYSS...
KAPON (KACLICK)
...BECAUSE WE WANTED TO KNOW WHAT EXACTLY YOU ARE TO THE BASKER-VILLES.

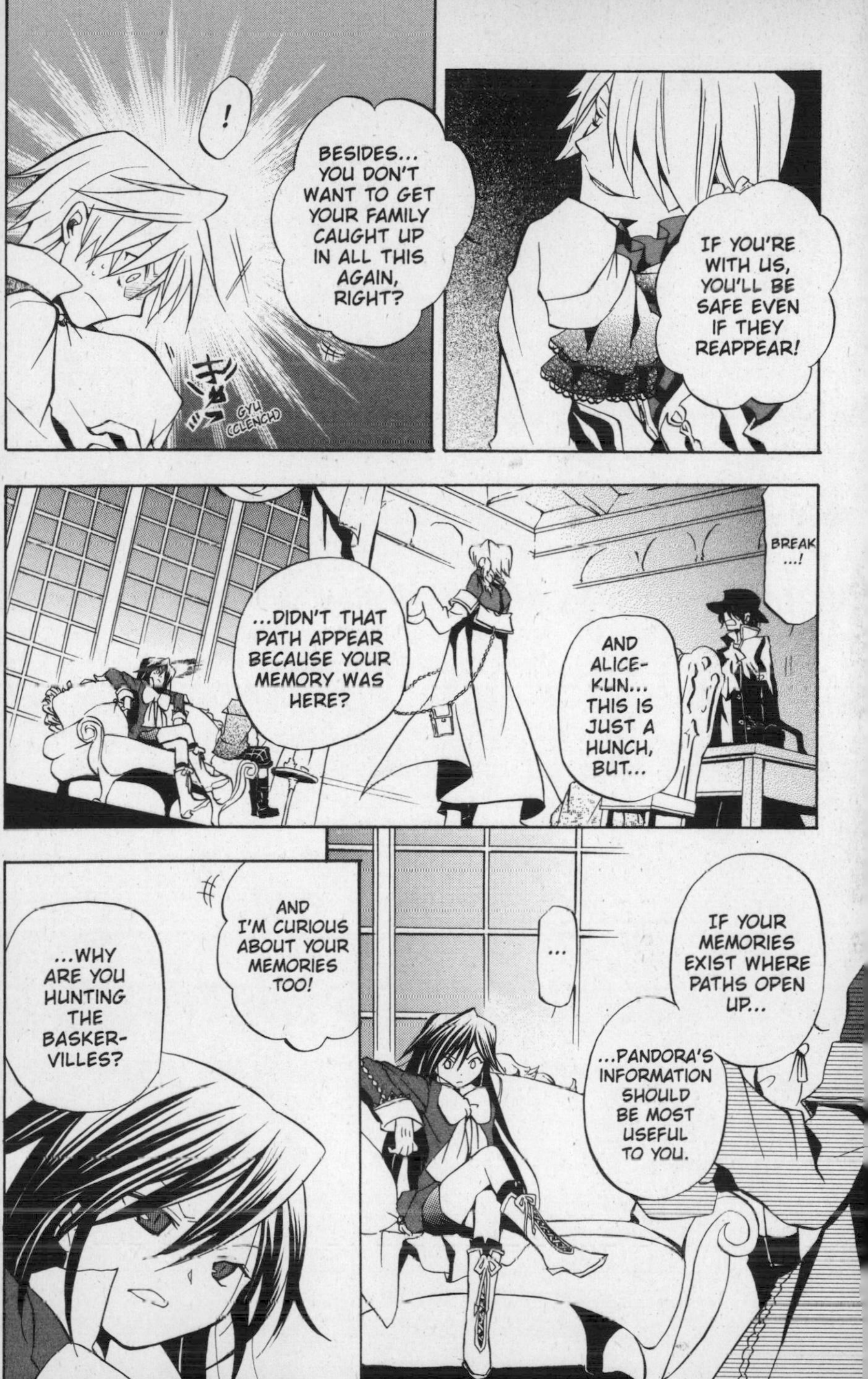
IF YOU'RE WITH US, YOU'LL BE SAFE EVEN IF THEY REAPPEAR!
BESIDES... YOU DON'T WANT TO GET YOUR FAMILY CAUGHT UP IN ALL THIS AGAIN, RIGHT?
!
GYU (CLENCH)
BREAK ...!
AND ALICE-KUN... THIS IS JUST A HUNCH, BUT...
...DIDN'T THAT PATH APPEAR BECAUSE YOUR MEMORY WAS HERE?
IF YOUR MEMORIES EXIST WHERE PATHS OPEN UP...
...PANDORA'S INFORMATION SHOULD BE MOST USEFUL TO YOU.
...
AND I'M CURIOUS ABOUT YOUR MEMORIES TOO!
...WHY ARE YOU HUNTING THE BASKERVILLES?

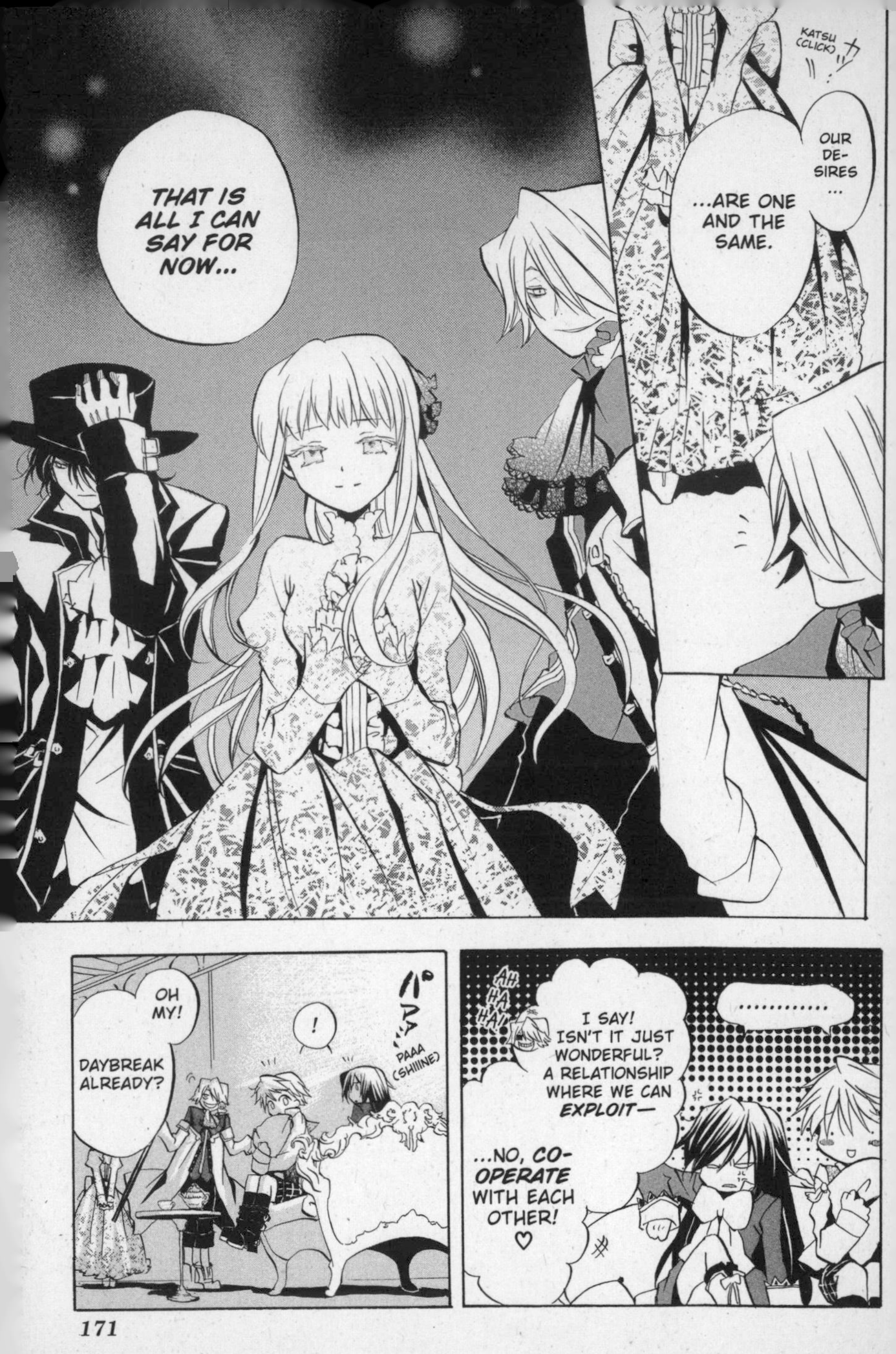
KATSU (CLICK)
OUR DE-SIRES...
...ARE ONE AND THE SAME.
THAT IS ALL I CAN SAY FOR NOW...
AH HA HA HA!
I SAY! ISN'T IT JUST WONDERFUL? A RELATIONSHIP WHERE WE CAN EXPLOIT—
...NO, CO-OPERATE WITH EACH OTHER! ♡
.............
PAAA (SHIIINE)
OH MY!
DAYBREAK ALREADY?
!

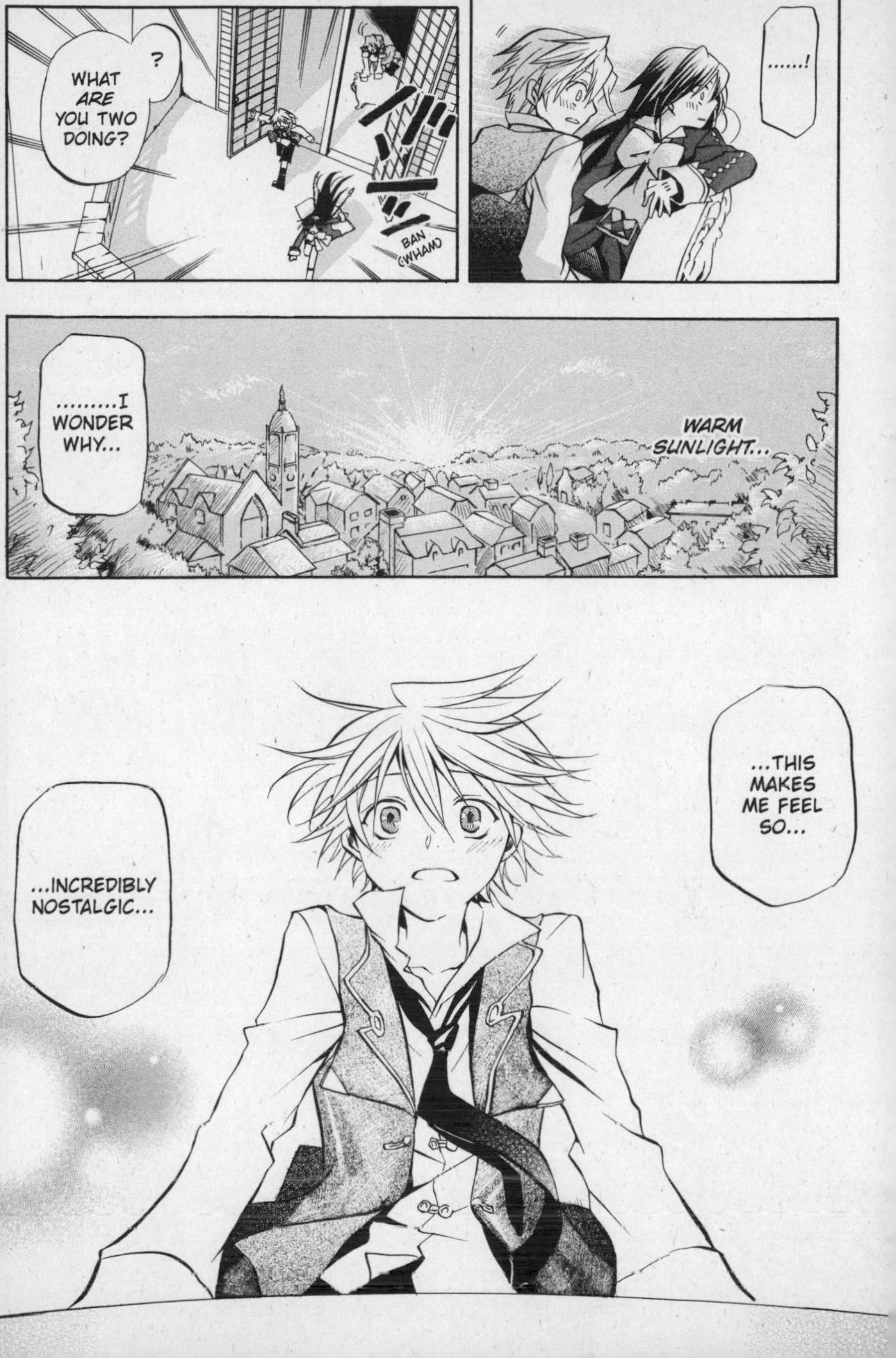
......!
?
WHAT ARE YOU TWO DOING?
BAN (WHAM)
WARM SUNLIGHT...
.........I WONDER WHY...
...THIS MAKES ME FEEL SO...
...INCREDIBLY NOSTALGIC...

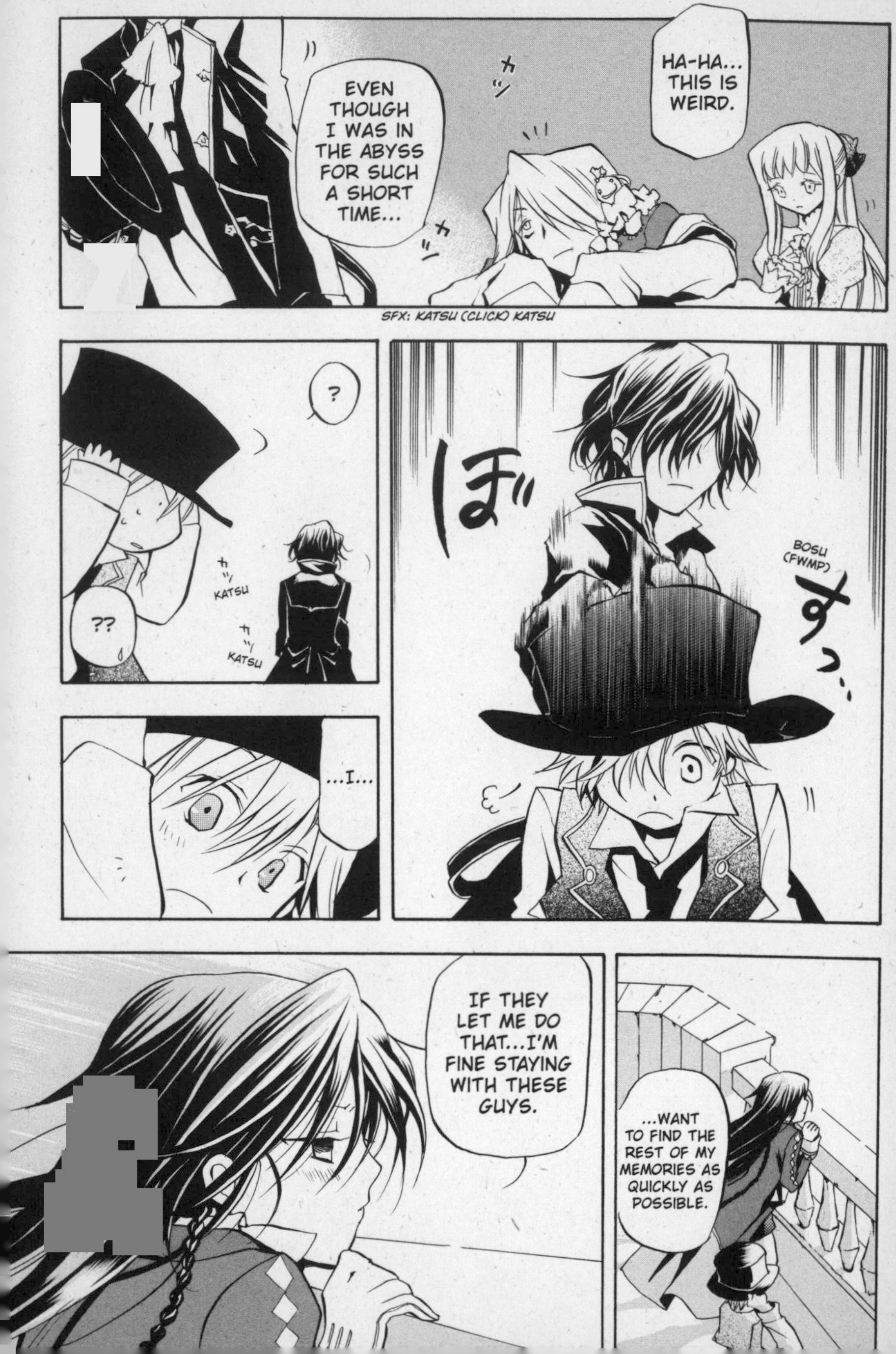
HA-HA... THIS IS WEIRD.
EVEN THOUGH I WAS IN THE ABYSS FOR SUCH A SHORT TIME...
SFX: KATSU (CLICK) KATSU
BOSU (FWMP)
?
KATSU
KATSU
??
...I...
...WANT TO FIND THE REST OF MY MEMORIES AS QUICKLY AS POSSIBLE.
IF THEY LET ME DO THAT...I'M FINE STAYING WITH THESE GUYS.

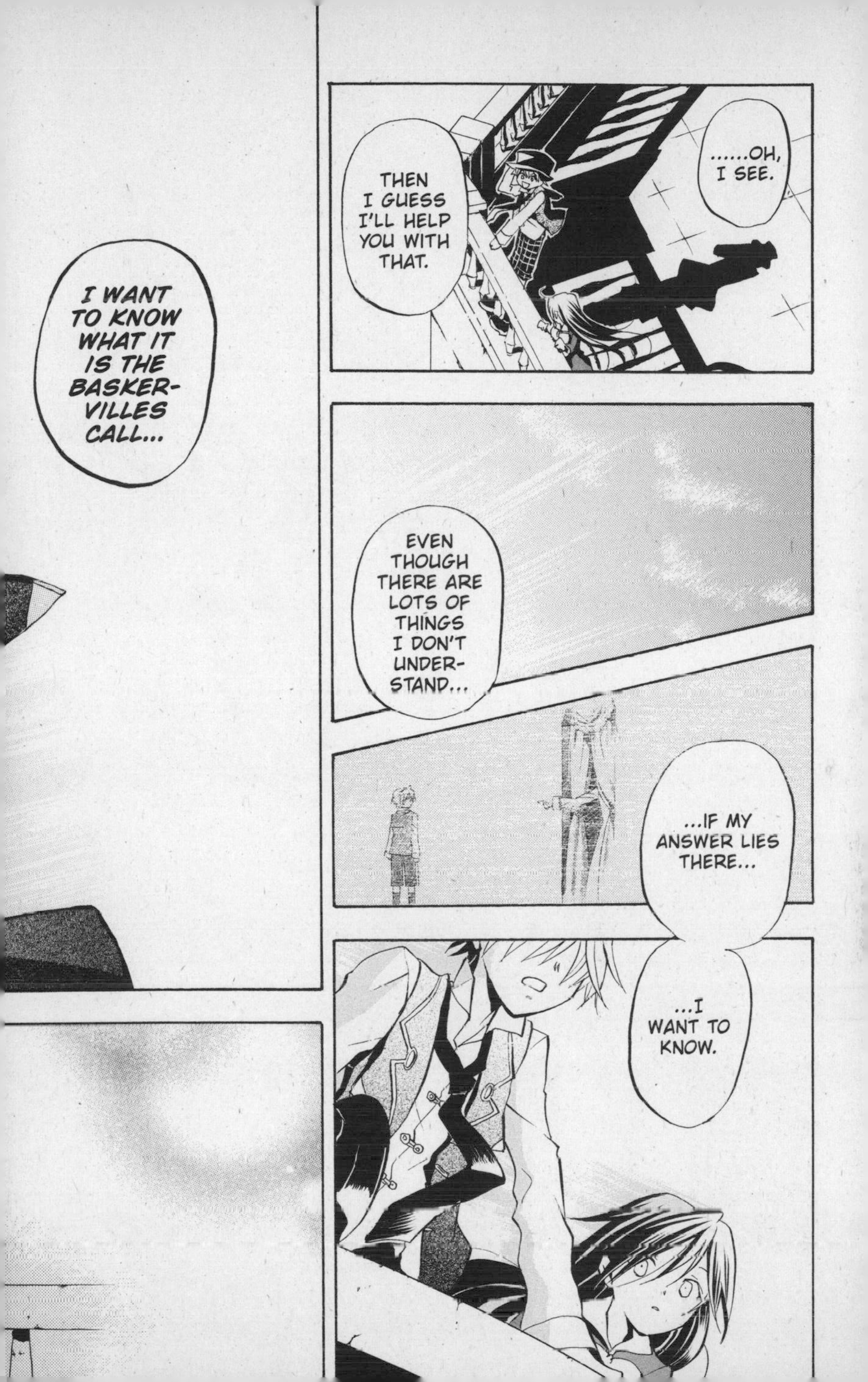
......OH, I SEE.
THEN I GUESS I'LL HELP YOU WITH THAT.
EVEN THOUGH THERE ARE LOTS OF THINGS I DON'T UNDER-STAND...
...IF MY ANSWER LIES THERE...
...I WANT TO KNOW.
I WANT TO KNOW WHAT IT IS THE BASKER-VILLES CALL...

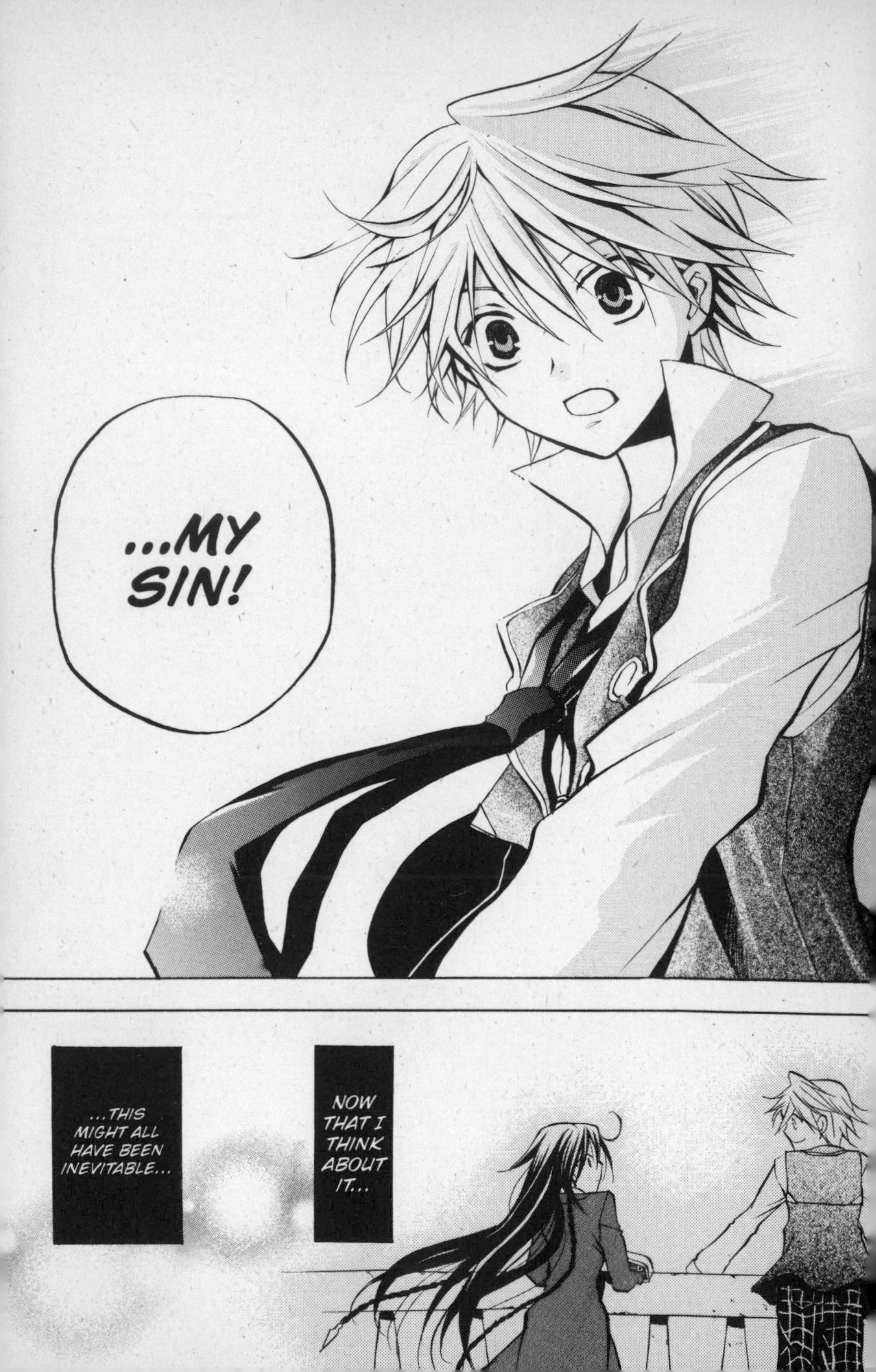
...MY SIN!
NOW THAT I THINK ABOUT IT...
...THIS MIGHT ALL HAVE BEEN INEVITABLE...

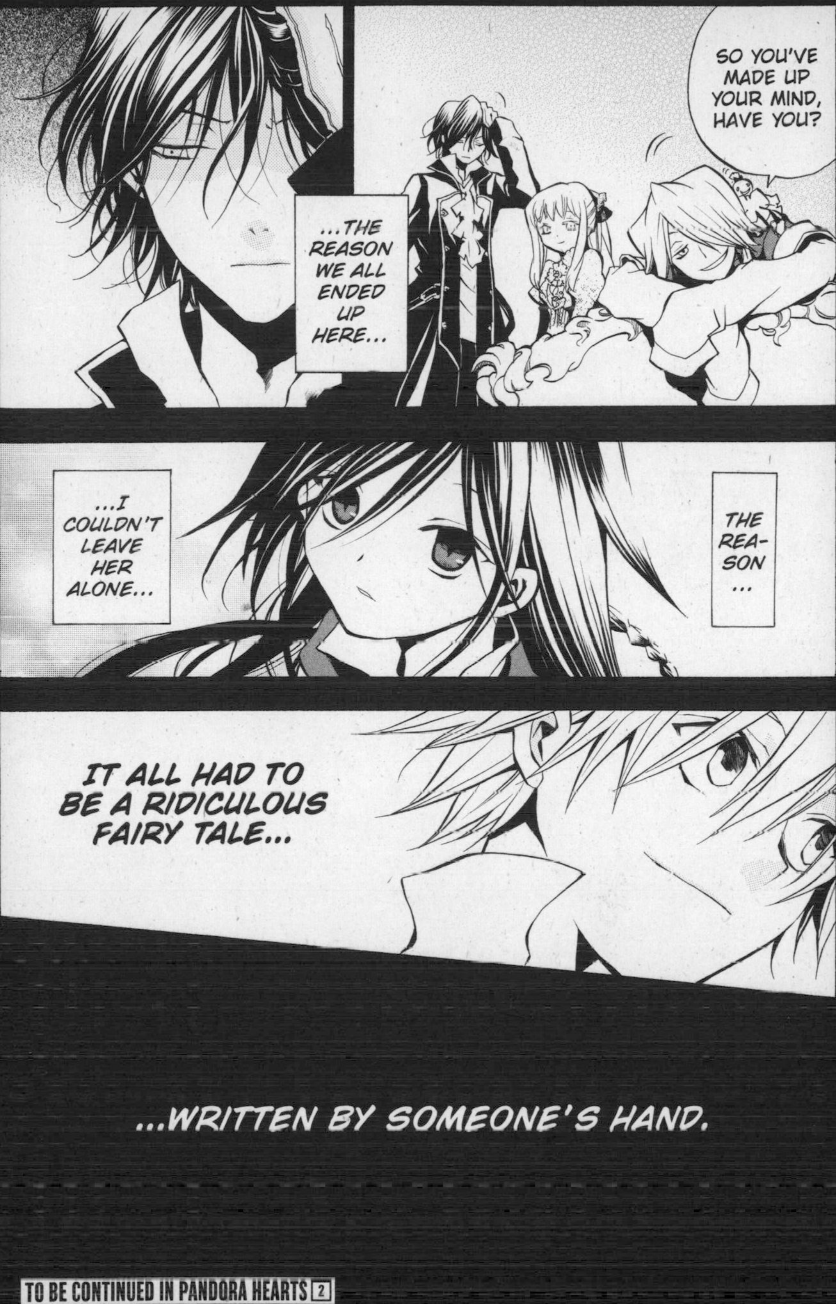
SO YOU'VE MADE UP YOUR MIND, HAVE YOU?
...THE REASON WE ALL ENDED UP HERE...
THE REA-SON...
...I COULDN'T LEAVE HER ALONE...
IT ALL HAD TO BE A RIDICULOUS FAIRY TALE...
...WRITTEN BY SOMEONE'S HAND.

TO BE CONTINUED IN PANDORA HEARTS 2

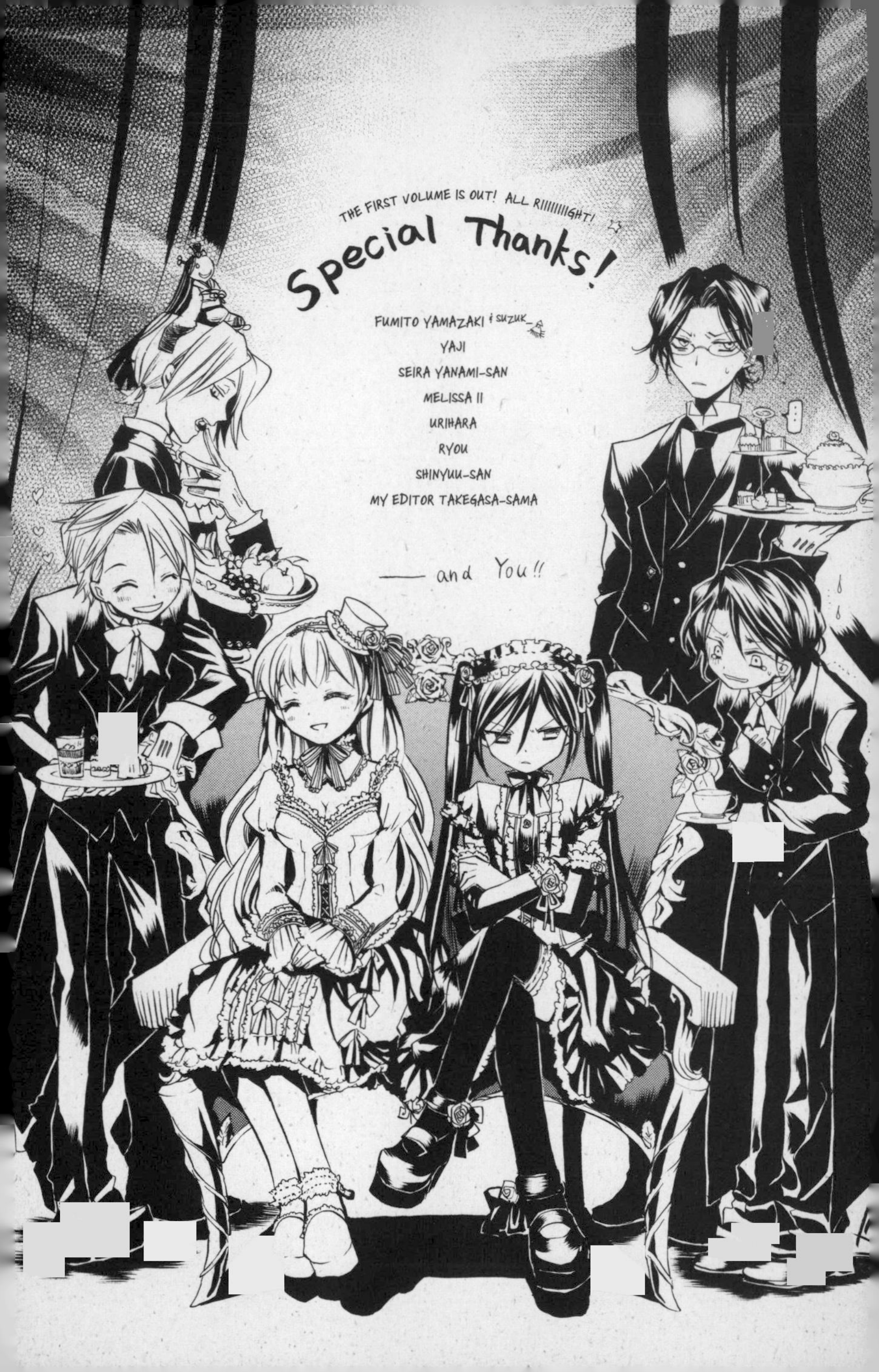
THE FIRST VOLUME IS OUT! ALL RIIIIIIIIIGHT!
Special Thanks!
FUMITO YAMAZAKI & SUZUK_
YAJI
SEIRA YANAMI-SAN
MELISSA II
URIHARA
RYOU
SHINYUU-SAN
MY EDITOR TAKEGASA-SAMA
—— and You!!

## ~ BECAUSE IT WAS TIME FOR AFTERNOON TEA ~

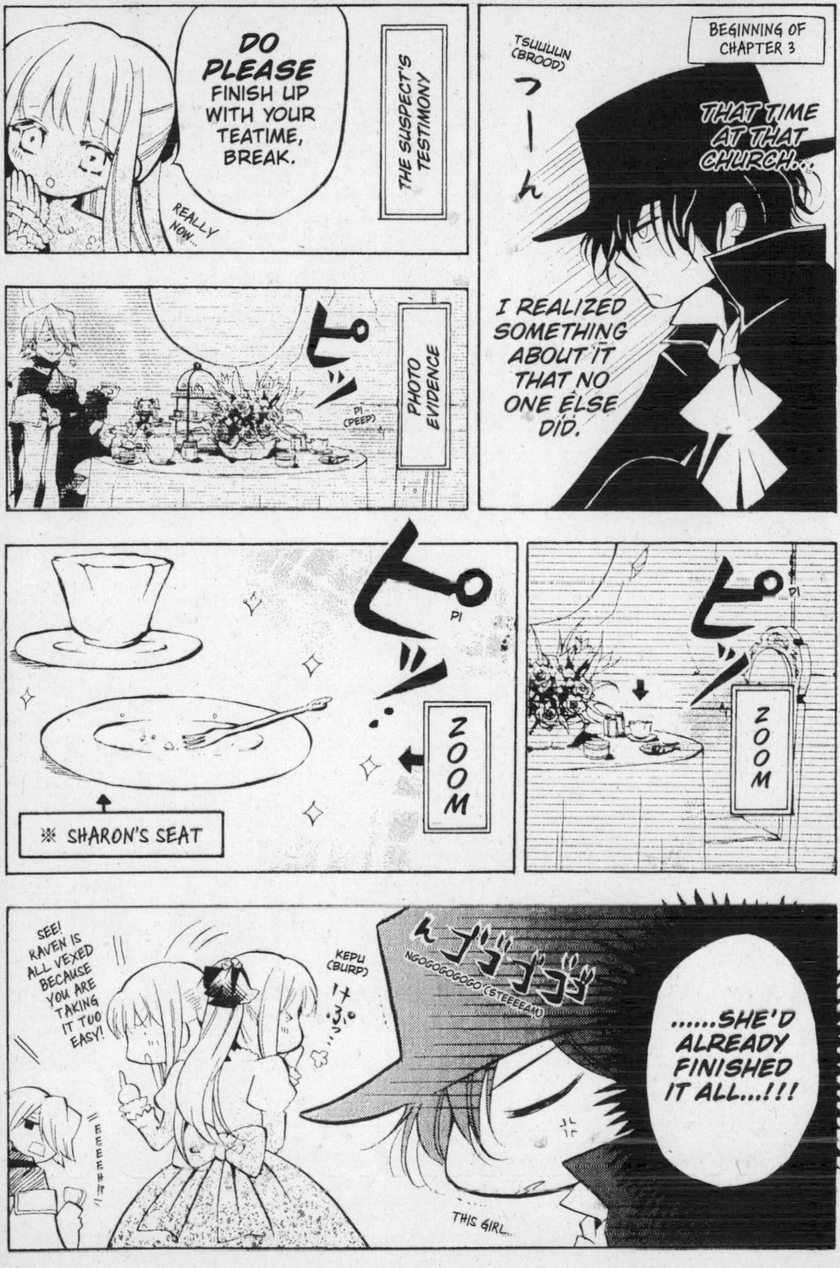
BEGINNING OF CHAPTER 3
TSUUUUN (BROOD)
つーん
THAT TIME AT THAT CHURCH...
I REALIZED SOMETHING ABOUT IT THAT NO ONE ELSE DID.
THE SUSPECT'S TESTIMONY
DO PLEASE FINISH UP WITH YOUR TEATIME, BREAK.
REALLY NOW...
PHOTO EVIDENCE
ピッ
PI (PEEP)
PI
ピッ
ZOOM
ZOOM
ピッ
PI
※ SHARON'S SEAT
......SHE'D ALREADY FINISHED IT ALL...!!!
NGOGOGOGOGO (STEEEEAM)
THIS GIRL...
KEPU (BURP)
SEE! RAVEN IS ALL VEXED BECAUSE YOU ARE TAKING IT TOO EASY!
EEEEEH!?

# BONUS COMIC ②

## ~ THE RED STRING OF FATE THAT BINDS YOU AND I ~

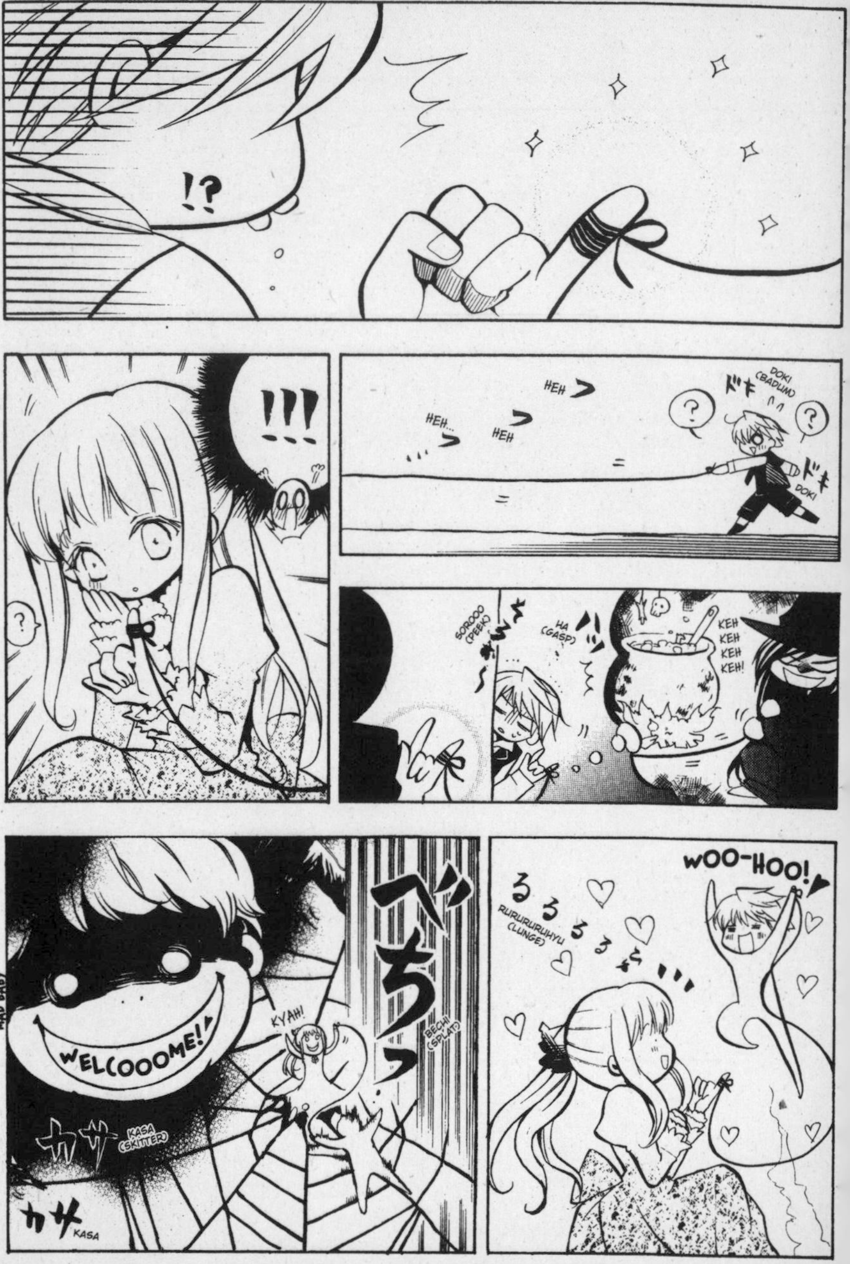
!?
DOKI (BADUMP)
ドキ
?
?
HEH
HEH
HEH...
...
ドキ
DOKI
KEH KEH KEH KEH!
ハッ
HA (GASP)
そろ~
SOROOO (PEEK)
...
!!!
?
WOO-HOO!♥
るるるるる
RURURURUHYU (LUNGE)
べちっ
BECHI (SPLAT)
KYAH!
WELCOOOME!♪
カサ
KASA (SKITTER)
カサ
KASA
MAD BABY

# TRANSLATOR'S NOTES ①

## COMMON HONORIFICS

**no honorific**: Indicates familiarity or closeness; if used without permission or reason, addresssing someone in this manner would constitute an insult.

**-san**: The Japanese equivalent of Mr./Mrs./Miss. If a situation calls for politeness, this is the fail-safe honorific.

**-sama**: Conveys great respect; may also indicate that the social status of the speaker is lower than that of the addressee.

**-kun**: Used most often when referring to boys (though it can be applied to girls as well), this indicates affection or familiarity. Occasionally used by older men among their peers, but it may also be used by anyone referring to a person of lower standing.

**-chan**: An affectionate honorific indicating familiarity used mostly in reference to girls; also used in reference to cute persons or animals of either gender.

### Mrs. Kate — page 9

The housekeeper is actually referred to as "Mrs." in the original, so we opted to keep the English honorific to match.

### onii-chan — page 17

An informal way of addressing an older brother (in this case, Oz) or unrelated young man who is older than the speaker.

### Duldee and Duldum — page 49

A play on the characters Tweedledee and Tweedledum, a pair of rotund brothers who appear in Lewis Carroll's *Through the Looking Glass and What Alice Found There*. They never disagree with one another and, as a result, are often portrayed as twins.

### shota — page 62

A young boy or an older male with extremely youthful features that lend him a boyish look. An interest in or attraction to this type of male is known in Japan as a "Shotarou complex" or *shotacon*.

## Zwei
*page 65*

The word for "two" in German; the name has significance in that Zwei oversees Duldum and Duldee who are regarded as twin brothers (as they are a play on the characters Tweedledee and Tweedledum from Lewis Carroll's *Through the Looking Glass and What Alice Found There*) and are always together as a pair.

## shinigami
*page 70*

Literally, a "god of death," the Japanese equivalent to the Grim Reaper.

## Alichino
*page 100*

One of the thirteen clawed devils that guard and torture those in the fifth ditch (filled with hot tar and reserved for those who use money for political gain) in the eighth circle of Hell in Dante's *Inferno*. The name is derived from the Italian word for "harlequin" (a popular clownish character from Italian improv theatre.)

## "The girl who molested me!"
*page 102*

Oz actually calls Alice a *sekuhara onna* ("sexual harassment girl") in the original edition.

## B-Rabbit
*page 107*

The "B" in Alice's other name stands for both "Bloody" and "Black."

I thought that youth was reserved for teenagers, but when I looked it up in a dictionary, "youth" was defined as extending all the way up until about the age of twenty-five. It's longer than I'd thought!!

But definition aside, I want to roar like a youth forever. That's how I feel these days.

## MOCHIZUKI'S MUSINGS

VOLUME 1

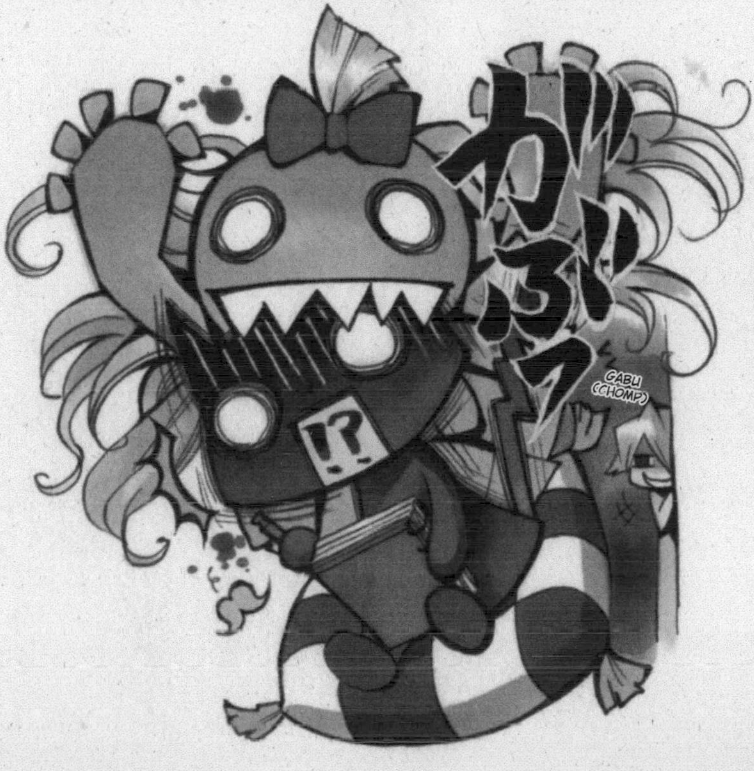
GABU (CHOMP)

PandoraHearts

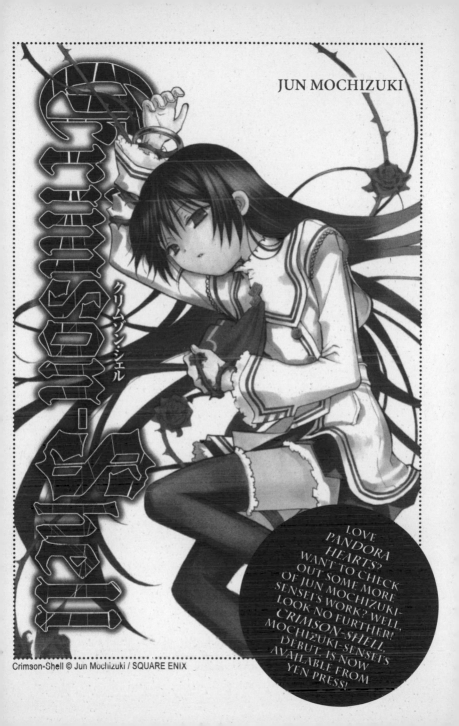

JUN MOCHIZUKI

Crimson-Shell

クリムゾン・シェル

LOVE PANDORA HEARTS? WANT TO CHECK OUT SOME MORE OF JUN MOCHIZUKI-SENSEI'S WORK? WELL, LOOK NO FURTHER! CRIMSON-SHELL, MOCHIZUKI-SENSEI'S DEBUT, IS NOW AVAILABLE FROM YEN PRESS!

PandoraHearts

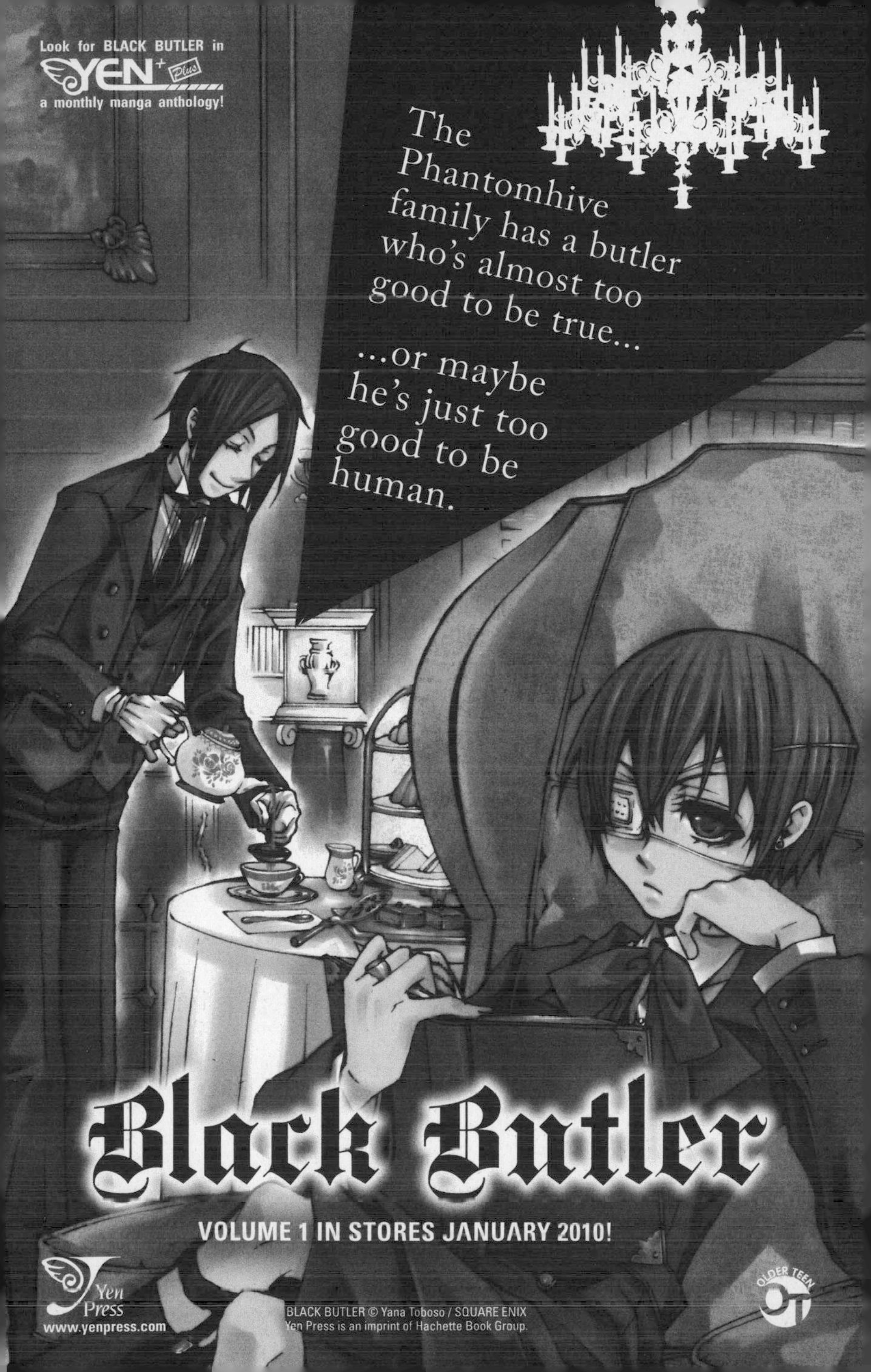
Look for BLACK BUTLER in
YEN+ Plus
a monthly manga anthology!
The Phantomhive family has a butler who's almost too good to be true...
...or maybe he's just too good to be human.
Black Butler
VOLUME 1 IN STORES JANUARY 2010!
Yen Press
www.yenpress.com
BLACK BUTLER © Yana Toboso / SQUARE ENIX
Yen Press is an imprint of Hachette Book Group.
OLDER TEEN
OT

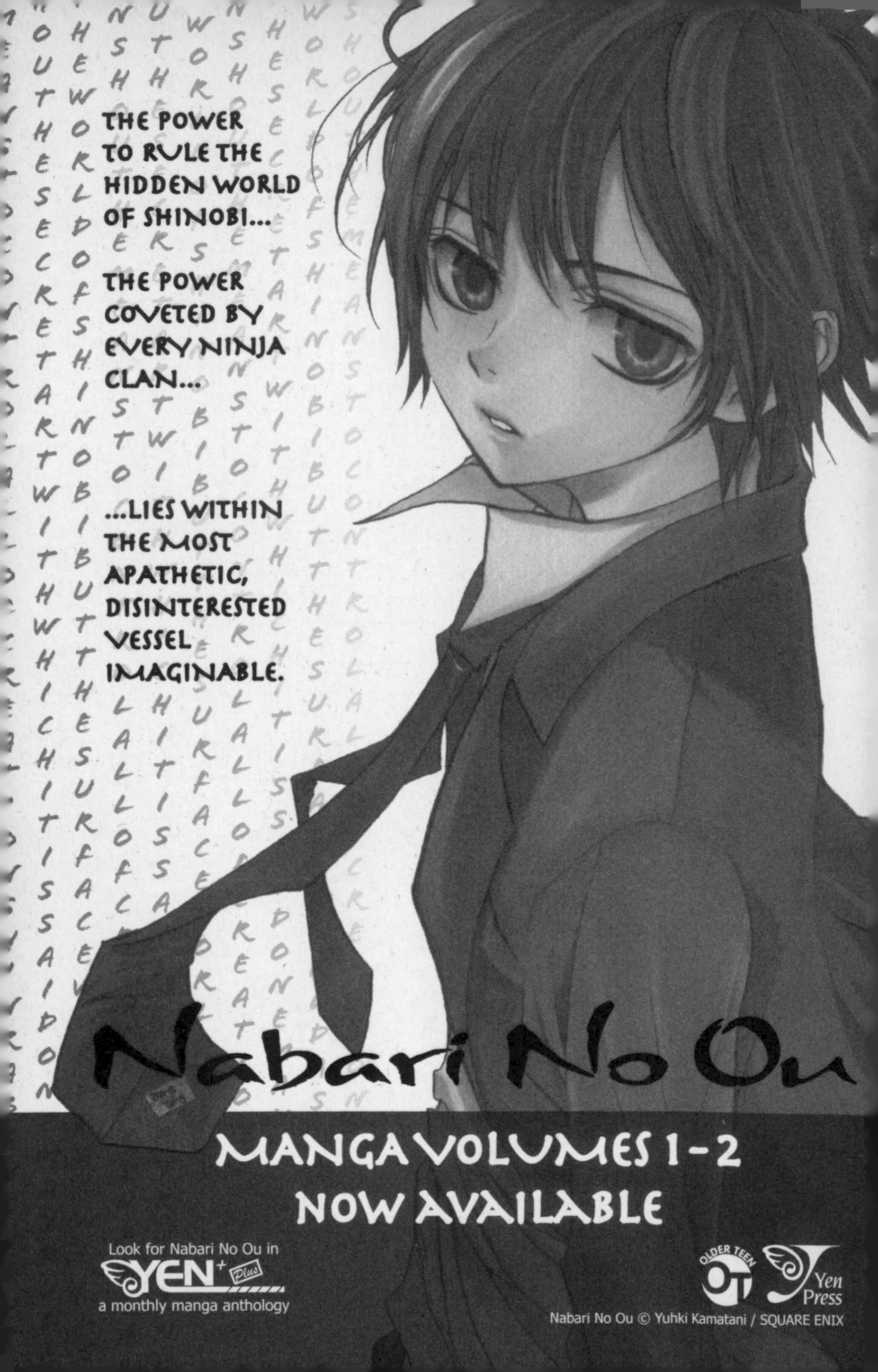
THE POWER TO RULE THE HIDDEN WORLD OF SHINOBI...
THE POWER COVETED BY EVERY NINJA CLAN...
...LIES WITHIN THE MOST APATHETIC, DISINTERESTED VESSEL IMAGINABLE.
Nabari No Ou
MANGA VOLUMES 1-2
NOW AVAILABLE
Look for Nabari No Ou in
YEN+ Plus
a monthly manga anthology
OLDER TEEN OT
Yen Press
Nabari No Ou © Yuhki Kamatani / SQUARE ENIX

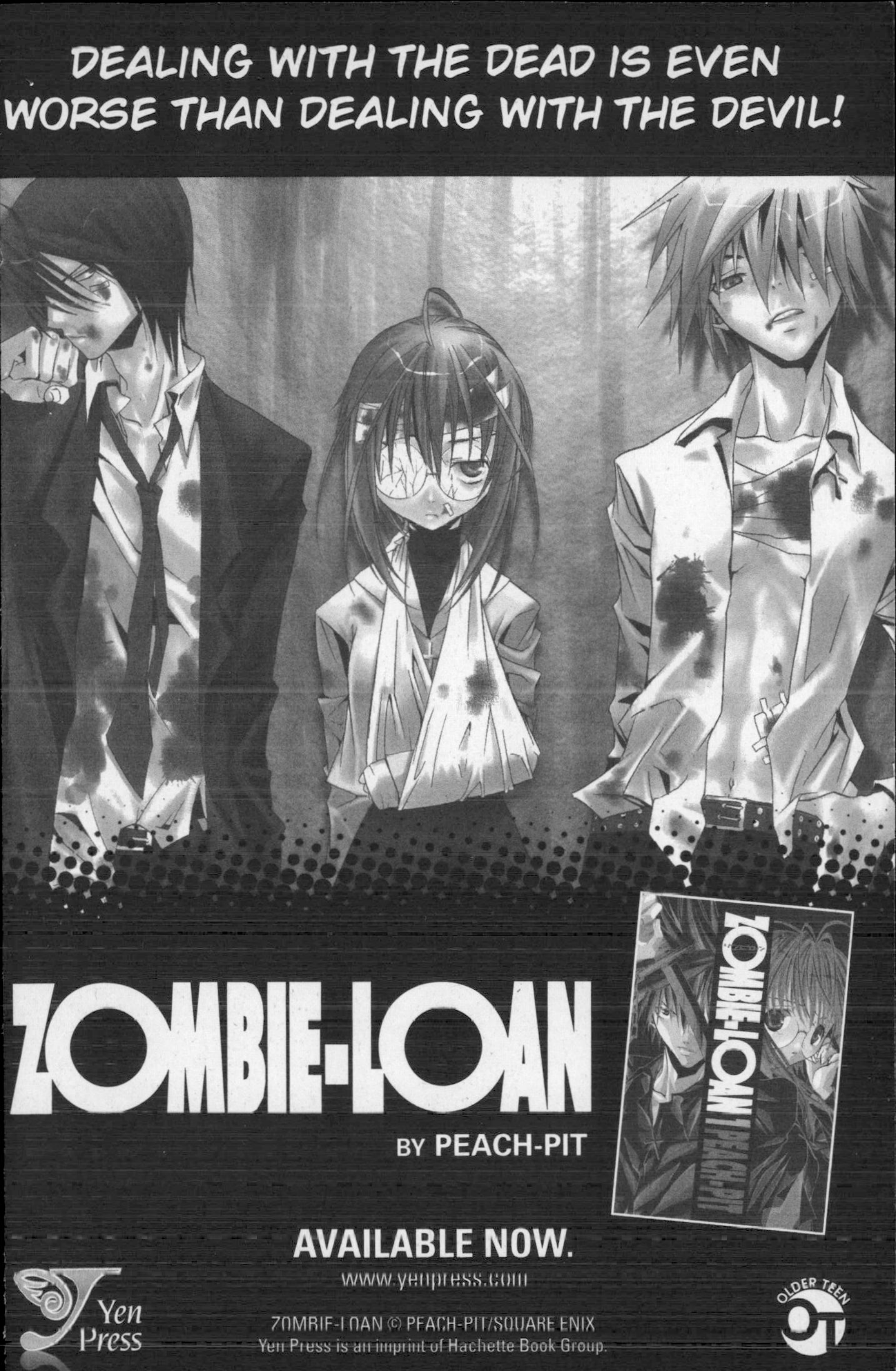
DEALING WITH THE DEAD IS EVEN
WORSE THAN DEALING WITH THE DEVIL!
ZOMBIE-LOAN
BY PEACH-PIT
AVAILABLE NOW.
www.yenpress.com
Yen Press
OLDER TEEN
OT
ZOMBIE-LOAN © PEACH-PIT/SQUARE ENIX
Yen Press is an imprint of Hachette Book Group.

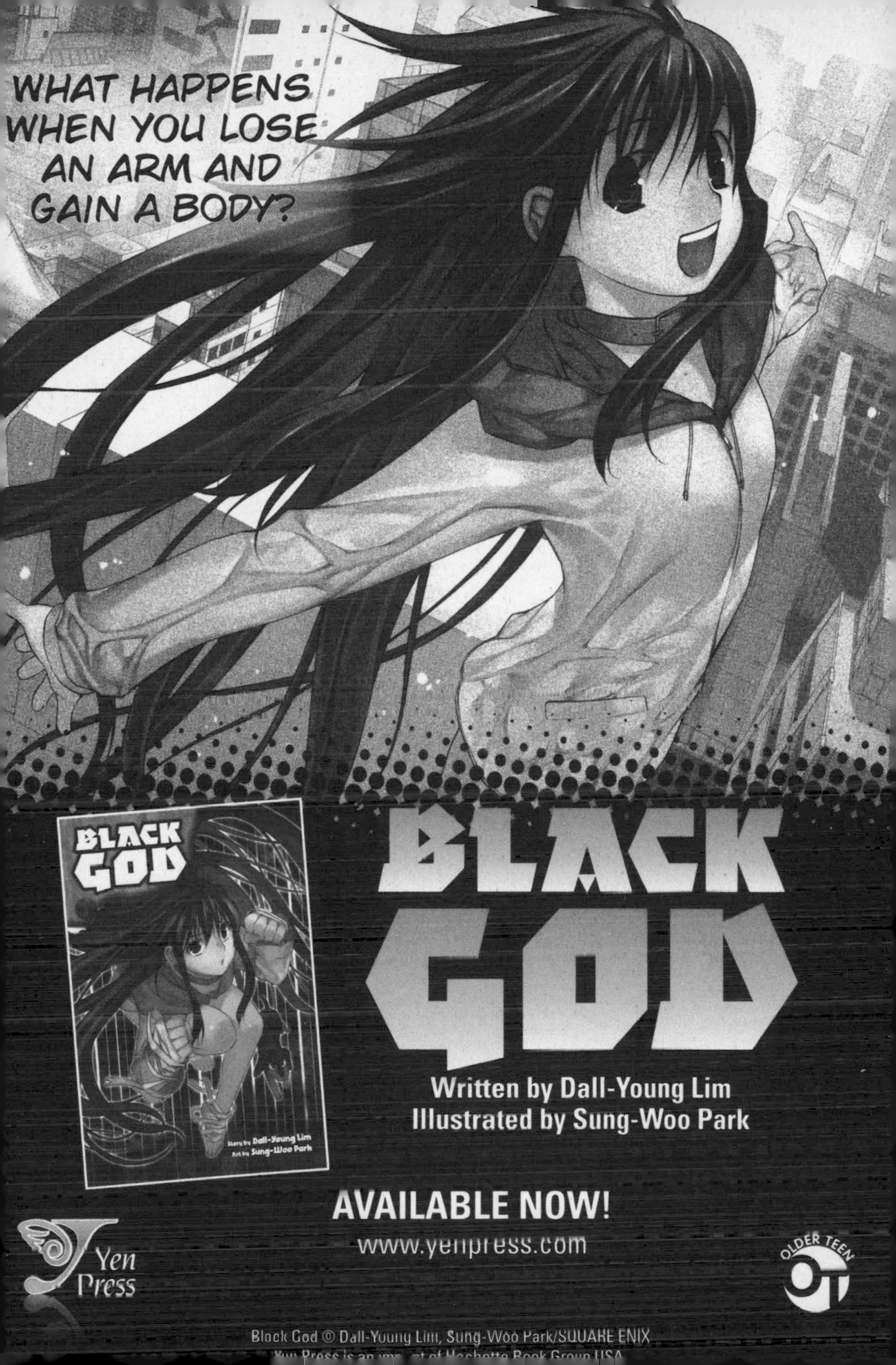
WHAT HAPPENS WHEN YOU LOSE AN ARM AND GAIN A BODY?
BLACK GOD
Story by Dall-Young Lim
Art by Sung-Woo Park
BLACK GOD
Written by Dall-Young Lim
Illustrated by Sung-Woo Park
AVAILABLE NOW!
www.yenpress.com
Yen Press
OLDER TEEN
OT
Black God © Dall-Young Lim, Sung-Woo Park/SQUARE ENIX

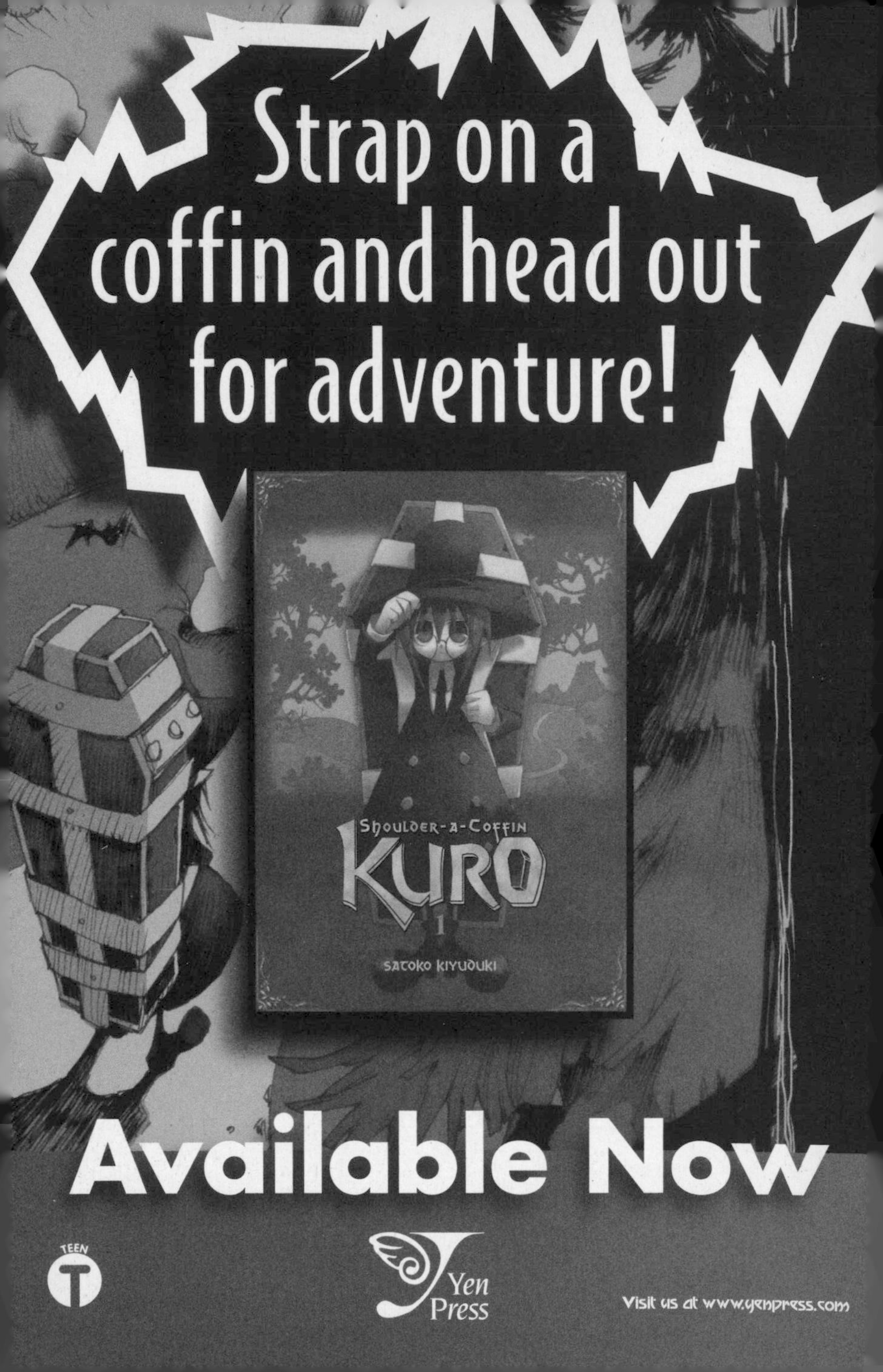
Strap on a coffin and head out for adventure!
Shoulder-a-Coffin
KURO
1
SATOKO KIYUDUKI
Available Now
TEEN
T
Yen Press
Visit us at www.yenpress.com

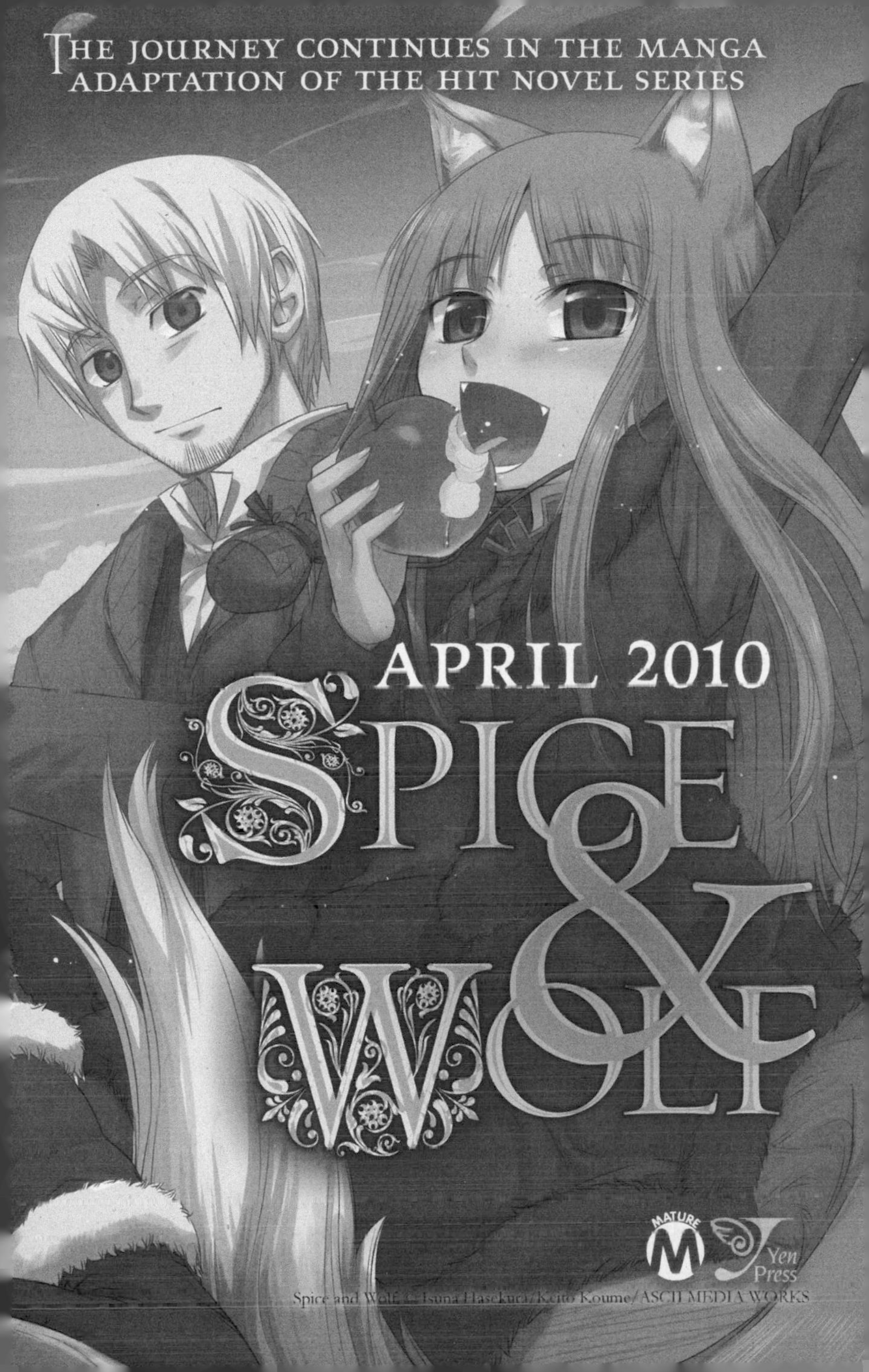
THE JOURNEY CONTINUES IN THE MANGA
ADAPTATION OF THE HIT NOVEL SERIES
APRIL 2010
SPICE & WOLF
MATURE
Yen Press
Spice and Wolf © Isuna Hasekura/Keito Koume/ASCII MEDIA WORKS

# PANDORA HEARTS ❶

## JUN MOCHIZUKI

Translation: Tomo Kimura  •  Lettering: Tania Biswas

PANDORA HEARTS Vol. 1 © 2006 Jun Mochizuki / SQUARE ENIX CO.,
LTD. All rights reserved. First published Japan in 2006 by SQUARE
ENIX CO., LTD. English translation rights arranged with SQUARE ENIX
CO., LTD. and Hachette Book Group through Tuttle-Mori Agency, Inc.
Translation © 2009 by SQUARE ENIX CO., LTD.

Yen Press
Hachette Book Group
237 Park Avenue, New York, NY 10017

www.HachetteBookGroup.com
www.YenPress.com

Yen Press is an imprint of Hachette Book Group, Inc. The Yen Press name
and logo are trademarks of Hachette Book Group, Inc.

First Yen Press Edition: December 2009

ISBN: 978-0-316-07607-4

10  9  8

BVG

Printed in the United States of America